Faye Levy was born and brought up in Washington, DC. She spent five years at the famous La Varenne cookery school in Paris, where she earned the 'Grand Diplôme' of the first graduating class, and developed and drafted recipes for the school's award-winning cookbooks.

Faye Levy is the recipient of numerous awards for her writing, including the International Association of Cooking Professionals/ Seagram Award for this book, which was also chosen by *Publishers Weekly* as one of their 'Best Books of the Year'.

Described by *Gourmet* Magazine as 'one of the finest cooks in the country' and by the *New York Times* as 'an expert chef', Faye Levy is a frequent contributor to major newspapers in the USA, and the author of 'The Basics' column for *Bon Appétit*. She lives in Santa Monica with her husband, Yakir. In their free time, they enjoy travelling around the world, tasting local specialities and discovering new dishes.

By the same author

Faye Levy's Chocolate Sensations
Classic Cooking Techniques
La Cuisine du Poisson (in French, with
    Fernard Chambrette)
French Cooking Without Meat (in Hebrew)
French Desserts (in Hebrew)
French Cakes, Pastries and Cookies (in Hebrew)
The La Varenne Tour Book

FAYE LEVY

Fresh From France

Vegetable Creations

GRAFTON BOOKS

A Division of the Collins Publishing Group

LONDON GLASGOW
TORONTO SYDNEY AUCKLAND

Grafton Books
A Division of the Collins Publishing Group
8 Grafton Street, London W1X 3LA

Published in paperback by Grafton Books 1990

First published in Great Britain by
Grafton Books 1989

First published in 1987 in the United States
by E. P. Dutton, a division of NAL Penguin Inc.,
2 Park Avenue, New York, N.Y. 10016

A CIP catalogue record for this book
is available from the British Library

ISBN 0-586-20447-4

Printed and bound in Great Britain by
Collins, Glasgow

Set in Garamond

To Chef Fernand Chambrette

Contents

Acknowledgements   xiv
Introduction   1

VEGETABLE TIMBALES, TERRINES, MOUSSES, AND SOUFFLÉS   7

Vegetable Timbales   9

Beetroot Timbales · Asparagus Timbales with Hollandaise Sauce · Carrot Timbales · Broccoli Timbales with Garlic Butter Sauce · Parsnip Timbales with Parsley Sauce · Spinach Timbales with Quick Cumin Hollandaise Sauce · Cauliflower Timbales with Tomato Butter Sauce · Turnip Timbales

Vegetable Terrines and Moulds   29

Tricoloured Vegetable Terrine with Creamy Basil-Garlic Sauce · Vegetable Terrine with Mushroom Mousse and Fresh Tomato Vinaigrette · Quick Spinach Pâté · Aubergine Savarin with Fresh Tomato Sauce · Spinach-Cauliflower Gâteau with Creamy Mushroom Sauce

Vegetable Mousses   43

Two-Tone Tomato Mousse · Avocado Mousse · Broccoli Bavarian · Cold Carrot Soufflé with Peas

Vegetable Soufflés   51

Spinach and Goat Cheese Soufflé · Pumpkin Soufflé · Individual Onion Soufflés · Broccoli and Mushroom Soufflé with Chives · Cauliflower Soufflé Pudding with Gruyère Cheese

VEGETABLE TARTS, PASTRIES, AND CRÊPES   61

Vegetable Quiches and Pie-Pastry Tarts   63

Bright Green Spinach Tart · Tomato and Goat Cheese Tartlets with Fresh Thyme · Cabbage Tart with Caraway Seeds · Creamy Mushroom Tart with Chives · Cauliflower Quiche with Onion and Gruyère Cheese · Swiss Chard and Tomato Tart

Savoury Vegetable Cream Puffs and Quenelles   76

Cheese Puff Crown with Asparagus · Cream Puffs with Carrot Purée · Brie Beignets · Baked Broccoli Gnocchi with Parmesan Cheese Sauce · Green Vegetable Quenelles with Mushroom Cream

Vegetable Pizzas and Country Tarts   88

Provençal Pizza · Ratatouille Pizza · Pipérade Pizza · Country Leek Tart · Festive Vegetable Tart · Alsatian Onion and Cream Cheese Tart

Vegetables in Puff Pastry   100

Spring Onion and Parmesan Croissants · Mushroom and Olive Pastry Rolls · Asparagus-Filled Pastry Cases with Watercress Sauce · Layered Vegetable Tourte · Cèpe Turnovers

Vegetable Crêpes   112

Buckwheat Crêpes with Creamy Vegetables · Spinach-Filled Crêpes with Crème Fraîche · Leek and Mushroom Crêpes · Crêpes with

Peppers, Onions and Peas in Curry Sauce · Aubergine Soufflé-Filled Crêpes with Red Pepper Sauce · Niçoise Baked Chick-Pea Pancake

Vegetable Canapés   126

Asparagus and Roquefort Canapés · Cucumber and Herbed Goat Cheese Canapés · Radish Flower Canapés · Tomato and Egg Canapés · Roasted Pepper Canapés

GRATINS, PURÉES, AND STUFFED VEGETABLES   131

Vegetable Gratins   133

Leek and Duxelles Gratin · Chicory Gratin with Cream Sauce and Walnuts · Pumpkin Gratin with Fresh Tomato Sauce · Cauliflower Gratin with Light Cheese Sauce · Layered Cabbage and Mushroom Gratin · Quick Broccoli Gratin with Gruyère and Nuts · Brussels Sprouts Baked in Mornay Sauce · Swiss Chard and Pepper Gratin with Tomatoes · Turnip and Onion Gratin with Parmesan

Vegetable Purées   148

Courgette Purée with Basil · Cauliflower and Potato Purée · Spinach Purée on Croûtes · Parsley Purée · Celeriac Purée · Creamy Carrot Purée · Green Pea Purée with Mint Butter

Stuffed Vegetables   157

Mushrooms Stuffed with Fresh Tomato Purée · Artichokes with Onion Compote · Artichokes Filled with Peas · Stuffed Aubergines with Pine Nut Pilaf and Tomato Curry Sauce · Aubergines with Tomatoes, Saffron, and Garlic · Aubergines Stuffed with Duxelles · Courgettes Stuffed with Red Pepper Purée · Tomatoes Filled with Artichoke and Rice Salad · Plum Tomatoes with Shallot Purée · Peppers Stuffed with Rice, Mushrooms, and Olives · Onions Stuffed with Spinach

GLAZED, BRAISED, STEAMED, AND POACHED VEGETABLES   173

Glazed Vegetables   175

Ginger-Glazed Carrots and Turnips · Butter-Glazed Carrots · Glazed Baby Onions and Courgette

Braised and Stewed Vegetables   179

Braised Chestnuts · Cream-Braised Cabbage with Leeks · Cabbage with Apples and Cider · Butter-Braised Chicory · Braised Fennel with Peppers and Olives · Asparagus and Carrots with Madeira · Flageolets with Green and Yellow Beans and Spring Onion Butter · Colourful Vegetable Blanquette · Mixed Mushroom Ragoût

Steamed Vegetables   190

Courgettes with Mint Butter · Asparagus with Beurre Blanc · Steamed Carrots with Pistachio Butter · Beetroot with Orange Hollandaise

Poached and Boiled Vegetables   197

Provençal Vegetable and Garlic Feast · Baby Vegetables with Herb Butter Sauce · Cauliflower in Rosemary-Scented Tomato Sauce · French Curried Cauliflower · Broccoli with Roquefort Sauce · Courgettes with Capers and Hazelnut Butter · Lyonnaise Green Beans · Green Beans with Delicate Garlic Butter · French Beans with Pesto Sauce · Brussels Sprouts with Creamy Mustard-Sage Sauce · Cabbage with Butter and Wine Vinegar · Artichokes with Tomato Béarnaise Sauce · Morels with Cream · White Beans with Tomatoes and Onions · Broad Beans in Garlic Cream

BAKED, GRILLED, SAUTÉED, AND FRIED
VEGETABLES 217

Baked and Grilled Vegetables 219

Courgette, Aubergine, and Tomato Slices Baked with Herbs · Baked Mushrooms with Escargot Butter and Walnuts · Artichokes and Baby Onions Antiboise · Baked Onions with Dill Butter · Provençal Baked Tomatoes · Baked Beetroot with Lemon Cream · Grilled Peppers with Garlic and Olive Oil · Grilled Aubergine with French Herbs · Grilled Mushrooms with Garlic Purée

Sautéed and Fried Vegetables 230

Medley of Vegetables with Fresh Thyme · Green Beans with Sautéed Walnuts · Carrots with Raspberry Vinegar · Sautéed Jerusalem Artichokes · Red and Green Cabbage Sauté with Goat Cheese · Sautéed Cucumbers with Dill · Garlic-Scented Courgettes with Celery · Sautéed Salsify with Fresh Herbs · Spinach, Leek, and Pumpkin Pancakes · Batter-Fried Vegetables with Rémoulade Sauce

POTATOES, RICE, AND PASTA 243

Potatoes 245

Potatoes with Vegetable Julienne Sauce · Potato and Cheese Gâteau · Steamed New Potatoes with Tarragon Butter · Light Potato Fritters with Pine Nuts · Potato Gratin with Cream · Potato Soufflé in Potato Skins · Baked Potato Cakes · Sautéed Potatoes with Peppers and Thyme · Creamy Potato Purée · Potato and Leek Pancakes · French Fried Sweet Potatoes

Rice 260

Rice with Peas and Basil · Rice with Sautéed Vegetables and Walnut Oil · Savoury Rice Pilaf with Aubergines · Mediterranean Saffron

Rice Pilaf with Vegetables · Creamy Rice Pilaf with Asparagus · Multicoloured Pilaf with Sweet Red Peppers and Walnuts · Rice Pilaf with Artichoke Hearts, Carrots, and Toasted Almonds · Brown Rice Pilaf with Tarragon · Rice Ring with Curried Aubergines

Pasta 275

Tomato Pasta with Goat Cheese and Garlic · Pasta with Fresh Peas and Saffron Butter Sauce · Pasta with Creamy Broccoli Purée · Fettucine with Morels and Asparagus · Spaghetti with Autumn Vegetables and Tomato-Tarragon Sauce · Pasta with Vegetable 'Noodles' · Creamy Pasta Gratin with Cheese · Baked Pasta with Aubergines · Pasta with Broccoli, Cauliflower, and Roquefort Sauce · Couscous Pilaf with Carrots, Peas, and Sautéed Mushrooms

VEGETABLE SOUPS 291

Hearty Vegetable Soups 293

Vegetable Bouillabaisse · Rich Onion Soup with Port · Creamy Onion Soup with Pasta · Country Spinach Soup · Provençal Vegetable Soup with Pasta and Pistou · Mushroom Cream Soup with Fresh Herbs · Vegetable Bourride with Aïoli · Southwestern Vegetable Soup with Vegetable Croutons

Vegetable Purée Soups 306

Fresh Pea Soup with Mint Cream · Touraine Chestnut Soup · Asparagus Soup with Olive Oil · Light Cauliflower Soup · Pumpkin and Pasta Soup · Pumpkin, Potato, and Leek Soup · Provençal Tomato Soup · Light Courgette Soup with Curry Puffs · Norman Potato-Shallot Soup · Carrot Soup with Chives

Vegetable Cream and Velouté Soups 321

Swiss Chard Soup with Toasted Hazelnuts · Leek Cream Soup with Diced Tomatoes · Sorrel Velouté Soup · Watercress Velouté Soup with Cheese Puffs · Cauliflower Velouté Soup with Broccoli · Red Pepper Velouté Soup · Vegetable Stock · Chicken Stock

VEGETABLE SALADS   335

Simple Vegetable Salads   339

Watercress Salad with Goat Cheese and Walnuts · Green Salad with Pine Nuts and Sherry Vinaigrette · Celeriac Salad with Mustard Dressing · Fennel Salad with Herbed Crème Fraîche · Cucumber Salad with Yogurt Herb Dressing · Escarole Salad with Roquefort Cheese · Summer Tomato Salad with Fresh Herbs · Leeks Mimosa with Hazelnuts · Marinated Green Bean Salad with Spring Onions · Warm Dandelion Salad with Mushrooms and Poached Eggs · Baby Artichokes with Hazelnut Oil Vinaigrette

Composed Vegetable Salads   352

Breton Vegetable Salad with Chive Mayonnaise · Sweetcorn Salad with Peppers · Tomatoes Stuffed with Mushroom Salad · Chicory and Beetroot Salad · Chick-Pea and Bean Salad with Tomatoes and Basil · Avocado and Mushroom Salad with Swiss Chard · Cauliflower and Tomato Salad with Garlic and Walnut Dressing · Artichoke, Asparagus, Green Bean, and Fresh Pea Salad with Tarragon Mayonnaise · Provençal Marinated Vegetables

Potato, Rice, and Pasta Salads   366

Potato and Beetroot Salad · Summer Potato and Green Bean Salad · Potato-Pepper Salad à la Provençale · Auvergne Potato Salad with Cantal Cheese · Potato Salad with Watercress · Potato, Asparagus, and Artichoke Salad · Rice Salad with Peas and Peppers · Rice Salad with Pyrénées Cheese, Mushrooms, and Tomatoes · Pasta Salad with Red Peppers, Broccoli, and Garlic Dressing · Mayonnaise · Crème Fraîche

A Note About the Author   382
Index   383

Acknowledgements

I would like to thank Anne Willan, president of La Varenne Cooking School in Paris, for enabling me to live in France for five wonderful years and giving me the most fabulous job any food lover could imagine – researching and drafting the recipes for such major books as *French Regional Cooking*, *The Observer French Cookery School*, and *Basic French Cookery*. During these years my beloved cooking teachers and associates at La Varenne – Master Chefs Fernand Chambrette, Albert Jorant, and Claude Vauguet – and Denis Ruffel of the excellent Parisian Patisserie Millet, shared with me their vast knowledge of the art of cooking, and I wish to convey my heartfelt appreciation to them.

I am also grateful to the people at *Bon Appétit* and *Gourmet* magazines for being open to my ideas. I originally developed some of the material here for these magazines. I learned so much from writing for them, and I feel that my work has benefited from the high standards they demand.

My sincere thanks to my editor, Carole DeSanti, for her support and encouragement, and for making the book clearer and easier to read; to Gregory Dinner for thinking of the series title, *Fresh from France*; and to Annie Horenn, Teri Appleton, Leona Fitzgerald, and Patsy Allen for their help in recipe testing.

Finally, a big thank-you to my husband and associate Yakir Levy for helping me write this book.

Fresh From France

VEGETABLE CREATIONS

Introduction

'In all of France, we are witnessing the triumph of vegetables.' This is how the famous French gastronome, Christian Millau, summed up vegetables' recent stardom. Of course vegetables have been an important part of French cooking for centuries, but never before have they been used so lavishly throughout the meal. Vegetables are being used today in imaginative new ways to add colour and excitement to contemporary menus.

Increasingly vegetables are emphasized in the names of the most exquisite creations. Where a dish was once called, for example, 'sole with white wine sauce', we might now say 'sole with white wine sauce and baby vegetables'. Some leading chefs will name the vegetable first, calling dishes *petits pois au homard* or 'green peas with lobster', for example. Elegantly prepared vegetables have become symbolic of fresh, light, and natural cuisine.

Our own markets offer a growing selection of fresh native produce and also many imported vegetables. It would be difficult, perhaps impossible, to think of a food that comes to us in as many flavours, shapes, and colours as vegetables. It is not surprising, therefore, when we are incorporating more and more vegetables into our diet, that everyone is looking for wonderful ways to prepare them.

People from all over the world travel to France to savour French food and to learn more about the greatest style of cooking in the Western world. Even more than in fashion and the arts, in fine cuisine the French set the tone, style, and standards. Major French culinary trends are soon followed in other countries.

French cuisine is constantly evolving. Seasoning techniques and cooking methods are crossing international borders, and cooks in France are continuously experimenting with and searching for superb vegetable dishes. The French have been actively exploring, matching, and marrying the favourite flavourings of nearby Mediterranean and North African countries, as well as those of the Orient, into their own repertoire.

In fine kitchens vegetables are treated with respect and are given the attention they deserve. French cooks have developed a set of rules for cooking the different types of vegetables so they retain maximum flavour and colour and acquire a pleasing texture. This book teaches these principles and will enable home cooks to reproduce France's finest vegetable dishes. It includes updated versions of the best vegetable dishes from traditional family cooking, country cooking, and classic cuisine, as well as innovative vegetable dishes in the style of contemporary French cuisine.

The recipes in this book do not include meat, and thus perfectly complement meat or fish as side dishes or first courses. Many are ideal main courses for elegant light meals 'à la française'.

Following are several hints on vegetable preparation techniques you may find informative.

Artichoke Hearts

To shape artichokes in bottoms or 'hearts': Squeeze juice of ½ lemon into bowl of cold water.

Break stem off one artichoke. Break off largest leaves at bottom. Put artichoke on its side on board.

Holding very sharp knife or small serrated knife against side of artichoke (parallel to leaves), cut lower circle of leaves off, up to edge of artichoke heart. Turn artichoke slightly after each cut. Rub exposed edges of artichoke heart with cut lemon.

Cut off central cone of leaves just above artichoke heart. Cut off leaves under base and trim base so it is round, removing all dark green areas.

Rub again with lemon. Put artichoke in bowl of lemon water. Repeat with remaining artichokes.

To cook artichoke hearts: Squeeze juice of ¼ to ½ lemon into a saucepan containing enough boiling salted water to generously cover artichokes.

Add artichoke hearts to water. Reduce heat to low, cover, and simmer about 15 minutes, or until tender when pierced with the point of a knife. Cool to lukewarm in liquid.

Using a teaspoon, scoop out hairlike choke from centre of each artichoke heart. Return artichokes to liquid until ready to use.

Asparagus

Very thin asparagus (about the thickness of a pencil) does not need to be peeled but other asparagus should be. Put an asparagus spear on a cutting board. Holding base of asparagus and beginning slightly below the tip, peel spear with a vegetable peeler all around. Cut off and discard about 1 cm/½ inch from the bottom of the spear; this part is tough.

Garlic

To peel a garlic clove easily put it on a board and hold the flat side of a large knife just above it. Hit the knife with your fist. The peel will be released and can be pulled off. If it remains partially attached at one end, cut it off at that end.

To chop a peeled clove of garlic, hit it vigorously by holding the flat side of a large knife above the garlic and pounding the knife until the garlic is crushed. Cut it several times in one direction with a small sharp knife. Slice it against the direction of the first cuts. Chop it further with an up-and-down motion of the large knife. For finely chopped garlic continue chopping until it is in very tiny pieces.

Herbs

To chop herbs, first rinse and dry thoroughly. Remove leaves from stems. Use a large, heavy chopping knife and a dry board. Holding the point of the knife down, move the handle up and down so that the knife blade goes through the herb several times, until it is chopped. For finely chopped herbs, continue chopping until the herb is in very tiny pieces.

Chives can be held together and snipped with scissors or thinly sliced, instead of being chopped. Dill can also be snipped.

Leeks

To clean leeks cut off the root ends, remove and discard the coarse outer leaves and about 2·5 cm/1 inch of the leek tops. Split each leek lengthwise with a sharp knife, beginning about 2·5 cm/1 inch from the root end and cutting towards the green end. Turn the leek round by about 90 degrees and split it again in the same way. Holding each leek by its root end, dip it repeatedly in a sinkful or large bowl of cold water. If dirt remains, soak the leeks in cold water for several minutes. Then separate the leaves under running water to rinse away any clinging dirt, and drain.

Mushrooms

To clean wild mushrooms gently rinse one at a time under cold running water; do not soak them in water. Dry mushrooms upside down on paper towels. Do not wash cultivated mushrooms; wipe with a clean damp cloth if necessary.

To slice mushrooms cut them in half, set cut side down on board, and slice thinly.

Onions and Shallots

To peel an onion cut off the root; do not cut off too much or the onion will begin to fall apart. Pull off the peel with the aid of a knife. Cut off the top.

To slice an onion cut it in half lengthwise from stem end to root end. Put it, cut side down, on a cutting board. Holding a sharp knife in your right hand, slice the onion – half crosswise, holding the knife against the curved fingers of your left hand and moving your left hand gradually back to guide the knife in cutting slices of an even thickness. The onion will be cut in half slices.

To chop an onion, cut it in half lengthwise from stem end to root end. Put it, cut side down, on a cutting board. Using a sharp knife, cut the onion in vertical slices, starting nearly at the root end and slicing towards the stem end but leaving the onion joined at its root end. Next cut the onion in several horizontal slices, still leaving it attached at the root end.

Slice the onion crosswise, beginning at the stem end, and form small cubes. Chop onion cubes further with an up-and-down motion of a chopping knife. For finely chopped onion, continue chopping until the onion is in very tiny pieces.

Onions and shallots can also be sliced or chopped in a food processor, according to the machine's instruction manual. If using a food processor, drain the chopped onion on paper towels before cooking so it will not be watery.

Spinach

To clean fresh spinach first remove stems by pulling them off the leaves; discard. Wash the leaves thoroughly by placing them in a sinkful of cold water, lifting them out into a bowl, and changing the water. Repeat rinsing if necessary until no dirt remains.

To substitute frozen spinach for fresh: Frozen spinach can be substituted for fresh in recipes calling for cooked puréed spinach, although the flavour and texture will not be quite as good because frozen spinach also contains stems. Because frozen spinach is already blanched it does not require cooking in water, but simply thawing; to save time, however, it can be cooked in boiling water until it thaws, then drained and squeezed according to the recipes.

Both fresh and frozen spinach vary in the amounts of actual cooked spinach obtainable from a certain weight. From 700 g/1½ lb of fresh spinach (weight including stems) I have most often obtained 200 ml/7 fl oz purée, but occasionally only 100 ml/4 fl oz. In comparing 275-g/10-oz packets of frozen spinach of different brands I have also found they give between 100 ml/4 fl oz and 200 ml/7 fl oz purée. To solve the problem, in recipes in which the exact quantity of purée is important, I have included it, even though in some cases part of the spinach will not be used.

Tomatoes

To peel: Before using tomatoes for cooking they are often peeled, seeded, and chopped. Using a sharp knife, cut the cores from the tomatoes. Turn the tomatoes over and slit the skin in an X-shaped cut. Fill a large bowl with cold water. Put the tomatoes in a pan containing enough boiling water to generously cover them and boil for about 10 to 15 seconds, or until the skin begins to pull away from the flesh along the cut. Remove the tomatoes with a slotted spoon and put them in the bowl of cold water. Leave for a few seconds. Remove the tomatoes and pull off the skins with the aid of the knife.

To seed: With a large knife, cut the tomatoes in half horizontally. Hold each half over a bowl, cut side down, and squeeze to remove the seeds.

To chop: With a chopping knife, cut the tomatoes several times in one direction, then in the other direction. Chop them further with an up-and-down motion of the knife.

Other Ingredients

In this book, unless otherwise specified, instructions are predicated on using the following ingredients:

· Unsalted, or sweet, butter is of higher quality than salted, but salted butter can be used in recipes unless the unsalted type is specified.

· Use large eggs unless otherwise specified.

· Where an ingredient is measured in tablespoons, they are always level.

· Use whole milk.

· For vegetable oil, use any neutral-flavoured oil, such as corn oil, safflower oil, sunflower seed oil, or peanut oil.

· Always use dry wine for cooking unless otherwise specified. The best wine to choose is one that you also like to drink, but there is no need to use expensive wines for cooking.

VEGETABLE TIMBALES, TERRINES, MOUSSES, AND SOUFFLÉS

Timbales, terrines, mousses, and soufflés are the most glamorous types of vegetable dishes. Vegetable soufflés and timbales are traditional favourites that have reached new heights in popularity, while vegetable mousses and terrines are modern creations.

Vegetable Timbales

Vegetable timbales are round moulds of baked creamy purées. They are sophisticated and elegant in appearance but at the same time quick and easy to prepare.

These versatile dishes can be prepared from a great variety of vegetables during all seasons of the year. Even humble vegetables such as parsnips or turnips acquire distinction and a delicious flavour when turned into timbales. Simply cooked foods, from poached fish fillets to sautéed chicken to grilled meat, become festive when accompanied by a bright green spinach timbale or a vivid orange carrot timbale.

The term *timbale* refers to both the moulds and to the foods cooked in them. Vegetable timbales are baked in special cylindrical timbale moulds, sometimes called *dariole* moulds, or in ramekins. The word *dariole* is also occasionally used to refer to these vegetable dishes.

Traditional recipes for timbales often use flour or bread crumbs to bind the vegetable mixtures together, but contemporary cooks prefer to use another technique. They treat timbales as savoury vegetable custards, in which the vegetable purée is the main ingredient, and the purée is thickened by reducing it with cream. Both classic and modern timbales make use of eggs to firm the mixture so it holds together when unmoulded.

When served as a first course timbales are generally accompanied by a sauce, which can be a tomato sauce, brown sauce, cream-based sauce, cheese sauce, or butter sauce. The colour and flavour of the sauce should complement the vegetable; its consistency should be smooth and flowing so it can be poured easily around the base of the timbales.

Timbales served as side dishes can be accompanied by whatever sauce is planned for the main course; there is no need to prepare a separate one. The rule for matching timbales with entrées is simple: select a timbale made of a vegetable that would ordinarily complement the main dish. Timbales of sweet vegetables such as carrots, beetroot, turnips or parsnips can be paired with beef, lamb, pork, or poultry; delicate ones such as asparagus are perfect with veal; spinach, cauliflower, and broccoli timbales go well with most foods.

With today's trend towards lighter eating, timbales can be the basis for unconventional main courses as well. Surround a broccoli timbale, for example, with garlic butter sauce topped by several steamed prawns for an elegant entrée. For a change-of-pace luncheon menu set a cool beetroot timbale on a bed of crisp green salad and accompany it with a light rice salad dressed with dill vinaigrette.

Hints

· When preparing timbale mixtures whisk the eggs only until smooth, not frothy. Whisking the eggs too vigorously creates foam that solidifies during baking and mars the smoothness of the timbales.

· Timbales, terrines and moulds are delicate and are therefore baked gently in a water bath to ensure a silky texture. The dishes are set in a large shallow pan in the oven. The pan is filled with hot water, and the moulds are then covered with a sheet of foil to protect their tops. The water moderates the oven temperature so the moulds bake slowly and evenly, and provides moisture so they do not dry out.

· When preparing a water bath, pull the oven shelf out slightly before adding water to the pan. After adding the water very carefully slide it back into the oven to avoid spilling water into the moulds.

· For proper cooking the water in a water bath should remain hot but not boiling. If it begins to boil the texture of the moulds becomes marred by small holes.

· Careful checking is essential when baking timbales and other baked moulds. Overcooking results in rubbery rather than soft, creamy timbales and may cause them to separate. Underbaked custards may stick or fall apart when unmoulded. When a timbale is ready its surface should be firm and springy to the touch. At this point carefully insert a skewer in the centre of the mixture, which is the last part to set; if it comes out clean the timbale is done. When making individual servings check each timbale to see if it is done, because the temperature may not be uniform throughout the oven.

· Unmould timbales while they are hot; otherwise the butter congeals on the moulds and makes the timbales stick. Hold the knife straight when running it around the sides of the timbale. If a timbale did not unmould neatly, use a metal spatula to smooth it; or spoon some sauce over it. Baked timbales can be unmoulded and kept warm for 15 to 30 minutes by being covered carefully with the moulds and set in a warm place. When serving a timbale on a plate with meat and sauce it is easiest to unmould the timbale on to the plate first, then add the main course and sauce.

BEETROOT TIMBALES
Timbales de betteraves

These new timbales have a delicately sweet flavour and make a lovely first course or side dish for light meats and poultry. For a spectacular presentation they can be served surrounded by a sauce, such as the mustard sauce suggested below or with Lemon Cream (page 225).

MAKES 4 OR 5 SERVINGS

BEETROOT TIMBALES

1 kg/2¼ lb baby beetroot	3 eggs
150 ml/¼ pint double cream, at room temperature	Salt and freshly ground pepper

MUSTARD SAUCE (OPTIONAL)

15 g/½ oz butter

2 shallots, finely chopped

3 tablespoons dry white wine

6 tablespoons Chicken Stock
  (page 333) or Vegetable Stock
  (page 332)

Salt and freshly ground pepper

300 ml/½ pint double cream

1½ to 2 tablespoons Dijon
  mustard

BEETROOT TIMBALES

Preheat oven to 190°C/375°F/gas 5. Generously butter four 8-cm/
3-inch ramekins or five timbale moulds, being careful to butter bases
thoroughly. Butter sheet of foil to cover them.

Put beetroot in medium or large saucepan, cover with water, add
pinch of salt and bring to boil. Cover, reduce heat to medium-low,
and cook for about 35 minutes, or until tender when pierced with a
small sharp knife. Slip off skins while rinsing with cold water. Cut off
root ends. Drain thoroughly in large strainer. Purée in food processor
or hand food mill until very smooth. Measure 450 ml/¾ pint purée.

Cook purée in a heavy, medium-size wide saucepan over low heat,
stirring often, for 5 minutes to evaporate excess moisture. Stir cream
into purée. Raise heat to high and bring to boil. Reduce heat to
medium and cook, stirring often, until cream is absorbed and
mixture is reduced to 450 ml/¾ pint. Transfer mixture to a bowl and
cool for 7 minutes.

Whisk eggs in a medium-size bowl until blended. Gradually whisk
in beetroot mixture. Season to taste with salt and pepper; season well
so timbales will not be bland.

Divide mixture among ramekins or moulds, tapping each on work
surface to pack down mixture. Smooth tops, set ramekins in roasting
pan and transfer to oven. Add enough boiling water to come halfway
up sides of ramekins. Set sheet of buttered foil atop ramekins.

Bake for about 40 to 50 minutes or until timbales are firm to the
touch and skewer inserted into centres comes out dry. If necessary
occasionally add hot water to roasting pan so that it does not become
dry. If water comes close to a boil, add a few tablespoons of cold
water.

MUSTARD SAUCE

Melt butter in a medium-size heavy saucepan over low heat. Add shallots and cook, stirring, for about 2 minutes or until softened. Add wine, stock, salt and pepper; simmer, stirring, until liquid is reduced to about 2 tablespoons.

Stir in cream and bring to a boil, stirring. Reduce heat to medium and cook, stirring often, until sauce is thick enough to coat a spoon; about 7 minutes. Set aside. (Sauce can be kept, covered, in refrigerator for up to 1 day.)

To Finish Timbales and Sauce:

When timbales are done, carefully remove moulds from water bath and cool on rack for 5 minutes. Run thin-bladed flexible knife around edge of each ramekin or mould. Set small plate atop one mould and invert. Holding them together, tap on towel-covered working surface. Gently lift off mould. Repeat with remaining moulds. Serve timbales hot or at room temperature.

Reheat sauce, if necessary, over medium heat, whisking. Reduce heat to low and whisk in 1½ tablespoons mustard. Taste, and add salt, pepper and more mustard if needed. Serve hot or at room temperature.

To serve, spoon 2 to 3 tablespoons sauce on plate around each timbale and tilt plate so sauce runs around it. Serve remaining sauce separately.

ASPARAGUS TIMBALES WITH HOLLANDAISE SAUCE
Timbales d'asperges, sauce hollandaise

In classic cuisine hollandaise sauce is a favourite accompaniment for poached asparagus. Here a quick version of the sauce surrounds the pale green asparagus timbales. Bright green asparagus tips provide a decorative finishing touch.   MAKES 4 OR 5 SERVINGS

ASPARAGUS TIMBALES

1·5 kg/3 lb medium-size asparagus
  spears
150 ml/¼ pint double cream, at
  room temperature

3 eggs
Salt and white pepper
Freshly grated nutmeg

QUICK HOLLANDAISE SAUCE

3 egg yolks, at room temperature
Pinch of salt
1 tablespoon strained fresh lemon
  juice

175 g/6 oz unsalted butter, cut in
  pieces
1 tablespoon hot water
Pinch of cayenne pepper

16 to 20 asparagus tips, for garnish

ASPARAGUS TIMBALES

Preheat oven to 190°C/375°F/gas 5. Generously butter four 8-cm/
3-inch ramekins or five small timbale moulds, being careful to butter
bases thoroughly. Butter sheet of foil to cover them.

Peel asparagus spears and cut into 5-cm/2-inch pieces, discarding
tough ends. In a medium-size saucepan, boil asparagus pieces,
uncovered, in boiling salted water, for about 3 to 5 minutes or until
tender when pierced with small sharp knife. Drain thoroughly.
Return asparagus to dry saucepan and cook over low heat, stirring
and mashing with wooden spoon, until excess liquid evaporates;
about 7 minutes. Place asparagus in large strainer. Press to remove
excess liquid; do not push asparagus pulp through strainer. Purée
asparagus in food processor until very smooth. Measure 450 ml/¾
pint.

Cook purée in heavy, medium-size wide saucepan over low heat,
stirring often, for 5 minutes to evaporate excess moisture. Stir cream
into purée. Raise heat to high and bring to boil. Reduce heat to
medium and cook, stirring often, until cream is absorbed and
mixture is reduced to 450 ml/¾ pint; about 5 minutes. Transfer
mixture to bowl and cool for 7 minutes.

Whisk eggs in medium-size bowl until blended. Gradually whisk
in asparagus purée. Season to taste with salt, pepper and nutmeg;
season well so timbales will not be bland.

Divide mixture among ramekins. Tap each on work surface to pack down. Smooth tops, set ramekins in roasting pan and transfer to oven. Add enough boiling water to come halfway up sides of ramekins. Set sheet of buttered foil atop ramekins.

Bake for about 35 minutes or until timbales are firm to the touch and a skewer inserted into centres comes out dry. If necessary occasionally add hot water to roasting pan so that it does not become dry. If water comes close to a boil, add a few tablespoons of cold water.

When timbales are done remove moulds from water bath. Cool on rack for 5 minutes. Carefully run thin-bladed flexible knife around edge of each ramekin or mould. Set small plate atop one ramekin and invert. Holding them together, tap on towel-covered working surface. Gently lift off ramekin. Repeat with remaining ramekins. Cover each timbale gently with a ramekin or mould while preparing garnish and sauce.

In a large pan of boiling salted water, cook 16 to 20 asparagus tips for about 2 minutes, or until barely tender and still bright green. Drain thoroughly.

QUICK HOLLANDAISE SAUCE

Prepare sauce a short time before serving. Combine egg yolks, salt and 2 teaspoons lemon juice in blender or food processor and process until lightened in colour and very well blended. Remove pusher from processor.

Place butter in small heavy saucepan; if possible use one with a lip to facilitate pouring melted butter into blender or processor. Set over medium-low heat, and warm until butter melts and sizzles. With blade of machine turning (at high speed if using blender), gradually pour hot butter, drop by drop, through top. After 2 or 3 tablespoons of butter have been added, pour remaining butter through in thin, steady stream, with blade of machine still turning. Add hot water and process briefly to mix. Blend in cayenne pepper and remaining lemon juice. Taste and adjust seasoning. Serve sauce immediately. (It can be transferred to bowl and kept warm for about 15 minutes on a rack set above hot water, but it must be whisked frequently. It can also be kept warm in a vacuum bottle. Sauce may thicken if it is kept warm and should be diluted with a little more hot water; whisk in 1 teaspoon at a time.)

To serve, remove ramekins, spoon 2 to 3 tablespoons sauce on plate around each timbale, and tilt plate so sauce runs evenly around it. Garnish with reserved asparagus tips, pointing outward. Serve remaining sauce separately.

CARROT TIMBALES
Timbales de carottes

Vivid orange carrot timbales make an impressive first course, especially when they are accompanied by a sauce of a contrasting colour, such as Watercress Sauce (page 104), or surrounded by Glazed Baby Onions and Courgette (page 177). Another delicious and attractive way to present them is to surround each with Herb Butter Sauce (page 201) and to set a steamed baby carrot on the sauce on each plate. As a side dish they are perfect with sautéed chicken or veal.

MAKES 4 SERVINGS

450 g/1 lb carrots, peeled and cut
   in medium-size slices
15 g/½ oz butter
3 eggs

6 tablespoons milk
Salt and freshly ground pepper
Pinch of sugar

Preheat oven to 200°C/400°F/gas 6. Generously butter four 8-cm/3-inch ramekins.

Put carrots in a saucepan, cover them with water, and add a pinch of salt. Bring to a boil, cover, and cook for about 15 minutes or until very tender. Drain thoroughly. Purée in a food processor until smooth.

Melt butter in saucepan used to cook carrots. Add carrot purée and cook over low heat, stirring often, for about 3 minutes, or until butter is absorbed and excess moisture evaporates. Remove from heat.

Whisk eggs with milk in a medium-size bowl. Gradually whisk in carrot purée. Season to taste with salt, pepper and sugar.

Divide carrot mixture among ramekins, tapping each to pack down mixture. Smooth top and set ramekins in a roasting pan in oven. Add enough boiling water to pan to come halfway up sides of ramekins. Bake for 35 to 40 minutes or until firm to the touch; a skewer inserted into centres should come out dry. Add water to roasting pan occasionally so that it does not become dry.

Remove ramekins from water bath and let cool 2 or 3 minutes. Carefully run a thin-bladed flexible knife around edge of each one. Set small plate atop one and invert. Holding them together, tap on towel-covered working surface. Gently lift off ramekin. Repeat with remaining three. Serve hot, at room temperature or cold.

BROCCOLI TIMBALES WITH GARLIC BUTTER SAUCE
Timbales de brocolis, beurre à l'ail

Tiny broccoli florets provide a bright green garnish for the light green timbales and their golden butter sauce.   MAKES 4 SERVINGS

BROCCOLI TIMBALES

*1 kg/2 lb broccoli, divided into
 medium-size florets, stalks
 reserved*
*150 ml/¼ pint double cream, at
 room temperature*

3 eggs
Salt and white pepper
Freshly grated nutmeg (optional)

GARLIC BUTTER SAUCE

2 tablespoons finely chopped garlic
*3 tablespoons finely chopped
 shallots*
4 tablespoons dry white wine
2 tablespoons white wine vinegar

2 tablespoons double cream
Salt and white pepper
*225 g/8 oz well-chilled unsalted
 butter, cut into 16 cubes*

*15 or 16 small broccoli florets, for
 garnish*

BROCCOLI TIMBALES

Preheat oven to 190°C/375°F/gas 5. Generously butter four 8-cm/ 3-inch ramekins, being careful to butter bases thoroughly. Butter sheet of foil to cover them.

Trim off bottom 5 cm/2 inches of broccoli stalk. Peel remaining stalk and cut in 1-cm/½-inch-thick slices. In a large saucepan of boiling salted water, cook broccoli florets and slices, uncovered, for about 8 minutes or until very tender. Drain, rinse with cold water and drain thoroughly. Purée broccoli in food processor or blender until very smooth.

Cook purée in a medium-size shallow, heavy saucepan over low heat, stirring often, for 5 minutes to evaporate excess moisture. Stir cream into purée. Raise heat to high and bring to boil. Reduce heat to medium and cook, stirring often, until cream is absorbed and mixture is reduced to 450 ml/¾ pint. Transfer to a bowl and cool for 7 minutes.

Whisk eggs in medium-size bowl until blended. Gradually add broccoli purée and season to taste with salt, pepper and nutmeg; season well so timbales will not be bland.

Divide mixture among ramekins. Tap each on work surface to pack down. Smooth tops and set ramekins in roasting pan in oven. Add enough boiling water to roasting pan to come halfway up sides of ramekins. Set sheet of buttered foil atop ramekins.

Bake for about 38 minutes or until timbales are firm to touch and skewer inserted into centres comes out dry. If necessary add hot water to roasting pan occasionally so that it does not become dry. If water comes close to a boil add a few tablespoons of cold water.

GARLIC BUTTER SAUCE

In small heavy saucepan, combine garlic, shallots, wine and vinegar. Cook over medium heat until liquid is reduced to about 2 table-spoons.

Reduce heat to low, add cream and simmer, whisking often, until mixture is reduced to about 3 tablespoons. Keep butter cubes in refrigerator until ready to use. (Reduction can be prepared several hours in advance and kept, covered, in refrigerator.)

To Finish Timbales and Sauce:

When timbales are done, remove from water bath. Cool on rack for 5 minutes. Carefully run thin-bladed flexible knife around edge of each ramekin. Set small plate atop one ramekin and invert. Holding them together, tap on towel-covered working surface. Gently lift off ramekin. Repeat with remaining ramekins. Cover each timbale gently with a ramekin while finishing sauce and garnish.

In medium-size saucepan of boiling salted water, blanch broccoli florets, uncovered, over high heat for about 2 minutes or until just tender. Drain thoroughly.

To finish sauce, bring garlic mixture to a simmer in a small heavy saucepan. Reduce heat to low and season lightly with salt and white pepper. Add 2 cubes of butter, whisking liquid constantly. When they are nearly blended into liquid add another cube, still whisking. Continue adding butter cubes, 1 or 2 at a time, whisking constantly. Sauce should thicken and should be pleasantly warm to touch. (If at any time sauce becomes too hot and drops of melted butter appear, immediately remove from heat and add 2 butter cubes off heat, whisking constantly. When temperature of sauce drops again to warm, return to low heat and continue whisking in remaining butter cubes.) Remove from heat as soon as last butter cube is added.

Strain sauce into a bowl. Taste and adjust seasoning.

(Sauce can be kept warm for about 15 minutes in its bowl set on rack above hot water, but it must be whisked frequently to prevent separation. It can also be kept warm in a vacuum bottle.)

To serve, remove ramekins, spoon 2 to 3 tablespoons sauce on plate around timbale, and tilt plate so sauce runs evenly around it. Set a few broccoli florets on each plate. Serve remaining sauce separately.

PARSNIP TIMBALES WITH PARSLEY SAUCE
Timbales de panais, sauce au persil

This is my favourite way to prepare parsnips. These timbales could change the minds of many people about this vegetable, even avowed parsnip haters. Serve the timbales with roast or grilled lamb, beef or chicken.   MAKES 4 OR 5 SERVINGS

PARSNIP TIMBALES

700 g/1½ lb parsnips
150 ml/¼ pint double cream, at
   room temperature

3 eggs
Salt and white pepper
Freshly grated nutmeg

PARSLEY SAUCE

4 medium-size shallots, finely
   chopped
1 bay leaf
6 tablespoons dry white wine
225 ml/8 fl oz Chicken Stock
   (page 333) or Vegetable Stock
   (page 332)

450 ml/¾ pint double cream
Salt and freshly ground pepper
Pinch of cayenne pepper
25 g/1 oz fresh parsley sprigs
   without stems

PARSNIP TIMBALES

Preheat oven to 190°C/375°F/gas 5. Generously butter five small timbale moulds or four 8-cm/3-inch ramekins, being careful to butter bases thoroughly. Butter sheet of foil to cover them.

Peel parsnips and cut crosswise into 1-cm/½-inch slices. Put parsnips in medium-size saucepan, cover them with water, add pinch of salt and bring to boil. Cover, reduce heat to medium and cook for about 20 minutes or until very tender. Drain thoroughly. Purée in food processor until very smooth. Measure 450 ml/¾ pint purée.

Cook measured purée in a medium-size heavy wide saucepan over low heat, stirring often, for 5 minutes to evaporate excess moisture. Stir cream into purée. Raise heat to high and bring to boil. Reduce heat to medium and cook, stirring often, until cream is absorbed and mixture is reduced to 450 ml/¾ pint. Transfer mixture to a bowl and cool for 7 minutes.

Whisk eggs in medium-size bowl until blended. Gradually whisk in parsnip purée. Season to taste with salt, pepper, and nutmeg; season well so timbales will not be bland.

Divide mixture among moulds. Tap each on work surface to pack down. Smooth tops, set moulds in roasting pan and transfer to oven. Add enough boiling water to roasting pan to come halfway up sides of moulds. Set sheet of buttered foil on top.

Bake for about 40 minutes or until timbales are firm to touch and skewer inserted into centre comes out dry. If necessary add hot water to roasting pan occasionally so that it does not become dry. If water comes close to a boil add a few tablespoons of cold water.

PARSLEY SAUCE

Combine shallots, bay leaf and wine in a large heavy saucepan and bring to boil over high heat. Add stock and bring to boil. Reduce heat to medium-high and cook, stirring often, until liquid is reduced to about 150 ml/¼ pint. Stir in cream, add a pinch of salt and pepper and bring to boil, stirring. Reduce heat to medium and cook, stirring often, until sauce is thick enough to coat spoon; about 7 minutes. Strain sauce, pressing seasonings against sides of strainer. (Sauce can be kept, covered, for up to 1 day in refrigerator.)

Reheat sauce, if necessary, in a medium-size saucepan over low heat, whisking. Remove from heat and add cayenne pepper. Chop parsley in food processor, add sauce, and purée until well blended. Return to saucepan and heat, stirring, for about 2 minutes, or until again thick enough to coat a spoon. Taste and adjust seasoning.

To Finish Timbales and Sauce:

When timbales are done remove moulds from water bath. Cool on rack for 5 minutes. Carefully run thin-bladed flexible knife around edge of each mould. Set small plate atop mould and invert. Holding them together, tap on towel-covered working surface. Gently lift off mould. Repeat with remaining moulds. Cover each timbale gently with a mould while finishing sauce.

Remove moulds from timbales, spoon 2 to 3 tablespoons sauce on plate around timbale, and tilt plate so sauce runs around it. Serve remaining sauce separately.

SPINACH TIMBALES WITH QUICK CUMIN HOLLANDAISE SAUCE
Timbales d'épinards, sauce hollandaise au cumin

These deep green timbales are served with cumin-flavoured hollandaise sauce, typical of the current fashion of French cooks of incorporating seasonings from other cuisines (in this case, from nearby Morocco) into their own. For extra colour garnish the top of each timbale with a very small spoonful of diced raw or cooked tomato. The timbales are also good served alone or with Garlic Butter Sauce (page 17), Beurre Blanc (page 192), or Fresh Tomato Sauce (page 38).   MAKES 4 OR 5 SERVINGS

SPINACH TIMBALES

1·75 kg/4 lb fresh spinach (leaves with stems)
200 ml/7 fl oz double cream, at room temperature

3 eggs
Salt and white pepper
Freshly grated nutmeg

QUICK CUMIN HOLLANDAISE SAUCE

3 egg yolks, at room temperature
1 teaspoon ground cumin, preferably fresh
Salt
1 tablespoon strained fresh lemon juice

175 g/6 oz unsalted butter, cut in pieces
1 tablespoon hot water
Pinch of cayenne pepper

SPINACH TIMBALES
Preheat oven to 190°C/375°F/gas 5. Generously butter four 8-cm/ 3-inch ramekins or five timbale moulds, being careful to butter bases thoroughly. Butter sheet of foil to cover them.

Remove stems from spinach and wash leaves thoroughly. In very large saucepan of boiling salted water over high heat, cook spinach, uncovered, pushing leaves down into water often, for about 3 minutes or until very tender. Rinse with cold water and drain thoroughly. Squeeze by handfuls until dry. Purée in food processor until very smooth.

Cook purée in medium-size shallow, heavy saucepan over low heat, stirring often, for 5 minutes to evaporate excess moisture. Stir cream into purée. Raise heat to high and bring to boil. Reduce heat to medium and cook, stirring often, until cream is absorbed, and mixture is reduced to 450 ml/¾ pint. Transfer to bowl and cool for 7 minutes.

Whisk eggs in medium-size bowl until blended. Gradually whisk in spinach purée. Season to taste with salt, pepper and nutmeg; season well so timbales will not be bland.

Divide mixture among ramekins. Tap each on work surface to pack down. Smooth tops, set ramekins in roasting pan and transfer to oven. Add enough boiling water to roasting pan to come halfway up sides of ramekins. Set sheet of buttered foil atop ramekins.

Bake for about 40 minutes or until timbales are firm to touch and skewer inserted into centres comes out dry. If necessary occasionally add hot water to roasting pan so that it does not become dry. If water comes close to a boil add a few tablespoons of cold water.

When timbales are done remove moulds from water bath. Cool on rack for 5 minutes. Carefully run thin-bladed flexible knife around edge of each ramekin. Set small plate atop one and invert. Holding them together, tap on towel-lined working surface. Gently lift off ramekin. Repeat with remainder. Cover each timbale gently with a ramekin or mould while preparing sauce.

QUICK CUMIN HOLLANDAISE SAUCE

Prepare sauce a short time before serving. Combine egg yolks, cumin, salt, and 2 teaspoons lemon juice in blender or food processor and process until lightened in colour and very well blended. Remove pusher from processor.

Place butter in small heavy saucepan; if possible use one with a lip to facilitate pouring melted butter into blender or processor. Set over medium-low heat and warm until butter melts and sizzles. With blade of machine turning (at high speed if using blender), gradually pour hot butter, drop by drop, through top. After 2 or 3 tablespoons of butter have been added pour remaining butter through in thin, steady stream, with blade of machine still turning. Add hot water and process briefly to mix. Blend in cayenne pepper and remaining lemon juice. Taste and adjust seasoning. Use immediately.

To serve, uncover timbales, spoon 2 to 3 tablespoons sauce on plate around them and tilt plate so sauce runs around it. Serve remaining sauce separately.

NOTE: Three 275-g/10-oz packets of frozen spinach can be substituted for fresh. Thaw completely, squeeze dry, and purée. Measure 450 ml/¾ pint purée. Continue as above with step of heating purée with cream.

CAULIFLOWER TIMBALES WITH
TOMATO BUTTER SAUCE
Timbales de chou-fleur, beurre à la tomate

These timbales, whether served hot or at room temperature, are also good with Fresh Tomato Vinaigrette (page 34) or with a green salad. For a different shape bake them in oval moulds. The tomato butter sauce here can be prepared ahead or while the timbales are baking, except for the final amount of butter which should be added a short time before serving.   MAKES 4 OR 5 SERVINGS

CAULIFLOWER TIMBALES

One 1-kg/2-lb head of cauliflower
150 ml/¼ pint double cream, at
    room temperature

3 eggs
Salt and white pepper
Freshly grated nutmeg (optional)

TOMATO BUTTER SAUCE

1 sprig fresh thyme
1 bay leaf
5 parsley stalks
15 g/½ oz unsalted butter
100 g/4 oz chopped onion
2 medium-size garlic cloves, finely
    chopped
700 g/1½ lb ripe tomatoes, peeled,
    seeded (juice reserved), and
    chopped

225 g/8 oz unsalted butter, well
    chilled, cut in 1-cm/½-inch
    pieces
2 teaspoons tomato paste
Salt and freshly ground pepper

CAULIFLOWER TIMBALES

Preheat oven to 190°C/375°F/gas 5. Generously butter four 8-cm/ 3-inch ramekins or five small timbale moulds, being careful to butter bases thoroughly. Butter sheet of foil to cover them.

Discard leaves and large stalk from cauliflower and divide it into medium florets. In a large saucepan of boiling salted water over high heat, cook cauliflower, uncovered, for about 8 minutes or until very tender. Drain, rinse with cold water and drain thoroughly. Purée in food processor until very smooth. Measure 450 ml/¾ pint purée.

Cook purée in medium-size heavy wide saucepan over low heat, stirring often, for 5 minutes to evaporate excess moisture. Stir cream into purée. Raise heat to high and bring to boil. Reduce heat to medium and cook, stirring often, until cream is absorbed and mixture is reduced to 450 ml/¾ pint. Transfer to a bowl and cool for 7 minutes.

In medium-size bowl, whisk eggs until blended. Gradually whisk in cauliflower purée. Season to taste with salt, pepper and nutmeg; season well so timbales will not be bland.

Divide mixture among ramekins. Tap each on work surface to pack down. Smooth tops, set ramekins in roasting pan and transfer to oven. Add enough boiling water to roasting pan to come halfway up sides of ramekins. Set sheet of buttered foil atop ramekins.

Bake for about 40 minutes or until timbales are firm to touch and skewer inserted into centres comes out dry. If necessary, add hot water to roasting pan occasionally so that it does not become dry. If water comes close to a boil add a few tablespoons cold water.

TOMATO BUTTER SAUCE

Tie thyme, bay leaf and parsley stems in a piece of cheesecloth to make a bouquet garni. Melt 15 g/½ oz butter in medium saucepan over low heat. Stir in onion and cook over low heat, stirring, for about 10 minutes or until soft but not brown. Add garlic and cook for 30 seconds. Stir in tomato and add bouquet garni. Raise heat to medium and cook, stirring often, for about 25 minutes, or until mixture is thick and reduced to about 300 ml/½ pint. Discard bouquet garni. (Tomato mixture can be prepared 1 day ahead up to this point and refrigerated.)

To Finish Timbales and Sauce:

When timbales are done remove moulds from water bath. Cool on rack for 5 minutes. Carefully run thin-bladed flexible knife around edge of each mould. Set small plate atop ramekin and invert. Holding them together, tap on towel-covered working surface. Gently lift off ramekin. Repeat with remainder. Cover each timbale gently with a ramekin while finishing sauce.

Transfer tomato mixture to small saucepan. Bring to a simmer. Reduce heat to low. Add 2 cubes of butter, whisking liquid constantly. When butter cubes are nearly blended into liquid, add another cube, still whisking. Continue adding butter cubes, 1 or 2 at a time, whisking constantly. Sauce should thicken and should be pleasantly warm to touch. Do not cook too long. Remove from heat as soon as last butter cube is added.

Strain 2 tablespoons reserved tomato juice into sauce. Strain sauce into another small saucepan, pressing on tomatoes with back of spoon to extract all liquid. Place over very low heat briefly just to rewarm, whisking constantly. Remove from heat. Whisk in tomato paste. Add salt and pepper to taste. Serve immediately.

To serve, remove ramekins, spoon 2 to 3 tablespoons sauce on plate around timbale and tilt plate so sauce runs around it. Serve remaining sauce separately.

TURNIP TIMBALES
Timbales de navets

Turnips gain glamour when turned into timbales and go very well with roast duck, chicken or lamb. If desired serve the timbales with Parsley Sauce (page 20). No sauce is needed if the timbales will be an accompaniment for a dish that already has its own sauce.

MAKES 4 OR 5 SERVINGS

800 g/1¾ lb small turnips
150 ml/¼ pint double cream, at
   room temperature
3 eggs

Salt and white pepper
Freshly grated nutmeg
1 teaspoon snipped chives, for
   garnish (optional)

Preheat oven to 190°C/375°F/gas 5. Generously butter four 8-cm/3-inch ramekins or five small timbale moulds, being careful to thoroughly butter bases. Butter sheet of foil to cover them.

Peel turnips and cut into quarters. Put in medium-size saucepan, cover with water, add pinch of salt and bring to boil. Cover, reduce heat to medium-low and cook about 12 minutes or until very tender. Drain thoroughly. Purée in food processor until very smooth. Measure 450 ml/¾ pint purée.

Cook measured purée in medium-size heavy wide saucepan over low heat, stirring often, for 5 minutes to evaporate excess moisture. Stir cream into purée. Raise heat to high and bring to boil. Reduce heat to medium and cook, stirring often, until cream is absorbed and mixture is reduced to 450 ml/¾ pint. Transfer to a bowl and cool for 7 minutes.

Whisk eggs in medium-size bowl until blended. Gradually whisk in turnip purée. Season to taste with salt, pepper and nutmeg; season well so timbales will not be bland.

Divide mixture among ramekins. Tap each on work surface to pack down. Smooth tops, set ramekins in roasting pan and transfer to oven. Add enough boiling water to roasting pan to come halfway up sides of ramekins. Set sheet of buttered foil atop ramekins.

Bake for about 45 minutes or until timbales are firm to touch and a skewer inserted into centres comes out dry. If necessary add hot water to roasting pan occasionally so that it does not become dry. If water comes close to a boil add a few tablespoons cold water.

When timbales are done remove ramekins from water bath. Cool on rack for 5 minutes. Carefully run thin-bladed flexible knife around edge of each one. Set small plate atop one and invert. Holding them together, tap on towel-covered working surface. Gently lift off ramekin. Repeat with remainder.

If desired, garnish each timbale with a small pinch of snipped chives.

Vegetable Terrines and Moulds

Today vegetable terrines, or vegetable pâtés, as they are often called, are displayed in the windows of the finest French *charcuteries*. There are several ways to prepare them. The terrines can be made from layers of vegetable purées held together by eggs and baked; or vegetables can be added in pieces to give a colourful confetti effect to the terrine. To hold the vegetable pieces together French cooks use either a mousseline of chicken, veal or ham; a vegetable aspic; or a vegetable mousse (as in Vegetable Terrine with Mushroom Mousse and Fresh Tomato Vinaigrette, page 33). Terrines bound with aspic or mousse do not require baking.

TRICOLOURED VEGETABLE TERRINE WITH CREAMY BASIL-GARLIC SAUCE
Terrine tricolore de légumes, crème au basilic et à l'ail

Three vegetable purées – spinach, carrot and turnip – make up this terrine, producing a striped pattern of green, orange and white. It is easiest to slice when cold. A platter of slices of this terrine, with the sauce served on the side, makes a lovely buffet dish.

MAKES 8 SERVINGS

TRICOLOURED VEGETABLE TERRINE

Spinach Layer

1·5 kg/3 lb fresh spinach (leaves with stems)

150 ml/¼ pint double cream, at room temperature

2 eggs

1 egg yolk

Salt and freshly ground pepper

Freshly grated nutmeg

Carrot Layer

450 g/1 lb carrots

6 tablespoons double cream, at room temperature

2 eggs

Salt and freshly ground pepper

Turnip Layer

450 g/1 lb small turnips

5 tablespoons double cream, at room temperature

2 eggs

Salt and white pepper

Freshly grated nutmeg

CREAMY BASIL-GARLIC SAUCE

3 large garlic cloves, finely chopped

4 tablespoons dry white wine

400 ml/14 fl oz double cream, plus a few teaspoons more if necessary

Salt and freshly ground pepper

4 tablespoons chopped fresh basil

A few drops fresh lemon juice

To Begin Spinach, Carrot, and Turnip Layers: Remove stems of fresh spinach and wash leaves thoroughly. In very large saucepan of boiling salted water, cook spinach, uncovered, over high heat, pushing leaves down into water often; about 3 minutes, or until very tender. Drain, rinse with cold water, and drain thoroughly. Squeeze by handfuls until dry. Purée in food processor until very smooth.

Peel carrots and cut in crosswise slices 1 cm/½ inch thick. Put carrots in medium-size saucepan, cover with water, add pinch of salt, and bring to boil. Cover, reduce heat to medium, and cook about 35 minutes, or until very tender. Drain thoroughly. Purée in food processor until very smooth.

Peel turnips and cut into quarters. Put in medium-size saucepan, cover with water, add pinch of salt, cover, and bring to boil. Reduce heat to medium-low and cook for about 20 minutes, or until very tender. Drain thoroughly. Purée in food processor until very smooth.

Preheat oven to 190°C/375°F/gas 5. Generously butter a 20- by 10-cm/8- by 4-inch loaf tin. Line base and sides of tin with parchment paper, letting paper extend slightly above edge of tin, and butter paper. Butter a sheet of foil to cover terrine.

To Enrich Each Layer with Cream: Cook spinach purée in medium-size heavy, wide saucepan over low heat, stirring often, for 5 minutes to evaporate excess moisture. Stir 150 ml/¼ pint cream into purée. Raise heat to high and bring to boil. Reduce heat to medium and cook, stirring often, until cream is absorbed and mixture is reduced to about 450 ml/¾ pint; about 5 minutes. Transfer to bowl.

Cook carrot purée in medium-size heavy, wide saucepan over low heat, stirring often, for 5 minutes to evaporate excess moisture. Stir 6 tablespoons cream into purée. Raise heat to high and bring to boil. Reduce heat to medium and cook, stirring often, until cream is absorbed and mixture is reduced to about 350 ml/12 fl oz; about 8 minutes. Transfer to bowl.

Cook turnip purée in medium-size heavy, wide saucepan over low heat, stirring often, for 5 minutes to evaporate excess moisture. Stir 5 tablespoons cream into purée. Raise heat to high and bring to boil. Reduce heat to medium and cook, stirring often, until cream is absorbed and mixture is reduced to about 350 ml/12 fl oz; about 12 minutes. Transfer to bowl.

To Complete Each Layer and Assemble Terrine: For spinach, whisk 2 eggs with 1 yolk in large bowl until blended. Gradually whisk in spinach mixture. Season to taste with salt, pepper, and nutmeg. For carrot layer, whisk 2 eggs in a bowl; whisk in carrot mixture. Season to taste with salt and pepper. For turnip layer, whisk 2 eggs in a bowl; whisk in turnip mixture. Season to taste with salt, pepper, and nutmeg. Season each well so terrine will not be bland.

Spread spinach mixture evenly in terrine. Tap on work surface to pack down. Spoon carrot mixture over spinach mixture and spread smooth. Last, spoon turnip mixture evenly on top. Smooth gently. Set terrine in roasting pan and transfer to oven. Add enough boiling water to come halfway up sides of terrine. Set sheet of buttered foil atop terrine.

Bake for about 2½ hours or until terrine is firm to touch when pressed gently and skewer inserted into centre comes out dry. During baking, add hot water to roasting pan occasionally so that it does not become dry. If water comes close to a boil, add a few tablespoons cold water.

CREAMY BASIL-GARLIC SAUCE

Combine garlic and wine in a large, heavy saucepan and bring to a boil over high heat. Reduce heat to medium-high and cook, stirring often, until liquid is reduced to about 2 tablespoons.

Stir in cream, add a pinch of salt and pepper, and bring to a boil, stirring. Reduce heat to medium and cook, stirring often, until sauce is thick enough to coat a spoon; about 7 minutes. (Sauce can be kept, covered, for up to 1 day in refrigerator.)

To Finish Terrine and Sauce:

When terrine is done, carefully remove it from water bath. For serving warm, cool terrine on rack for at least 30 minutes. If necessary, carefully run a metal spatula around edge of terrine. Set oval or rectangular platter atop loaf tin and invert both. Gently lift off pan. Carefully peel off paper. Slice very gently with point of a thin-bladed sharp knife in 2-cm/¾-inch slices. Slices are fragile, especially when warm. With aid of a spatula, set each slice on a plate. Serve warm, at room temperature, or cold.

If sauce was prepared in advance, and will be served hot, reheat in a small saucepan over low heat, whisking.

Add basil. Flavour with a few drops of lemon juice and a little freshly ground pepper. If sauce is too thick, stir in a few teaspoons cream. Taste and adjust seasoning. Serve the sauce hot or at room temperature.

Spoon 2 to 3 tablespoons sauce on plate around slice of terrine and tilt plate so sauce runs around it. Serve remaining sauce separately.

NOTE: Two 275-g/10-oz packets of frozen spinach can be substituted for fresh. Thaw completely, squeeze dry, and purée. Measure 350 ml/12 fl oz purée. Continue as above, with step of heating purée with cream.

VEGETABLE TERRINE WITH MUSHROOM MOUSSE AND FRESH TOMATO VINAIGRETTE
Terrine de légumes à la mousse de champignons, vinaigrette à la tomate

The Troisgros brothers started the fashion of serving vegetable terrines in fine restaurants and their terrine is indeed delicious. For our elegant, light terrine, a creamy white mushroom mousse flecked with herbs is layered with a variety of fresh vegetables. The vegetables are lined up in rows so they dot each slice. When the terrine is cut you see the mosaic pattern of colourful vegetables – golden carrots, asparagus, green beans, and peas. I find this terrine tastier than other 'vegetable' terrines bound by meat mixtures. Perfect for warm weather, the terrine requires no baking and is served cold or at room temperature.

The tomato vinaigrette is a favourite accompaniment for vegetable terrines in starred restaurants. It is also marvellous with simply cooked vegetables. MAKES 8 SERVINGS

VEGETABLE TERRINE
Vegetables

3 fairly thin carrots of even thickness, about 20 cm/8 in long (about 150 g/5 oz)	*75 g/3 oz green or yellow beans, ends removed, broken in 3 pieces*
5 medium asparagus spears, peeled	*450 g/1 lb fresh peas, shelled*

Mushroom Mousse

450 ml/¾ pint double cream	*6 tablespoons water*
175 g/6 oz very white mushrooms,	*1½ tablespoons chopped tarragon*
halved and sliced	*1½ tablespoons chopped parsley*
Salt and freshly ground pepper	*1 tablespoon snipped chives*
15 g/½ oz powdered gelatine	

FRESH TOMATO VINAIGRETTE

700 g/1½ lb large ripe, very red	*Salt and freshly ground pepper*
tomatoes	*200 ml/7 fl oz plus 2 or 3*
1½ tablespoons white wine vinegar	*tablespoons extra virgin olive oil*
or herb vinegar	*1 tablespoon chopped tarragon*
	1 tablespoon chopped parsley

VEGETABLES

Cut off tapering ends of carrots so each carrot is of even thickness. Put carrots in a medium-size saucepan of salted water and bring to a simmer. Cover and cook for about 30 minutes, or until carrots are very tender when pierced with sharp knife. Drain thoroughly.

In a sauté pan of boiling salted water to generously cover, cook asparagus, uncovered, for about 3 minutes, or until just tender. Drain very thoroughly.

In a medium-size saucepan containing enough boiling salted water to generously cover, cook beans, uncovered, over high heat for about 5 minutes, or until just tender. Rinse with cold water and drain very thoroughly.

In a medium-size saucepan of boiling salted water, cook peas for about 5 minutes, or until just tender. Rinse with cold water and drain very thoroughly.

MUSHROOM MOUSSE

Bring 350 ml/12 fl oz cream to a simmer in a large, heavy saucepan. Refrigerate remaining cream and chill a medium bowl for whipping it. Add mushrooms, salt, and pepper to simmering cream. Reduce heat to low and cook, uncovered, stirring often, for about 30 minutes, or until mushrooms are very tender and cream is well flavoured.

Transfer mushrooms to a food processor using slotted spoon. Process with short bursts of food processor until mushrooms are coarsely chopped. Return to pan of cream. (If using blender, process mushrooms together with cream.)

Sprinkle gelatine over 6 tablespoons very hot water in a small cup and let stand for 5 minutes to soften. Bring mushrooms in cream to a boil and remove from heat. Add gelatine and stir thoroughly to dissolve completely. Transfer to a bowl. Cool to room temperature. Stir in herbs.

Whip remaining cream in chilled bowl until soft peaks form. Fold into mushroom mixture. (Mixture should be thick enough so mushrooms do not fall to bottom; if it is not thick enough, refrigerate for a few minutes, stirring often so it does not set.) Taste and adjust seasoning; mixture should be well seasoned so it will not be bland after chilling.

To Assemble Terrine:
Lightly oil a 20- by 10-cm/8- by 4-inch loaf tin. When layering vegetables with mousse, do not let pieces of vegetable touch side of pan; vegetable pieces should be surrounded by mousse.

To layer vegetables with mousse, spoon about 200 ml/7 fl oz mushroom mousse into loaf tin. Arrange carrots in pan lengthwise, with thicker end of centre carrot in opposite direction from other two. Spoon 200 ml/7 fl oz mushroom mousse over carrots. Arrange peas on top in one layer. Carefully spoon 6 tablespoons mushroom mousse over peas. Arrange beans on top in one layer, in four lengthwise rows. Carefully spoon 6 tablespoons mushroom mousse over beans. Arrange asparagus on top, with tips of alternating spears pointing in opposite directions. Spoon remaining mousse over asparagus. Cover and refrigerate for 4 hours. (Terrine can be kept for up to 2 days in refrigerator.)

FRESH TOMATO VINAIGRETTE
Peel, cut into halves, and seed tomatoes. Then cut each half into quarters, salt lightly, and leave in strainer for 15 minutes to drain well.

Finely chop tomato pieces, transfer to a medium-size bowl, add vinegar, salt, and pepper, and whisk until smooth. Gradually whisk in all but 1 tablespoon olive oil, drop by drop. The sauce should remain thick and emulsified. Taste and add remaining tablespoon oil, if desired. Add herbs, taste, and adjust seasoning. Serve at room temperature.

To Finish and Serve:
To unmould terrine, run a thin-bladed flexible knife around its edge, gently pushing mixture slightly from edge of mould to let in air. Dip mould, nearly to depth of contents, in warm, not hot, water for about 10 seconds. Dry outside of mould, and set a long platter on top. Holding platter and mould firmly together, flip quickly so terrine is upside down. Shake mould gently downwards; terrine should slip from mould on to platter. If terrine remains in mould, repeat dipping procedure. Carefully remove mould by lifting it straight up. Refrigerate terrine until ready to serve.

To serve, cut in 2-cm/¾-inch slices using a sharp, heavy knife, cutting cleanly through vegetables. Set on plates. Spoon a little tomato vinaigrette next to each slice.

QUICK SPINACH PÂTÉ
Pâté d'épinards minute

The French term *pâté* is now used interchangeably with *terrine*, but this recipe illustrates the other type of pâté – a flavourful spread. Serve this bright green pâté with fresh or toasted French bread or with lightly salted crackers.   MAKES ABOUT 4 SERVINGS

700 g/1½ lb spinach (leaves with stems)
25 g/1 oz butter
Salt and freshly ground pepper
Freshly grated nutmeg

8 tablespoons Crème Fraîche (page 381) or bought crème fraîche
1 tablespoon chopped parsley (optional)

Remove spinach stems and wash leaves thoroughly. In a large saucepan of boiling salted water, cook spinach, uncovered, over high heat, pushing leaves down into water often, until very tender, about 3 minutes. Rinse with cold water and squeeze dry by handfuls.

Melt butter in medium-size saucepan. Add spinach, salt, pepper, and nutmeg, and cook over medium heat, stirring, for about 2 minutes, or until spinach absorbs butter and any excess liquid has evaporated. Remove from heat and cool to room temperature.

Purée spinach in food processor with 3 tablespoons crème fraîche. Stir in remaining crème fraîche. Add parsley, if desired. Taste for seasoning; the spread should be generously seasoned with nutmeg. (Pâté can be kept, covered, for 1 day in refrigerator.) Serve in a bowl or a ramekin at room temperature.

NOTE: Instead of crème fraîche, you can use 6 tablespoons sour cream mixed with 2 tablespoons double cream.

AUBERGINE SAVARIN WITH FRESH TOMATO SAUCE
Savarin d'aubergines, sauce tomate

This ring-shaped aubergine dish is named for the familiar cake of the same form. In France it's popular to make use of aubergine slices with their skin on to line a mould and form an attractive pattern. Small Japanese aubergines are ideal because they can be cut in thin slices and their peels are not tough. Choose straight rather than curved ones for this savarin so it will be easy to slice them lengthwise. The dried mushrooms used in the filling are available at speciality food shops.

MAKES 6 FIRST-COURSE SERVINGS,
OR 2 TO 3 MAIN-COURSE SERVINGS

FRESH TOMATO SAUCE

2 large sprigs fresh thyme, or ½
 teaspoon dried thyme
1 bay leaf
2 tablespoons extra virgin olive oil

2 medium-size garlic cloves, finely
 chopped
700 g/1½ lb ripe tomatoes, peeled,
 seeded, and chopped
Salt and freshly ground pepper
1 tablespoon tomato paste

AUBERGINE SAVARIN

15 g/½ oz dried cèpes or porcini
 mushrooms
6 Japanese aubergines (about 600
 g/1¼ lb)
About 200 ml/7 fl oz olive oil

Salt and freshly ground pepper
2 medium-size garlic cloves, finely
 chopped
3 tablespoons chopped parsley
4 eggs
4 tablespoons freshly grated
 Parmesan cheese

FRESH TOMATO SAUCE

Wind a piece of kitchen string around fresh thyme and bay leaf several times and tie them together to make a bouquet garni; if using dried thyme, wrap it and bay leaf in a piece of cheesecloth and tie tightly. Heat oil in a medium-size heavy saucepan over low heat. Add garlic and cook, stirring occasionally, for 30 seconds. Add tomatoes, bouquet garni, salt, and pepper. Combine well and bring mixture to a boil. Reduce heat to low and cook, uncovered, stirring occasionally, for about 40 minutes, or until tomatoes are very soft and sauce is thick. Discard bouquet garni. Stir tomato paste into sauce.

Purée sauce in a food processor or blender until smooth. Taste and adjust seasoning. (The sauce may be kept, covered, for up to 3 days in refrigerator.)

AUBERGINE SAVARIN

Soak mushrooms in a bowl of hot water, covered, for 30 minutes or until softened. Drain, rinse, and pat them dry. Chop them in very small pieces and reserve.

Cut caps off 4 aubergines. Cut off a lengthwise slice at one side and cut aubergines in 6-mm/¼-inch lengthwise slices so that each slice has a rim of peel.

Heat 3 tablespoons oil in a large frying pan over medium-high heat until it is very hot. Add enough aubergine slices to make one layer and sauté them for 1 minute on each side, or until they are just tender. Drain them and pat them dry on paper towels. Add 3 tablespoons oil to pan, heat oil until it is hot, and sauté remaining aubergine in batches the same way, adding more oil between batches as necessary so that pan is never dry; you will need about 4 tablespoons more oil.

Lightly oil a 1-litre/2-pint ring mould. Line it with about 20 sautéed aubergine slices, placing them crosswise in mould with their more attractive side facing down and wider end of each slice resting on outer edge of mould; overlap slices slightly so there are no holes.

Preheat oven to 180°C/350°F/gas 4. Cut remaining aubergines and any remaining pieces of first ones in 1-cm/½-inch dice. You will need 400 g/14 oz of diced aubergine. Measure any oil left from sautéing slices and add enough to make 2 tablespoons. Heat it in a medium-size frying pan, add diced aubergine and a small pinch of salt and pepper, and sauté over medium heat for 2 minutes. Reduce heat to low, cover, and cook, stirring often, for 15 minutes or until very tender. Stir in reserved mushrooms, add garlic, and cook, stirring, for 1 minute. Transfer to a bowl and let cool to lukewarm. Stir parsley, eggs, and cheese into aubergine mixture, taste, and add salt and pepper, if needed.

Spoon mixture into prepared ring mould. Cover with a sheet of foil, set it in a roasting pan, and add enough very hot water to come halfway up sides of mould. Bake for 45 minutes, or until a skewer inserted in several places comes out clean. Remove mould from pan of water and let it cool on a rack for 10 minutes.

Cut off any aubergine ends sticking up above filling in mould and place them on filling. Run a thin-bladed flexible knife around outer and inner edges of ring. Unmould ring on to a round platter. Spoon hot tomato sauce into centre of ring. Serve savarin hot; leftovers are also good cold.

SPINACH-CAULIFLOWER GÂTEAU
WITH CREAMY MUSHROOM SAUCE
Gâteau d'épinards et chou-fleur, sauce aux
champignons

This festive layered vegetable cake, decorated with carrot 'coins', can be assembled at leisure and served hot or at room temperature.

To feature it as the star of a menu highlighting vegetables accompany it by fresh bread and serve a light salad, such as Marinated Green Bean Salad with Spring Onions (page 348) or Chicory and Beetroot Salad (page 357), followed by a simple fruit dessert.

MAKES 3 TO 5 MAIN-COURSE SERVINGS,

OR 6 TO 8 APPETIZER SERVINGS

SPINACH-CAULIFLOWER GÂTEAU

2 medium-size carrots of uniform thickness, trimmed, peeled, and thinly sliced

1·25 kg/2½ lb cauliflower (about 2 small heads), trimmed of leaves and large stalk, divided into medium-size florets

40 g/1½ oz butter

3 tablespoons double cream

1 kg/2 lb fresh spinach (leaves with stems)

4 eggs

2 tablespoons chopped fresh dill

5 tablespoons fine, dry bread crumbs

Salt and white pepper

Freshly grated nutmeg

CREAMY MUSHROOM SAUCE

20 g/¾ oz butter

100 g/4 oz button mushrooms, halved and cut in thin slices

Salt and freshly ground pepper

225 ml/8 fl oz double cream

1 tablespoon chopped parsley

SPINACH-CAULIFLOWER GÂTEAU

Put carrots in medium-size saucepan; add enough water to cover and a pinch of salt. Bring to boil. Reduce heat to low, cover, and simmer until very tender; about 7 minutes. Drain.

In large saucepan of boiling salted water, boil cauliflower, uncovered, for about 7 minutes, or until very tender. Drain, rinse with cold water, and drain. Purée in food processor or blender until very smooth. Melt 25 g/1 oz butter in large heavy saucepan. Add cauliflower purée and cook over medium heat, stirring very often, for about 10 minutes, or until butter is absorbed and purée is dry. Add 2 tablespoons cream and cook, stirring, for 2 minutes. Transfer to bowl and cool to room temperature.

Remove spinach stems and wash leaves thoroughly. In very large saucepan of boiling salted water, cook spinach, uncovered, over high heat, pushing leaves down into water often, until very tender; about 3 minutes. Rinse with cold water and squeeze dry by handfuls. Purée in food processor until very smooth. Melt 15 g/½ oz butter in large heavy saucepan. Add spinach purée and cook over low heat, stirring, for about 3 minutes, or until butter is absorbed and purée is dry. Add 1 tablespoon cream and cook, stirring, for 30 seconds. Transfer to second bowl and cool to room temperature. (Carrots, cauliflower purée, and spinach purée can be prepared up to 8 hours in advance and kept covered in refrigerator.)

Beat 2 eggs and add to bowl of cauliflower. Add dill and 4 tablespoons bread crumbs, and season to taste with salt and white pepper. Beat remaining 2 eggs and add to spinach. Add 1 tablespoon bread crumbs and season to taste with salt, white pepper, and nutmeg.

Preheat oven to 190°C/375°F/gas 5. Heavily butter a 1-litre/2-pint soufflé dish. Line base with foil, press in foil smoothly, and butter. Arrange carrot slices of uniform size, side by side, in two concentric rings on base of dish. Set one carrot slice in centre. (Reserve remaining carrot slices for other uses.)

Spoon 350 ml/12 fl oz cauliflower purée carefully over carrots. Spread smooth with rubber spatula. Tap dish on work surface so contents settle. Spoon spinach purée by tablespoons over cauliflower and spread to smooth layer. Spoon remaining cauliflower purée by tablespoons over spinach purée and spread to smooth layer. (Layers must be added carefully so each remains distinct.)

Set soufflé dish in roasting pan and add enough boiling water to come to one-third of height of dish. Set piece of buttered foil on top. Bake, adding more boiling water to water bath if it evaporates, for about 2 hours, or until gâteau is set and a skewer inserted into centre comes out clean. (Mixture should not stick to your fingers when pressed on top.) Remove from oven. (Gâteau can be kept warm in water bath for 30 minutes.) Remove from water bath and let stand for 10 minutes. If desired, let cool to room temperature.

CREAMY MUSHROOM SAUCE

In a medium-size frying pan, melt butter over medium-high heat. Add mushrooms, salt, and pepper. Sauté, tossing often, for about 4 minutes, or until mushrooms are tender and lightly browned and any liquid that escapes from them has evaporated. Add cream, reduce heat to medium-low, and simmer, stirring often, until sauce is thick enough to coat a spoon; about 5 minutes. (Sauce can be prepared up to 8 hours in advance and kept covered in refrigerator. Reheat in saucepan over low heat; thin if necessary with 1 or 2 tablespoons cream.) Stir in parsley. Taste and adjust seasoning.

To serve, carefully run a thin-bladed flexible knife around sides of vegetable gâteau and unmould on to round platter. Carefully peel off foil. Serve sauce separately. When cutting, place a metal spatula or pie server underneath the gâteau so wedges stay whole.

Vegetable Mousses

Mousses made of purées of colourful cooked vegetables make creamy, fresh-tasting appetizers. Like fruit mousses, they are held together with a little gelatine and enriched with whipped cream. They can be formed into an impressive soufflé, as in Cold Carrot Soufflé with Peas (page 48), or can be unmoulded from a ring mould, as in Two-Tone Tomato Mousse (below). Vegetable Bavarians are a special type of mousse, modelled on the pattern of dessert Bavarian creams.

TWO-TONE TOMATO MOUSSE
Mousse de tomates

The two layers of this mousse – one of deep red colour and the other creamy – are both made from the same fresh tomato mixture.

MAKES 4 TO 6 SERVINGS

1 tablespoon vegetable oil
1 medium-size garlic clove, finely chopped
1·25 kg/2½ lb ripe tomatoes, peeled, seeded (juice reserved), and finely chopped
1½ teaspoons fresh thyme, or ½ teaspoon dried thyme

1 bay leaf
Salt and freshly ground pepper
1 tablespoon chopped fresh basil, or 1 teaspoon dried basil (optional)
1 to 2 teaspoons tomato paste (optional)
7 g/¼ oz powdered gelatine

3 hard-boiled eggs, cut in half
200 ml/7 fl oz double cream, well
   chilled

Fresh French bread or toast, for
   serving

Heat oil in a large frying or sauté pan over medium heat. Add garlic and sauté, stirring, for 30 seconds. Add tomatoes, thyme, bay leaf, salt, and pepper. Cook over medium heat, stirring often, for about 20 minutes, or until tomatoes are soft and mixture is thick and smooth. Discard bay leaf. Stir in basil. If a deeper colour is desired, stir in tomato paste.

Put about 225 ml/8 fl oz of mixture into a medium-size bowl (for red tomato layer) and remaining mixture into a larger bowl (for creamy layer).

Pour 4 tablespoons reserved tomato juice into a small heatproof bowl, and sprinkle with gelatine. Leave for 5 minutes to soften. Set bowl over a saucepan of hot water over very low heat, and stir for about 5 minutes, or until dissolved.

Stir 2 tablespoons of gelatine into tomato mixture reserved for red layer. Combine thoroughly to be sure gelatine is evenly distributed. Taste and adjust seasoning. Overseason slightly to avoid blandness after chilling. Stir remaining gelatine into second tomato mixture in large bowl; combine thoroughly.

Refrigerate the medium-size bowl of red tomato mixture for 5 minutes, or set in a bowl of ice cubes and water to chill, stirring often to prevent it from setting at sides and bottom. Lightly oil a 1-litre/2-pint ring mould or other decorative mould.

Spoon chilled red tomato mixture into mould. Arrange egg halves on top at regular intervals, being careful not to let them touch sides of mould. Chill mould 10 minutes, leaving second bowl of tomato mixture at room temperature. Chill bowl for whipping cream.

Whip cream in chilled bowl until soft peaks form. Fold it into remaining tomato mixture. If mixture sets before cream is added, whisk it first until smooth, and whisk in cream. Taste for seasoning; overseason slightly. Carefully spoon it into mould, without moving eggs. Smooth with a rubber spatula, making sure to push mixture into cracks between mould and eggs. Refrigerate for at least 2 hours, or until set. (The mousse can be kept, covered, for up to 8 hours in refrigerator.)

To unmould mousse, run a thin-bladed flexible knife around its edge, gently pushing mixture slightly from edge of mould to let in air. If using a ring mould, run knife around central part of ring. Dip mould, nearly to depth of contents, in warm, not hot, water for about 10 seconds. Dry mould. Set a round platter on top of mould. Holding them firmly together, flip quickly so mould is upside down. Shake mould gently downward; mousse should slip from mould on to platter. If mousse remains in mould, repeat dipping procedure. Carefully remove mould by lifting it straight up. Refrigerate mousse until ready to serve.

Serve with fresh French bread or toast.

AVOCADO MOUSSE
Mousse d'avocats

Avocado halves are often used in France as attractive containers for a variety of luxurious salads or for mousses, as in this recipe. If desired set each avocado half on a bed of lettuce and decorate with a few Niçoise olives.   MAKES 4 SERVINGS

2 large ripe avocados
*1 tablespoon strained fresh lemon
   juice, or to taste*
2 teaspoons chopped parsley
1 tablespoon snipped chives
Salt
Pinch of cayenne pepper

3 tablespoons water
1 teaspoon powdered gelatine
*4 tablespoons double cream, well
   chilled*
*3 small cherry tomatoes, or 2 small
   plum tomatoes, for garnish*
*French bread or toast, for an
   accompaniment*

Cut avocados in half carefully. Remove each stone by hitting it with heel of a sharp knife so that it sticks in stone; then lift stone up. Carefully remove avocado pulp with a spoon, reserving shells to use as serving containers.

In a food processor, purée avocado pulp with lemon juice. Transfer to a medium-size bowl and stir in parsley, 2 teaspoons chives, salt, and cayenne pepper to taste.

Pour water into a small cup and sprinkle gelatine over it. Let stand for 5 minutes. Set cup in a pan of hot water over low heat, and stir until gelatine is dissolved. Whisk into avocado purée. Cool to room temperature. Chill small bowl for whipping cream.

Whip cream in chilled bowl until soft peaks form. Fold it into avocado mixture. Cover by setting cling film directly on surface of mousse. Refrigerate for 1 hour or until thick. (The mousse can be prepared up to 4 hours in advance but no longer because it will discolour.)

To serve, cut tomatoes in crosswise slices. Spoon mousse into avocado halves. Smooth tops.

Arrange row of tomato slices lengthwise down middle of each avocado half. Sprinkle tomatoes with remaining chives. Serve with French bread or toast.

BROCCOLI BAVARIAN
Bavarois de brocolis

Although Bavarian creams are traditionally sweet, French chefs now make savoury Bavarians as well, using vegetables. This pale green Bavarian is prepared in the same way as a dessert Bavarian but, of course, without sugar and with vegetable purée as the flavouring. Small briefly cooked broccoli florets provide a bright garnish and pleasantly textured accompaniment.   MAKES 8 SERVINGS

1 kg/2 lb broccoli
4 tablespoons water
7 g/¼ oz plus 1½ teaspoons
   powdered gelatine
3 egg yolks, at room temperature

225 ml/8 fl oz milk
Salt and white pepper
Freshly grated nutmeg
225 ml/8 fl oz double cream, well
   chilled

Remove about 25 small florets from broccoli, refrigerate and reserve for garnish. Divide remaining broccoli into medium-size florets. Peel thick stalk with paring knife and cut in slices about 6 mm/¼ inch thick.

In a large saucepan of boiling salted water, cook broccoli florets (except those reserved for garnish) and slices, uncovered, over high heat for about 7 minutes, or until very tender. Drain, rinse gently with cold water until completely cooled, and drain thoroughly.

Purée in food processor until very smooth. Return purée to saucepan and cook over low heat, stirring, for 5 minutes to dry it slightly.

Pour water in small bowl and sprinkle gelatine over it. Let stand for 5 minutes.

Whisk egg yolks in medium bowl. Bring milk to a simmer in a small heavy saucepan. Gradually pour milk into yolks, whisking. Return to saucepan and cook over low heat, stirring constantly, until slightly thickened so it just begins to coat a spoon; on an instant-read thermometer, it should reach 66°C/150°F. (It will not be as thick as sweet *crème anglaise*.) Remove from heat and immediately whisk in gelatine. Pour into large bowl. Whisk in broccoli purée. Season to taste with salt, white pepper, and nutmeg.

Cool broccoli mixture to room temperature. Lightly oil a 1.25-litre/2¼-pint ring mould. Chill a large bowl for whipping cream.

Whip cream in chilled bowl until soft peaks form. Fold cream into broccoli purée. Taste and add more salt, pepper, and nutmeg, if needed. Overseason slightly to avoid blandness after chilling. Fold in seasoning thoroughly and spoon mixture into prepared mould.

Refrigerate for about 4 hours or until set. Cover after top sets. (Mould can be kept for up to 1 day in refrigerator.)

In a medium-size saucepan of boiling salted water, boil florets reserved for garnish, uncovered, over high heat for about 2 minutes, or until barely tender and still bright green. Drain, rinse gently with cold water until well cooled, and drain thoroughly.

To unmould Bavarian, run a thin-bladed flexible knife around edge of mould, gently pushing mixture slightly from edge to let in air. Run knife around central part of ring as well. Dip mould, nearly to depth of contents, in warm, not hot, water for about 10 seconds. Dry mould. Set a round platter on top. Holding them firmly together, flip quickly so mould is upside down. Shake mould gently downwards; mixture should slip from mould on to platter. If mixture remains in mould, repeat dipping procedure. Carefully remove mould by lifting it straight up. Spread if necessary to smooth. Refrigerate Bavarian until ready to serve.

To serve, garnish centre or outer edge with blanched broccoli florets. If placing them in centre, arrange one layer in centre of ring and put remaining florets on top, with their flower ends pointing outward.

COLD CARROT SOUFFLÉ WITH PEAS
Soufflé froid aux carottes et aux petits pois

This soufflé resembles a dessert soufflé in appearance but is actually a festive first course in disguise. The creamy carrot mousse is layered with a green pea mousse for a ribboned effect.   MAKES 8 SERVINGS

15 g/½ oz butter
White part of 1 medium-size leek, chopped
1 kg/2 lb carrots, peeled and cut into 2·5-cm/1-inch chunks
750 ml/1¼ pints water
1 bay leaf

Salt and freshly ground pepper
275 g/10 oz shelled fresh or frozen peas
7 g/¼ oz plus 1 teaspoon powdered gelatine
350 ml/12 fl oz double cream, well chilled

GARNISH

Reserved carrots and peas
4 tablespoons double cream, well chilled

Pinch of salt

Melt butter in a large saucepan, add leek, and cook over low heat, stirring, for about 7 minutes, or until softened. Add carrots, water, bay leaf, salt, and pepper. Bring to a boil. Cover, reduce heat to low, and cook for about 25 minutes, or until carrots are very tender. Do not drain.

Cut a 64-cm/25-inch sheet of greaseproof paper and fold it in half. Wrap paper around a 1-litre/2-pint glass soufflé dish so that it extends about 5 cm/2 inches above rim to make a collar. Fasten tightly with sticky tape.

In a large saucepan of boiling salted water, cook peas for about 5 minutes for fresh or 2 minutes for frozen peas, or until just tender. Remove about 50 g/2 oz peas with slotted spoon; these will be left whole. Continue cooking remaining peas for about 2 more minutes, or until tender enough to purée. Meanwhile, drain reserved peas and rinse well; set aside. Drain remaining peas and rinse well. Purée with 2 tablespoons carrot cooking liquid and transfer to a bowl.

Discard bay leaf from carrots. Set aside 3 pieces carrot for garnish. Remove carrot and leek pieces with slotted spoon, reserving liquid. Pour 4 tablespoons cooking liquid into a small bowl and cool to room temperature. Pour 225 ml/8 fl oz remaining liquid into a medium-size saucepan.

Purée carrot and leek pieces until smooth. Return to dry saucepan and dry purée over low heat, stirring constantly, for about 5 minutes. Transfer to a large bowl.

Chill a large bowl for whipping cream. Sprinkle gelatine over the carrot liquid in the small bowl. Let stand for 5 minutes to soften. Bring carrot liquid in pan to boil and remove from heat. Add softened gelatine and whisk until gelatine is completely dissolved.

Pour 3 tablespoons gelatine mixture into pea purée, stirring vigorously. Pour remaining gelatine into carrot purée, stirring vigorously.

Set bowl of carrot mixture in a bowl of ice cubes and water, stirring often to prevent mixture from setting at sides and bottom of bowl, until completely cool but not set.

Whip cream in chilled bowl until soft peaks form. Fold 450 ml/¾ pint whipped cream into carrot purée and remaining cream into pea purée. Fold all but 1 tablespoon of peas into pea mixture. Taste each and adjust seasoning; mixtures should be slightly overseasoned so soufflé will not be bland after chilling. Fold in seasoning thoroughly.

Spoon about 600 ml/1 pint of carrot mousse into prepared dish.

Spoon all of pea mousse carefully over carrot layer. Refrigerate for 20 minutes, keeping remaining carrot mixture at room temperature. Spoon remaining carrot mousse carefully on top of pea layer. Smooth top. Refrigerate for about 5 hours, or until set. (Mousse can be kept overnight; keep remaining carrot pieces and peas separately, covered.)

For Garnish: Chill a small bowl for whipping cream. Cut reserved carrot pieces into small dice about size of peas. Whip 4 tablespoons cream with pinch of salt in chilled bowl until stiff.

To serve, carefully peel off and discard paper from soufflé dish. Using a piping bag and small star tip, pipe an even number of rosettes of whipped cream on top of soufflé near edge. Decorate with small pieces of carrot and peas by setting them on top of alternating rosettes. Serve cold.

Vegetable Soufflés

To many soufflés are the symbol of French cooking because they are delicate, rich yet light, and have the reputation of being difficult to prepare. Actually they are quite simple to make and do not involve techniques different from those required for making many cakes.

Vegetable soufflés are made basically of vegetable purée mixed with cream sauce, enriched with egg yolks, and lightened with beaten egg whites. Although they can be made without the sauce, the soufflés taste moister and more creamy when it is included. Vegetable soufflés are delicious when flavoured with cheeses, as in Spinach and Goat Cheese Soufflé (page 52).

Although soufflés are generally baked in a soufflé dish, they can be baked in individual dishes or even inside crêpes, as in Aubergine Soufflé-Filled Crêpes with Red Pepper Sauce (page 122).

When prepared to the French taste soufflés should be soft and moist inside, so that the inner part acts almost as a sauce for the outer, firmer section. Still, baking is to taste, and the soufflé can be baked a bit longer if desired.

It is well known that soufflés do not wait for the guests, but the soufflé base can be made ahead, so that only the whipping of the egg whites and baking must be done at the last minute.

SPINACH AND GOAT CHEESE SOUFFLÉ
Soufflé aux épinards au fromage de chèvre

The wonderful French goat cheese blends beautifully with vegetables, which balance its richness. In this savoury soufflé it provides a creamy and tangy complement to the spinach.   MAKES 4 SERVINGS

*450 g/1 lb fresh spinach (leaves
    with stems)*
100 g/4 oz creamy goat cheese
40 g/1½ oz unsalted butter
3 tablespoons plain flour

225 ml/8 fl oz milk
Salt and freshly ground pepper
Freshly grated nutmeg
3 egg yolks, at room temperature
4 egg whites, at room temperature
Pinch of cream of tartar

Butter a 1-litre/2-pint soufflé dish, making sure to butter rim well. Position rack in lower third of oven and preheat to 220°C/425°F/gas 7.

Remove spinach stems and wash leaves thoroughly. In a large saucepan of boiling salted water, cook spinach, uncovered, over high heat, pushing leaves down into water often, for about 3 minutes, or until very tender. Drain, rinse thoroughly with cold water, and drain. Squeeze by handfuls until dry. Purée in food processor until finely chopped.

If goat cheese has a dark rind, remove it. Crumble cheese or cut in small pieces.

In a small heavy saucepan, melt butter over low heat, add flour, and cook, whisking constantly, for about 2 minutes, or until foaming but not browned. Remove from heat. Gradually whisk in milk, bring to a boil over medium-high heat, whisking, reduce heat to low, and cook, whisking often, for 2 minutes. Remove from heat and add small pinches of salt, pepper, and nutmeg. Whisk in spinach purée and goat cheese. Bring to a boil.

Remove from heat and vigorously whisk in egg yolks, one by one. Heat yolk mixture over low heat, whisking constantly, for about 2 minutes or until slightly thickened; do not overcook or let mixture boil or yolks may curdle. Taste and add more salt, pepper, and nutmeg, if needed. (Mixture can be kept, covered, for up to 8 hours in refrigerator.)

Have a round heatproof platter ready near oven. If soufflé mixture is cold, heat it in a small saucepan over low heat, whisking, until just warm. Remove from heat.

In a large bowl, beat egg whites with cream of tartar at medium speed until soft peaks form. Continue beating at high speed until whites are stiff but not dry.

Quickly fold about one-quarter of whites into spinach mixture. Spoon this mixture over remaining whites and fold in lightly but quickly, just until mixture is blended.

Transfer mixture to prepared soufflé dish and smooth top. Bake for about 20 minutes, or until puffed and browned; when you gently move oven rack, soufflé should shake very slightly in centre. Do not overbake or soufflé may burn on top and may shrink. Set soufflé dish on prepared platter and serve immediately.

NOTE: About one 275-g/10-oz package frozen spinach can be substituted for fresh. Thaw spinach completely, squeeze it dry, and purée it in a food processor. Measure about 150 ml/¼ pint purée and use it for soufflé.

PUMPKIN SOUFFLÉ
Soufflé à la courge rouge

A beautiful bright orange colour and delicate flavour and texture make this soufflé a favourite starter to a dinner. Whole garlic cloves are steamed alongside the pumpkin to provide a pleasant background taste.   MAKES 4 SERVINGS

700 g to 1 kg/1½ to 2 lb pumpkin
Pinch of salt
5 large garlic cloves, unpeeled
40 g/1½ oz butter
30 g/1¼ oz plain flour

100 ml/4 fl oz plus 1 tablespoon
    milk
White pepper
Freshly grated nutmeg
4 egg yolks, at room temperature
5 egg whites, at room temperature
Pinch cream of tartar

Remove seeds and strings from pumpkin. Cut pumpkin into approximately 5-by-5-by-2·5-cm/2-by-2-by-1-inch chunks.

Bring at least 2·5 cm/1 inch of water to a boil in base of pan with a steamer. Boiling water should not reach holes in bottom part of steamer. Put pumpkin in 1 layer in steamer above boiling water and sprinkle lightly with salt. Add garlic cloves. Cover, and steam about 14 minutes, or until pumpkin is tender. Remove pumpkin, and reserve garlic. Cut off skin and discard it. Purée flesh in food processor until very smooth.

Butter a 1-litre/2-pint soufflé dish, making sure to butter rim well. Position rack in lower third of oven and preheat to 220°C/425°F/gas 7.

Put pumpkin purée in a very heavy medium-size saucepan, preferably one that is lined with enamel. Bring to a boil, reduce heat to medium, and cook, stirring often, for about 12 minutes, or until purée is reduced to 350 ml/12 fl oz. Be careful; mixture spatters and burns easily. Set aside.

In a medium-size shallow, heavy saucepan, melt butter over low heat, add flour, and cook, whisking constantly, for about 2 minutes, or until foaming but not browned. Remove from heat. Whisk in milk and reduced purée, and bring nearly to a boil, whisking. (Mixture will barely bubble and will be too thick to come to a full boil.) Reduce heat to low and cook, whisking constantly, for 5 minutes. Peel and crush garlic; stir into mixture. Add a small pinch of salt, white pepper, and nutmeg.

Remove from heat and vigorously whisk in egg yolks, one by one. Return to low heat and cook, whisking, 3 minutes, or until mixture thickens; do not overcook or let mixture boil or yolks may curdle.

Taste and adjust seasoning. (Mixture can be kept, covered, for up to 8 hours in refrigerator.)

Have a round heatproof platter ready near oven.

If soufflé mixture is cold, heat it in a small saucepan over low heat, whisking, until just warm. Remove from heat.

In a large bowl, beat egg whites with cream of tartar at medium speed until soft peaks form. Continue beating at high speed until whites are stiff but not dry.

Quickly fold about one-quarter of whites into pumpkin mixture. Spoon this mixture over remaining whites, and fold in lightly but quickly, until just blended.

Transfer to prepared soufflé dish and smooth top. Bake for about 18 minutes or until puffed and browned; when you gently move oven rack, soufflé should shake very slightly in centre. Do not overbake or soufflé may burn on top and may shrink. Set soufflé dish on prepared platter and serve immediately.

INDIVIDUAL ONION SOUFFLÉS
Petits soufflés à l'oignon

When onions cook very slowly and gently in butter they acquire a wonderful slightly sweet flavour. They are used as the base for these savoury soufflés.   MAKES 4 SERVINGS

50 g/2 oz butter	*2 tablespoons plain flour*
600 g/1¼ lb onions, halved and thinly sliced	*200 ml/7 fl oz milk*
2 sprigs fresh thyme, or ½ teaspoon dried thyme	*4 egg yolks, at room temperature*
Pinch of salt and freshly ground pepper	*5 egg whites, at room temperature*
	Pinch of cream of tartar

Melt half the butter in a medium sauté pan over very low heat. Add onions, thyme, salt, and pepper, and mix well. Cover with a round of buttered foil and a lid. Cook, stirring occasionally, for about 45 minutes, or until onions are soft enough to be easily crushed with a spoon. If you used fresh thyme, remove sprigs. If there is liquid in pan, uncover and cook over medium heat, stirring, until dry.

Butter four 300 ml/½ pint soufflé dishes, making sure to butter rims well. Position rack in lower third of oven and preheat to 220°C/425°F/gas 7.

In a small heavy saucepan, melt remaining butter over low heat, add flour, and cook, whisking constantly, for about 2 minutes, or until foaming but not browned. Remove from heat. Gradually whisk in milk and bring to a boil over medium-high heat, whisking. Add a small pinch of salt and pepper, reduce heat to low, and cook, whisking often, for 5 minutes. Remove from heat, and stir in onions. Bring to a boil, stirring.

Remove from heat and vigorously whisk in egg yolks, one by one. Cook over low heat, whisking constantly, for about 3 minutes or until thickened. Do not overcook or let boil or yolks may curdle. Taste and adjust seasoning. (Mixture can be kept, covered, for up to 8 hours in refrigerator.)

Have four heatproof plates ready near oven. Put soufflé dishes on a baking sheet.

If soufflé mixture is cold, heat it in a small saucepan over low heat, whisking, until just warm. Remove from heat.

In a large bowl, beat egg whites with cream of tartar at medium speed until soft peaks form. Continue beating at high speed until whites are stiff but not dry.

Quickly fold about one-quarter of whites into onion mixture. Spoon this over remaining whites and fold in lightly but quickly, until just blended.

Transfer to prepared soufflé dishes and smooth tops. Bake for about 12 minutes, or until puffed and browned; when you gently move oven rack, soufflés should shake very slightly in centre. Do not overbake or soufflés may burn on top and may shrink. Set soufflé dishes on plates and serve immediately.

BROCCOLI AND MUSHROOM SOUFFLÉ
WITH CHIVES
Soufflé de brocolis et champignons à la ciboulette

Broccoli was not common in France until it began appearing on the tables of fine restaurants with the beginning of nouvelle cuisine in the early seventies. This soufflé is flavoured with broccoli purée and dotted with sautéed mushrooms for a contrasting texture.

MAKES ABOUT 4 SERVINGS

450 g/1 lb broccoli, divided into medium-size florets, stalk reserved
50 g/2 oz butter
100 g/4 oz mushrooms, halved and thinly sliced
Salt and freshly ground pepper
3 tablespoons plain flour

200 ml/7 fl oz plus 2 tablespoons milk
Freshly grated nutmeg
4 egg yolks, at room temperature
2 tablespoons snipped chives
5 egg whites, at room temperature
Pinch of cream of tartar

Butter a 1-litre/2-pint soufflé dish, making sure to butter rim well. Position rack on bottom third of oven and preheat to 220°C/425°F/gas 7.

Trim off 5 cm/2 inches of broccoli stalk. Peel remaining stalk and cut into 1-cm/½-inch slices. In a large saucepan of boiling salted water, cook broccoli florets and slices, uncovered, over high heat for about 7 minutes, or until very tender. Drain, rinse with cold water, and drain thoroughly. Purée broccoli in a food processor or blender until very smooth. Measure 225 ml/8 fl oz purée. Return purée to saucepan and cook over medium heat, stirring, for about 3 minutes to dry.

Melt 15 g/½ oz butter in a medium-size frying pan over medium-high heat. Add mushrooms, salt, and pepper, and sauté for 2 or 3 minutes, or until lightly browned and any liquid that comes out of mushrooms evaporates.

In a small heavy saucepan over low heat, melt remaining butter, add flour, and cook, whisking constantly, for about 2 minutes or until foaming but not browned. Remove from heat. Gradually whisk in milk. Bring to a boil over medium-high heat, whisking. Reduce heat to low, and cook, whisking constantly, for 2 minutes. Remove from heat and whisk in broccoli purée and a small pinch of salt, pepper, and nutmeg. Bring to a boil, stirring.

Remove from heat and vigorously whisk in egg yolks, one by one. Return to low heat and cook, whisking, for 2 to 3 minutes or until slightly thickened. Do not overcook or let mixture boil or yolks may curdle. Taste and adjust seasoning. Stir in mushrooms. (Mixture can be kept, covered, for up to 8 hours in refrigerator.)

Have a round heatproof platter ready near oven. If soufflé mixture is cold, heat it in a small saucepan over low heat, stirring, until just warm. Remove from heat and stir in chives.

In a large bowl, beat egg whites with cream of tartar at medium speed until soft peaks form. Continue beating at high speed until whites are stiff but not dry.

Quickly fold about one-quarter of whites into broccoli mixture. Spoon over remaining whites, and fold in lightly but quickly, until just blended.

Transfer mixture to prepared soufflé dish and smooth top. Bake for about 18 minutes, or until soufflé is puffed and lightly browned; when you gently move oven rack, soufflé should shake very slightly in centre. Do not overbake or soufflé may burn on top and may shrink. Set soufflé dish on prepared platter and serve immediately.

CAULIFLOWER SOUFFLÉ PUDDING
WITH GRUYÈRE CHEESE
Pudding soufflé de chou-fleur au fromage de Gruyère

A soufflé pudding is not quite as fragile as a soufflé because it is baked slowly in a water bath and thus does not fall as much as it cools. This soufflé pudding can be served with Fresh Tomato Sauce (page 38).

MAKES 4 TO 6 SERVINGS

1 large cauliflower, trimmed of
   leaves and large stalk, and
   divided into medium-size florets
450 ml/¾ pint milk
¼ onion, sliced
10 black peppercorns
1 bay leaf
40 g/1½ oz butter
30 g/1¼ oz plain flour

Salt and freshly ground white
   pepper
Freshly grated nutmeg
200 ml/7 fl oz Crème Fraîche
   (page 381), bought crème
   fraîche or double cream
4 eggs, separated, at room
   temperature
Pinch of cream of tartar
100 g/4 oz Gruyère cheese, grated

Preheat oven to 190°C/375°F/gas 5. Butter a 1·25-litre/2¼-pint soufflé dish or other deep baking dish.

In large saucepan of boiling salted water, cook cauliflower, uncovered, for about 7 minutes, or until very tender. Drain, rinse with cold water, and drain thoroughly. Purée in food processor or blender until very smooth.

In a medium-size saucepan, bring milk to a boil, add onion, peppercorns, and bay leaf, and remove from heat. Cover and let stand for about 10 minutes so that milk can absorb flavour from seasonings. Strain.

In a medium-size heavy saucepan over low heat, melt butter, add flour, and cook, whisking constantly, for about 2 minutes, or until foaming but not browned. Remove from heat and gradually whisk in milk. Bring to a boil over medium-high heat, whisking. Add small pinch of salt, pepper, and nutmeg. Reduce heat to low and cook, whisking often, for 5 minutes. Add crème fraîche or double cream and bring to a boil, whisking. Remove from heat.

Stir in cauliflower purée. Beat in egg yolks. Taste and add more salt, pepper, and nutmeg, if needed. (Mixture can be prepared 4 hours in advance; dab top with a small piece of butter to prevent a skin from forming and keep covered in refrigerator.)

In a large bowl, beat egg whites with cream of tartar at medium speed until soft peaks form. Continue beating at high speed until whites are stiff but not dry.

Quickly fold about one-quarter of whites into onion mixture.

Spoon this over remaining whites, add Gruyère cheese, and fold in lightly but quickly, just until blended.

Transfer mixture to prepared soufflé dish and smooth top. Set dish in roasting pan and transfer to oven. Add enough boiling water to come halfway up sides of soufflé dish.

Bake for about 30 to 40 minutes, or until a thin-bladed knife inserted into centre comes out dry. Serve hot, from the dish.

NOTE: If desired, mixture can be baked and served in individual ramekins instead of a large dish; it will require 20 to 25 minutes of baking time.

VEGETABLE TARTS, PASTRIES, AND CRÊPES

Presenting vegetables in pastry is a good way to make them the stars of any meal or party. Vegetables are perfect partners for pastry as they provide a light complement to rich crusts. Whether they are paired with elaborate puff pastry feuilletés for special occasions or with simple crêpes for everyday dinners, vegetables can always serve as a colourful, elegant filling.

In France pastry is usually made with white flour, but if you prefer to use whole-meal tart or pie cases, the fillings in this chapter will be fine with your favourite whole-meal pastry recipes.

Vegetable Quiches and Pie-Pastry Tarts

Vegetables baked in pie pastry as quiches or tarts are favourite items of *pâtisseries* and *charcuteries* in France. The most popular fillings are made of mushrooms, spinach, onions and leeks, but the vegetables used vary with the seasons. Cheeses add a zesty touch to Tomato and Goat Cheese Tartlets with Fresh Thyme and to numerous other vegetable tarts. At Androuet, the famous Parisian cheese shop and restaurant specializing in cheese, I feasted on a savoury onion and Roquefort tart.

Hints

· For best results pie pastry should rest both before being rolled out and again before baking.

· Because custard fillings are very moist the pastry for tarts and quiches is often prebaked so it will not become soggy once the filling is added.

BRIGHT GREEN SPINACH TART
Tarte aux épinards

Puréed spinach gives this tart a vivid green filling with a firmer texture than that of a quiche. To ensure the delicate flakiness of the *pâte brisée*, or French pie pastry, the tart case is baked briefly before the filling is added.

MAKES 6 SERVINGS

PASTRY CASE

2 egg yolks   ¼ teaspoon salt
2 tablespoons iced water   100 g/4 oz cold unsalted butter,
200 g/7 oz plain flour   cut into bits

SPINACH FILLING

1·25 kg/2½ lb fresh spinach   Salt and freshly ground pepper
   (leaves with stems)   Freshly grated nutmeg
3 eggs   300 ml/½ pint double cream
2 egg yolks

PASTRY CASE

To make dough in processor: Beat egg yolks with iced water. Combine flour and salt in a food processor fitted with a metal blade. Process briefly to blend. Scatter butter pieces over mixture. Mix, using on/off turns, until mixture resembles coarse bread crumbs. Pour egg yolks and water evenly over mixture in processor. Process with on/off turns, scraping down occasionally, until dough forms sticky crumbs that can easily be pressed together but do not come together in a ball. If crumbs are dry, sprinkle on ½ teaspoon of water, and process with on/off turns until dough forms sticky crumbs. Add more water in same way, ½ teaspoon at a time, if crumbs are still dry. Using a rubber spatula, transfer dough to a sheet of cling film, wrap it, and push it together. Shape dough into a flat disc.

To make dough by hand: Beat egg yolks with iced water. In a large bowl combine flour and salt, add butter, and cut butter through until it forms fine crumbs. Add egg yolks and water and toss until liquid is incorporated, adding more iced water by ½ teaspoons, if necessary, to form dough into a ball. Knead dough lightly with heel of hand against a smooth surface for just a few seconds and press it gently into a ball. Dust dough with flour and wrap it in cling film. Shape dough into a flat disc.

Refrigerate dough for 1 or 2 hours. (Dough can be kept up to 2 days in refrigerator.)

Butter a 23–25-cm/9–10-inch fluted tart tin with a removable base. Let dough soften for 1 minute at room temperature. Set dough on a cool, lightly floured surface. Tap it firmly several times with a heavy rolling pin to flatten it. Roll it out, flouring often and work-ing as quickly as possible, to a circle about 3 mm/⅛ inch thick. Roll up dough loosely around rolling pin and unroll it over tin. Gently ease dough into tin. (If dough tears, use a piece hanging over rim of tin to patch it up.)

Using your thumb, gently push down dough a little bit at top edge of tart tin, making top edge of dough thicker than remainder. Roll the rolling pin across tin to cut off dough at edges. With your finger and thumb, push up top edge of dough all round tin so it is about 6 mm/¼ inch higher than rim of tin. Prick bottom of case lightly with a fork and refrigerate for 30 minutes. (Tart case can be kept, covered, for up to 2 days in refrigerator; or it can be frozen.)

Position rack in lower third of oven and preheat to 220°C/425°F/gas 7. Line pastry case with foil and fill with rice, beans or pie crust weights. Set on a baking sheet and bake for 10 minutes. Carefully remove rice, beans, or weights and paper, and bake for 8 to 10 more minutes or until lightly browned. Transfer tart tin to a rack and let case cool. Move baking sheet to centre of oven. Reduce oven temperature to 180°C/350°F/gas 4.

SPINACH FILLING

Remove stems of spinach and wash leaves thoroughly. In a large saucepan of boiling salted water, cook spinach, uncovered, over high heat, pushing leaves down into water often, about 3 minutes, or until very tender. Rinse with cold water and drain thoroughly. Squeeze by handfuls until dry. Purée in food processor until very finely chopped.

In a bowl, whisk eggs with yolks and pinches of salt, pepper, and nutmeg. Stir in cream and chopped spinach. Taste and add more salt, pepper, and nutmeg, if needed.

Return pastry case to baking sheet in oven. Ladle spinach mixture slowly into tart. Bake for 30 minutes, or until filling is set. Let cool on a rack for 10 minutes. Set tart on an upside-down flat-bottomed bowl and remove pan rim. (The tart can be kept, covered, for 1 day in refrigerator; before serving, heat it in a cool oven.) Serve warm or at room temperature.

NOTES

· Three 275-g/10-oz packets of frozen spinach can be substituted for fresh. Thaw spinach completely, squeeze it dry, and purée it in a food processor. Measure 300 ml/½ pint purée. (With some brands two packets will be enough.)

· Tart can also be baked in a pie dish.

TOMATO AND GOAT CHEESE
TARTLETS WITH FRESH THYME
Tartelettes aux tomates et au fromage de chèvre

Freshly cooked tomatoes and cubes of creamy goat cheese make a colourful, luscious filling for these small pastries. Tartlets make a lovely individual portion but the filling can also be baked in a large tart case.　　　　　　　　　　　　　　　　MAKES 12 SMALL TARTLETS

PASTRY CASES

2 egg yolks
3 tablespoons plus ½ teaspoon iced
    water
260 g/9 oz plain flour

¼ teaspoon salt
175 g/6 oz cold unsalted butter,
    cut into bits

TOMATO AND GOAT CHEESE FILLING

3 sprigs fresh thyme
1 bay leaf
25 g/1 oz unsalted butter
1 small onion, finely chopped
700 g/1½ lb ripe tomatoes, peeled,
    seeded, and chopped
Salt and freshly ground pepper

75 g/3 oz creamy goat cheese
1½ teaspoons fresh thyme leaves,
    or ½ teaspoon dried thyme
1 egg
3–4 tablespoons double cream

PASTRY CASES

To make pastry in processor, whisk egg yolks with 3 tablespoons iced water. Combine flour and salt in a food processor fitted with a metal blade. Process briefly to blend. Scatter butter pieces over mixture. Mix using on/off turns until mixture resembles coarse breadcrumbs. Pour egg yolks evenly over mixture in processor. Process with on/off turns, scraping down occasionally, until dough forms sticky crumbs that can easily be pressed together but does not come together in a ball. If crumbs are dry, sprinkle on ½ teaspoon of water and process with on/off turns until dough forms sticky crumbs. Add more water in same way, ½ teaspoon at a time, if crumbs are still dry.

To make pastry by hand, see Bright Green Spinach Tart, page 63.

Using a rubber spatula, transfer dough to a sheet of cling film, wrap it, and push it together. Shape dough into a flat disc. Refrigerate dough for 1 or 2 hours. (Dough can be kept up to 2 days in refrigerator.)

Butter twelve fluted 7·5-cm/3-inch round tartlet tins. Let dough soften for 1 minute at room temperature before rolling it. Set dough on a cold, lightly floured surface. Tap it firmly with a heavy rolling pin several times to flatten it. Roll it out, flouring often and working as quickly as possible, until it is slightly less than 6 mm/¼ inch thick. Set eight tartlet tins next to each other. Roll up dough loosely around rolling pin and unroll it over tins. With a small ball of dough (from edge of sheet of dough) dipped in flour, gently press dough into tartlet tins.

Using your thumb, gently push down dough a little bit at top edge of each tin, making top edge of dough thicker than remaining dough. Roll the rolling pin across tins to cut off dough at edges. With your finger and thumb, press up edge of dough around each tin so it extends slightly above rim. Prick dough all over with a fork. Cover lined tins and refrigerate for at least 30 minutes; also refrigerate scraps. Roll out remaining dough and scraps, and line remaining tartlet pans. (Tartlet shells can be kept, covered, for up to 2 days in refrigerator; or they can be frozen for several weeks.)

TOMATO AND GOAT CHEESE FILLING

Position rack in lower third of oven and preheat to 200°C/400°F/gas 6. Wrap thyme sprigs and bay leaf in a piece of cheesecloth and tie tightly to make a bouquet garni. In a large frying pan, melt butter over low heat. Add onion and cook, stirring, for about 10 minutes, or until soft but not brown. Add tomatoes, bouquet garni, and small pinches of salt and pepper. Raise heat to medium and cook, stirring often, for about 20 minutes, or until mixture is very thick and most of moisture has evaporated. Remove bouquet garni.

If goat cheese has a dark rind, remove it. Cut cheese in 6-mm/¼-inch dice.

Set tartlets on a baking sheet. Spoon in 1 tablespoon of tomato mixture and spread smooth. Put 4 cheese cubes in centre. Sprinkle with a few thyme leaves.

Whisk egg with cream and salt and pepper to taste until blended. Spoon 1½ to 2 teaspoons egg and cream mixture over tomatoes, using enough to just cover without running over side of tartlet.

Bake for 15 minutes. Reduce oven temperature to 180°C/350°F/gas 4, and bake about 18 minutes longer, or until filling sets and puffs and pastry is golden brown. Serve warm or at room temperature. (The tartlets can be kept, covered, for up to 1 day in refrigerator. Warm them in a cool oven before serving.)

NOTE: For small hors d'oeuvres, the pastry and filling can be baked in smaller tartlet tins; for a more substantial first course, use larger ones.

CÈPE TARTLETS

For each tartlet, use 1 tablespoon cèpe duxelles filling, as in Cèpe Turnovers (see page 109), instead of Tomato and Goat Cheese Filling. Top cèpe filling with 1½ to 2 teaspoons egg and cream mixture, as above. Bake as above.

CABBAGE TART WITH CARAWAY SEEDS
Tarte aux choux au grains de carvi

The cabbage in this tart is surprisingly delicate in taste because it is boiled only briefly and then heated in butter. It is topped with a savoury mixture of sour cream and double cream, which gives a flavour reminiscent of that of crème fraîche.   MAKES 6 SERVINGS

One 25-cm/10-inch Pastry
  Case (page 64)

CABBAGE FILLING

½ medium-size head green	*1 egg yolk*
cabbage (about 450 g/1 lb),	*3–4 tablespoons sour cream*
cored, rinsed, and cut in thin	*Freshly grated nutmeg*
strips	*175 ml/6 fl oz double cream*
15 g/½ oz butter	*1 teaspoon caraway seeds*
Salt and freshly ground pepper	*25 g/1 oz Gruyère cheese, grated*
2 eggs	

Prepare dough and prebake crust according to the instructions given in recipe for Bright Green Spinach Tart, page 63. Reduce oven temperature to 180°C/350°F/gas 4.

CABBAGE FILLING

In a large pan of boiling salted water, boil cabbage, uncovered, over high heat for 5 minutes, or until tender. Rinse under cold running water, and drain. Squeeze out excess liquid.

In a large frying pan, melt butter over low heat, add cabbage, and cook, stirring often, for 2 minutes, or until butter is absorbed. Add salt and pepper to taste. Transfer cabbage to a bowl and let it cool to room temperature.

In a bowl, whisk eggs with yolk, sour cream, ½ teaspoon salt, ⅛ teaspoon pepper, and nutmeg. Beat in double cream. Taste mixture and add more salt, pepper, and nutmeg, if needed.

Spoon cabbage into case. Sprinkle evenly with caraway seeds. Return shell to baking sheet in oven. Ladle egg mixture slowly over cabbage and sprinkle with Gruyère. Bake tart for 30 minutes, or until it is puffed, golden, and set. Let cool on a rack for 10 minutes. Set tart on an upside-down flat-bottomed bowl and remove tart tin rim. (The tart can be kept, covered, for 1 day in refrigerator; warm it before serving in a cool oven.) Serve warm or at room temperature.

CREAMY MUSHROOM TART WITH CHIVES
Tarte aux champignons à la ciboulette

This pastry is inspired by a favourite tart at La Varenne in Paris. Unlike other mushroom tarts, which make use of sautéed sliced mushrooms, the chopped mushrooms used in this version flavour the creamy filling much more intensely.   MAKES 4 TO 6 SERVINGS

One Pastry Case (page 64)

MUSHROOM FILLING WITH CHIVES

25 g/1 oz butter
1 medium-size onion, finely chopped
225 g/8 oz mushrooms, finely chopped
2 tablespoons plain flour
225 ml/8 fl oz double cream

1 egg, beaten with a pinch of salt, for glaze

3 tablespoons milk
Salt and freshly ground pepper
Freshly grated nutmeg
3 egg yolks
2 tablespoons finely snipped chives

Prepare dough according to the instructions given in recipe for Bright Green Spinach Tart, page 63. Reserve one-quarter of dough in refrigerator to make a lattice; roll out the remainder and line a buttered 20-cm/8-inch fluted tart tin with removable base. Prick bottom of case lightly with a fork and refrigerate for 30 minutes, or freeze for 15 minutes. Cut any long scraps of dough in strips about 6 mm/¼ inch wide and 23 cm/9 inches long. Roll out remaining dough into a thin sheet and cut in strips of same size. Refrigerate strips side by side on a plate for about 15 minutes. (Tart case can be kept, covered, for up to 1 day in refrigerator; if chilled strips become too stiff to handle, remove them briefly so they soften slightly before using.)

MUSHROOM FILLING WITH CHIVES

In a large sauté pan or deep frying pan, melt butter over low heat. Add onion and cook, stirring often, for about 7 minutes, or until soft but not brown. Add mushrooms, increase heat to high, and cook, stirring often, until liquid has evaporated.

Remove mushroom mixture from heat, sprinkle in flour, and stir well. Reduce heat to low and cook, stirring, for 1 minute. Stir in cream and milk and season with salt, pepper, and nutmeg. Raise heat to medium and cook, stirring, until mixture comes to a boil and thickens. Reduce heat to low and continue cooking for 2 minutes. Remove from heat and let cool.

When filling is lukewarm, stir in egg yolks and chives. Taste, and add more salt, pepper, and nutmeg, if needed. Let cool completely.

To assemble Pastry Case and Filling:

Position rack in lower third of oven, set a baking sheet on rack, and preheat oven to 220°C/425°F/gas 7. Spoon cool filling into tart case. Brush rim of case lightly with egg glaze. Arrange 5 or 6 parallel strips at equal intervals above filling. Press gently to stick each strip to dough lining tin. Arrange 5 or 6 more strips intersecting first group at an angle so they form diamond shapes. Also stick these to dough lining tin. Remove excess from ends of strips by pressing against edge of tart tin. Gently brush strips with egg glaze.

Put tart on hot baking sheet and bake for 10 minutes. Reduce oven temperature to 200°C/400°F/gas 6 and bake for 20 to 25 minutes more, or until pastry browns and filling sets. Let cool on a rack for 10 minutes. Set tart on an upside-down flat-bottomed bowl and remove tart tin rim. (The tart can be kept, covered, for 1 day in refrigerator; warm it before serving in a cool oven.) Serve warm or at room temperature.

CAULIFLOWER QUICHE WITH ONION AND GRUYÈRE CHEESE
Quiche au chou-fleur

The classic quiche originated in Lorraine, a region in eastern France, and was topped with bacon and onions. Quiche now is part of the repertoire of many cuisines and appears in countless versions. In this one the cauliflower florets show through the creamy, cheesy topping.

MAKES 6 TO 8 SERVINGS

One *23-cm/9-inch or 25-cm/10-inch*
    Pastry Case (page 64)

CAULIFLOWER, ONION, AND GRUYÈRE FILLING

25 g/1 oz butter
2 medium-size onions, halved and thinly sliced
Salt and freshly ground pepper
700 g/1½ lb cauliflower, divided into large florets

3 eggs
6 tablespoons milk
225 ml/8 fl oz double cream
Freshly grated nutmeg
100 g/4 oz Gruyère cheese, grated

Prepare dough and line a 23-cm/9-inch or 25-cm/10-inch fluted tart tin with a removable rim or a pie tin as in Bright Green Spinach Tart, page 63. Prebake crust and reduce oven temperature in the same way.

CAULIFLOWER, ONION, AND GRUYÈRE FILLING
In a medium-size frying pan, melt butter over low heat. Add onions and a pinch of salt and pepper, and cook, stirring often, for about 10 minutes, or until soft but not brown.

Meanwhile, in a large saucepan of boiling salted water, cook cauliflower florets, uncovered, over high heat for 3 minutes. Remove gently to a colander and rinse with cold water. Remove stalks and divide large florets into very small ones.

In a bowl, whisk eggs with milk, cream, and salt, pepper, and nutmeg to taste.

Spoon onions into cooled pastry case. Arrange a ring of cauliflower florets near its edge, with flower end of each one facing outward. Arrange another circle of florets, with flower ends resting on stalk ends of first circle. Continue arranging rings of florets until pie case is covered. Put a few florets in centre. Sprinkle cauliflower with half the grated cheese.

Return case to baking sheet in oven. Ladle egg and cream mixture slowly over cauliflower and sprinkle with remaining cheese. Bake tart for 30 minutes, or until it is puffed, golden, and set; when you touch filling gently, it should not stick to your finger. Do not overbake or filling may separate. Let cool on a rack for 10 minutes. Set tart on an upside-down flat-bottomed bowl and remove tart tin rim. (The quiche can be kept, covered, for 1 day in refrigerator. Warm it in a cool oven before serving.) Serve warm or at room temperature.

SWISS CHARD AND TOMATO TART
Tarte aux blettes et aux tomates

Two fillings – one of Swiss chard and one of tomato and onion – are layered in this vegetable tart. It is filled entirely with vegetables and does not contain custard. There is no need to prebake the crust because the vegetables are cooked until thick and do not soak into the pastry. MAKES 6 TO 8 SERVINGS

PASTRY CASE

1 egg yolk	1/4 teaspoon salt
2 to 3 tablespoons iced water	90 g/3 1/2 oz cold unsalted butter,
170 g/6 oz plain flour	cut into bits

SWISS CHARD, TOMATO, AND ONION FILLING

450 g/1 lb Swiss chard
40 g/1½ oz unsalted butter
Salt and freshly ground pepper
2 tablespoons olive oil
1 medium-size onion, halved and
  sliced
275 g/10 oz ripe tomatoes, peeled,
  seeded, and chopped

1 teaspoon fresh thyme, or ¼
  teaspoon dried thyme
1 large garlic clove, finely chopped
50 g/2 oz Gruyère cheese, cut into
  fine strips
25 g/1 oz freshly grated Parmesan
  cheese

PASTRY CASE

To make pastry case, follow instructions in recipe for Bright Green Spinach Tart (page 64). Use a buttered 20-cm/8-inch fluted tart tin. Prick bottom of case lightly with a fork and refrigerate for 30 minutes. (Tart case can be kept, covered, for up to 2 days in refrigerator; or it can be frozen.)

SWISS CHARD, TOMATO, AND ONION FILLING

Remove chard leaves from stalks, and discard stalks or reserve for other uses. Rinse leaves thoroughly. Pile chard leaves and cut in half lengthwise, then crosswise, into 1-cm/½-inch-wide strips.

In a large frying pan, melt 25 g/1 oz butter over low heat. Add about half of chard and a pinch of salt and pepper. Cook, stirring often, about 6 minutes, or until tender. Remove with tongs, add remaining chard and a little salt and pepper and cook it also until tender. Return all of chard to pan and heat, stirring, 1 minute. Transfer to a plate and cool to room temperature.

In a medium-size frying pan, heat oil and remaining butter over low heat. Add onion and a pinch of salt and pepper and cook, stirring often, for about 15 minutes, or until very tender but not browned. Add tomatoes and thyme. Raise heat to medium-high and cook, stirring often, for about 15 minutes, or until juice from tomatoes has evaporated and mixture is dry. Stir in garlic. Taste and adjust seasoning. Cool to room temperature.

Preheat oven to 200°C/400°F/gas 6. Heat a baking sheet in oven. Spread chard evenly in tart case. Scatter Gruyère cheese strips evenly over mixture. Cover chard with tomato mixture. Sprinkle with Parmesan cheese.

Set tart on baking sheet in oven. Bake for about 40 minutes, or until pastry is brown at sides and filling browns on top. Let cool on a rack for 10 minutes. Set tart on an upside-down flat-bottomed bowl and remove tart tin rim. (The tart can be kept, covered, for 1 day in refrigerator. Warm it in a cool oven before serving.) Serve hot or warm.

Savoury Vegetable Cream Puffs and Quenelles

Cream puffs and quenelles are made of choux pastry, which is extremely versatile and can be baked, poached or fried. The dough puffs when baked and leaves a hollow for filling. Fillings can be hot cooked vegetables in a sauce, vegetable purées, or even cool vegetable salads with a rich mayonnaise-type dressing.

For vegetable quenelles, or light dumplings, the pastry itself is flavoured with the vegetables and poached or baked, then served with a creamy sauce. When a mixture of this type is deep-fried instead, it creates a totally different effect. The result is little round *beignets*, which puff and become lightly crisp on the outside and soft inside, as in Brie Beignets (page 81) flavoured with celery.

CHEESE PUFF CROWN WITH ASPARAGUS
Gougère aux asperges

Gougère originated in the Burgundy region and these cheese puffs traditionally accompanied tastings of the great red wines. Small *gougères* are often served at fine restaurants as a treat while diners are looking over the menu. This vegetable version makes a festive first course or luncheon main course. MAKES 4 TO 6 SERVINGS

CHOUX PASTRY WITH CHEESE

50 g/2 oz plus 1 tablespoon plain
  flour
6 tablespoons water
¼ teaspoon salt
50 g/2 oz unsalted butter, cut in 8
  pieces

3 eggs
Pinch of freshly ground pepper
50 g/2 oz Gruyère cheese, cut in
  tiny cubes

ASPARAGUS CREAM FILLING

350 ml/12 fl oz water
225 g/8 oz medium-size asparagus
  spears (about 9 spears), peeled
  and cut in 2·5-cm/1-inch pieces
1 tablespoon finely chopped
  shallots
40 g/1½ oz butter

3 tablespoons plain flour
6 tablespoons milk
Salt and white pepper
Freshly grated nutmeg
6 tablespoons double cream
25 g/1 oz Gruyère cheese, grated

CHOUX PASTRY WITH CHEESE

Position rack in lower third of oven and preheat to 200°C/400°F/
gas 6. Lightly butter a 23-cm/9-inch or 25-cm/10-inch round gratin
dish or other heavy shallow baking dish. Sift flour on to a piece of
greaseproof paper.

In a small, heavy saucepan, combine water, salt, and butter and
cook over low heat, stirring constantly, until butter melts. Raise
heat to medium-high and bring to a boil. Remove from heat.
Immediately add flour all at once and stir quickly with a wooden
spoon until mixture is smooth. Set pan over low heat and beat
mixture for about 30 seconds.

Remove from heat and cool for about 3 minutes. Add 1 egg and
beat it thoroughly into mixture. Add second egg and beat mixture
until it is smooth. Beat third egg in a small bowl. Gradually beat 1 or
2 tablespoons of this egg into dough, adding enough so that dough
becomes very shiny and is soft enough to just fall from spoon.

Add a pinch of salt to remaining egg and beat until blended;
reserve for glaze.

Beat pepper and cubes of cheese into dough.

Using two tablespoons, shape mounds of dough of about 4-cm/

1½-inch diameter, spacing them at edge of gratin dish so they nearly touch each other. Brush them with egg glaze.

While puffs bake, prepare filling as directed below. Bake puffs about 35 minutes, or until dough is puffed and browned; cracks that form during baking should be golden. Mounds will join and form a crown.

ASPARAGUS CREAM FILLING

In a medium-size saucepan, bring the water to a boil, and add a pinch of salt. Add asparagus and cook, uncovered, over high heat for about 5 minutes, or until just tender. Remove asparagus with a slotted spoon, reserving liquid. Rinse with cold water and drain well.

Measure 6 tablespoons asparagus cooking liquid. Boil measured liquid with shallots until reduced by half. Cover and reserve.

In a small heavy saucepan, melt butter over low heat, stir in flour, and cook, whisking constantly, for about 2 minutes, or until foaming but not browned. Remove from heat. Gradually add reduced asparagus cooking liquid and milk. Bring to a boil over medium-high heat, whisking. Add a small pinch of salt, pepper, and nutmeg. Stir in cream and bring to boil, reduce heat to low, and cook, whisking often, until mixture is thick enough to coat a spoon; about 5 minutes.

Reserve 8 asparagus tips for garnish. Add remaining asparagus pieces to sauce, bring to a simmer, and remove from heat. Stir in Gruyère. Taste, and add more salt, pepper, and nutmeg if needed. Spoon filling into baking dish, in centre of baked crown.

Garnish with asparagus spears pointing from centre outward like spokes of a wheel. Serve immediately by separating puffs with a knife and serving filling with a spoon.

CREAM PUFFS WITH CARROT PURÉE
Choux à la purée de carottes

Cream puffs filled with a vegetable purée make a delicious first course. Besides carrot, other colourful purées such as spinach or broccoli make flavourful fillings.   MAKES 6 SERVINGS, ABOUT 18 PUFFS

CARROT PURÉE

600 g/1¼ lb carrots, peeled and   Salt
  cut in 1-cm/½-inch slices

CHOUX PASTRY

50 g/2 oz plain flour   40 g/1½ oz unsalted butter, cut in
6 tablespoons cooking liquid from   pieces
  carrots   2 to 3 eggs
¼ teaspoon salt
Freshly ground pepper

TO FINISH CARROT PURÉE

½ teaspoon sugar   50 g/2 oz unsalted butter, softened

CARROT PURÉE

Put carrots in a medium-size saucepan with enough water to cover and a pinch of salt; bring to boil. Reduce heat to medium-low, cover, and simmer for 25 to 30 minutes, or until carrots are very tender and can be easily pierced with sharp knife.

Remove carrots from liquid with slotted spoon, reserving cooking liquid. Purée carrots in a food processor, food mill, or blender until smooth. (If using blender, purée in small amounts and use a little liquid with each batch.)

CHOUX PASTRY

Position rack in lower third of oven and preheat to 220°C/425°F/gas 7. Lightly butter baking sheet. Sift flour on to a piece of greaseproof paper.

Combine 6 tablespoons of reserved carrot cooking liquid, salt, pepper, and butter in a small heavy saucepan. Cook over low heat, stirring constantly, until butter melts. Raise heat to medium-high and bring to a boil. Remove from heat. Immediately add flour all at once and stir quickly with a wooden spoon until mixture is smooth. Set pan over low heat and beat mixture for about 30 seconds.

Remove from heat and cool for about 3 minutes. Add 1 egg and beat it thoroughly into mixture. Using a fork, beat second egg in a small bowl. Gradually beat 1 or 2 tablespoons of this egg into dough, adding enough so that dough becomes very shiny and is soft enough to just fall from spoon. To check, scoop up about one-third of dough on wooden spoon, hold spoon sideways and wait for dough to fall; if it falls into pan in 10 to 15 seconds, it is ready; if it takes longer or does not fall, add a little more egg.

Reserve remaining egg for glaze. (If no egg remains, beat a third egg with a pinch of salt and set aside to use for glaze.)

Using a piping bag and 1-cm/½-inch plain nozzle, shape mounds of dough about 3 cm/1¼ inches in diameter, spacing them about 5 cm/2 inches apart on baking sheet. Alternatively, take 1 table-spoon dough and, with another tablespoon, push it on to baking sheet; continue with remaining dough. Using a pastry brush, coat each mound of dough with beaten egg, gently pushing down any points.

Bake puffs in preheated oven for about 25 minutes, or until golden brown and firm; cracks that form during baking should also turn golden brown. To test for doneness, remove one from oven and cut open. Interior should be slightly moist.

To Finish:
Put carrot purée in a saucepan and stir constantly over low heat for 5 minutes, or until dry. Add sugar and salt to taste, and stir until dissolved. Remove from heat and stir in butter until it is absorbed.

When puffs are baked, cut them in half horizontally with a serrated knife. Let cool for 5 minutes. Fill bottom half of each puff generously with carrot purée, so that purée shows when top half is put back in place. Serve warm as a first course.

BRIE BEIGNETS
Beignets de Brie

Beignets of vegetables and cheese are great appetizers. These pair celery with Brie and are held together by choux pastry, which makes them puff when they are fried.

MAKES 4 TO 6 SERVINGS

1 large celery stick	*About 2 eggs*
225 ml/8 fl oz water	*50 g/2 oz Brie cheese, cut in tiny*
50 g/2 oz plus 1 tablespoon plain	*cubes*
flour	*Freshly ground black pepper*
¼ teaspoon salt	*Pinch of cayenne pepper*
40 g/1½ oz unsalted butter, cut in	*Oil for deep-frying (at least 1·25*
pieces	*litres/2¼ pints)*

Review the hints on deep-frying on page 231 before proceeding.

Peel celery with vegetable peeler to remove strings. Cut in very fine dice.

In a small saucepan, bring water to a boil, add celery, and boil, uncovered, over high heat for about 3 minutes, or until tender. Drain well, reserving cooking liquid and celery separately.

Sift flour on to a piece of greaseproof paper.

Combine 6 tablespoons reserved celery cooking liquid, salt, and butter in a small heavy saucepan. Cook over low heat, stirring constantly, until butter melts. Raise heat to medium-high and bring to a boil. Remove from heat. Immediately add flour all at once and stir quickly with a wooden spoon until mixture is smooth. Set pan over low heat and beat mixture for about 30 seconds.

Remove from heat and cool for about 3 minutes. Add 1 egg and beat it thoroughly into mixture. Beat second egg in a small bowl. Gradually beat this egg by tablespoons into dough, adding enough so that dough becomes very shiny and is soft enough to just fall from spoon. To check, scoop up about one-third of dough on wooden spoon, hold spoon sideways and wait for dough to fall; if it falls into pan in 10 to 15 seconds, it is ready; if it takes longer or does not fall, add a little more egg.

Beat in Brie cubes and celery. Add black pepper and cayenne, taste, and adjust seasoning.

In a deep fryer or large deep, heavy saucepan, heat oil to 180°C/350°F on a thermometer for deep-frying. Preheat oven to lowest setting. Take about 1 teaspoon dough, dip second teaspoon in hot oil and use it to push dough from spoon into oil. Continue making more beignets in same way. Do not crowd.

Fry for about 3 to 4 minutes, or until they are golden brown. Remove with slotted spoon to paper towels on heatproof tray. Put in preheated oven while frying rest.

Transfer beignets to platter lined with doily. Serve immediately.

BAKED BROCCOLI GNOCCHI WITH PARMESAN CHEESE SAUCE
Gnocchis parisienne aux brocolis

This is a new vegetable version of the familiar Parisian gnocchi. Here they are enriched with a colourful purée of fresh broccoli. Classic Parisian gnocchi, which are small balls of poached choux pastry coated with a creamy cheese sauce, have always been associated in my mind with the fabulous food shop Fauchon in Paris, where I tasted them for the first time. The gnocchi in this recipe are baked instead of being poached because the broccoli purée makes them softer than the classic ones.

MAKES 3 MAIN COURSE OR 6 APPETIZER SERVINGS

BROCCOLI GNOCCHI

800 g/1¾ lb broccoli	*50 g/2 oz unsalted butter, cut in 4*
50 g/2 oz plus 2 tablespoons plain	* pieces*
* flour*	*2 eggs*
6 tablespoons milk	*Freshly ground pepper*
¼ teaspoon salt	*Freshly grated nutmeg*

PARMESAN CHEESE SAUCE

25 g/1 oz unsalted butter
15 g/½ oz plain flour
350 ml/12 fl oz milk
Salt and white pepper
Freshly grated nutmeg

3–4 tablespoons double cream
25 g/1 oz freshly grated Parmesan
  cheese
Pinch of cayenne pepper

2 tablespoons freshly grated
  Parmesan cheese, for topping

BROCCOLI GNOCCHI

Peel central stalk of broccoli by cutting off tough outer layer and discarding small stems. Cut peeled stalk into 1-cm/½-inch slices. Cut remaining broccoli in medium-size florets. Reserve 225 g/8 oz small broccoli florets, each with about 2 cm/¾ inch of stem, for garnish. In a large saucepan of boiling salted water, cook broccoli slices and florets, uncovered, over high heat until very tender; about 7 minutes. Drain thoroughly. Purée in food processor or in blender until very smooth. Return to saucepan and cook over medium heat, stirring, until dry; about 3 minutes.

Sift flour on to piece of greaseproof paper. Combine milk, ¼ teaspoon salt, and butter in small heavy saucepan, and cook over low heat until butter melts. Increase heat, bring to boil, and remove from heat. Add flour immediately and stir quickly with wooden spoon until mixture is smooth. Beat mixture over low heat for 30 seconds. Remove from heat and let cool for 2 minutes. Using wooden spoon, beat 1 egg thoroughly into flour mixture. Repeat with other egg; at first mixture will seem separated but keep beating and it will come together.

Beat broccoli purée into choux pastry in four portions. Scrape mixture carefully from sides and bottom of pan to make sure there is no unmixed dough. Add pepper and nutmeg, taste, and adjust seasoning. Cover tightly with cling film and refrigerate for 30 minutes.

Butter two 20-cm/8-inch gratin dishes or heavy shallow baking dishes. Preheat oven to 190°C/375°F/gas 5. Using two teaspoons, shape broccoli mixture into egg-shaped dumplings by taking heaped teaspoon of mixture on one spoon and using second spoon to push it on to dish, leaving 1 cm/½ inch between dumplings. Cover dish tightly with buttered foil. Bake until surface of dumplings is firm; about 15 minutes. Let cool. Release gnocchi gently from dish using metal spatula but leave in baking dish.

PARMESAN CHEESE SAUCE
In small heavy saucepan, melt butter over low heat, add flour and cook, whisking constantly, until foaming but not browned; about 2 minutes. Remove from heat. Gradually stir in milk. Bring to boil over medium-high heat, whisking. Add a small pinch of salt, white pepper, and nutmeg. Reduce heat to low and cook, whisking often, for 5 minutes. Add cream and bring to boil, reduce heat to low, and cook, whisking often, for 5 minutes.

Remove from heat and stir in Parmesan cheese. Add cayenne pepper. Taste and add more salt, pepper, and nutmeg, if needed.

Spoon sauce carefully over each gnocchi to coat it completely. Sprinkle with Parmesan cheese. (Dish can be prepared ahead and kept for 1 day in refrigerator. Let it reach room temperature before continuing.)

Bake at 190°C/375°F/gas 5 until sauce is bubbling; about 10 minutes. Remove from oven; preheat grill. Meanwhile, in medium-size saucepan of boiling salted water, blanch reserved broccoli florets over high heat until crisp-tender and drain thoroughly.

Grill baked gnocchi just until sauce is light golden. Garnish with blanched florets. Serve hot, from baking dishes.

GREEN VEGETABLE QUENELLES WITH MUSHROOM CREAM
Quenelles de légumes vertes à la crème de champignons

Quenelles are light French dumplings. I made these based on the classic formula for fish quenelles. The blend of vegetables and herbs gives these quenelles an intriguing pale-green colour and a delicate flavour.   MAKES 6 SERVINGS

GREEN VEGETABLE QUENELLES

Vegetable-Herb Mixture

One 150 g/5 oz bunch watercress
450 g/1 lb fresh spinach (leaves with stems)
2 tablespoons parsley sprigs
1 tablespoon chopped fresh tarragon

1 medium-size courgette, coarsely grated (150 g/5 oz)
1 tablespoon butter
1 medium-size onion, minced
Salt

Choux Pastry

50 g/2 oz plus 2 tablespoons plain flour
6 tablespoons milk
¼ teaspoon salt

50 g/2 oz unsalted butter, cut in 4 pieces
2 large eggs
Freshly ground pepper

MUSHROOM CREAM

25 g/1 oz butter
100 g/4 oz mushrooms, halved and thinly sliced
Salt and freshly ground pepper

350 ml/12 fl oz double cream
Pinch of cayenne pepper
1 tablespoon chopped fresh tarragon

GREEN VEGETABLE QUENELLES

Vegetable-Herb Mixture
Remove leaves from watercress, discarding stems. Remove and discard spinach stems and wash leaves thoroughly. In a large saucepan of boiling salted water, cook spinach, uncovered, over high heat, pushing leaves down into water often; about 1 minute. Add watercress and boil for 1 minute. Drain, rinse with cold water, and drain. Squeeze by handfuls until dry. Put in food processor and add parsley sprigs. Purée in food processor until finely chopped. Transfer to bowl and add tarragon.

Squeeze excess juice from grated courgette. In medium-size frying pan over low heat, melt butter, add onion, and cook for about 10 minutes, or until soft but not brown. Add courgette and cook over medium heat, stirring, for about 3 minutes or until liquid evaporates. Add to spinach mixture.

Choux Pastry

Sift flour on to piece of greaseproof paper. Combine milk, salt, and butter in small heavy saucepan and cook over low heat until butter melts. Increase heat, bring to boil, and remove from heat. Add flour immediately and stir quickly with wooden spoon until mixture is smooth. Beat mixture over low heat for 30 seconds. Remove from heat and let cool for 2 minutes. Using wooden spoon, beat 1 egg thoroughly into flour mixture. Repeat with second egg; at first mixture will seem separated but keep beating and it will come together.

Beat vegetable mixture into choux pastry in four portions. Scrape mixture carefully from sides and bottom of pan to make sure there is no unmixed dough. Add pepper, taste, and adjust seasoning.

Bring about 4 cm/1½ inches salted water to a simmer in sauté pan or other shallow pan. Using two teaspoons, shape vegetable mixture into egg-shaped dumplings by taking heaped teaspoon of mixture on one spoon and using second teaspoon to give it a neat round shape. Tap spoon on edge of pan to drop dumpling into water. Continue adding dumplings but not enough to crowd. Adjust heat so water just moves but does not simmer. Poach, uncovered, for 20 minutes. With slotted spoon, remove carefully and transfer to tray lined with paper towels. Repeat with remaining dumpling mixture.

Butter two 20-cm/8-inch gratin dishes or heavy, shallow baking dishes. Preheat oven to 190°C/375°F/gas 5.

MUSHROOM CREAM

In large heavy frying pan, melt butter over medium-high heat. Add mushrooms, salt, and pepper, and sauté until lightly browned. Add cream and bring to boil. Cook, stirring often, until sauce is thick enough to coat a spoon; about 6 minutes. Add cayenne pepper and tarragon. Taste and adjust seasoning.

Put quenelles in prepared dishes. (Dish can be prepared ahead and kept, covered, for 1 day in refrigerator. Keep sauce separately. Let quenelles reach room temperature and reheat sauce before continuing.)

Spoon sauce carefully over each quenelle. Bake for about 10 minutes, or until sauce begins to bubble. Serve hot, from baking dishes.

Vegetable Pizzas and Country Tarts

Pizza-like tarts have long been popular in French regional cooking and are among the easiest of pastries to make. The base can vary from a simple oil-enriched yeast dough similar to that of Italian pizza, to a rich brioche-type dough, as in Festive Vegetable Tart. They can be baked in a tart tin, like Provençal Pizza, or on a baking sheet, like Alsatian Onion and Cream Cheese Tart.

Fillings vary enormously and can include many vegetables, but do not necessarily contain tomatoes or cheese. Actually yeast dough can be used as a base for custardy, quiche-type vegetable fillings just as successfully as pie pastry.

PROVENÇAL PIZZA
Pissaladière

The original version of this French pizza was prepared without tomatoes, but many cooks add them when they are in season for their bright colour and delicious flavour.

MAKES 4 TO 6 SERVINGS

PIZZA DOUGH

7 g/¼ oz dried yeast, or 15 g/½ oz   200 g/7 oz plain flour
   fresh yeast   ¾ teaspoon salt
6 tablespoons lukewarm water   1 extra-large egg

ONION AND TOMATO TOPPING

4 tablespoons olive oil

5 medium-size onions, thinly sliced

Salt and freshly ground pepper

1 kg/2 lb ripe tomatoes, peeled, seeded, and chopped

1 bay leaf

1½ teaspoons fresh thyme, or ½ teaspoon dried thyme

1 tablespoon chopped fresh basil (optional)

50 g/2 oz can anchovy fillets, drained (optional)

50 g/2 oz black olives, preferably Niçoise or other oil-cured olives, stoned and halved

PIZZA DOUGH

To make dough in a food processor: Sprinkle dry yeast or crumble fresh yeast over 4 tablespoons of the water in a cup or small bowl and let stand for 10 minutes. Stir until smooth. In food processor fitted with dough blade or metal blade, process flour and salt briefly to mix them. Add remaining water and egg to yeast mixture. With blades of processor turning, pour in yeast-liquid mixture. If dough is too dry to come together, add 1 extra tablespoon of water and process again. Process for 1 minute to knead dough.

To make dough by hand: Sift flour into a bowl and make a well in centre. Sprinkle dry yeast or crumble fresh yeast into well. Pour 4 tablespoons of the water over yeast and let stand for 10 minutes. Stir until smooth. Add remaining water, egg, and salt, and mix with ingredients in middle of well. Stir in flour and mix thoroughly to obtain a fairly soft dough. If dough is dry, add 1 extra tablespoon water. Knead dough vigorously, slapping it on working surface until it is smooth and elastic. If it is very sticky, flour it occasionally while kneading.

Lightly oil a medium-size bowl. Add dough, turning to coat entire surface. Cover with cling film or with lightly dampened tea towel. Let dough rise in a warm, draught-free area for about 1 hour, or until doubled in volume.

ONION AND TOMATO TOPPING

In a frying pan, heat 3 tablespoons oil over low heat and add onions and a pinch of salt and pepper. Cover, and cook over low heat, stirring occasionally, for about 30 minutes, or until very tender. Taste and adjust seasoning.

In another frying pan or sauté pan, heat 1 tablespoon olive oil over medium heat. Stir in tomatoes, bay leaf, thyme, and a pinch of salt and pepper. Cook, stirring occasionally, for about 20 minutes, or until mixture is dry. Discard bay leaf; stir in basil. Taste and adjust seasoning.

Oil a 25-cm/10-inch tart tin. Roll out dough on a floured surface, or with oiled hands pat it out in tin. Line tin with dough.

Fill dough with onion mixture. Spread tomato mixture on top. Arrange anchovy fillets in a lattice and set olives in spaces. Let rise in a warm place for 15 minutes. Preheat oven to 190°C/375°F/gas 5.

Bake pizza for about 30 minutes, or until dough is golden brown and firm but not hard. Serve hot.

RATATOUILLE PIZZA
Pizza à la ratatouille

Ratatouille is a traditional vegetable stew that has remained one of the most popular French vegetable dishes. There are many versions, some sautéed, some stewed, and some including potatoes. Recently chefs have been using ratatouille as a filling for pastries. In this recipe it is paired with pizza. The vegetables are cooked separately before being briefly simmered together so that they keep their form and colour and make an attractive topping for the pizza. The ratatouille can also be served on its own, hot or cold.

MAKES 6 TO 8 SERVINGS

PIZZA DOUGH

7 g/¼ oz dried yeast
225 ml/8 fl oz plus 2 tablespoons
  lukewarm water

390 g/14 oz plain flour
1½ teaspoons salt
2 tablespoons olive oil

RATATOUILLE

3 sprigs fresh thyme, or ¾
   teaspoon dried thyme
2 sprigs fresh rosemary, or ½
   teaspoon dried rosemary
1 bay leaf
7 tablespoons olive oil
600 g/1¼ lb ripe tomatoes, peeled,
   seeded, and chopped
Salt and freshly ground pepper
1 large onion, halved and thinly
   sliced

1 small green pepper, seeded and
   cut into strips
1 small red pepper, seeded and cut
   into strips
225 g/8 oz courgettes (3 small),
   thickly sliced
1 small aubergine
3 large garlic cloves, finely chopped
1½ tablespoons chopped fresh basil

Extra olive oil, to finish
Basil leaves, for garnish (optional)

PIZZA DOUGH

To make dough in a food processor: Sprinkle yeast over 4 tablespoons water in a cup or small bowl and let stand for 10 minutes. Stir until smooth. In food processor fitted with dough blade or metal blade, process flour and salt briefly to mix them. Add remaining water and oil to yeast mixture. With blades of processor turning, pour in yeast-liquid mixture. If dough is too dry to come together, add 1 tablespoon water and process again. Process for 1 minute to knead dough.

To make dough by hand: Sift flour into a bowl and make a well in centre. Sprinkle dry yeast or crumble fresh yeast into well. Pour 4 tablespoons water over yeast and let stand for 10 minutes. Stir until smooth. Add remaining water, oil, and salt, and mix with ingredients in middle of well. Stir in flour and mix well, to obtain a fairly soft dough. If dough is dry, add 1 tablespoon extra water. Knead dough vigorously, slapping it on working surface, until it is smooth and elastic. If it is very sticky, flour it occasionally while kneading.

Lightly oil a medium-size bowl. Add dough, turning to coat entire surface. Cover with cling film or with lightly dampened tea towel. Let dough rise in a warm, draught-free area for about 1 hour, or until doubled in volume.

RATATOUILLE

Wrap thyme, rosemary, and bay leaf in a piece of cheesecloth to make a bouquet garni. In a medium-size heavy saucepan or stew pan, heat 1 tablespoon of the oil over medium-high heat. Add tomatoes, salt, pepper, and bouquet garni, and cook, stirring often, for 20 minutes. Remove bouquet garni.

In a large sauté pan, heat 2 tablespoons oil over low heat. Add onion and cook for 5 minutes. Add peppers and cook over medium-low heat, stirring often, about 10 minutes. Add courgette, reduce heat to low, and cook for about 5 minutes, or until barely tender.

Peel aubergine and cut in 6-mm/¼-inch-thick slices. Cut any large slices in half. In a frying pan, heat 2 tablespoons oil over medium-high heat. Add half of aubergine slices and sauté for about 2 minutes per side, or until just tender. Repeat with another 2 tablespoons oil and remaining slices.

Stir garlic into tomato mixture and transfer it to courgette and pepper mixture, then add aubergine slices. Mix very gently. Bring to a boil, cover, reduce heat to low, and simmer for 5 minutes to blend flavours. Uncover, raise heat to medium-high, and cook for about 5 minutes to evaporate excess liquid. Mixture should be thick and all vegetables should be tender; a few aubergine slices may be falling apart. Stir in chopped basil. Taste and adjust seasoning. Cool in pan, not in a bowl, so mixture stays dry.

Oil two baking sheets. Knead dough again briefly, divide it in two parts, and put each on a baking sheet. With oiled hands, pat each portion of dough into a 25-cm/10-inch circle, with rims slightly higher than centres.

Spread half of ratatouille over each circle of dough, setting some of pepper and courgette pieces on top and leaving about 1 cm/½ inch of dough at edge uncovered. Brush edge of dough with olive oil and sprinkle some over topping.

Preheat oven to 200°C/400°F/gas 6. Let pizzas rise for about 15 minutes.

Bake in preheated oven for 20 minutes, or until dough is golden brown and firm but not hard. Serve hot. Garnish, if desired, with small leaves of basil.

PIPÉRADE PIZZA
Pizza à la pipérade

Pipérade is a pepper mixture from the Basque area of southern France. Generally it is used as a flavouring for omelettes and scrambled eggs. Here it makes a wonderful, bright-red topping for a new pizza.

MAKES 6 TO 8 SERVINGS

Pizza Dough (page 90), *using*
   vegetable oil instead of olive oil

PIPÉRADE TOPPING

1 fresh chilli pepper	2 garlic cloves, chopped
3–4 tablespoons vegetable oil	700 g/1½ lb ripe tomatoes, peeled,
1 large onion, chopped	seeded, and chopped
2 red peppers (about 350 g/12 oz),	Salt and freshly ground pepper
seeded and diced	

Prepare pizza dough following instructions in recipe for Ratatouille Pizza, page 90.

   Lightly oil a medium-size bowl. Add dough, turning to coat entire surface. Cover with cling film or with lightly dampened tea towel. Let dough rise in a warm draught-free area about 1 hour, or until doubled in volume.

PIPÉRADE TOPPING

Wear rubber gloves if you are sensitive to chilli peppers. Discard seeds and ribs from chilli pepper and finely chop. Wash your hands, cutting board, and knife immediately.

   In a deep frying pan, heat 3 tablespoons oil over low heat, add onion, and cook, stirring often, for about 5 minutes, or until soft but not brown. Add red peppers, garlic, and chilli, and cook, stirring often, about 7 minutes, or until peppers soften.

   Add tomatoes and a pinch of salt and pepper and raise heat to medium. Cook, uncovered, stirring often, about 30 minutes, or until mixture is thick. Taste and adjust seasoning.

Oil two baking sheets. Knead the dough again briefly, divide in two, and put each part on baking sheet. With oiled hands, pat dough into two 25-cm/10-inch circles, with rims slightly higher than centres.

Spread pipérade over dough, using half for each pizza, and leaving about 1 cm/½ inch of dough uncovered. Again push up dough so rim is higher than centre. Brush edge of dough with oil and sprinkle some oil over topping.

Preheat oven to 200°C/400°F/gas 6. Let pizzas rise about 15 minutes.

Bake for about 20 minutes, or until dough is golden brown and firm but not hard. Serve hot.

COUNTRY LEEK TART
Tarte campagnarde aux poireaux

Leek tarts are favourites in Champagne and northern France. This one is enriched with mushrooms and baked in a buttery crust, which is an easy version of brioche. If serving the tart as a main course a good appetizer is Endive and Beetroot Salad, which originated in the same area of France.　　MAKES 4 MAIN-COURSE OR 6 APPETIZER SERVINGS

BUTTERY YEAST DOUGH

7 g/¼ oz dried yeast	2 eggs, at room temperature
3 tablespoons lukewarm water	¾ teaspoon salt
225 g/8 oz plain flour	50 g/2 oz unsalted butter, at room temperature, cut in 8 pieces

LEEK FILLING

25 g/1 oz dried mushrooms	1 egg yolk
1 kg/2 lb leeks	200 ml/7 fl oz double cream
40 g/1½ oz butter	Freshly grated nutmeg
Salt and freshly ground pepper	25 g/1 oz Gruyère cheese, grated
2 eggs	

BUTTERY YEAST DOUGH

To make dough in mixer with dough hook: Combine yeast and warm water in small bowl and leave for 10 minutes. Stir well with fork. Sift 200 g/7 oz flour into bowl of heavy-duty mixer fitted with dough hook. Add yeast mixture, eggs, and salt and mix at medium-low speed, scraping dough down occasionally from bowl and hook, about 7 minutes, or until dough is well blended and just begins to cling to hook. Dough will be soft. (If dough seems too wet, beat in remaining flour 1 tablespoon at a time.) Knead by mixing at medium speed, scraping down twice, for about 5 minutes or until dough is smooth, clings to hook, and almost cleans sides of bowl. Scrape down from hook. Add half butter pieces and mix at medium-low speed until dough is thoroughly blended; about 3 minutes. Add remaining butter and mix again until blended; 3 more minutes. Dough will be soft and sticky.

To make dough in food processor: Sprinkle yeast over warm water in a small bowl and let stand for 10 minutes. Combine flour and salt in a food processor fitted with dough blade or metal blade. Process briefly to blend. Add eggs. With blades of processor turning, quickly pour in yeast mixture. Process for 1 minute to knead dough. Add butter and process just until it is absorbed. Dough will be soft and sticky.

Lightly oil a medium bowl. Add dough, turning to coat entire surface. Cover with cling film or with lightly dampened tea towel. Let dough rise in a warm, draught-free area about 1 hour, or until doubled in volume.

LEEK FILLING

Soak mushrooms in hot water to cover until tender; about 20 minutes. Lift into strainer, rinse, and drain well. Cut into 6-mm/ ¼-inch pieces.

Use white and light green parts of leeks for filling. Cut leeks in half lengthwise, rinse well, and cut into 6-mm/¼-inch slices crosswise. Soak sliced leeks in cold water to cover for 5 minutes to remove any dirt. Lift into colander or large strainer, rinse, and drain well.

In a large heavy frying pan, melt butter over low heat, add leeks and salt and pepper to taste, cover, and cook, stirring often, for 15 minutes. Add mushrooms, cover, and cook, stirring occasionally, until leeks are very soft but not brown; about 5 more minutes. If any liquid remains in pan, uncover and cook over medium-high heat, stirring, until mixture is dry. Transfer leek and mushroom mixture to large bowl and let cool to room temperature.

Combine eggs, egg yolk, cream, and nutmeg in medium-size bowl and whisk until blended. Mix with leek mixture, taste, and adjust seasoning.

Position rack in centre of oven and preheat to 220°C/425°F/gas 7. Butter 23-cm/9-inch round fluted tart tin with removable bottom. Lift dough and let it fall lightly into bowl a few times to knock out air. Transfer dough to tart tin with aid of rubber spatula. With oiled knuckles, push dough outward from centre toward rim, to line tin. Push dough against rim of pan with oiled fingers, so tart has border about 1 cm/½ inch thick at top edge. Set tart tin on baking sheet. Ladle leek mixture carefully into tart. With side of finger, gently push up edge of dough again so it is slightly higher than rim of tin. Sprinkle filling with grated cheese. Let tart rise in warm draught-free area for 10 minutes.

Bake tart for 15 minutes. Reduce oven temperature to 180°C/350°F/gas 4 and bake for about 25 minutes longer, or until filling is set and lightly browned. Let cool on rack for 15 minutes and remove tart tin rim by setting pan on an overturned bowl. (Tart can be baked up to 4 hours ahead and kept at room temperature.) Serve tart warm or at room temperature.

FESTIVE VEGETABLE TART
Tarte aux légumes

This tart is filled mainly with vegetables, with just a little custard topping. Peas, yellow courgette, asparagus, and other colourful vegetables can be added when in season. MAKES ABOUT 6 SERVINGS

Buttery Yeast Dough (page 94)

VEGETABLE FILLING

2 medium-size carrots, peeled	1 small red pepper
White and light green part of 2 large leeks, cleaned	175 g/6 oz mushrooms, halved and cut in thin slices
2 small courgettes	2 eggs
1 medium-size celery stick, peeled	6 tablespoons double cream or milk
50 g/2 oz butter	White pepper
Salt and freshly ground pepper	Freshly grated nutmeg

Prepare dough and let rise as in Country Leek Tart.

VEGETABLE FILLING

Cut carrots, leeks, and courgettes in pieces about 4 cm/1½ inches long. Cut these pieces in thin lengthwise slices, and each slice in thin lengthwise strips. Also cut celery in thin strips.

In a large frying pan, melt half the butter over low heat. Add carrots, leeks, celery, salt, and pepper. Cover and cook, stirring often, for 15 minutes. Add courgettes and cook, uncovered, for about 3 minutes, or until all vegetables are tender.

Preheat grill. Grill pepper about 5 cm/2 inches from heat source, turning often with tongs, for about 15 to 20 minutes or until blistered and charred. Transfer to plastic bag and close bag. Let stand for 10 minutes and then peel. Cut pepper in half and remove core. Drain well in colander, and pat dry. Cut in thin strips and add to vegetable mixture. Taste and adjust seasoning.

In a medium-size frying pan, melt remaining butter over medium heat. Add mushrooms, salt, and pepper to taste, and sauté, stirring often, for about 3 minutes, or until tender.

Combine eggs, cream, and salt, white pepper, and nutmeg to taste in a medium-size bowl and whisk until blended.

Position rack in centre of oven and preheat to 200°C/400°F/gas 6. Butter a 23-cm/9-inch round fluted tart tin with removable bottom. Lift dough and let it fall lightly into bowl a few times to knock out air. Transfer dough to tart tin with aid of rubber spatula. With oiled knuckles, push dough outward from centre towards rim, to line tin. Push dough against rim of tin with oiled fingers, so tart has border about 1 cm/½ inch thick at top edge. Set tart on a baking sheet.

Scatter mushrooms over dough and top evenly with vegetable mixture. Ladle cream mixture carefully over vegetables. Let tart rise in warm draught-free area for 10 minutes.

Bake for about 40 to 45 minutes, or until dough browns and filling sets. Let cool on a rack for 15 minutes and remove tart tin rim by setting pan on an overturned bowl. (Tart can be baked up to 4 hours ahead and kept at room temperature; it can also be frozen. Heat in cool oven before serving.) Serve tart warm or at room temperature.

ALSATIAN ONION AND CREAM CHEESE TART
Tarte alsacienne à l'oignon et au fromage frais

This is a northern French 'pizza'. A soft creamy cheese is used in Alsace, but cream cheese softened with sour cream and double cream is a fine substitute. In some traditional versions, thin strips (lardons) of bacon are scattered on top before baking, but the tart has plenty of flavour without them.   MAKES 8 SERVINGS

*Pizza Dough (page 90), using
    melted unsalted butter instead of
    olive oil*

ONION AND CREAM CHEESE TOPPING
*40 g/1½ oz butter
2 medium-size onions, finely
    chopped (about 275 g/10 oz)
100 g/4 oz cream cheese, at room
    temperature*

*6 tablespoons sour cream
6 tablespoons double cream
2 egg yolks
Salt and white pepper
Freshly grated nutmeg*

Prepare pizza dough following instruction in recipe for Ratatouille Pizza, page 90.

ONION AND CREAM CHEESE TOPPING

In a medium-size frying pan, melt butter over low heat, add onions, and cook for about 7 minutes, or until soft but not brown. Cool to room temperature.

Whisk cheese until smooth. Gradually beat in sour cream and double cream. Add egg yolks, and salt, pepper, and nutmeg to taste. Stir in onions, taste, and add more seasonings if needed.

Position rack in centre of oven and preheat to 200°C/400°F/gas 6. Oil a large baking sheet about 43 × 28 cm/17 × 11 inches (or two smaller ones). Knead dough again briefly and put it on baking sheet. With oiled hands, pat dough out to cover, giving it a rim slightly higher than the centre. It should make a thin layer. When dough is nearly patted out, let it rest for 2 or 3 minutes before continuing.

Spread topping over dough, leaving a rim of about 1 cm/½ inch at sides uncovered by filling. Let tart rise for about 15 minutes.

Bake tart in preheated oven for about 22 to 25 minutes, or until topping is golden brown and dough is firm but not hard. Serve hot.

Vegetables in Puff Pastry

A rich vegetable filling served in a puff pastry case may be today's most popular first course at the finest restaurants. Generally noble vegetables such as asparagus or wild mushrooms are the favourites, and they are moistened with a rich butter or cream-based sauce.

Puff pastry is rather time-consuming to prepare, but fortunately good-quality puff pastry can now be bought ready-made, making it easier to prepare a variety of delectable savoury pastries at home. You can match the quality of the pastry hors d'oeuvres prominently displayed in fine food shops in France and make the delicious first courses served at good restaurants.

Puff pastry can be baked in a multitude of shapes, from round bouchées, to square, rectangular or diamond-shaped feuilletés or crescent-shaped turnovers. It can also be used to make impressive tourtes, such as Layered Vegetable Tourte, filled with roasted red peppers, spinach and sautéed mushrooms.

SPRING ONION AND PARMESAN CROISSANTS
Croissants au parmesan et aux oignons nouveaux

Savoury croissants have become popular in recent years, as has purchased puff pastry, which simplifies the making of these croissants. Serve these small pastries as an hors d'oeuvre, as part of a buffet, or as an accompaniment for soups.   MAKES ABOUT 24 PASTRIES

25 g/1 oz unsalted butter
100 g/4 oz sliced spring onions
  (white and green parts)
75 g/3 oz freshly grated Parmesan
  cheese
Pinch of cayenne pepper

Pinch of freshly grated nutmeg
450 g/1 lb good-quality puff
  pastry, well chilled
1 egg, beaten with a pinch of salt

In a medium-size frying pan, melt butter over low heat, add onions, and cook, stirring, for about 4 minutes, or until soft but not brown. Cool completely.

Mix grated cheese with cayenne pepper and nutmeg. Sprinkle two baking sheets very lightly with water. Keep puff pastry refrigerated until ready to use.

Work with half the pastry, keeping rest refrigerated. On a cold, lightly floured surface, roll pastry out into an 18-by-34-cm/7-by-13½-inch rectangle about 3 mm/⅛ inch thick. Work quickly so pastry does not soften, moving it often and flouring it occasionally to prevent sticking. Brush pastry lightly with beaten egg and sprinkle with half the cheese mixture. Press cheese so it will adhere.

Using heel of a large knife, cut pastry lengthwise into two strips, each about 9 cm/3½ inches wide. Cut each strip into triangles in which two sides are approximately equal, making each cut across width of strip; first triangle will be pointing up, second one will be touching it and pointing down, and so on, so that all of strip is cut into triangles and there are no scraps. Flour knife occasionally if it begins to stick to pastry. Spoon about ½ teaspoon onions near one side of one triangle. Roll up tightly in direction of point opposite it. Press to attach to point. Repeat with remaining triangles.

Transfer pastries to one of prepared baking sheets and curve both ends to form a croissant. Refrigerate for at least 30 and preferably 60 minutes, or keep pastries in freezer until ready to bake. Continue shaping croissants from remaining pastry.

Preheat oven to 220°C/425°F/gas 7. Brush pastries with beaten egg. Bake for about 12 minutes, or until puffed and brown. (The pastries can be kept for 2 days in an airtight container, or they can be frozen.) Serve warm or at room temperature.

MUSHROOM AND OLIVE PASTRY
ROLLS
Roulés aux champignons et aux olives

Cylinders of filled puff pastry, with both ends dipped in a generous quantity of grated Gruyère cheese, are a common attraction in the windows of *charcuteries* throughout France. Generally a meat filling is used, but I am certain that many will find this luscious vegetable filling even tastier. These make delightful hors d'oeuvres at parties.

MAKES ABOUT 24 SMALL PASTRIES

MUSHROOM-OLIVE FILLING

50 g/2 oz Niçoise or other black olives, stoned and cut into quarters

65 g/2½ oz unsalted butter

100 g/4 oz small mushrooms, halved and thinly sliced

Salt and freshly ground pepper

600 g/1¼ lb good-quality puff pastry, well chilled

1 egg, beaten with pinch of salt, for glaze

4 tablespoons plain flour

450 ml/¾ pint milk

Freshly grated nutmeg

Pinch of cayenne pepper

1 egg

100 g/4 oz Gruyère cheese, finely grated

2 tablespoons double cream

150 g/5 oz Gruyère cheese, finely grated

MUSHROOM-OLIVE FILLING

If using Niçoise or other oil-cured black olives (but not olives in brine) put them in a small saucepan, cover with water, and bring to a boil. Drain thoroughly.

In a medium-size frying pan, melt 25 g/1 oz of the butter over medium heat, add mushrooms and salt and pepper to taste, and sauté for about 5 minutes, or until tender.

In a medium-size heavy saucepan, melt remaining butter over low heat, stir in flour, and cook, whisking constantly, for about 2 minutes, or until foaming but not browned. Remove from heat. Gradually whisk in milk, and bring to a boil over medium-high heat, whisking. Add a small pinch of salt, pepper, and nutmeg. Reduce heat to low and cook, whisking often, for about 5 minutes, or until very thick. Add cayenne pepper. Set aside 6 tablespoons of sauce for spreading on finished pastries and dab top with a small piece of butter to prevent a skin from forming. Let cool completely.

Remove remaining sauce from heat and let cool slightly. Add egg and whisk it in vigorously. Return to very low heat and cook, whisking constantly, for a few seconds. Do not overcook or egg will scramble. Add olives and mushrooms. Dab top of mixture with a small piece of butter. Let cool completely. Add Gruyère, taste and adjust seasoning.

To Assemble and Bake Pastry Rolls:

Sprinkle water on two baking sheets, preferably having a nonstick coating. Roll out half of dough on a cool, lightly floured surface until just under 6 mm/¼ inch thick. Trim edges so that dough forms an even rectangle. Spoon a row of filling mixture along edge of one long side of rectangle. Carefully roll dough over once from long side so that filling is enclosed. Using a pastry brush, apply water on dough in a thin line alongside rolled section. Roll filled section over slightly in order to stick it to dough brushed with water. Using heel of a heavy knife, cut this roll off from rest of dough.

Cut roll into smaller pieces about 4 cm/1½ inches long, and transfer to prepared baking sheets. Refrigerate. Continue making rolled pieces with remaining dough and filling. Refrigerate for about 30 minutes, or freeze for 15 minutes, or until firm.

Position rack in centre of oven and preheat to 220°C/425°F/gas 7. Brush all pastry rolls with beaten egg. Bake for about 15 minutes, or until puffed and browned; do not worry if some of filling begins to come out, but reduce heat to 190°C/375°F/gas 5 if they begin to burn. (The pastries can be kept for 12 hours at room temperature, or they can be frozen. Reheat in a cool oven before serving.)

To finish, whisk cream into reserved sauce. Adjust seasoning.

Spread both open ends of cylinders with a thin layer of reserved sauce and dip each side in grated cheese. Serve hot, warm, or at room temperature.

ASPARAGUS-FILLED PASTRY CASES
WITH WATERCRESS SAUCE
Bouchées aux asperges, sauce au cresson

Bouchées, or round puff pastry cases, have long been a popular pastry in France, both in tiny cocktail size for hors d'oeuvres and larger sizes for a first course. Their charm lies in the variety of textures presented – the flaky pastry, tender filling, and creamy sauce. Asparagus is regarded as a 'noble' vegetable and therefore makes an ideal choice for a luxurious filling. By using purchased pastry, shaping the bouchées ahead, and preparing the sauce in advance as well, the total amount of work and last-minute fuss are kept to a minimum.

MAKES 6 SERVINGS

600 g/1¼ lb good-quality puff
    pastry, well chilled
1 egg, beaten with a pinch of salt

12 medium-size asparagus spears,
    peeled
Salt

WATERCRESS SAUCE

About 225 g/8 oz watercress
350 ml/12 fl oz double cream
15 g/½ oz butter
3 medium-size shallots, finely
    chopped
200 ml/7 fl oz dry white wine

200 ml/7 fl oz asparagus cooking
    liquid or Vegetable Stock (see
    recipe, page 332)
Salt and freshly ground pepper
A few drops fresh lemon juice

Sprinkle baking sheet with water. Roll out half the pastry dough on a cool, lightly floured surface until about 6 mm/¼ inch thick. Using a 7-cm/3-inch fluted round cutter, cut six rounds of dough. Turn over three rounds and transfer to baking sheets. Brush these rounds with beaten egg. Using a 5-cm/2-inch cutter cut out centres of three of the rounds. (Save these for scraps.) Turn resulting rings over and set them on top of rounds on baking sheet. Press gently so they adhere. Refrigerate for 1 hour, or freeze for 30 minutes. Repeat with remaining dough and refrigerate. (Cases can be kept for 1 day in refrigerator. Scraps can be refrigerated or frozen and used for lining tart tins or for other recipes.)

Preheat oven to 220°C/425°F/gas 7. Brush rings carefully with beaten egg without letting it drip into centre or on to baking sheet. Using a small sharp knife, mark crisscross lines on rings. Bake for about 20 minutes, or until pastry cases puff and brown. Using a sharp knife, carefully remove small 'hat' that forms in centre of case and reserve it. If uncooked dough remains inside, remove it with a spoon. Transfer pastries to a rack. (They can be kept overnight in an airtight container or can be frozen.)

Cut 6-cm/2½-inch-long asparagus tips from stems. Cut stems in about 1-cm/½-inch pieces, discarding tough ends.

Put asparagus pieces into medium-size saucepan containing enough boiling salted water to cover them generously. Return to boil and cook, uncovered, for about 2 minutes, or until asparagus is just tender when pierced with a small sharp knife. Drain, reserving 200 ml/7 fl oz cooking liquid for sauce. Rinse with cold running water until cool and drain thoroughly.

WATERCRESS SAUCE

Cut off leafy section of watercress; discard thick stems. Put leafy section into a large saucepan of boiling salted water. Return to a boil and cook for 1 minute. After rinsing well with cold water, drain, pressing hard to extract excess liquid. Purée cooked watercress in a food processor or blender with 6 tablespoons cream, scraping down often and continuing to purée until mixture turns a fairly uniform green. Push watercress purée through a strainer, pressing firmly to make sure it goes through and using a rubber spatula to scrape it from underside of strainer.

Melt butter in a medium-size saucepan over low heat. Add shallots and cook, stirring, 1 minute. Add wine and bring to boil. Cook, stirring often, until wine is reduced to about 4 tablespoons. Add asparagus liquid and boil until mixture is again reduced to about 4 tablespoons. Stir in remaining cream and pinch of salt and pepper. Reduce heat to medium and simmer, stirring often, until sauce is thick enough to coat a spoon; about 7 minutes. Stir in watercress purée and simmer for 1 minute. Strain sauce, pressing firmly on solids. Taste and adjust seasoning.

Before serving, reheat bouchées in cool oven. Reheat asparagus by steaming above boiling water or by plunging into a medium-size saucepan of boiling salted water for about 30 seconds. Drain well. Reserve asparagus tips for garnish. Reheat sauce, add a few drops lemon juice, and taste again.

To serve, set bouchées on small rimmed plates or individual gratin dishes. Fill with asparagus stem pieces. Spoon in a little sauce. Garnish with asparagus tips and set pastry 'hat' on at an angle. Spoon a little sauce on each plate around bouchée. Serve immediately.

LAYERED VEGETABLE TOURTE
Tourte feuilletée aux légumes

The French often prepare tourtes of vegetables, which have a double crust and thus are different from tarts, which are open-faced. This version is a tall, glamorous puff pastry pie with colourful vegetable layers baked in a springform tin. Under the name '*tourte milanaise*' or '*tourte de Paris*', versions of this pastry can be found at the finer *charcuteries* in France. Although it includes several components, they can be prepared ahead; it is best to assemble and bake the tourte on the day it will be served.   MAKES 6 TO 8 SERVINGS

1 kg/2¼ lb good-quality puff
   pastry, well chilled

BÉCHAMEL SAUCE

25 g/1 oz unsalted butter   *Salt and freshly ground white*
2 tablespoons plain flour   *pepper*
225 ml/8 fl oz milk   *Freshly grated nutmeg*

LAYERED VEGETABLE FILLING

4 eggs

Salt and freshly ground pepper

65 g/2½ oz butter

1·5 kg/3 lb fresh spinach (leaves
   with stems)

100 g/4 oz Gruyère cheese, grated

75 g/3 oz thinly sliced Gruyère
   cheese

Freshly grated nutmeg

3 red peppers

225 g/8 oz mushrooms, thinly
   sliced

1 teaspoon fresh thyme, or ¼
   teaspoon dried thyme

1 egg, beaten with salt, for glaze

To make pastry case, lightly butter the sides of a 20-cm/8-inch springform tin. On a cool, floured surface, roll out two-thirds of puff pastry about 6 mm/¼ inch thick, and cut a circle about 33 cm/13 inches in diameter. Line prepared tin with pastry round. Smooth sides with your fingers. Using a sharp knife, cut off excess pastry at sides, leaving about 2·5 cm/1 inch of excess. Prick bottom of case lightly with a fork and refrigerate for 30 minutes. Roll out remaining puff pastry about 6 mm/¼ inch thick and cut in a 23-cm/9-inch-diameter circle. Place circle on a lightly floured baking sheet and refrigerate.

BÉCHAMEL SAUCE

In a small heavy saucepan, melt butter over low heat. Add flour and cook, whisking constantly, for about 2 minutes, or until foaming but not browned. Remove from heat. Gradually whisk in milk. Bring to boil over medium-high heat, whisking. Add a small pinch of salt, white pepper, and nutmeg. Reduce heat to low and cook, whisking often, for about 5 minutes, or until thick. Taste and adjust seasoning.

Transfer sauce to a bowl, dab top with a small piece of butter, and cool completely.

LAYERED VEGETABLE FILLING

Beat eggs with a pinch of salt and pepper. Melt 15 g/½ oz butter in a 20-cm/8-inch frying pan, preferably nonstick, over medium-high heat. Add half the egg mixture and stir briefly. Stop stirring and let mixture set to make a flat omelette. Remove from pan. Wipe clean. Melt another 15 g/½ oz butter in pan. Add remaining egg mixture and make another omelette.

Remove spinach stems and wash leaves thoroughly. In a large saucepan of boiling salted water, cook spinach, uncovered, over high heat, pushing leaves down into water often; about 3 minutes or until tender. Drain, rinse with cold water, and drain thoroughly.

Squeeze spinach by handfuls until dry, then press between paper towels to be sure it is dry. Finely chop. In a large sauté pan, melt 15 g/½ oz butter over medium heat. Add spinach and salt, pepper, and nutmeg to taste. Sauté, stirring, for about 5 minutes. Adjust seasoning.

Preheat grill. Grill peppers about 5 cm/2 inches from heat source, turning often with tongs, for 15 to 20 minutes, or until they are blistered and charred. Transfer to plastic bag and close bag. Let stand for 10 minutes. Peel, cut in half, and remove cores. Drain well in colander. Pat dry with paper towels and cut each half in 4 pieces.

In a medium-size frying pan, melt remaining butter over medium heat. Add mushrooms, salt and pepper to taste, and thyme; sauté, stirring often, for about 3 minutes, or until tender. (Tourte components can be prepared 1 day ahead and each covered and refrigerated separately; pastry should also be covered.)

To Assemble the Tourte:

Sprinkle one-quarter of the grated Gruyère cheese on pastry base. Put 1 omelette on top. Whisk béchamel sauce until smooth. Gently spread 6 tablespoons over omelette. Top with half the spinach. Sprinkle with two-thirds of remaining Gruyère. Arrange half the peppers on top and spoon all of mushrooms over peppers. Top with second omelette. Gently spread another 6 tablespoons béchamel over omelette. Top with remaining spinach, then with all of Gruyère slices, followed by remaining peppers. Sprinkle with remaining grated cheese.

Position rack in lower third of oven and preheat to 200°C/400°F/ gas 6. Brush edge of tourte thoroughly with egg glaze. Set pastry round on top, pressing firmly to stick it to sides. Cut off excess pastry with knife. Crimp edge decoratively. Brush top with egg glaze. Using point of a small sharp knife, score top in curved lines from centre outwards, cutting through only a few pastry layers. Make three small slits in top, this time cutting through to filling, so steam can escape.

Refrigerate tourte for 15 minutes. Set on a baking sheet, and bake for about 45 minutes. Reduce oven temperature to 180°C/350°F/gas 4 and bake for 15 minutes more, until pastry is well browned.

Let tourte rest for about 30 minutes. Remove sides of springform tin. (Tourte can be kept for 1 day in refrigerator but is best on day it is baked.) Serve at room temperature.

NOTES

· Cooked fresh spinach can be replaced by two 275-g/10-oz packets frozen spinach. Thaw spinach and squeeze dry. Purée and continue as above.

· Puff pastry scraps can be used to make small pastries such as Spring Onion and Parmesan Croissants (see page 100).

CÈPE TURNOVERS
Chaussons aux cèpes

Duxelles, a flavourful mixture of chopped sautéed mushrooms, can be made not only with plain mushrooms, but with wild ones as well. Here a duxelles made of cèpes is used as a filling for puff pastry turnovers. As with all filled pastries, avoid the temptation to put too generous an amount of filling in the turnovers or they will burst open. These are small turnovers that are good as an hors d'oeuvre, but they can be made larger and served as a first course.

MAKES ABOUT 40 PASTRIES

CÈPE DUXELLES FILLING

225 g/8 oz fresh cèpes, or 50 g/2   2 tablespoons finely chopped
  oz dried cèpes   parsley
15 g/½ oz butter   1 tablespoon unseasoned bread
2 shallots, finely chopped   crumbs
Salt and freshly ground pepper   1 egg yolk
3 tablespoons double cream for
  fresh cèpes, or 6 tablespoons for
  dried cèpes

1 kg/2 lb good-quality puff pastry,   1 egg, beaten with a pinch of salt
  well chilled

CÈPE DUXELLES FILLING

Thoroughly rinse fresh cèpes and cut off ends of stems; pat dry. Soak dried cèpes in hot water to cover for about 20 minutes, or until tender. Lift into strainer, rinse, and drain well. Finely chop fresh or dried cèpes.

In a medium-size frying pan, melt butter over low heat, add shallots, and cook, stirring, for 1 minute. Add cèpes and a small pinch of salt and pepper. Raise heat to medium-high and cook, stirring often, for 5 minutes for fresh cèpes, or until liquid they render evaporates; cook for only 1 minute if dried. Stir in cream and bring to a boil. Simmer, stirring often, for about 2 minutes, or until mixture is thick and cream has been absorbed.

Transfer mixture to a bowl. Stir in parsley and bread crumbs. Cool to lukewarm. Add egg yolk and beat until mixture is blended. Taste and adjust seasoning. Cover and refrigerate for 30 minutes. (Mixture can be kept for up to 1 day in refrigerator.)

To Assemble Turnovers:

Sprinkle two baking sheets with water. Roll out half the dough on a cool, lightly floured surface until about 3 mm/⅛ inch thick. Using an 8-cm/3-inch-diameter cutter, cut circles of dough, reserving scraps. Roll each circle to elongate it slightly into an oval. Put 1 teaspoon filling in centre of each. Brush half of oval, around a narrow end, with beaten egg. Fold in half to enclose filling, joining second side to egg-brushed side. Press to seal well. Set turnovers on the prepared baking sheets. Refrigerate for at least 30 minutes; or wrap and keep pastries in freezer until ready to bake. Continue shaping turnovers from remaining pastry. Make turnovers from scraps too, after refrigerating them for at least 30 minutes.

Preheat oven to 220°C/425°F/gas 7. Defrost frozen turnovers briefly. Brush turnovers with beaten egg. With point of a sharp knife, mark a few decorative lines in a half-sunburst pattern on each turnover, cutting through a few layers of pastry but not all the way to the filling.

Bake pastries for about 10 minutes. Reduce oven temperature to 190°C/375°F/gas 5 and bake for about 12 minutes, or until puffed and brown. (The pastries can be kept for 2 days in an airtight container, or they can be frozen.) Serve warm or at room temperature.

Vegetable Crêpes

One of the joys of strolling in Paris is purchasing a crêpe from an outdoor vendor. The crêpe is first quickly heated on a griddle with a pat of butter. Next it is topped with a selection of ingredients – grated Gruyère cheese, cooked vegetables, strips of ham, beaten egg, or a combination of these, for example – and heated until the filling is warm. Finally the crêpe is folded in quarters and wrapped in paper in a cone shape for easy holding. My own favourite at some Parisian crêperies is a filling of Roquefort cheese mixed with chopped walnuts and butter. The result is the finest fast food imaginable.

Crêpes are available throughout France as snacks but are a speciality of the region of Brittany, where they are still more popular than anywhere else. They make delicious and convenient wrappings for almost any vegetable. The batter for these thin French pancakes takes only a minute to make, whether it is done in a food processor, a blender, or in a bowl with a whisk. With a stack of crêpes on hand in the refrigerator or the freezer the busy cook can easily prepare a festive treat for a light meal or a snack. Crêpes can be turned into an elegant first course or luncheon dish or can be enjoyed in a more casual setting right out of the pan. They can enclose a great variety of vegetable fillings, from classic spinach with crème fraîche to elegant aubergine soufflé.

For a savoury snack many people are fond of the hearty taste of buckwheat crêpes, whereas white-flour crêpes are preferred for pairing with delicate fillings. For most purposes they are interchangeable.

One of the most delicious ways to dress up leftovers is to turn them into crêpe fillings. Basically any cooked vegetables and any flavouring can be used, according to what is available and your imagination. The only rule for fillings is that all the ingredients should be tender and in small pieces, and their flavours should harmonize well. The filling should be moistened with melted butter, a fragrant oil such as olive or hazelnut, or a little sauce – tomato, cream or cheese. The sauce can also accompany the filled crêpes, as in Crêpes with Peppers, Onions, and Peas in Curry Sauce.

Crêpe batter can be cooked in a frying pan, but the low sides of a crêpe pan make turning them easy. Traditional crêpe pans made of cast iron or rolled steel produce crêpes that are lacier, moister, and more attractively browned than those cooked in other pans. These heavy pans need to be seasoned with oil before they are used the first time, so the crêpes will not stick. Crêpe pans with a nonstick surface are lighter and do not require buttering before the batter is added. There also are crêpe pans that are dipped in the batter and cook the crêpes on the bottom of the pan. Which type of pan to select is a matter of personal choice.

The technique for cooking crêpes perfectly can be mastered quite easily after making just a few. They key is regulating the heat and the thickness of the batter so that the crêpes will be thin and lacy.

Hints

· To season a cast-iron or rolled-steel crêpe pan brush it with vegetable oil and bake it at your oven's lowest setting for 2 to 4 hours.

· Do not wash cast-iron or rolled-steel crêpe pans after use. To clean them, rub them well with paper towels while they are still warm.

· Before cooking the crêpe batter have all the utensils ready near the crêpe pan and burner: a plate for stacking them, a spatula for turning them, and a metal tablespoon.

· A few small holes in a crêpe give a lacy effect and are fine; but if the crêpes have many large holes, the pan is probably too hot and the heat should be reduced slightly.

· Gratin dishes are ideal for baking filled crêpes. Either large or individual dishes can be used.

BUCKWHEAT CRÊPES WITH CREAMY VEGETABLES
Galettes de sarrasin aux légumes

Buckwheat crêpes are a speciality of Brittany, a region bordering the Atlantic. If you have these crêpes on hand it is easy to whip up a delicious light main course. That is part of the reason they have long been so popular, both as street snacks and at home, throughout France. The vegetables can be varied according to the season and stirred into the cream sauce, which can then be enclosed inside any unsweetened crêpe.   MAKES 10 TO 12 CRÊPES, 4 TO 6 SERVINGS

BUCKWHEAT CRÊPES

70 g/2½ oz buckwheat flour
35 g/1¼ oz plain flour
3 eggs
300 ml/½ pint milk, or a little
   more if needed

¾ teaspoon salt
About 50 g/2 oz unsalted butter

CREAMY VEGETABLE FILLING

25 g/1 oz butter
15 g/½ oz plain flour
300 ml/½ pint milk
Salt and freshly ground white
   pepper
Freshly grated nutmeg
4 tablespoons double cream or
   Crème Fraîche (see page 381)

Pinch of cayenne pepper
About 450 g/1 lb diced cooked
   vegetables, one or a mixture of
   the following: cauliflower,
   broccoli, spinach, Swiss chard,
   or mushrooms

25 g/1 oz butter, melted, for
   brushing crêpes

BUCKWHEAT CRÊPES

To prepare crêpe batter and cook crêpes, follow directions in Spinach-Filled Crêpes with Crème Fraîche (page 116), substituting flours in this recipe. Sift buckwheat flour with plain flour. Reserve 12 crêpes for this recipe.

CREAMY VEGETABLE FILLING

In a medium-size heavy saucepan, melt butter over low heat. Add flour and cook, whisking constantly, for about 2 minutes, or until foaming but not browned. Remove from heat. Gradually stir in milk. Bring to boil over medium-high heat, whisking. Add a small pinch of salt, white pepper, and nutmeg. Reduce heat to low and cook, whisking often, for 3 minutes. Add cream and bring to a boil. Reduce heat to low and cook, whisking often, for about 5 minutes, or until thick. Add cayenne pepper, stir in diced vegetables, taste and adjust seasoning.

Preheat oven to 220°C/425°F/gas 7. Butter one large shallow baking dish or two 20-cm/8-inch gratin dishes or other shallow baking dishes. On lower third of the less attractive side of each crêpe, spoon 2 tablespoons filling and roll up in cigar shape, beginning at edge with filling. Arrange crêpes in single layer in buttered dish and brush with melted butter. (Crêpes can be prepared up to this point and kept, covered, for up to 1 day in refrigerator. Bring crêpes to room temperature and preheat oven before continuing.)

Bake in preheated oven for about 10 minutes, or until hot and sauce is bubbling. Serve immediately.

SPINACH-FILLED CRÊPES WITH CRÈME FRAÎCHE
Crêpes aux épinards à la crème

The spinach filling gives these crêpes an interesting appearance; its green colour can be seen through the thin, lacy exterior. Be sure to season the filling generously with nutmeg; spinach and nutmeg are a favourite French flavour combination.   MAKES 4 TO 6 SERVINGS

CRÊPES

100 g/4 oz plain flour	3/4 teaspoon salt
3 eggs	About 50 g/2 oz unsalted butter
300 ml/1/2 pint milk, or a little more if needed	

SPINACH FILLING AND CHEESE TOPPING

800 g/1 3/4 lb fresh spinach (leaves with stems)	75 g/3 oz Gruyère cheese, grated
50 g/2 oz unsalted butter	Salt and freshly ground pepper
6–9 tablespoons Crème Fraîche (see page 381), bought crème fraîche or double cream	Freshly grated nutmeg

CRÊPES

To prepare batter in food processor: Combine eggs, 3 tablespoons milk, flour, and salt in work bowl and mix, using several on/off turns; batter will be lumpy. Scrape down sides and bottom of work bowl. With machine running, pour remaining milk through feed tube and process batter for about 15 seconds. Scrape down sides and bottom of work bowl thoroughly. Blend batter for about 15 seconds.

To prepare batter in blender: Combine eggs, all the milk, flour, and salt in blender. Mix on high speed for about 1 minute or until batter is smooth.

To prepare batter in bowl: Sift flour into medium-size bowl. Push flour to sides of bowl, leaving large well in centre. Add eggs, salt, and 3 tablespoons milk and whisk ingredients in well briefly until blended. Using whisk, stir flour gently and gradually into egg mixture until smooth. Gradually add remaining milk.

Strain batter if it is lumpy. Cover and let stand at room temperature for about 1 hour. (Batter can be refrigerated, covered, for up to 1 day. Bring to room temperature before continuing.)

In small saucepan, melt butter over low heat. Gradually add 2 tablespoons melted butter to crêpe batter, stirring constantly with a whisk. Pour remaining butter into a small cup. Skim off foam to clarify. (Batter should have consistency of double cream. If it is too thick, gradually add more milk, about 1 teaspoon at a time. If too much liquid was added and crêpe batter is too thin, sift 2 or 3 tablespoons plain flour into another bowl and gradually stir batter into it.)

Heat crêpe pan or frying pan with 15-cm/6-inch base over medium-high heat. Sprinkle with few drops of water. If water immediately sizzles, pan is hot enough. Brush pan lightly with some clarified butter; if using nonstick crêpe pan, no butter is needed. Remove pan from heat and hold it near bowl of batter. Working quickly, pour 2 tablespoons of batter to one edge of pan, tilting and swirling pan until its base is covered with thin layer of batter. Immediately pour any excess batter back into bowl.

Return pan to medium-high heat. Loosen edges of crêpe with spatula, discarding any pieces of crêpe clinging to sides of pan. Cook until bottom browns lightly. Slide spatula under it and turn carefully. Cook until second side browns lightly in spots. Slide crêpe on to plate. Top with sheet of foil, if desired. Reheat pan for a few seconds. Continue making crêpes with remaining batter, stirring it occasionally. If the first crêpes are too thick, whisk a teaspoon of milk or water into the batter. Adjust heat and add more clarified butter to pan if necessary. If batter thickens on standing, very gradually add a little more milk, about 1 teaspoon at a time. Pile crêpes on plate as they are done. Reserve 10 or 12 crêpes for this recipe. (Crêpes can be kept, wrapped tightly, for up to 3 days in refrigerator, or they can be frozen. Bring them to room temperature before using to avoid tearing them.)

SPINACH FILLING AND CHEESE TOPPING

Remove spinach stems and wash leaves thoroughly. In a very large saucepan of boiling salted water, cook spinach, uncovered, over high heat, pushing leaves down into water often, about 3 minutes, or until very tender. Rinse with cold water and drain. Squeeze by handfuls until dry and chop coarsely.

In a medium-size saucepan, melt half the butter over medium heat, add spinach, and cook, stirring, until most of spinach liquid evaporates. Remove from heat and stir in 6 tablespoons cream. If mixture is thick, stir in more cream. Add half the cheese. Season to taste with salt, pepper, and nutmeg.

Lightly butter a large shallow baking dish or 2 medium-size baking dishes. On lower third of less attractive side of each crêpe, spoon about 2 tablespoons filling and roll up in cigar shape, beginning at edge with filling. Arrange crêpes in one layer in buttered dish. Sprinkle with remaining cheese. Cut remaining butter in small bits and scatter them over crêpes. (Crêpes can be prepared up to this point and kept, covered, for up to 1 day in refrigerator. Bring to room temperature and preheat oven before continuing.)

Preheat oven to 180°C/350°F/gas 4. Bake crêpes for about 15 minutes, or until cheese melts and filling is hot.

LEEK AND MUSHROOM CRÊPES
Crêpes aux poireaux et aux champignons

Sautéed vegetables make a rich, juicy filling for crêpes that is easy to prepare. This mixture of sautéed mushrooms and leeks is flavoured with olive oil, white wine and garlic.   MAKES ABOUT 6 SERVINGS

12 Crêpes (page 116), using
   vegetable oil instead of butter

LEEK AND MUSHROOM FILLING

700 g/1½ lb leeks
25 g/1 oz unsalted butter
Salt and freshly ground pepper
2 teaspoons fresh thyme, or ½
   teaspoon dried thyme

3 tablespoons plus 1 teaspoon olive
   oil
225 g/8 oz mushrooms, halved and
   thinly sliced
1 tablespoon finely chopped garlic
3–4 tablespoons white wine

1 tablespoon olive oil, for brushing
   crêpes

Prepare crêpes according to the instructions in Spinach-Filled Crêpes with Crème Fraîche, page 116. Reserve 12 crêpes for this recipe.

LEEK AND MUSHROOM FILLING

Use only white and light green parts of leeks for filling; reserve dark green parts for stock if desired. Cut leeks in half lengthwise, rinse well, and slice into 6-mm/¼-inch pieces. Soak sliced leeks in cold water to cover for 5 minutes to remove any sand. Lift into colander or large strainer, rinse, and drain well.

Preheat oven to 200°C/400°F/gas 6 if planning to serve crêpes as soon as they are ready. In a medium-size heavy frying pan, melt butter over medium heat, add leeks, pinch of salt and pepper, and thyme. Cook, stirring often, until leeks are very soft but not brown; about 15 minutes. If any liquid remains in pan, cook over medium-high heat, stirring, until it evaporates. Transfer leek mixture to a large bowl.

Wipe pan clean. Add 2 tablespoons olive oil and heat over medium-high heat. Add mushrooms, salt and pepper to taste, and sauté, stirring often, about 6 minutes, or until any liquid that escapes from mushrooms has evaporated and they begin to brown. Add 1 teaspoon olive oil, quickly stir in garlic, and sauté for 30 seconds. Add white wine and bring to boil, stirring. Cook over high heat until wine is completely absorbed by mushroom mixture. Remove from heat and transfer to leek mixture. Mix very well. Stir in 1 tablespoon olive oil and a pinch of pepper. Taste and adjust seasoning.

Lightly oil a large shallow baking dish or 2 medium-sized baking dishes. On lower third of less attractive side of each crêpe, spoon about 2 tablespoons filling, and roll up in cigar shape, beginning at edge with filling. Arrange crêpes in one layer in oiled dish and brush with 1 tablespoon olive oil. (Crêpes can be prepared up to this point and kept, covered, for up to 1 day in refrigerator. Bring to room temperature and preheat oven before continuing.)

Bake crêpes in preheated oven for about 12 minutes, to heat filling. Serve immediately.

CRÊPES WITH PEPPERS, ONIONS AND PEAS IN CURRY SAUCE
Crêpes aux poivrons, oignons et petits pois, sauce curry

A colourful garnish of peas and peppers in a spicy but creamy French curry sauce is spooned over the rolled crêpes and hints at the vegetable filling inside. Other vegetables that are good with curry, such as cauliflower, carrots, sautéed aubergine and courgette, can also be used.

MAKES 6 SERVINGS

12 *Crêpes (page 116), 18 cm/7 inches in diameter*

PEPPER, ONION, AND PEA MIXTURE

25 g/1 oz butter
2 medium-size onions, halved and cut in thin slices
Salt and freshly ground pepper
1 red pepper, cored, seeded, and cut in thin strips

450 ml/¾ pint water
700 g/1½ lb fresh peas, shelled, or 225 g/8 oz frozen peas

CURRY SAUCE

25 g/1 oz butter
15 g/½ oz plain flour
1½ teaspoons curry powder
6 tablespoons cooking liquid (from vegetables above)

225 ml/8 fl oz milk
Salt and freshly ground pepper
Pinch of cayenne pepper
6 tablespoons double cream, to finish sauce

15 g/½ oz unsalted butter, melted, for brushing crêpes

Prepare crêpes according to the instructions in Spinach-Filled Crêpes with Crème Fraîche, using an 18-cm/7-inch crêpe pan and about 3 tablespoons batter to make each crêpe. Reserve 12 crêpes for this recipe.

PEPPER, ONION, AND PEA MIXTURE

In a medium-size sauté pan, melt butter over low heat, add onions and salt and pepper to taste, and mix well. Cover with a circle of buttered foil and a lid. Cook, stirring occasionally, for about 10 minutes. Add strips of red pepper, cover, and continue cooking, stirring occasionally, for about 20 minutes, or until onions and pepper are very soft but not brown. Remove from pan to bowl with slotted spoon.

Add water to pan and bring to a boil. Add a dash of salt and peas, and boil, uncovered, until just tender; about 8 minutes for fresh peas or 4 minutes for frozen peas. Drain, reserving 6 tablespoons liquid for sauce. Reserve 2 tablespoons peas and 3 pepper strips for garnish. Cut reserved pepper strips in small dice.

CURRY SAUCE

In a small heavy saucepan, melt butter over low heat. Add flour and curry powder, and cook, whisking constantly, for about 2 minutes, or until foaming. Remove from heat and gradually whisk in reserved vegetable cooking liquid and milk. Bring to a boil over medium-high heat, whisking. Add small pinches of salt, pepper, and cayenne pepper. Reduce heat to low and cook, whisking often, for 5 minutes.

Drain any liquid that the vegetables may have rendered while sauce was being prepared. Stir 6 tablespoons of sauce into vegetables. Reserve remaining sauce separately.

To Assemble Crêpes:

Preheat oven to 220°C/425°F/gas 7. Butter a large oval baking dish or other shallow baking dish. On lower third of less attractive side of each crêpe, spoon 3 tablespoons filling, and roll up in cigar shape, beginning at edge with filling. Arrange crêpes in single layer in buttered dish and brush with melted butter. (Crêpes can be prepared up to this point and kept, covered, for up to 1 day in refrigerator; sauce and garnish vegetables should be reserved, covered, in separate bowls. Bring crêpes and garnish vegetables to room temperature and preheat oven before continuing.)

Bake crêpes in preheated oven for about 10 minutes, or until hot and sauce begins to bubble.

In a small saucepan, bring reserved sauce just to a boil. Remove from heat and whisk in cream. Return to boil. Reduce heat and simmer, whisking, for about 1 minute, or until sauce thickens slightly. Taste and adjust seasoning.

To serve, transfer crêpes to plates and spoon a little sauce over centre of each. Sprinkle reserved vegetables over sauce.

AUBERGINE SOUFFLÉ-FILLED CRÊPES
WITH RED PEPPER SAUCE
*Crêpes soufflées à l'aubergine, sauce aux poivrons
rouges*

Crêpes with soufflé fillings make elegant vegetable first or main courses. As with any soufflé, these should be baked just before serving. Fortunately their baking time is very brief. If desired serve these with Fresh Tomato Sauce (page 38) instead of Red Pepper Sauce, or on their own, without sauce.   MAKES 6 SERVINGS

12 Crêpes (page 116)

RED PEPPER SAUCE

2 medium-size red peppers
6 tablespoons dry white wine
6 tablespoons white wine vinegar
4 sprigs fresh thyme, or ¾
   teaspoon dried thyme

Salt and freshly ground pepper
225 g/8 oz well-chilled unsalted
   butter, cut into 1-cm/½-inch
   pieces

AUBERGINE SOUFFLÉ

450 g/1 lb aubergines
3 tablespoons vegetable or olive oil
20 g/¾ oz butter
15 g/½ oz plain flour
6 tablespoons milk
Salt and freshly ground pepper

Pinch of freshly grated nutmeg
2 egg yolks, at room temperature
4 egg whites, at room temperature
Pinch cream of tartar
2 tablespoons freshly grated
   Parmesan cheese

Prepare crêpes according to the instructions in Spinach-Filled Crêpes with Crème Fraîche. Reserve 12 crêpes for this recipe.

RED PEPPER SAUCE

Preheat grill. Grill peppers about 5 cm/2 inches from heat source, turning often with tongs, for about 15 to 20 minutes, or until they are blistered and charred. Transfer to plastic bag and close. Let stand for 10 minutes. Peel, cut in half, and remove cores. Drain well in colander. Pat dry and purée in food processor until very fine.

In medium-size saucepan, combine wine, vinegar, and thyme and bring to boil. Cook over medium-high heat until liquid is reduced to 3 tablespoons. Strain into small heavy saucepan. Add pepper purée and bring to boil. Keep butter pieces in refrigerator until ready to finish sauce. (Sauce can be prepared up to 1 day ahead to this point and kept, covered, in refrigerator.)

AUBERGINE SOUFFLÉ

Preheat oven to 220°C/425°F/gas 7. Cut aubergines in half and score flesh lightly with sharp knife. Pour 2 tablespoons oil into heavy baking dish. Put aubergines in dish, cut side up, and spoon remaining oil over. Bake for 5 minutes. Turn aubergine halves over and bake for another 30 minutes, or until flesh is tender when pierced with a knife.

In small heavy saucepan, melt butter over low heat, add flour, and cook, whisking constantly, about 2 minutes, or until foaming but not browned. Remove from heat and gradually whisk in milk. Bring to a boil over medium-high heat, whisking. Add small pinches of salt, pepper, and nutmeg. Reduce heat to low and cook, whisking often, for 2 minutes. Sauce will be very thick.

Scoop flesh from aubergine skins and put flesh in strainer to drain well. Finely chop with a knife and whisk into sauce. Heat mixture briefly. Remove from heat and whisk in egg yolks, one by one. Return to low heat and cook, whisking constantly, until mixture thickens slightly. Add pepper and adjust seasoning. (Mixture can be prepared ahead; dot with butter to prevent skin from forming, cover, and refrigerate for up to 1 day. Warm over low heat briefly, whisking, then remove from heat and proceed.)

Before serving, preheat oven to 220°C/425°F/gas 7. Oil two heatproof platters or shallow baking dishes.

In a large bowl, beat egg whites with cream of tartar at medium speed until soft peaks form. Continue beating at high speed until whites are stiff but not dry.

Quickly fold about one-quarter of whites into aubergine mixture. Spoon this mixture over remaining whites, add cheese, and fold in lightly but quickly, just until mixture is blended.

Working quickly, spoon 2 tablespoons of mixture on to less attractive side of each crêpe, fold in half without pressing on filling, and transfer to prepared dishes in a single layer. (Crêpes can be kept for up to 30 minutes in refrigerator but are best if baked as soon as possible.) Bake for about 10 minutes, or until filling puffs; do not overbake or filling will dry out.

To Assemble and Serve:
Set pan of red pepper sauce over low heat and bring to simmer, whisking. Season lightly with salt and pepper. Add 2 pieces of chilled butter and whisk quickly until just incorporated. Whisk in remaining butter 1 piece at a time without stopping, adding each only after previous piece is just nearly incorporated. Remove from heat as soon as last butter piece is incorporated. Taste and adjust seasoning. Keep sauce warm by placing saucepan on a rack above hot but not boiling water, or put in a vacuum flask.

To serve, set two crêpes on each plate and spoon a little sauce next to them. Serve immediately. Serve any remaining sauce separately.

NIÇOISE BAKED CHICK-PEA PANCAKE
Socca

This pancake is made of a crêpe-like batter containing chick-pea flour. A speciality of Nice, it is served as a snack at markets and informal restaurants that resemble pizzerias. Chick-pea flour is available at Indian markets and at speciality food shops.

MAKES 4 SERVINGS

125 g/4½ oz chick-pea flour (also	½ teaspoon salt
called garbanzo flour)	4 tablespoons olive oil
225 ml/8 fl oz water	Freshly ground black pepper

Preheat oven to 220°C/425°F/gas 7. Pour chick-pea flour into a medium-size bowl and make a well in centre. Add water to well and whisk chick-pea flour into it. Add salt and 2 tablespoons of olive oil. Strain to remove any lumps, pressing on mixture.

Pour remaining 2 tablespoons olive oil into a heavy gratin dish 23 cm/9 inches in diameter. Heat in oven for 5 minutes, open oven door, and carefully pour batter into dish, standing back because hot oil can splatter. Bake for 10 minutes. Transfer to grill and cook until surface browns in a few places. Cut in wedges, sprinkle with freshly ground black pepper, and serve.

Vegetable Canapés

Although canapés are not usually made with pastry some chefs do prepare them on thin bases of puff pastry. These dainty open-face sandwiches make it possible to enjoy tasty combinations without the need to prepare or roll pastry, and play a role similar to an hors d'oeuvre. Vegetables make perfect toppings for light and colourful canapés. Any type of bread can be used, so long as it is not sweet.

Butter, whether plain or flavoured with herbs, is the most common spread for the bread base, but for a change try homemade cheese spreads or mayonnaise. Fresh, marinated or cooked vegetables can serve as the topping. Generally the vegetable acts as garnish as well so that there is no need for further decoration.

ASPARAGUS AND ROQUEFORT CANAPÉS
Canapés aux asperges et au roquefort

The asparagus sits on a spread made of a traditional pair – Roquefort cheese and walnuts – with a little butter to soften the flavour.

MAKES 6 CANAPÉS

12 very thin asparagus spears
Salt
12 walnut halves

25 g/1 oz Roquefort cheese, at
   room temperature
25 g/1 oz unsalted butter, softened

6 thin slices good-quality white
  bread, crusts discarded

Cut asparagus spears so they are slightly shorter than bread slices. In a medium-size saucepan of boiling salted water to generously cover, cook asparagus tips over high heat for about 2 minutes, or until just tender. Drain carefully, rinse with cold water until chilled, and drain. Set on paper towels to dry.

Finely chop 6 walnut halves. Mash Roquefort cheese and beat it thoroughly with softened butter. Stir in chopped walnuts. Spread Roquefort mixture on bread slices.

To arrange asparagus decoratively on canapés, cut each spear in two pieces and arrange them in a cross on bread. Put a walnut half in the centre. (The canapés can be kept, covered with cling film, for up to 8 hours in refrigerator.) Serve at room temperature.

CUCUMBER AND HERBED GOAT CHEESE CANAPÉS
Canapés aux concombres et au fromage de chèvre

These canapés make use of a popular cheese spread from Burgundy. Cream cheese can be substituted for the goat cheese. To make a simple vegetable hors d'oeuvre the cheese mixture can be spread on cucumber slices instead of being spread on bread.

MAKES 8 TO 10 CANAPÉS

100 g/4 oz creamy goat cheese, at
  room temperature
3 to 4 tablespoons Crème Fraîche
  (page 381), double cream, or
  sour cream
2 tablespoons finely chopped
  parsley
1½ tablespoons snipped chives

2 teaspoons chopped fresh
  tarragon, or ¾ teaspoon dried
  tarragon
Salt (optional) and freshly ground
  pepper
½ cucumber
8 to 10 thin slices French bread or
  good-quality white bread

Remove any dark rind from goat cheese by scraping gently with a knife. Using a wooden spoon, beat cheese with 2 tablespoons cream until smooth. Stir in enough remaining cream to obtain a spreading consistency.

Stir in parsley, half the chives, and tarragon. Add a pinch of pepper. Goat cheese is often salty, so taste spread before adding salt. Cover and refrigerate overnight so that flavours blend.

Peel cucumber and remove centre with a corer. Cut cucumber in thin slices – they will be ring-shaped. Spread on paper towels to remove excess moisture.

Using a round cutter of same diameter as cucumber slices, cut bread into circles. Spread with goat cheese mixture and set cucumber slice on top. Sprinkle remaining chives in centre of rings.

RADISH FLOWER CANAPÉS
Canapés aux fleurs de radis

Slices of baby radishes arranged like a flower, with a stem of spring onion, complete this easy and attractive canapé. It has a very fresh vegetable taste.

MAKES 6 CANAPÉS

6 thin slices French bread or
good-quality white bread
25 g/1 oz lightly salted butter

6 small radishes, thinly sliced
2 spring onions, green part only

Use an oval cutter to cut bread or use a knife to cut off corners, giving slice of bread an oval shape. Spread with butter.

At one end of bread arrange 5 radish slices, slightly overlapping each other, in a flower shape.

Cut strips of spring onion for stems and diagonal pieces of onion for leaves. Arrange a stem with 3 leaves on each bread slice. (The canapés can be kept, covered with cling film, for up to 8 hours in refrigerator.) Serve at room temperature.

TOMATO AND EGG CANAPÉS
Canapés aux tomates et aux oeufs

Half the round of bread is covered with a tomato wedge and the other with a wedge of egg, both facing each other. These simple canapés will add colour to any buffet. MAKES 8 CANAPÉS

8 thin slices good-quality white
   bread, crusts removed
2–3 tablespoons Mayonnaise (see
   page 379) or commercial
   mayonnaise

1 teaspoon snipped chives
2 hard-boiled eggs
2 ripe tomatoes, about same size as
   eggs

Cut bread into 8-cm/3-inch circles with a round cutter. Mix mayonnaise with chives and spread on bread. Cut eggs and tomatoes in lengthwise quarters.

On one side of each bread slice, set a quarter egg with cut side facing inward. On other side of slice, set a quarter tomato, with cut side facing inward. Serve as soon as possible; if these are made in advance juice from tomatoes will begin to soak into bread.

ROASTED PEPPER CANAPÉS
Canapés aux poivrons grillés

These canapés feature the vibrant flavours of Provence – peppers, Niçoise olives, and fine olive oil. MAKES 8 CANAPÉS

1 medium-size red pepper
2 teaspoons olive oil
40 g/1½ oz unsalted butter
1½ teaspoons finely chopped
   parsley
Salt and freshly ground pepper

8 thin slices good-quality white
   bread, crusts removed
4 black olives, preferably Niçoise,
   halved and stoned

Preheat grill. Grill pepper about 5 cm/2 inches from heat source, turning often with tongs, for 15 to 20 minutes, or until blistered and charred. Transfer to plastic bag and close bag. Let stand for 10 minutes. Peel, cut in half, and remove cores. Drain well in colander and pat dry.

Cut pepper in strips about 1 cm/½ inch wide and cut off uneven ends on the diagonal. Put in a bowl, sprinkle with olive oil, and toss until coated. Let stand for about 30 minutes.

Soften butter and stir in parsley and salt and pepper to taste. Spread on bread. Put 2 pepper strips in a cross on each bread slice and set an olive half in the centre. (The canapés can be kept, covered with cling film, for up to 8 hours in refrigerator.) Serve at room temperature.

GRATINS, PURÉES, AND STUFFED VEGETABLES

Gratins, purées, and stuffed vegetables are festive and proudly served both at home and in all types of restaurants. While gratins and stuffed vegetables are special forms of baked vegetables, purées are usually prepared from boiled or steamed vegetables.

The role of these types of vegetable dishes in the menu is versatile. All are perfect accompaniments for simply prepared foods, such as sautéed, grilled, or roasted poultry, fish, or meat. Gratins and stuffed vegetables also make an inviting main dish for a lunch, brunch or light dinner.

Vegetable Gratins

Coating a cooked vegetable with a flavourful sauce, sprinkling it with a simple topping and browning it in the oven transforms it into a tempting gratin that is both attractive and elegant. A staple of French home cooking, gratins have long played a role similar to our casseroles. Since they can be assembled in advance and are baked and served in the same dish, gratins make menu planning easy. Many time-conscious cooks prepare a double quantity of vegetables in order to serve half with butter on one day, and the rest as a gratin on the next.

It is the crust that forms during baking that gives the gratin its name. The French *gratiner* means to bake until crusty. *Gratin* has been extended to mean any dish, most often of vegetables and usually sprinkled with a topping, that obtains a crusty surface after being baked or grilled. Depending on the topping used the crust can be delicate or crunchy. The traditional topping is grated Parmesan or Gruyère cheese, or bread crumbs. Other flavourful grating cheeses, such as French Cantal or Pyrénées, add a new touch. Chopped nuts give a crunchier topping.

Even the humblest of vegetables becomes enticing when transformed into a gratin. Green leafy vegetables and members of the onion, cabbage, and marrow families all make delicious gratins; so do artichoke hearts, asparagus, aubergines, and mushrooms. Although gratins are usually made with one vegetable, they can also be composed of multicoloured layers as in Swiss Chard and Pepper Gratin with Tomatoes.

In traditional recipes Mornay sauce, a thick cheese sauce enriched with egg yolks, was used most often for gratins. It is still quite popular, but today many cooks prefer lighter cheese sauces and cream sauces or, for a Mediterranean touch, fresh tomato sauce. Instead of a sauce, olive oil, melted butter or cream can be sprinkled on the vegetables so they remain moist, as in Quick Broccoli Gratin with Gruyère and Nuts.

After the vegetables are cooked they are drained thoroughly in a strainer or colander. If vegetables are not well drained, liquid adhering to them dilutes the sauce or moistening ingredient.

Gratins have given their name to a special baking dish, called a *gratin dish* or sometimes an *au gratin dish*. It is round or oval and is usually made of enamel-coated cast iron or earthenware. The dish is shallow so that the vegetable mixture can be spread in a relatively thin layer, which permits it to heat quickly and to have plenty of crust. Because gratin dishes are designed for both baking and serving, they are handsome and colourful. Other heavy, shallow baking dishes can be substituted.

LEEK AND DUXELLES GRATIN
Gratin de poireaux et duxelles

I learned to prepare this dish when I was training in the kitchen of a Parisian restaurant called La Ciboulette, or Chives. The chef would put his 'signature' on each savoury dish, including vegetable gratins like this, by sprinkling chives over it.   MAKES 4 TO 6 SERVINGS

CREAM SAUCE

25 g/1 oz butter
2 tablespoons plain flour
350 ml/12 fl oz milk
Salt and white pepper

Freshly grated nutmeg
3–4 tablespoons double cream
Pinch of cayenne pepper

700 g/1½ lb leeks
25 g/1 oz unsalted butter

2 tablespoons finely chopped
   shallots

350 g/12 oz mushrooms, finely   50 g/2 oz Gruyère cheese, coarsely
   chopped   grated

CREAM SAUCE

In a medium-size heavy saucepan, melt butter over low heat, add flour, and cook, whisking constantly, for about 2 minutes or until foaming but not browned. Remove from heat. Gradually whisk in milk. Bring to boil over medium-high heat, whisking. Add small pinches of salt, white pepper, and nutmeg. Reduce heat to low and cook, whisking often, for 5 minutes. Whisk in cream and bring to boil. Cook over low heat, whisking often, until sauce thickens and coats a spoon heavily; about 7 minutes. Remove from heat and add cayenne pepper. Taste and adjust seasoning. If not using immediately, dab surface of sauce with a small piece of butter to prevent a skin from forming.

To Prepare Vegetables and Assemble Gratin:

Use white and light green parts of leeks only. Starting about 2·5 cm/1 inch from root end of leeks, cut them in quarters lengthwise, leaving them still joined at root end and cutting towards top. Soak leeks in cold water to cover for 5 minutes. Rinse well to remove any remaining dirt.

Preheat oven to 220°C/425°F/gas 7. Put leeks into a large saucepan containing enough boiling salted water to cover them generously. Return to boil. Cook, uncovered, until leeks are just tender when pierced with a small sharp knife; about 7 minutes for small leeks or 10 minutes for large. Drain leeks gently, rinse with cold running water until cool, and drain thoroughly.

In a large frying pan, melt butter over low heat. Add shallots and cook, stirring, for about 1½ minutes, or until tender. Add mushrooms, a little salt, and pepper to taste, raise heat to medium-high, and cook, stirring often, for about 8 minutes, or until most of liquid that mushrooms render has evaporated and mixture is very dry. Butter a medium-size heavy gratin dish or other shallow baking dish. Spread mushroom mixture in even layer in dish.

If leeks are small or medium-size, cut them in half lengthwise; if they are large, cut them in quarters by continuing cuts made previously to clean them. Cut in 8-cm/3-inch lengths, pat them dry, and arrange them in dish in one layer on top of mushrooms.

Spoon sauce carefully over leeks to coat completely. Sprinkle evenly with cheese. (Gratin can be prepared ahead and kept for 1 day in refrigerator; bring to room temperature before continuing.)

Bake until sauce is beginning to bubble; about 7 minutes if sauce was still hot, or about 10 minutes if ingredients were at room temperature. Heat grill and grill just until cheese is lightly browned (about 1 minute), turning dish if necessary so cheese browns evenly. Serve hot, from baking dish.

CHICORY GRATIN WITH CREAM SAUCE AND WALNUTS
Gratin d'endives aux noix

A versatile vegetable, chicory is delicious raw in salads, braised with butter, or poached and baked in cream sauce, as in this gratin.

MAKES 4 SERVINGS

450 g/1 lb chicory
300 ml/½ pint hot Cream Sauce
    (page 134)
2 tablespoons freshly grated
    Parmesan or Gruyère cheese

25 g/1 oz coarsely chopped walnuts
    (optional)

Preheat oven to 220°C/425°F/gas 7. Remove any damaged leaves from chicory and trim bases very slightly, removing any brown parts.

Put chicory into a large saucepan containing enough boiling salted water to cover it generously. Return to boil. Cook, uncovered, for about 8 minutes, or until just tender when pierced with a small sharp knife. Rinse with cold running water until cool and drain thoroughly. Press gently to remove excess water and cut in half lengthwise.

Butter a medium-size heavy gratin dish or other shallow baking dish. In prepared dish, arrange chicory halves, cut side down, in one layer. Spoon sauce carefully over them to coat completely. Sprinkle evenly with cheese and walnuts. (Gratin can be kept, covered, for 1 day in refrigerator; bring to room temperature before continuing.)

Bake until sauce begins to bubble; about 7 minutes if sauce was still hot, or about 10 minutes if ingredients were at room temperature. If top is not brown, transfer dish to grill and cook just until cheese is lightly browned (about 1 minute), checking often and turning dish if necessary so cheese browns evenly. Serve hot, from baking dish.

SPINACH GRATIN WITH CREAM SAUCE

Omit walnuts. Substitute 700 g/1½ lb fresh spinach (leaves with stems) or one 275-g/10-oz packet frozen spinach for chicory. If using fresh spinach, pull off and discard stems. Put leaves in a large saucepan containing enough boiling salted water to cover them generously. Return to boil. Cook, uncovered, for about 2 minutes, or until just tender and wilted. Drain, rinse with cold running water until cool and drain. Squeeze spinach by handfuls to remove as much water as possible and chop coarsely. If using frozen spinach, let it thaw, squeeze as above, and chop coarsely.

PUMPKIN GRATIN WITH FRESH TOMATO SAUCE
Gratin de courge à la sauce tomate

Fresh tomato sauce adds a lively Mediterranean flavour and bright colour to gratins and turns the humble pumpkin into a delightful dish. If you like, substitute fragrant oregano or marjoram for the thyme in the sauce.

MAKES 4 SERVINGS

FRESH TOMATO SAUCE

2 tablespoons olive oil

2 medium-size garlic cloves, finely chopped

1 kg/2 lb ripe tomatoes, peeled, seeded, and chopped

Salt and freshly ground pepper

700 g/1½ lb pumpkin

¾ teaspoon fresh thyme, or ¼ teaspoon dried thyme

1 bay leaf

1 tablespoon tomato paste

Pinch of sugar (optional)

2 tablespoons freshly grated Parmesan cheese

FRESH TOMATO SAUCE

Heat olive oil in a heavy large saucepan over low heat. Add garlic and cook, stirring, for about 30 seconds, without letting it brown. Add tomatoes, salt, pepper, thyme, and bay leaf and stir well to combine with garlic mixture. Bring to a boil over high heat. Reduce heat to low and cook, uncovered, stirring occasionally, for about 1 hour, or until tomatoes are very soft and sauce is thick.

Discard bay leaf. Purée sauce in a food processor until smooth. Return sauce to saucepan and whisk in tomato paste. Bring to a boil. Reduce heat to low and cook, stirring occasionally, until sauce is very thick and reduced to 300 ml/½ pint; about 10 minutes. Taste and add sugar if sauce is too tart. Taste and adjust seasoning.

Preheat oven to 220°C/425°F/gas 7. Remove seeds and strings from pumpkin and cut into medium-sized chunks. Put them into a large saucepan containing enough boiling salted water to cover generously. Return to boil. Cook, uncovered, for about 10 minutes, or until just tender when pierced with a small sharp knife. Put in colander and rinse with cold running water until cool. Cut off skin, return to colander, and drain thoroughly.

Butter a medium-size heavy gratin dish or other shallow baking dish. Arrange pumpkin pieces in one layer in prepared dish. Spoon sauce carefully over pieces to coat them completely. (Gratin can be kept, covered, for 1 day in refrigerator; bring to room temperature before continuing.)

Sprinkle with cheese. Bake until sauce begins to bubble; about 7 minutes if sauce was still hot, or about 10 minutes if ingredients were at room temperature. If top is not brown, transfer dish to grill and cook for about 1 minute, or just until cheese is lightly browned, checking often and turning dish if necessary so cheese browns evenly. Serve hot, from baking dish.

CELERY GRATIN WITH TOMATO SAUCE

Substitute 350 g/12 oz celery for pumpkin. Peel to remove strings. Cut crosswise in 5-cm/2-inch pieces. Cook in water for only 4 minutes.

CAULIFLOWER GRATIN WITH LIGHT CHEESE SAUCE
Gratin de chou-fleur au fromage

A classic combination, cauliflower with cheese sauce is a good accompaniment for roast beef or veal. Or it can be made the focus of a meal by being paired with a rice dish, such as Rice with Peas and Basil (see page 261), and a fresh vegetable salad.   MAKES 4 SERVINGS

LIGHT CHEESE SAUCE

25 g/1 oz butter
2 tablespoons plain flour
350 ml/12 fl oz milk
Salt and white pepper
Freshly grated nutmeg

3–4 tablespoons double cream
Pinch of cayenne pepper
25 g/1 oz freshly grated Parmesan cheese

1 cauliflower (about 700 g/1½ lb)

2 tablespoons freshly grated Parmesan cheese

LIGHT CHEESE SAUCE

In medium-size heavy saucepan, melt butter over low heat, add flour, and cook, whisking constantly, for about 2 minutes, or until foaming but not browned. Remove from heat. Gradually whisk in milk. Bring to boil over medium-high heat, whisking. Add a small pinch of salt, white pepper, and nutmeg. Reduce heat to low and cook, whisking often, for 5 minutes. Whisk in cream and bring to boil. Cook over low heat, whisking often, until sauce thickens and coats a spoon heavily; about 7 minutes. Remove from heat and add cayenne pepper. Taste and adjust seasoning. Dab surface of sauce with butter if not using immediately.

Before using, bring sauce to boil. Remove from heat. Whisk in Parmesan.

Preheat oven to 220°C/425°F/gas 7. Divide cauliflower into medium-size florets, discarding stalk and green leaves. Put florets into a large saucepan containing enough boiling salted water to cover generously. Return to boil. Cook, uncovered, for about 7 minutes, or until florets are just tender when pierced with a small sharp knife. Drain, rinse with cold running water until cool, and drain thoroughly.

Butter a heavy 20-cm/8-inch gratin dish or other shallow baking dish. Arrange florets in one layer in prepared dish. Spoon sauce carefully over them to coat completely. Sprinkle evenly with 2 tablespoons cheese. (Gratin can be kept, covered, for 1 day in refrigerator; bring to room temperature before continuing.)

Bake until sauce begins to bubble; about 7 minutes if sauce was still hot, or about 10 minutes if ingredients were at room temperature. If top is not brown, transfer dish to grill and cook just until cheese is lightly browned (about 1 minute), checking often and turning dish if necessary so cheese browns evenly. Serve hot, from baking dish.

BROCCOLI GRATIN WITH LIGHT CHEESE SAUCE
Substitute 700 g/1½ lb broccoli for cauliflower. Boil for only about 4 minutes.

CABBAGE GRATIN WITH LIGHT CHEESE SAUCE
Substitute 600 g/1¼ lb cabbage (1 very small or ½ large head) for cauliflower. Cut out and discard core. Shred cabbage leaves coarsely and boil for only about 5 minutes. After draining, squeeze gently to remove excess water.

NOTE: Both cauliflower and broccoli are fragile vegetables. To avoid crushing their florets, they should be drained as gently as possible after cooking and rinsed under a thin stream of water so they will not fall apart.

LAYERED CABBAGE AND MUSHROOM GRATIN
Gratin de choux et champignons

This gratin is made with cream rather than with sauce. Serve it with grilled chicken breasts or other light meats.   MAKES 4 TO 6 SERVINGS

½ large-size head of green
  cabbage (about 600 g/1¼ lb),
  cored, rinsed, finely shredded
300 ml/½ pint double cream
Salt and freshly ground pepper
¼ teaspoon freshly grated nutmeg,
  or to taste

25 g/1 oz unsalted butter
225 g/8 oz mushrooms, halved and
  thinly sliced
2 tablespoons freshly grated
  Parmesan cheese

In a large pan of boiling salted water, cook cabbage for 3 minutes. Drain thoroughly and return cabbage to pan. Stir in 6 tablespoons cream and salt and pepper to taste. Cover and simmer over low heat for 5 minutes. Uncover and simmer over medium heat for 10 minutes. Reduce heat to low and simmer, stirring often, for 10 minutes, or until cream is completely absorbed and mixture appears dry. Add nutmeg and adjust seasoning. Preheat oven to 220°C/ 425°F/gas 7.

In a medium-size frying pan, melt butter over medium-high heat, add mushrooms with salt and pepper to taste, and sauté, stirring, for about 4 minutes, or until browned and tender. Add remaining cream and simmer over medium-high heat, stirring, for 3 minutes, or until cream is completely absorbed and mushrooms appear quite dry.

Taste and adjust seasoning. (Mixtures can be kept, covered, for 1 day in refrigerator; reheat each over low heat before continuing.)

Butter a heavy 20-cm/8-inch gratin dish or other shallow baking dish. Spread mushroom mixture in an even layer in prepared dish. Spoon cabbage mixture carefully on top to avoid moving mushrooms, and spread until smooth. Sprinkle with grated cheese.

Bake for about 5 minutes, or until heated through. Grill for 1 or 2 minutes, or until cheese is golden.

QUICK BROCCOLI GRATIN WITH GRUYÈRE AND NUTS
Gratin de brocolis au gruyère et aux noix

This gratin has a crunchy topping and is ready in minutes. Serve it with roast or grilled chicken, or to accompany Aubergines Stuffed with Duxelles.   MAKES 4 SERVINGS

700 g/1½ lb broccoli
50 g/2 oz unsalted butter, melted
Salt and freshly ground pepper
50 g/2 oz Gruyère cheese, coarsely
    grated

25 g/1 oz coarsely chopped walnuts
    or toasted hazelnuts
2 tablespoons unseasoned bread
    crumbs

Preheat oven to 220°C/425°F/gas 7. Divide broccoli into medium florets, discarding stalks and leaves. Put florets into large saucepan containing enough boiling salted water to cover them generously. Return to boil. Cook, uncovered, for about 4 minutes, or until just tender. Gently rinse with cold running water until cool and drain thoroughly.

Butter a shallow 20-cm/8-inch gratin dish or other heavy baking dish. In prepared dish, arrange broccoli in one layer, stems pointing inward. Sprinkle with 2 tablespoons melted butter and with a pinch of salt and pepper. Mix cheese, nuts, and bread crumbs and sprinkle evenly on top. Sprinkle with remaining melted butter.

Bake for about 8 minutes, or until cheese melts. If topping is not brown, grill about 1 minute, or just until lightly browned, checking often and turning dish if necessary so topping browns evenly. Serve hot, from baking dish.

BRUSSELS SPROUTS BAKED IN MORNAY SAUCE
Choux de bruxelles Mornay

If you think you don't like Brussels sprouts, try them this way. They taste best when served with creamy sauces, which tame their assertive flavour. Egg yolks in the sauce give the gratin a golden colour.   MAKES 4 SERVINGS

*350 g/12 oz Brussels
  sprouts*

MORNAY SAUCE

20 g/¾ oz butter   *Freshly grated nutmeg*
1½ tablespoons plain flour   *25 g/1 oz freshly grated Parmesan*
225 ml/8 fl oz milk   *cheese*
Salt and white pepper   *2 egg yolks*

*2 tablespoons freshly grated
  Parmesan cheese for topping*

Preheat oven to 220°C/425°F/gas 7. Trim sprouts, removing tough bases and any yellow leaves. Put sprouts into a large saucepan containing enough boiling salted water to cover them generously. Return to boil. Cook, uncovered, for about 10 minutes, or until they are just tender when pierced with a small sharp knife. Drain, rinse with cold running water until cool and drain thoroughly.

MORNAY SAUCE
In a small heavy saucepan, melt butter over low heat, add flour, and cook, whisking constantly, for about 2 minutes, or until foaming but

not browned. Remove from heat. Gradually whisk in milk. Bring to boil over medium-high heat, whisking. Add a small pinch of salt, white pepper, and nutmeg. Reduce heat to low and cook, whisking often, for 5 minutes.

Remove from heat and whisk in cheese. Quickly whisk in egg yolks. Taste and adjust seasoning.

Butter a heavy 20-cm/8-inch gratin dish or other shallow baking dish. In prepared dish, arrange Brussels sprouts in one layer. Spoon sauce carefully over them to coat completely. Sprinkle evenly with 2 tablespoons cheese. (Gratin can be kept, covered, for 1 day in refrigerator; bring to room temperature before continuing.)

Bake until sauce begins to bubble; about 7 minutes if sauce was still hot, or about 10 minutes if ingredients were at room temperature. If top is not brown, transfer dish to grill and cook with door partly open just until cheese is lightly browned (about 1 minute), checking often and turning dish if necessary so cheese browns evenly. Serve hot, from baking dish.

COURGETTES BAKED IN MORNAY SAUCE

Substitute about 350 g/12 oz small courgettes for Brussels sprouts. Cut them in half lengthwise. Cut each half crosswise in 6-cm/2½-inch pieces. Boil for 4 minutes. Drain thoroughly.

SWISS CHARD AND PEPPER GRATIN
WITH TOMATOES
Gratin de blettes et poivrons aux tomates

A favourite in southern France, Swiss chard is often cooked with olive oil and tomatoes, as in this gratin. Chard can be cooked like spinach and is a quicker substitute because it has much larger leaves and so takes less time to clean. MAKES 6 SERVINGS

700 g/1½ lb Swiss chard, rinsed
    thoroughly
6 tablespoons olive oil
100 g/4 oz finely chopped onion
800 g/1¾ lb ripe tomatoes, peeled,
    seeded, and finely chopped
4 anchovy fillets, rinsed and
    chopped (optional)
3 small garlic cloves, finely
    chopped
Salt and freshly ground pepper

2 small red peppers (about 225 g/
    8 oz)
1 medium-size green pepper (about
    150 g/5 oz)
3 tablespoons unseasoned bread
    crumbs
3 tablespoons coarsely chopped
    blanched almonds, or 2
    tablespoons freshly grated
    Parmesan cheese

Preheat oven to 200°C/400°F/gas 6. Cut chard leaves from stems, discarding stems. Pile chard leaves, cut them in half lengthwise and then crosswise in strips 1 cm/½ inch wide. In medium-size saucepan of boiling salted water, cook, uncovered, for about 3 minutes, or until just tender. Drain thoroughly. Squeeze by handfuls to remove excess moisture.

In a large frying pan, heat 2 tablespoons olive oil over medium heat, stir in onion, and cook for about 7 minutes, or until soft but not brown. Stir in tomatoes and anchovies. Raise heat to high and cook, stirring constantly for about 12 minutes, or until mixture becomes dry. Stir in garlic, add ground pepper, and adjust seasoning.

Cut peppers in half lengthwise, core, and remove ribs. Cut them crosswise and cut each piece into strips 6 mm/¼ inch wide. In large frying pan, heat 2 tablespoons of olive oil over medium-low heat, add peppers, salt and pepper to taste, and cook, tossing often; about 7 minutes, or until tender.

Lightly coat a heavy 20-cm/8-inch gratin dish or other shallow baking dish with olive oil. Spread chard in dish. Spoon tomato mixture on top and smooth. Spoon pepper mixture evenly over tomatoes. (Gratin can be kept, covered, for 1 day in refrigerator; bring to room temperature before continuing.)

Scatter bread crumbs, then almonds or cheese, evenly over vegetables. Sprinkle with remaining 2 tablespoons olive oil. Bake for about 15 minutes, or until vegetables are heated through and beginning to bubble at bottom. If topping is not brown, grill for about 1 minute, or just until lightly browned, checking often and turning dish if necessary so topping browns evenly. Serve hot, from baking dish.

TURNIP AND ONION GRATIN WITH PARMESAN
Gratin de navets et oignons au parmesan

In this unusual dish the sweetness of turnips and onions is balanced by the sharpness of the Parmesan cheese. Serve it with roast chicken or grilled steak.

MAKES 4 SERVINGS

700 g/1½ lb small turnips
4 tablespoons olive oil
2 medium-size onions, thinly sliced
Salt and freshly ground pepper
1½ teaspoons fresh thyme, or ½
  teaspoon dried thyme

2 large garlic cloves, finely chopped
8 tablespoons freshly grated
  Parmesan cheese

Peel turnips thickly, cut them in half, then in 6-mm/¼-inch-thick slices. Put in large saucepan, cover with water, add salt, and bring to boil. Reduce heat to low, cover, and simmer for about 7 minutes, or until just tender.

Preheat oven to 220°C/425°F/gas 7. In a large frying pan, heat 2 tablespoons oil over low heat, and add onions, salt, pepper, and thyme. Cover and cook, stirring often, for about 25 minutes, or until tender. Stir in garlic, then gently stir in turnip slices. Cook over low heat for 2 minutes. Adjust seasoning, taking into account that Parmesan cheese will add a salty flavour.

Coat a heavy 20-cm/8-inch gratin dish or shallow baking dish with olive oil. Transfer half of vegetable mixture to dish. Sprinkle with 4 tablespoons cheese, then with 1 tablespoon of oil. Spoon remaining vegetable mixture on top. Sprinkle with remaining cheese, then with remaining oil.

Bake for about 15 minutes, or until hot. If cheese is not brown, grill for about 1 minute, or just until lightly browned, checking often and turning dish if necessary so cheese browns evenly. Serve hot, from baking dish.

Vegetable Purées

Vegetable purées add style and colour to any plate and are loved not only at simple restaurants but at the most sumptuous of tables. At Taillevent, the renowned Parisian restaurant, I enjoyed a stunning dish of Carré d'Agneau Rôti aux Trois Purées (roast rack of lamb with three purées). The silky-smooth texture of purées enables us to perceive the taste of the vegetable even more intensely. Depending on how they're seasoned and served, purées can take on a character all their own or dramatically alter an otherwise straightforward dish.

Simply cooked foods, from poached fish fillets to hard-boiled eggs to grilled meats, look especially festive and appetizing served on a bed of colourful vegetable purée. Lightly steamed scallops or prawns set on bright green spinach purée or fresh tomato purée make an elegant main course. The French like to serve roasted or grilled meats and game dishes such as venison with a selection of different-coloured purées, so that each plate looks like an artist's palette.

The versatility of purées is apparent in the many roles they can play in a meal. Although their obvious function is as side dishes, they can also be eaten as appetizers if served in pastry, as in Cream Puffs with Carrot Purée, on toast, as a stuffing for vegetables, or even as part of a sauce for pasta. They can also be turned into mousses, timbales, and soufflés.

Purées can be made quickly and easily. They can be reheated and therefore make meal planning simple. Because they can be made from cooked vegetables left from the day before they are also economical.

To be made into purées green vegetables such as spinach, asparagus and broccoli are cooked quickly, uncovered, in a large amount of boiling salted water so they conserve as much as possible of their colour and fresh taste. Root vegetables are not in danger of losing their colour and sometimes have over-strong flavours, so are started off in cold water. Some vegetables, such as aubergine or sweet peppers, are baked or grilled instead. Steamed vegetables can also be made into purées.

When the vegetable can be pierced very easily with the tip of a sharp knife it is soft enough to be puréed. It should be more tender than for serving whole or in pieces and not at all crunchy. It should not, however, be cooked beyond this point or its flavour will be watery and, in the case of a green vegetable, its colour will be less vivid.

In France purées used to be made by pushing cooked vegetables through a sturdy sieve, but today most home cooks use a food processor, blender, or hand-operated food mill.

The easiest way to purée vegetables is in the food processor. If a blender is used, the vegetable should be processed in small batches with a few tablespoons of the cooking liquid or the cream in the recipe and should be pushed down the sides of the blender often to be sure it becomes smoothly puréed.

Many vegetable purées are heated until the excess water in the vegetable evaporates so they thicken. This method intensifies the flavour of the vegetable. If a purée will be tossed with pasta, it should be thinned with a generous amount of milk, cream, or stock so that it becomes sauce-like and coats the pasta, as in Pasta with Creamy Broccoli Purée. A very thick purée is best for stuffing vegetables or filling pastry so the filling will not run out. For serving as a side dish a purée of medium thickness is best.

Butter and cream give purées a wonderful taste, but olive oil adds a distinct flavour that is a pleasant change. Spices and herbs can also be added, but with a light hand so that the character of the vegetable predominates.

COURGETTE PURÉE WITH BASIL
Purée de courgettes au basilic

Resembling pesto, this zesty purée is enriched with a little olive oil and has a deep green colour. It can be served topped with hard-boiled or fried eggs or with sautéed croutons. Courgette purée also makes a lovely accompaniment to grilled fish or chicken.   MAKES 4 SERVINGS

700 g/1½ lb small courgettes
3 tablespoons extra virgin olive oil
2 medium-size garlic cloves, finely
   chopped

2 tablespoons fresh basil leaves
Salt and freshly ground pepper
Pinch of cayenne pepper

In a large saucepan of boiling salted water to generously cover, cook whole courgettes for about 10 minutes, or until tender enough to be easily puréed. Cut in 2·5-cm/1-inch pieces, crush very lightly with spoon, and drain very thoroughly in colander for about 15 minutes.

In a medium-size frying pan, heat 2 tablespoons olive oil over low heat, add garlic, and sauté for 30 seconds. Add courgettes and cook over medium heat, stirring, for about 5 minutes.

Purée mixture in food processor together with basil. With motor running, add remaining olive oil. (Purée can be kept, covered, for 1 day in refrigerator.)

Reheat purée gently in saucepan. If mixture is too thin, cook over medium heat, stirring, until thickened. Add salt, pepper, and cayenne pepper to taste. Serve hot.

CAULIFLOWER AND POTATO PURÉE
Purée de chou-fleur

Potatoes harmonize well with most vegetables and are often combined with one or even several to make delicately flavoured purées, as in this recipe. Besides cauliflower other favourite partners are turnips, celeriac, onions and fennel. Serve this purée with white meats, especially veal, turkey or chicken.   MAKES 4 SERVINGS

225 g/8 oz white boiling potatoes
1 medium-size cauliflower (about
*   700 g/1½ lb), divided into*
*   medium-size florets*
6 to 9 tablespoons double cream or
*   milk*

About 50 g/2 oz unsalted butter
Salt and white pepper
Freshly grated nutmeg
1 tablespoon snipped chives
*   (optional)*

Peel potatoes and cut each in two or three pieces. Put in a non-aluminium saucepan and add water to just cover and a pinch of salt. Cover, bring to boil, and simmer over medium heat for 20 to 25 minutes, or until potatoes are very tender.

Meanwhile, in a large pan of boiling salted water, boil cauliflower, uncovered, over high heat for about 10 minutes, or until very tender.

Drain both vegetables thoroughly. Purée potatoes and cauliflower in a food mill; if using a food processor, add a few tablespoons cream or milk and purée as briefly as possible.

Return purée to saucepan used to cook potatoes. Add 40 g/1½ oz butter and 2 tablespoons cream or milk to purée and season to taste with salt, pepper, and nutmeg. Heat over low heat, stirring vigorously with a wooden spoon, until purée is light and smooth. (Purée can be kept, covered, for 1 day in refrigerator. Reheat over low heat before continuing.)

Gradually beat in enough of remaining cream or milk so purée is soft but not soupy. If using milk, beat in remaining butter. Taste and adjust seasoning. Sprinkle with chives, if desired. Serve hot.

SPINACH PURÉE ON CROÛTES
Croûtes à la purée d'épinards

The flavour of fresh spinach is vital for the taste of this appetizer or accompaniment. Not too much time need be spent washing large quantities of spinach leaves, though, because the spinach purée is spread on toasted *croûtes* of bread so that a little goes a long way.

MAKES 4 SERVINGS

600 g/1¼ lb fresh spinach (leaves with stems)
100 g/4 oz butter
2 tablespoons double cream
Salt and freshly ground pepper
Freshly grated nutmeg

16 slices very thin French bread (baguette)
2 tablespoons coarsely grated Gruyère cheese

Remove spinach stems and wash leaves thoroughly. In large saucepan of boiling salted water, cook spinach, uncovered, over high heat, pushing leaves down into water often, until very tender; about 2 minutes. Rinse with cold water and squeeze by handfuls until dry. Purée in food processor or chop with large knife until very fine.

In a medium-size saucepan, heat 15 g/½ oz butter over low heat until very hot, add spinach, and stir until heated through. Stir in cream and heat until it is absorbed by spinach. Stir in 25 g/1 oz butter and continue cooking just until absorbed. Season to taste with salt, pepper, and nutmeg. (Spinach purée can be kept, covered, for 1 day in refrigerator; reheat gently before continuing.)

Preheat oven to 220°C/425°F/gas 7. Put bread slices on a baking sheet. Soften remaining butter and spread on both sides of slices. Bake in preheated oven for 5 minutes. Turn slices over and bake for 3 more minutes.

Divide spinach purée among bread slices, spreading it evenly over them. Sprinkle with cheese. Return to oven and bake for 7 minutes, or until cheese melts and mixture is very hot. Serve immediately.

PARSLEY PURÉE
Purée de persil

Parsley is used here as a vegetable. It is really amazing how flavourful it is. Blanching keeps its bright green colour. Serve this purée as a part of a selection of purées, or to accompany fish or seafood.

MAKES 4 TO 6 SERVINGS

350 g/12 oz parsley   *50 g/2 oz butter*
200 ml/7 fl oz double cream   *Salt and freshly ground pepper*

Remove small parsley sprigs, discarding large stems. In a large saucepan of boiling salted water, cook sprigs, uncovered, over high heat for 1 minute. Drain, rinse under cold running water until cold, and drain thoroughly. Squeeze by handfuls until dry.

Purée parsley in a food processor or blender until very finely chopped. Add 6 tablespoons cream and purée until smooth.

In a small saucepan, melt butter over low heat, add parsley mixture and heat until hot. Stir in remaining cream and salt and pepper to taste, and heat gently, stirring, for about 2 minutes, or until cream is absorbed. Taste and adjust seasoning. (Purée can be kept for up to 2 hours at room temperature and reheated.) Serve a spoonful of purée for each serving.

CELERIAC PURÉE
Purée de céleri-rave

Celeriac is excellent not only raw in salad, but cooked and made into a creamy purée. Serve it with warm hard-boiled or poached eggs, or with roast or grilled chicken, duck or lamb.   MAKES 6 SERVINGS

½ *lemon*
1 *kg/2 lb celeriac*
2 *medium-size boiling potatoes*

200 *ml/7 fl oz milk*
40 *g/1½ oz butter*
Salt and freshly ground pepper

Squeeze lemon juice into a bowl of water. Peel celeriac, removing all brown parts. Cut in half, then in slices about 1 cm/½ inch thick. Put each slice into lemon water as it is cut.

Remove celeriac slices from lemon water and put in a large saucepan. Add enough water to cover generously, taking into account that potatoes will also be added to saucepan. Add a pinch of salt and bring to a boil. Cook over medium heat for about 10 minutes.

Meanwhile, peel potatoes and cut each in two or three pieces. Add to saucepan containing celeriac and cook for about 20 minutes, or until potatoes and celeriac are very tender. Drain thoroughly.

Purée potatoes and celeriac in a food mill; if using a food processor, add a few tablespoons of milk and purée as briefly as possible.

Return purée to saucepan. Add butter, salt, pepper, and 3 tablespoons milk and stir over medium heat for 2 or 3 minutes. Gradually add enough of remaining milk so that purée is soft but not runny. Taste and adjust seasoning. (Purée can be kept warm for about 30 minutes by setting saucepan in another saucepan of warm water over low heat; pour a little milk over purée to prevent a skin from forming and stir it in just before serving.) Serve hot.

CREAMY CARROT PURÉE
Purée de carottes

Beautiful colour and concentrated carrot flavour make this purée one of the most popular. It adds liveliness to any plate, and makes a delicious accompaniment to sautéed or roasted poultry or poached or baked fish, alone or in combination with other purées.

MAKES 6 SERVINGS

1 kg/2 lb carrots	*Salt and freshly ground pepper*
15 g/½ oz butter	*Pinch of sugar (optional)*
3–4 tablespoons double cream, or	
2 to 3 tablespoons milk, at room	
temperature	

Peel carrots and cut in 1-cm/½-inch slices. In medium-size saucepan, cover carrots with water, add pinch of salt, and bring to boil. Cover, reduce heat to medium, and cook for about 35 minutes, or until very tender when pierced with a sharp knife. Drain thoroughly in large strainer. Purée in a food processor until very smooth.

In a medium-size saucepan, melt butter over low heat, add purée, and heat thoroughly. Gradually stir in cream and cook until it is absorbed. Season to taste with salt, pepper, and sugar. (Purée can be kept, covered, for 2 days in refrigerator.) Serve hot.

GREEN PEA PURÉE WITH MINT BUTTER
Purée de petits pois au beurre de menthe

This purée takes a little time to prepare with fresh peas but can be made very quickly if frozen peas are used. It is delicious with grilled lamb or chicken.   MAKES 4 SERVINGS

1½ tablespoons chopped fresh mint	*50 g/2 oz butter, softened*
leaves	*Salt and freshly ground pepper*
1·5 kg/3 lb fresh peas in pods,	*4 tablespoons double cream*
shelled, or 600 g/1¼ lb frozen	*Pinch of sugar*
peas	

To make mint butter, thoroughly mix mint leaves with butter and season to taste with salt and pepper. (Mint butter can be kept for 1 day in refrigerator.)

In a saucepan of boiling salted water, cook fresh peas for 7 minutes, frozen peas for 3 minutes, or until they are just tender. Rinse under cold running water and drain thoroughly.

Purée peas in a food processor in two batches, adding 2 tablespoons cream to each batch. (Purée can be kept, covered, for up to 1 day in refrigerator.)

In a medium-size saucepan, heat purée, stirring, until hot. Stir in mint butter and remove from heat as soon as butter is absorbed. Add sugar, taste and adjust seasoning.

Stuffed Vegetables

Stuffed vegetables can be served as first courses, side dishes, or, according to a custom in Provence, a selection of them can become the main course. Many stuffed vegetables are good hot or cold.

Some vegetables seem to have been created to be stuffed. For many people, stuffing is the preferred way to prepare aubergines, courgettes and peppers. Unlike cooks in the eastern end of the Mediterranean area, who like to stuff their vegetables whole, French chefs cut aubergines and courgettes in half lengthwise and scoop out the pulp, leaving boat-shaped shells.

The French acknowledge the Middle Eastern and Italian origins of some of their favourite stuffed vegetable recipes by qualifying them, for example, as *à l'orientale*, as in Aubergine with Tomatoes, Saffron, and Garlic, *à l'égyptienne*, or *à la napolitaine*.

Popular stuffings for vegetables are those based on rice or vegetables mixed with bread crumbs, often with the addition of the pulp of the vegetable that is being stuffed. A classic duxelles mixture of chopped mushrooms cooked in butter remains a modern favourite. These types of mixtures are being substituted more and more for meat stuffings. Provençal cooks like to flavour their stuffings with their three favourite ingredients, labelled by some French food writers the 'holy Mediterranean trio': onions, garlic and tomatoes. Saffron, fragrant herbs, and grated Parmesan or Gruyère cheese are also well-liked seasonings for vegetable fillings.

MUSHROOMS STUFFED WITH FRESH TOMATO PURÉE
Champignons à la tomate concassée

Spinach purée (see recipe for Spinach Purée on Croûtes, page 152) is another fabulous filling for mushrooms. The two versions of stuffed mushrooms can be presented alternating on a platter around a roast chicken as a colourful garnish.   MAKES 4 TO 6 SERVINGS

FRESH TOMATO PURÉE

2 tablespoons olive oil
1 small onion or 2 shallots, finely
    chopped
700 g/1½ lb ripe tomatoes, peeled,
    seeded, and chopped
Salt and freshly ground pepper
1 sprig of fresh thyme, or ¼
    teaspoon dried thyme

1 bay leaf
5 parsley stalks
1 tablespoon chopped fresh basil,
    or 1 teaspoon dried basil
    (optional)

450 g/1 lb large mushrooms   25 g/1 oz butter

FRESH TOMATO PURÉE
In a sauté pan, heat olive oil over low heat. Add onion or shallots and cook, stirring often, until softened. Add tomatoes and salt and pepper to taste. Tie thyme, bay leaf, and parsley together with string or in a piece of cheesecloth to make a bouquet garni and add it to tomatoes. Cook over medium heat, stirring often, for about 20 minutes, or until mixture is very thick. Discard bouquet garni. (Purée can be kept, covered, for 2 days in refrigerator; reheat before continuing.) Add basil and adjust seasoning.

Meanwhile, preheat oven to 190°C/375°F/gas 5. Remove mushroom stems and clean caps. Put caps, rounded side down, in a lightly oiled shallow baking dish. Sprinkle them lightly with salt and pepper. Fill with tomato purée and dot with butter.

Bake stuffed mushrooms for 10 to 15 minutes, or until mushrooms are tender and filling is hot. Serve hot.

NOTE: An equal weight of canned tomatoes (a 400 g/14 oz and a 225 g/8 oz can) can be substituted for fresh ones. Drain them, remove as many seeds as possible, and chop.

ARTICHOKES WITH ONION COMPOTE
Artichauts à la compote d'oignons

'Compotes' are vegetables that are cooked for a long time over very low heat so they become delicate and meltingly tender. Most often they are made from vegetables in the onion family. Here the sweetness of the white onions is balanced by the cream and flavoured with a touch of wine vinegar. The onion compote can be served as a separate vegetable dish to accompany roast or sautéed chicken, veal or beef.

MAKES 6 SERVINGS

1 lemon   *6 artichokes*

ONION COMPOTE
50 g/2 oz butter   *2 tablespoons double cream*
700 g/1½ lb white onions, halved   *1 to 2 teaspoons white wine*
   and thinly sliced   *vinegar (optional)*
Salt and freshly ground pepper

Squeeze juice of ½ lemon into medium-size bowl of cold water. Break off stems and largest leaves of artichoke bottoms. Cut off lower circle of leaves, up to edge of artichoke heart. Rub exposed edges of artichoke heart with cut lemon. Cut off central cone of leaves just above artichoke heart. Cut off leaves under base and trim so it is round, removing all dark green areas. Rub again with lemon. Put each artichoke in bowl of lemon water as it is finished.

Squeeze any juice remaining in lemon into medium-size saucepan of boiling salted water, add artichoke hearts, cover, and simmer over low heat for about 15 minutes, or until tender when pierced with a knife. Cool to lukewarm in liquid. Using a teaspoon, scoop out choke from centre of each artichoke heart. Return artichokes to liquid until ready to use.

ONION COMPOTE
In a heavy saucepan, flameproof casserole, or stew pan, heat butter over low heat, and add onions, a pinch of salt, and pepper. Cover and cook, stirring often, for 45 minutes. Uncover and cook, stirring very often, for about 25 minutes longer, or until onions are tender enough to crush easily with a wooden spoon and are golden; be careful not to let them burn.

Preheat oven to 200°C/400°F/gas 6. Stir in cream, raise heat to high, and cook until bubbling. Reduce heat to very low and simmer, stirring often, for about 5 minutes, or until cream is completely absorbed. (Compote can be kept, covered, for 1 day in refrigerator; reheat in saucepan over low heat.)

Stir in vinegar, if desired, and heat until absorbed. Taste and adjust seasoning.

Butter a baking dish and set artichoke hearts in it. Spoon onion compote into each artichoke. Bake in preheated oven for 10 minutes to heat through.

ARTICHOKES FILLED WITH PEAS
Fonds d'artichauts farcis Clamart

This classic garnish for roast meat is named for Clamart, a suburb of Paris once famous for its delicious peas. Artichokes and peas are a well-loved combination in other dishes as well. Sometimes they are cooked together and served as a stew.   MAKES 4 SERVINGS

1 lemon	25 g/1 oz butter
4 artichokes	1 teaspoon sugar
275 g/10 oz freshly shelled or frozen peas	Salt

Prepare and cook artichokes as in Artichokes with Onion Compote (page 159).

In a large pan of boiling salted water, cook fresh peas for about 5 minutes, or until just tender. Cook frozen peas only about 1 or 2 minutes. Drain well. Melt the butter in a sauté pan, add peas, sugar, and salt to taste, and heat gently.

Reheat artichokes in their liquid. Drain thoroughly. To serve, carefully spoon peas into artichokes.

STUFFED AUBERGINES WITH PINE NUT PILAF AND TOMATO CURRY SAUCE
Aubergine farcie pilaf aux pignons, sauce tomate au curry

Aubergine is most delicious when it is thoroughly cooked and fork-tender. Unlike many other vegetables, it should not be under-cooked with the aim of leaving it *al dente*. MAKES 4 SERVINGS

TOMATO CURRY SAUCE

2 tablespoons olive oil	Salt and freshly ground pepper
2 garlic cloves, finely chopped	2 teaspoons tomato paste
1½ teaspoons curry powder	
700 g/1½ lb ripe tomatoes, peeled, seeded, and chopped	

RICE PILAF WITH PINE NUTS

2 tablespoons vegetable oil
½ medium-size onion, finely
   chopped
100 g/4 oz long-grain white rice
225 ml/8 fl oz hot water
Salt and freshly ground pepper

40 g/1½ oz pine nuts or slivered
   almonds
2 tablespoons chopped flat-leaf
   parsley (optional)

2 medium-size aubergines (450 g/
   1 lb each), unpeeled

2 tablespoons olive oil

TOMATO CURRY SAUCE

In a large saucepan, heat olive oil over low heat, add garlic, and cook, stirring occasionally, for about 30 seconds, or until soft but not browned. Add curry powder and cook, stirring, for 30 seconds. Add tomatoes and salt and pepper to taste, and stir well to combine with curry mixture. Bring to boil, reduce heat to low, and cook, uncovered, stirring occasionally, for about 30 minutes, or until tomatoes are very soft. Add tomato paste.

Purée sauce in food processor or blender until smooth. Taste and adjust seasoning. (Sauce can be prepared for up to 2 days ahead and kept, covered, in refrigerator.)

RICE PILAF WITH PINE NUTS

In a medium-size frying pan, heat 1 tablespoon vegetable oil over low heat, add onion, and cook, stirring, for about 10 minutes, or until soft but not brown. Add rice and sauté, stirring, for about 2 minutes, or until grains turn opaque. Add water and salt and pepper to taste. Bring to a boil, stir once, and cover. Reduce heat to low and cook, without stirring, for 18 minutes. Taste rice; if not yet tender, simmer for 2 more minutes. Remove from heat. Let stand, covered, for 10 minutes. (Pilaf can be prepared up to 1 day ahead and kept, covered, in refrigerator.)

In a small heavy frying pan, heat remaining vegetable oil over medium-low heat, add pine nuts or almonds and pinch of salt and sauté, tossing them often with slotted spoon, for about 2 minutes or until lightly browned. Set aside and reserve at room temperature. Add nuts and parsley to rice and gently stir with a fork.

To Finish:
Preheat oven to 230°C/450°F/gas 8. Remove green caps from aubergines and cut in half lengthwise. Score flesh of each half lightly to
make a border about 8 mm/⅜ inch from skin, using point of sharp
knife. Score lightly 3 times in centre of each half. (This enables heat
to penetrate more evenly.) Place in a lightly oiled roasting pan or
shallow baking dish, cut side up. Sprinkle cut surface with salt and 1
tablespoon olive oil. Bake for about 25 minutes, or until flesh is
tender when pierced with knife. Let cool slightly. Reduce oven
temperature to 180°C/350°F/gas 4.

Cut aubergines gently along scored border and remove pulp
carefully with spoon, taking care not to pierce skin. Drain shells for 5
minutes in colander. Transfer shells to oiled shallow baking dish,
so they touch each other, or to four individual baking dishes. Chop
flesh and add to pilaf. Taste and adjust seasoning. Spoon mixture
into shells. Sprinkle with remaining tablespoon olive oil.

Bake for about 15 minutes, or until aubergine is very tender and
hot. Reheat sauce. If using individual baking dishes, spoon sauce
around base of aubergines. If using large dish, divide sauce among
four plates and set aubergine halves on top.

AUBERGINES WITH TOMATOES, SAFFRON, AND GARLIC
Aubergines farcies à l'orientale

Saffron is the reason this dish is called in French *à l'orientale*. In
classic cuisine the spice is associated with the flavours of the East.
Try making this part of a Mediterranean vegetable feast by serving it
with Onions Stuffed with Spinach, Courgettes Stuffed with Red
Pepper Purée, and Rice Salad with Pyrénées Cheese, Mushrooms,
and Tomatoes.   MAKES 4 SERVINGS

2 medium aubergines (450 g/1 lb
    each), unpeeled
Salt
4 tablespoons olive oil
450 g/1 lb ripe tomatoes, peeled,
    seeded, and chopped
Freshly ground pepper

Large pinch of saffron strands,
    crushed (about 1/4 teaspoon)
2 garlic cloves, finely chopped
1 tablespoon unseasoned bread
    crumbs
2 tablespoons chopped fresh parsley

GARNISH (OPTIONAL)

8 black olives, cut in half
    lengthwise
2 tablespoons finely diced fresh
    tomato

4 small sprigs parsley

Preheat oven to 230°C/450°F/gas 8. Remove green caps from aubergines and cut in half lengthwise. Score flesh of each half lightly to
make a border about 8 mm/3/8 inch from skin, using point of sharp
knife. Score lightly 3 times in centre of each half. (This enables heat
to penetrate more evenly.) Place in a lightly oiled roasting pan or
shallow baking dish, cut side up. Sprinkle cut surface with salt and 2
tablespoons olive oil. Bake for about 25 minutes, or until flesh is
tender when pierced with knife.

Meanwhile, in medium-size frying pan, heat 1 tablespoon olive oil
over medium-high heat. Add tomatoes, salt, and pepper. Cook,
stirring occasionally, for about 15 minutes, or until mixture is dry.
Reduce heat to low, stir in saffron, and cook for 1 minute.

Let aubergines cool slightly. Cut gently along scored border and
remove pulp carefully with spoon, taking care not to pierce skin.
Drain pulp for 5 minutes in colander. If shells are watery, drain them
also. Return shells to baking dish.

Chop removed aubergine flesh and add to tomato mixture. Add
garlic, bread crumbs, and parsley. Adjust seasoning; mixture should
be well seasoned with salt and pepper.

Spoon mixture into aubergine shells. Sprinkle with remaining 1
tablespoon olive oil. Bake for about 15 minutes, or until aubergine is
very tender and hot. Serve hot, warm, or at room temperature.

Garnish: Make a row of 4 olive halves, rounded side down, along centre of each aubergine half. Put a spoonful of diced tomato at one end and top tomato with a parsley sprig.

AUBERGINES STUFFED WITH DUXELLES
Aubergines farcies à la duxelles

For this simple dish both the aubergines and the mushroom stuffing are precooked. The purpose of the final baking is just to warm them and lightly brown the topping. The duxelles mixture also makes an excellent filling for courgettes.   MAKES 4 SERVINGS

1·25 kg/2½ lb small or medium-size aubergines	*Salt*

DUXELLES

15 g/½ oz butter	*Salt and freshly ground pepper*
2 shallots, finely chopped	*2 tablespoons chopped fresh parsley*
275 g/10 oz mushrooms, very finely chopped	
3 tablespoons fresh bread crumbs	*3 tablespoons melted butter or vegetable oil*

Preheat oven to 230°C/450°F/gas 8. Leave aubergines unpeeled; cut them in half lengthwise. Score flesh of each half lightly to make a border about 8 mm/⅜ inch from skin, using a sharp knife. Score lightly 3 times in centre of each half. (This enables heat to penetrate more evenly.) Sprinkle cut surface with salt. Place in a lightly oiled roasting pan or shallow baking dish, cut side up. Bake for about 20 to 25 minutes, or until flesh is tender when pierced with a knife. Let cool slightly.

Cut aubergines gently along scored border and remove pulp carefully with a spoon, taking care not to pierce skin. Put shells in a buttered gratin dish. Chop flesh.

DUXELLES

In a medium-size frying pan, melt butter over low heat, add shallots, and cook until soft but not brown. Stir in mushrooms and sprinkle with salt and pepper. Raise heat and cook, stirring constantly, for about 7 minutes, or until mixture is dry. Stir in parsley. Add chopped aubergine to mushroom mixture. Taste and adjust seasoning.

Spoon stuffing into aubergine shells. Sprinkle with bread crumbs, then with melted butter or oil. Bake for 10 to 15 minutes, or until hot. If bread crumbs have not browned in that time, place under grill for a few seconds to brown. Serve hot.

COURGETTES STUFFED WITH RED
PEPPER PURÉE
Courgettes à la purée de poivrons rouges

Courgette boats make an attractive container for serving vegetable purées and are also good stuffed with carrot, spinach, or tomato purée. The striking red pepper purée can be served on its own, especially as a zesty accompaniment for chicken, turkey or lamb.

MAKES 6 SERVINGS

4 red peppers
3–4 tablespoons virgin olive oil
¼ teaspoon dried thyme

Salt and freshly ground pepper
6 small courgettes (about
700 g/1½ lb), trimmed

Preheat grill. Grill peppers about 5 cm/2 inches from heat, turning them slightly every few minutes, until their skin blisters on all sides and turns black; about 15 to 20 minutes. Put peppers in a plastic bag, close bag, and let stand for 10 minutes. Peel peppers, remove seeds and ribs, and cut into 3 or 4 pieces.

In a frying pan, heat 2 tablespoons olive oil over medium heat. Add peppers, thyme, and pinch of salt and pepper. Sauté peppers for 1 minute on each side.

Remove mixture from pan and purée peppers until very smooth in a food processor or blender. Taste and adjust seasoning. (Purée can be kept, covered, for 1 day in refrigerator; reheat before continuing.)

Preheat oven to 200°C/400°F/gas 6. In a large saucepan of boiling salted water, cook courgettes for 2 minutes. Rinse under cold running water and drain thoroughly. Cut each in half lengthwise. With a small sharp knife, carefully scoop out seeds, leaving a boat-shaped shell; be careful not to pierce the sides.

Put courgettes in an oiled shallow baking dish. Rub cut surfaces with remaining oil, and sprinkle with salt and pepper. Bake for 5 minutes.

Spoon pepper purée evenly into shells. Bake for 10 more minutes, or until ends of courgettes are tender when pierced with a sharp knife. Serve hot or at room temperature as a first course or side dish.

TOMATOES FILLED WITH ARTICHOKE
AND RICE SALAD
Tomates farcies salade de riz aux artichauts

For this cool, colourful dish, a variety of vegetables, such as small broccoli florets or sautéed sliced mushrooms, can be added to the rice filling.   MAKES 6 SERVINGS

6 large tomatoes, ripe but firm   4 to 6 artichokes

RICE PILAF

1 tablespoon vegetable oil   ½ teaspoon curry powder
15 g/½ oz butter   450 ml/¾ pint hot water
1 small onion, finely chopped   Salt and freshly ground pepper
200 g/7 oz long-grain rice

VINAIGRETTE

2 tablespoons white wine vinegar   Salt and freshly ground pepper
6 tablespoons vegetable oil

150 g/5 oz cooked fresh or frozen   6 basil leaves (optional), cut in
   peas   thin strips
1 small celery stick, peeled and   ½ green pepper, seeded and diced
   finely diced

Cut tomatoes in half horizontally. Remove interior with a teaspoon, but leave a layer of pulp attached to skin to form a shell. Turn tomatoes over on a plate and leave to drain for about 30 minutes. Prepare and cook artichoke hearts according to the instructions in Artichokes with Onion Compote (page 159) and dice them.

RICE PILAF

In a medium-size frying pan, heat oil and butter over low heat, add onion, and cook, stirring, for about 10 minutes, or until soft but not brown. Add rice and sauté, stirring, for about 2 minutes, or until grains turn opaque. Add curry powder, water, and salt and pepper. Bring to a boil, stir once, and cover. Reduce heat to low and cook, without stirring, for 18 minutes. Taste rice; if not yet tender, simmer for 2 more minutes. Remove from heat. Let stand, covered, for 10 minutes. Fluff with fork.

VINAIGRETTE

In a small bowl, stir vinegar, salt, and pepper with a whisk; whisk in oil. Taste and adjust seasoning.

In a bowl, combine rice with diced artichoke hearts, peas, celery, basil, and green pepper. Mix gently. Add vinaigrette and mix thoroughly. Taste and adjust seasoning. Refrigerate until ready to serve. Just before serving, fill tomato halves with rice salad.

PLUM TOMATOES WITH SHALLOT PURÉE
Olivettes au four à la purée d'échalotes

Velvety smooth shallot purée has a superb rich flavour that is perfectly complemented by the slight tartness of the baked tomato. These tomatoes make an elegant accompaniment for lamb or veal.

MAKES 4 SERVINGS

*225 g/8 oz shallots, peeled and cut
  in half*
40 g/1½ oz butter
Salt and freshly ground pepper
*8 ripe plum tomatoes (about
  350 g/12 oz)*

1 teaspoon vegetable oil
3 tablespoons double cream
*About 1 teaspoon finely snipped
  chives, or a few small parsley
  sprigs (optional), for garnish*

Preheat oven to 200°C/400°F/gas 6. In a medium-size saucepan, cover shallots with water, bring to a boil, and cook for 2 minutes. Drain thoroughly.

In a medium-size heavy sauté pan, melt butter over low heat, add shallots, a pinch of salt, and pepper, and cover. Cook, stirring often, for about 20 minutes, or until shallots are very tender; be careful not to let them burn.

Meanwhile, cut tomatoes in half lengthwise and scoop out interior with melon-ball cutter. Oil shallow baking dish in which tomatoes can fit in one layer. Put tomato halves in baking dish. Sprinkle with salt, pepper and a little oil. Bake for about 10 minutes, or until just tender. Carefully pour out juices from inside tomato halves. Pat insides dry with paper towel.

Purée shallots in a food processor. Put purée in a small heavy saucepan and stir over low heat. Add cream and continue to stir until absorbed. Taste and adjust seasoning.

Spoon shallot purée carefully into tomatoes, using 2 or 3 teaspoons purée for each tomato half, according to its size.

Return tomatoes to oven. Bake for about 7 minutes, or until

tomatoes are very tender. If desired, garnish each with chives or parsley sprig. Serve hot or warm. If any shallot purée remains, reheat it and serve it separately.

NOTE: Tomatoes can also be served standing on their ends. Instead of cutting them in half, cut a thin slice off wider end so it will balance. Then cut off top fourth of tomato, leaving it partially attached to be a 'hat'. They will hold less purée, so allow about 450 g/1 lb tomatoes.

PEPPERS STUFFED WITH RICE, MUSHROOMS, AND OLIVES
Poivrons farcis à la basquaise

Full of the flavours and colours of southern France, these peppers are roasted before being stuffed and therefore need to be baked only briefly with the stuffing.   MAKES 8 SERVINGS

8 red or green peppers, or 4 of each
175 g/6 oz long-grain white rice
Salt and freshly ground pepper
4 tablespoons vegetable or olive oil
100 g/4 oz mushrooms, halved and
   cut in thin slices
1 medium-size onion, finely
   chopped

450 g/1 lb ripe tomatoes, peeled,
   seeded, and chopped
2 teaspoons fresh thyme, or ¾
   teaspoon dried thyme
1 tablespoon chopped fresh basil
   leaves
50 g/2 oz stoned black olives, diced

Preheat grill. Grill peppers about 5 cm/2 inches from heat, turning them slightly every few minutes, until their skin blisters on all sides and turns black; about 15 to 20 minutes. Put peppers in a plastic bag, close bag, and let stand for 10 minutes. Peel peppers, leaving them whole. Carefully cut out cores. With a teaspoon, carefully remove seeds, leaving pepper intact, if possible. Pour out any liquid. Preheat oven to 200°C/400°F/gas 6.

In a large saucepan, bring about 1·25 litres/3 pints water to a boil and add a pinch of salt. Add rice, stir once, and boil, uncovered, for about 12 to 14 minutes, or until tender; check by tasting. Rinse with cold water and leave in a strainer to drain for 5 minutes.

In a medium-size frying pan, heat 1 tablespoon oil over high heat, add mushrooms and salt and pepper to taste, and sauté, stirring, for about 3 minutes, or until lightly browned. Set aside.

Add another tablespoon of oil to pan and lower heat. Add onion and cook, stirring, for about 10 minutes, or until soft but not brown. Add tomatoes and thyme and cook over medium-high heat, stirring often, for about 12 minutes, or until dry.

Gently mix tomatoes, mushrooms, basil, and diced olives with rice. Add 1 tablespoon oil. Taste and adjust seasoning. Spoon carefully into peppers, packing lightly.

Oil two 20-cm/8-inch-square shallow baking dishes or a large gratin dish. Put peppers on their sides in prepared dishes. Sprinkle with remaining oil. Bake for about 15 minutes, or until very tender. Serve hot, warm, or at room temperature.

ONIONS STUFFED WITH SPINACH
Oignons farcis aux épinards

Onions are amusing to stuff; after being briefly precooked, they can easily be separated into layers and each one can enclose a little stuffing. Long baking gives the stuffed onions a delicate flavour.

MAKES 4 SERVINGS

4 medium-size onions (about 700 g/1½ lb), peeled
700 g/1½ lb fresh spinach (leaves with stems)
50 g/2 oz butter
1 egg

2 tablespoons double cream
2 tablespoons unseasoned bread crumbs
Salt and freshly ground pepper
Freshly grated nutmeg
1 tablespoon vegetable oil

Preheat oven to 180°C/350°F/gas 4. In a large pan of boiling salted water, cook onions for about 15 minutes, or until somewhat tender when pierced with a small sharp knife. Drain and leave until cool enough to handle.

Cut off about one-quarter of onion at stem end. Carefully cut off root end. Beginning at stem end, scoop out centre of onion with a small sharp knife and spoon, leaving a fairly thick shell of at least 4 layers of onion. Carefully separate shell into cases, each of 1 or 2 layers of onion; those with 1 layer will be more delicate and tender, but those with 2 layers keep their shape better. Put cases in a lightly oiled large gratin dish or other heavy shallow baking dish. Chop onion centres and tops.

Discard spinach stems. Wash leaves, put in a large pan of boiling salted water, and cook for 1 minute, until just tender. Rinse under cold running water and drain thoroughly. Squeeze out as much liquid as possible and coarsely chop.

In a medium-size frying pan or sauté pan, melt 40 g/1½ oz butter over low heat, add chopped onion, and cook for about 10 minutes, or until tender. Add spinach and cook, stirring often, for about 2 minutes. Transfer to a bowl and let cool slightly. Add egg, cream, and bread crumbs. Season to taste with salt, pepper, and nutmeg.

Spoon stuffing into onion cases without packing. Discard any extra cases. Sprinkle onions with 1 tablespoon oil, cover with foil, and bake for 45 minutes. Uncover, dot stuffing with remaining butter, and bake for about 30 minutes, or until onions are very tender when pierced with a sharp knife. Serve hot or warm.

NOTE: If desired, substitute one 275-g/10-oz packet frozen spinach for fresh. Thaw completely, then squeeze as above.

GLAZED, BRAISED, STEAMED, AND POACHED VEGETABLES

Very fresh vegetables are one of the best assurances of delicious vegetable dishes. In some of the finest restaurants the owners are proud of having their own vegetable gardens. Of course this is not practical for most people, but the sooner a vegetable is cooked after purchase the better.

Careful cooking is the other key to enjoying vegetables at their best. Vegetables should be cooked so that they are slightly crisp yet tender, with just a little bite. They should not be undercooked so that their texture is hard and their flavour still raw; neither should they be overcooked so that they become flavourless and flabby.

Although there are countless French vegetable recipes, the most frequently used method for cooking vegetables as an accompaniment is the simplest and quickest: they are boiled, poached, or steamed, then drained and tossed with a little salt, freshly ground pepper and fine-quality butter.

Another quick way to season cooked vegetables, which is used in southern France, is to sprinkle a small amount of extra virgin olive oil over them. Sometimes the olive oil, or a flavoured oil with thyme, garlic, rosemary, or even hot peppers, is provided in a cruet so that people can pour their own. The vegetable might then be served with a wedge of lemon. The versatile vinaigrette is another simple but popular seasoning for freshly cooked hot vegetables.

For the purpose of cooking, the French often divide vegetables into green vegetables, which are most often boiled, and root vegetables, which are poached or glazed. The category of 'green' vegetables includes not only the leafy ones but also asparagus, green beans, leeks, and even cauliflower. Other vegetables, such as courgettes, aubergines, peppers, tomatoes and mushrooms, which we call 'Mediterranean vegetables', are most often cooked by other methods and are discussed in the next chapter.

Glazed Vegetables

Glazing is a special cooking technique somewhere between poaching and sautéing. The vegetable is cooked with water, butter, and often a little sugar until it softens, the water evaporates, and the butter and sugar form a delicious glaze. It is best suited to root vegetables, especially carrots, turnips, and baby onions.

GINGER-GLAZED CARROTS AND TURNIPS
Carottes et navets glacés au gingembre

'Turned' vegetables, carved in oval shapes, are popular in French restaurants because they cook evenly and look beautiful. Serve these vegetables with roast duck or chicken.   MAKES 3 TO 4 SERVINGS

600 ml/1 pint Chicken Stock (page 333) or Vegetable Stock (page 332)

4 tablespoons finely chopped peeled fresh ginger root

4 medium-size thin carrots, of uniform size and shape (about 275 g/10 oz)

3 small turnips, of uniform size and shape (about 275 g/10 oz)

Pinch of salt

1½ teaspoons sugar

40 g/1½ oz unsalted butter

Freshly ground pepper

Bring stock to boil with 2 tablespoons ginger. Simmer, uncovered, over medium-low heat for 30 minutes. Strain, pressing ginger.

Cut carrots in 4-cm/1½-inch lengths. Trim each piece to oval, rounding off corners. Cut turnips in quarters from top to bottom and trim each piece to oval shape. (Trimmings of carrots, but not of turnips, can be saved for use in stock.)

Put carrots in small saucepan in which they fit in one layer and add about 300 ml/½ pint ginger-flavoured stock, or enough to barely cover them. Add salt, 1 teaspoon sugar, 25 g/1 oz butter, and remaining 2 tablespoons ginger. Bring to boil, reduce heat to medium, and simmer, uncovered, for about 15 minutes, or until carrots are tender. Leave until cool enough to handle. Remove carrots, leaving ginger in liquid. Boil liquid until reduced to 4 tablespoons. Strain liquid, pressing ginger. Return liquid and carrots to saucepan.

Put turnips in another small saucepan in which they fit in one layer and add the remaining ginger-flavoured stock, or enough to barely cover turnips. Add salt, remaining sugar, and remaining butter. Bring to a boil, reduce heat to medium, and simmer, uncovered, for about 7 minutes, or until turnips are barely tender. Remove gently with slotted spoon. Boil liquid until reduced to 3–4 tablespoons. Add liquid and turnips to saucepan of carrots.

Reheat vegetables in their liquid, uncovered, over medium-high heat, tossing often. Serve hot.

BUTTER-GLAZED CARROTS
Carottes Vichy

This classic carrot recipe remains the favourite French way to prepare the vegetable. The sugar gives just a touch of sweetness and does not produce candied carrots. MAKES 4 SERVINGS

8 medium-size carrots, peeled
Pinch of salt
1½ teaspoons sugar

40 g/1½ oz unsalted butter
1 tablespoon chopped parsley
(optional)

To turn carrots to an olive shape, cut into 5-cm/2-inch lengths. If carrots are wide, cut each piece into quarters lengthwise. Shape each piece in an oval or olive shape, rounding off corners.

Put carrots in a medium-size sauté pan and cover with water. Add salt, sugar, and butter. Bring to a boil, reduce heat to medium, and simmer, uncovered, for about 20 minutes, or until carrots are tender. If liquid has not evaporated by this time, continue to cook over medium-low heat, shaking pan often, until liquid evaporates and carrots become coated with a buttery glaze. Transfer to a serving dish and sprinkle with parsley, if desired.

GLAZED BABY ONIONS AND COURGETTE
Petits oignons et courgette glacés

These glazed vegetables can be served with any poultry or meat, or can be spooned around Carrot Timbales (page 16) for a delicious and attractive accompaniment. MAKES 2 GENEROUS OR 4 SMALL SERVINGS

12 baby onions of uniform size
(about 225 g/8 oz)
Salt and freshly ground pepper
25 g/1 oz unsalted butter

3 tablespoons water
1 small courgette (about 100 g/
4 oz)
1 teaspoon sugar

Put unpeeled onions in a heavy saucepan in which they can fit in one layer. Cover with water and bring just to a boil. Drain, rinse with cold water until they cool completely, and peel.

Return onions to saucepan with a pinch of salt and pepper, butter, and 3 tablespoons water. Cover and cook over low heat, shaking pan occasionally, 15 to 20 minutes, or until tender.

Cut courgette into quarters lengthwise, then into 2·5-cm/1-inch pieces.

Sprinkle onions with sugar and cook, uncovered, over medium heat, shaking pan often, until liquid is reduced to a buttery glaze of a syrupy consistency. Reduce heat to medium-low. Add courgettes, cover, and cook for about 5 minutes, or until barely tender.

Braised and Stewed Vegetables

For these techniques vegetables are cooked in a relatively small amount of liquid or sometimes, as in the case of Butter-Braised Chicory, without any liquid at all. They are generally cooked until very tender, rather than crisp-tender as when boiled or steamed.

Often stewing and braising involve a flavour exchange between the vegetable and its cooking liquid, which can then be made into a sauce for the vegetable. Unlike braised or stewed meats, the vegetables are not usually browned before the liquid is added.

Vegetables can also enhance one another. Combining several in a stew can produce a delightful creation with contrasting tastes, textures, and colours. Dried beans, for example, seem lighter when they are matched with fresh vegetables, as in Flageolets with Green and Yellow Beans and Spring Onion Butter. To ensure that each vegetable in a stew is perfectly cooked, fragile ones are often precooked separately until nearly tender and then all are heated together briefly so their flavours blend.

BRAISED CHESTNUTS
Marrons braisés

Peeling fresh chestnuts is time-consuming, but they are a real treat and in France are holiday fare. Braised chestnuts are usually served with turkey, duck or chicken.

MAKES 2 TO 3 SERVINGS

350 g/12 oz large fresh chestnuts   *Salt and freshly ground pepper*
350 ml/12 fl oz Chicken Stock   *15–25 g/½–1 oz unsalted butter*
  (page 333) or Vegetable Stock
  (page 332)
1 small celery stick, broken in two

Put chestnuts in a medium-size saucepan and add enough water to cover them by about 2·5 cm/1 inch. Bring to full boil and cook for 1 minute. Remove one nut with slotted spoon and peel by first cutting base and pulling off outer skin, and then pulling and scraping off inner skin. Continue with remaining nuts, removing from water one by one.

Put chestnuts in a medium-size saucepan with stock, celery, salt, and pepper. Bring to a boil, reduce heat to low, cover, and simmer for about 15 minutes, or until chestnuts are just tender when pierced with point of a knife; do not overcook, or they will fall apart. Uncover and leave in liquid until ready to use. (Chestnuts can be kept in their liquid, covered, for up to 2 days in refrigerator.)

To serve, reheat chestnuts in their cooking liquid in covered saucepan over low heat. Discard celery and chestnut-cooking liquid. Add butter to chestnuts and shake over low heat until blended. Taste and adjust seasoning. Serve hot.

CREAM-BRAISED CABBAGE WITH LEEKS
Choux braisés à la crème et aux poireaux

Among many people, cabbage has a bad reputation. Yet cabbage is such a great favourite of the French that they even use the word for it as a term of endearment, calling loved ones '*mon petit chou*' or 'my little cabbage'. Combining cabbage with mild ingredients, especially butter and cream, is a popular way to moderate its nature, as in this recipe, in which it becomes extremely rich and delicate. Serve this dish as a base for baked or poached eggs or to accompany poultry or fish.

MAKES 4 TO 6 SERVINGS

1 medium-size head of green
  cabbage (about 1 kg/2 lb),
  cored and rinsed
40 g/1½ oz butter
Salt and freshly ground white
  pepper

750 ml/1¼ pints milk
White and light green parts of 2
  large leeks, halved lengthwise,
  washed well, and thinly sliced
  crosswise
225 ml/8 fl oz double cream

Cut cabbage in thin strips. In a large heavy casserole of boiling salted water, cook cabbage, uncovered, over high heat for 5 minutes. Rinse under cold water and drain thoroughly. Gently squeeze dry.

In a casserole, over low heat, melt 25 g/1 oz butter. Stir in cabbage and salt and pepper to taste. Add milk, cover, and cook, stirring occasionally, for about 20 minutes, or until very tender.

In a heavy frying pan, melt remaining butter over low heat. Add leeks, salt and pepper to taste, and cook, stirring occasionally, for about 10 minutes, or until soft but not brown.

When cabbage is tender, uncover and cook over high heat, stirring often, until it absorbs milk. Stir in cream and simmer for 5 minutes, or until thickened. Stir in leeks. Taste and adjust seasoning.

CABBAGE WITH APPLES AND CIDER
Choux à la normande

In this rich country dish from Normandy the cabbage becomes slightly sweet and olive green in colour. Serve it with sausages or roasted or braised meats.

MAKES 4 TO 6 SERVINGS

1 medium-size head of green
    cabbage (about 1 kg/2 lb),
    cored and rinsed
225 ml/8 fl oz dry cider
3–4 tablespoons water
1 whole clove

Salt and freshly ground pepper
Freshly grated nutmeg
2 Golden Delicious apples, peeled,
    cut in half, and cored
100 g/4 oz unsalted butter, cut in
    pieces, at room temperature

Cut cabbage in thin strips. In a large heavy casserole of boiling salted water, cook cabbage, uncovered, over high heat for 5 minutes. Rinse under cold water and drain thoroughly. Gently squeeze dry.

Return cabbage to casserole and add cider, water, clove, and salt, pepper, and nutmeg to taste.

Cut each apple half in 4 wedges, add to casserole, and bring liquid to a boil. Reduce heat to low, cover, and simmer for about 20 minutes, or until cabbage and apples are tender. Uncover and cook over high heat, stirring gently, until nearly all liquid is evaporated. Try not to let all of the apples fall apart. Remove from heat and discard clove. Stir butter into cabbage mixture. Taste and adjust seasoning. To serve, spoon cabbage on to a heated platter or plates and set apple wedges on top.

BUTTER-BRAISED CHICORY
Endives braisées

Chicory is good not only in salads but also cooked. Braising, the most popular technique in France for cooking the vegetable, gives it a flavour completely different from raw. It is slightly bitter and somewhat of an acquired taste, but delightful. This dish makes a good partner for roast chicken as it can go in the oven while the chicken is roasting.   MAKES 3 TO 4 SERVINGS

450 g/1 lb chicory
25 g/1 oz unsalted butter

Salt and freshly ground pepper

Preheat oven to 200°C/400°F/gas 6. Trim any brown spots from chicory leaves and from bases. Spread butter in a heavy ovenproof saucepan just large enough to contain chicory in one layer. Set chicory in saucepan and sprinkle with salt and pepper.

Cover very tightly and cook over medium heat until butter begins to sizzle. Transfer to oven and bake for about 30 minutes. Turn over, cover tightly, and continue baking for 20 to 30 minutes more, or until chicory is very tender when pierced with a small sharp knife near base; cooking time varies with size of chicory. Check occasionally to be sure it does not burn. Serve hot.

BRAISED FENNEL WITH PEPPERS AND OLIVES
Fenouil braisé aux poivrons et aux olives

Fennel is generally braised whole but this way is quicker and enables the fennel to gain more flavour from the olive oil and peppers. Serve with chicken, veal or lamb.   MAKES 4 SERVINGS

2 medium-size fennel bulbs (about 600 g/1¼ lb)	2 tablespoons olive oil
2 medium-size red peppers	Salt and freshly ground pepper
	50 g/2 oz stoned black olives

Remove stalks and any browned outer leaves and cut each fennel bulb into quarters. Cut off and discard core from each piece. Holding layers together, cut each fennel piece in 6-mm/¼-inch slices lengthwise, to obtain long strips. Cut peppers in half lengthwise and remove core and ribs. Cut in half crosswise and cut each half into lengthwise strips about 6 mm/¼ inch wide.

Heat olive oil in large frying pan over low heat. Add fennel, salt and pepper to taste, and stir well. Cover and cook, stirring occasionally, for 15 minutes. Add peppers, cover, and continue cooking for about 10 minutes, or until vegetables are tender. Taste and adjust seasoning. Remove to platter. Top with olives and serve.

ASPARAGUS AND CARROTS WITH MADEIRA
Asperges et carottes au madère

This colourful stew is wonderful served over rice or alongside sautéed
or roast poultry.   MAKES 4 SERVINGS

3 medium-size carrots (about 275 g/10 oz), peeled, cut in 5-cm/2-inch pieces	15 g/½ oz butter
	2 medium-size shallots, finely chopped
700 g/1¼ lb asparagus	4 tablespoons Madeira
Pinch of salt	6 tablespoons double cream

Cut thick carrot pieces in quarters lengthwise and thin pieces in half
lengthwise. Put carrot pieces in medium-size saucepan, cover with
water, and add pinch of salt. Bring to a boil, cover, and simmer for
about 15 minutes, or until barely tender.

Trim and peel asparagus and cut off tough ends. Remove asparagus
tips, cut stems in half crosswise, then lengthwise, if necessary, so
they will be of same thickness as carrots.

Add asparagus stem pieces to barely tender carrots and simmer for
7 minutes longer, or until tender. Drain cooking liquid into a
measuring jug. Reserve 225 ml/8 fl oz. Cover saucepan to keep
vegetables warm.

In a medium-size frying pan, melt butter over low heat, add
shallots, and cook, stirring, for about 1 minute. Add reserved
vegetable-cooking liquid and boil, stirring, until reduced to about 4
tablespoons. Add Madeira and bring to a boil, add cream, and
simmer over medium heat, stirring often, until thick enough to coat
a spoon.

At same time, put asparagus tips in a pan of boiling salted water
and cook, uncovered, over high heat for about 5 minutes, or until
just tender. Drain thoroughly and reserve 8 tips for garnish. Add
carrots, asparagus stems, and remaining asparagus tips to sauce and
heat for 2 or 3 minutes over low heat. Taste and adjust seasoning.

Spoon into a serving dish and garnish with reserved tips.

FLAGEOLETS WITH GREEN AND YELLOW BEANS AND SPRING ONION BUTTER

Flageolets aux haricots verts et au beurre d'oignons nouveaux

Pale green flageolets are aristocrats in the dried bean family and have a more delicate flavour than other types of dried beans. They are imported from France and are available in speciality shops. This is a new version of the traditional French recipe for *haricots panachés*, made of equal amounts of flageolet beans and green beans and used to accompany roast or grilled lamb. Serve it according to this custom or on its own as a first course or light main course.   MAKES 4 SERVINGS

225 g/8 oz dried flageolet beans
1 bay leaf

¼ teaspoon dried thyme
1 litre/1¾ pints water

SPRING ONION BUTTER

1½ to 2 medium-size spring onions, trimmed, cut into 2·5-cm/1-inch pieces, and patted dry

100 g/4 oz unsalted butter, at room temperature

175 g/6 oz green beans, ends removed, broken in half
175 g/6 oz yellow/French beans, ends removed, broken in half

1 small garlic clove, finely chopped
Salt and freshly ground pepper

Soak flageolets in 750 ml/1¼ pints cold water in a cool place for 8 hours, or overnight. Drain and rinse.

Combine flageolets with bay leaf, thyme, and water in a medium-size saucepan. Bring to a boil, reduce heat to low, cover, and cook for about 1½ hours, or until just tender. (Flageolets can be kept in their cooking liquid for 1 day in refrigerator. Reheat before continuing.) Drain thoroughly, reserving 2 tablespoons cooking liquid. Discard bay leaf.

SPRING ONION BUTTER

In food processor fitted with steel knife, finely chop spring onions. (The amount you use in spring onion butter depends on how strong a flavour you like. For a strong onion flavour, use 2 onions. For a more delicate flavour, use only 1½.) Add butter and process until blended; colour will be light green with dots of deeper green. Do not overprocess or butter will melt. Refrigerate for about 30 minutes, or until firm.

Meanwhile, cook green and yellow beans, uncovered, separately, each in a medium-size saucepan of boiling salted water over high heat for about 7 minutes, or until barely tender. Drain thoroughly.

In a frying pan, combine flageolets with the reserved 2 tablespoons of their liquid, garlic, and salt and pepper to taste. Cook over low heat, stirring gently, for 2 minutes. Add cooked beans and mix.

Reserve 15 g/½ oz spring onion butter and cut in 2 pieces. With pan of beans over low heat, gently stir in remaining spring onion butter, about 25 g/1 oz at a time, heating just until butter is absorbed. Taste and adjust seasoning. Transfer to serving dish and place remaining spring onion butter on top. Toss when serving.

COLOURFUL VEGETABLE
BLANQUETTE
Blanquette de légumes

In classic cuisine *blanquette* refers to a creamy veal or lamb stew. I find this formula excellent for preparing a sumptuous vegetable dish as well.   MAKES 4 SERVINGS

225 g/8 oz small mushrooms
450 ml/¾ pint Chicken Stock
   (page 333) or Vegetable Stock
   (page 332)
6 tablespoons dry white wine

1 large lemon, cut in half (if using
   fresh artichokes)
2 medium-size artichokes, or 8
   frozen artichoke heart pieces,
   thawed

225 g/8 oz Swiss chard, leaves
  only, rinsed thoroughly
100 g/4 oz button onions
100 g/4 oz mange-tout peas
225 g/8 oz baby carrots, scraped,
  larger ones halved crosswise
225 g/8 oz small courgettes,
  quartered lengthwise and cut in
  5-cm/2-inch pieces

300 ml/½ pint double cream
1 tablespoon chopped fresh
  tarragon
1 tablespoon snipped chives
1 tablespoon chopped parsley
Salt and freshly ground pepper
A few drops fresh lemon juice

Remove stems from mushrooms. Combine stems with stock and wine in a medium-size saucepan. Bring to a boil, reduce heat to low, and simmer, uncovered, for 15 minutes. Strain stock and reserve; discard mushroom stems.

If using fresh artichokes, squeeze juice of ½ lemon into medium-size bowl of cold water. Break off stems and largest leaves of artichoke bottom. Put artichoke on its side on board. Holding very sharp knife or small serrated knife against side (parallel to leaves), cut lower circle of leaves off, up to edge of artichoke heart. Turn artichoke slightly after each cut. Rub exposed edges of artichoke heart with cut lemon. Cut off central cone of leaves just above artichoke heart. Cut off leaves under base and trim so it is round, removing all dark green areas. Rub again with lemon. Put each artichoke in bowl of lemon water as it is finished.

Squeeze any juice remaining in lemon into medium-size saucepan of boiling salted water, add artichoke hearts, cover, and simmer over low heat until tender when pierced with knife; about 15 minutes for fresh and about 7 minutes for frozen. Cool to lukewarm in liquid. Using a teaspoon, scoop out choke from centre of each fresh artichoke heart. Return artichokes to liquid until ready to use. Cut each fresh artichoke into 4 pieces. (Stock mixture and artichokes in their liquid can be kept for 1 day in refrigerator. Reheat artichokes in their liquid and drain them.)

Pile chard leaves, cut them in half lengthwise and then crosswise into 1-cm/½-inch strips. In a large saucepan of boiling salted water, cook, uncovered, over high heat for about 3 minutes, or until just tender. Rinse under cold water, drain well, and press gently to remove excess liquid.

Put pearl onions in a medium-size saucepan, cover with water, and bring to a boil. Boil for 1 minute, rinse under cold water, drain well, then peel.

Remove ends and strings from mange-tout peas. In a large saucepan of boiling salted water to generously cover, cook, uncovered, over high heat until they turn bright green; no more than 1 minute; they should remain crisp. Rinse under cold water and drain well.

Bring strained stock to a boil in a medium-size shallow saucepan. Add baby carrots and simmer, covered, over medium heat for about 15 minutes, or until they are just tender. Remove with a slotted spoon. Add mushroom caps and onions, cover, and simmer over medium heat for about 10 minutes, or until onions are just tender. Remove with slotted spoon. Add courgettes, cover, and simmer for about 4 minutes, or until just tender. Remove with slotted spoon.

Bring vegetable cooking liquid to a boil in a sauté pan. Whisk cream into cooking liquid and bring to a boil over medium-high heat, whisking. Boil, stirring often, until sauce is thick enough to coat spoon; about 6 minutes. Stir in chard, using a fork. Stir in remaining vegetables and reheat just to simmer. Cook over low heat for 1 minute, stirring gently. Remove from heat. Add tarragon, chives, parsley, and salt, pepper, and lemon juice to taste. Toss gently, taste and adjust seasoning. Serve in gratin dishes or shallow bowls.

MIXED MUSHROOM RAGOÛT
Ragoût de champignons

If you can get any wild mushrooms, such as chanterelles or cèpes, include them in this richly flavoured ragoût. The dish makes a wonderful topping for white rice, grilled steaks or poached eggs.

MAKES 4 SERVINGS

1 tablespoon vegetable oil
50 g/2 oz butter
1 large shallot, finely chopped
225 g/8 oz button mushrooms,
  halved and thinly sliced

Salt and freshly ground pepper
4 tablespoons Madeira
1 tablespoon chopped parsley

In a large heavy frying pan, heat oil and butter over medium heat. Stir in shallot, then mushrooms, and salt and pepper to taste. Sauté, tossing often, for about 4 minutes, or until mushrooms are just tender.

Add Madeira and simmer over medium heat, stirring, for about 3 minutes, or until it is absorbed by mushrooms. Taste and adjust seasoning, transfer to a serving dish, sprinkle with parsley, and serve.

Steamed Vegetables

Cooking vegetables by the moist heat of steam is favoured by many cooks because it preserves more of their nutrients. In France steaming was not very much a part of classic restaurant cuisine, except for a few dishes like *pommes vapeur* or steamed new potatoes. Home cooks, however, have long valued steaming. The folding steamer is a standard piece of equipment even in the simplest of French homes.

Most vegetables can be successfully steamed. Because steaming locks in flavours, it is better for mild-tasting rather than strong-flavoured vegetables. Steaming usually takes a little longer than boiling.

Fresh steamed vegetables are delicious on their own but can be enhanced with a little plain butter or flavoured butter, as in Steamed Carrots with Pistachio Butter, or with a sauce, as in Beetroot with Orange Hollandaise.

In all steamers the food is placed on a rack above boiling liquid and is not in direct contact with the liquid. The pan is covered to keep in the steam. Several types of steamers are available. The French folding steamer rack can be set in any deep saucepan with a tight cover to turn it into a steamer. Chinese bamboo or metal steamers are convenient because the trays can be stacked and several different vegetables can be steamed at once and each removed according to its cooking time. A couscous pot can also be used. For cooking small amounts of vegetables steamers can be improvised by setting a metal colander or strainer in a large saucepan and covering it tightly.

Hints

· It is essential to drain steamed or boiled vegetables well so they will not be watery, especially if they will be served with a sauce, because excess liquid would dilute it.

· Vegetables can be boiled or steamed a day ahead, refrigerated, and reheated in a little butter in a sauté pan or skillet. But they taste best when freshly cooked.

· For the most even cooking use a large steamer in which the food can fit in one layer. If the vegetables are piled up, the steam cannot reach those in the centre. If using a small steamer, steam the vegetables in several batches if possible, so that each forms one layer.

· When steaming vegetables be sure they are well clear of the surface of the boiling water, so that when it bubbles vigorously it will not boil them. Be sure the water is boiling before the vegetables are added. Steam vegetables over high heat so the water continues to boil and to provide a constant flow of steam. Cover the vegetables in the steamer tightly so that the steam is kept in. When checking them, uncover as briefly as possible. Steam is very hot – when uncovering the steamer, hold the cover away from you in order to avoid it.

· During steaming check occasionally to be sure most of the water has not evaporated. If the level of the water is low add boiling water. Have a kettle of hot water ready for this purpose.

COURGETTES WITH MINT BUTTER
Courgettes au beurre de menthe

Be sure to use courgettes that are fresh – they should be firm and smooth. Although they do not appear to spoil quickly they become bitter after a few days. This very quick, simple vegetable dish can be spooned over rice or served with fish, chicken or lamb.

MAKES 4 TO 6 SERVINGS

1 tablespoon chopped fresh mint
leaves
40 g/1½ oz unsalted butter,
softened

Salt and freshly ground pepper
700 g/1½ lb courgettes, cut into
quarters lengthwise

Thoroughly mix mint leaves with butter and season to taste with salt
and pepper. Let stand at room temperature.

Bring at least 2·5 cm/1 inch of water to a boil in base of steamer.
Place courgettes on steamer rack in one layer or in a metal colander
above boiling water. Sprinkle with salt, cover tightly, and steam for
about 5 minutes, or until just tender.

Transfer briefly to paper towels to drain, then to a serving plate.
Top with spoonfuls of mint butter and serve.

ASPARAGUS WITH BEURRE BLANC
Asperges au beurre blanc

This is a favourite first course in fine restaurants when asparagus is in
season. White asparagus is more available in France than green, but
both types are well liked. If you have an asparagus cooker, in which
the asparagus spears cook standing up so that the bases are boiled and
the more tender tips steamed, use it rather than a steamer for this
dish.   MAKES 6 SERVINGS

BEURRE BLANC

2 large shallots, finely chopped
2 tablespoons white wine vinegar
3 tablespoons dry white wine
2 tablespoons double cream

Salt and freshly ground white
pepper
225 g/8 oz cold unsalted butter,
cut into 16 pieces

1·5 kg/3 lb asparagus

Salt

BEURRE BLANC

In a small heavy non-aluminium saucepan, simmer shallots in vinegar and wine over medium heat until liquid is reduced to about 2 tablespoons. Reduce heat to low, stir in cream, and simmer, whisking occasionally, until mixture is reduced to about 3 tablespoons. Season lightly with salt and white pepper. Cover and reserve. (The mixture can be kept, covered, for 1 hour at room temperature.) Keep butter in refrigerator until ready to use.

Peel asparagus stems thoroughly and cut off about 1 cm/½ inch of bases. Rinse well.

Bring at least 2·5 cm/1 inch of water to boil in base of steamer. Put asparagus in steamer above boiling water. Sprinkle with salt, cover, and steam for about 5 minutes, or until just tender when pierced with a sharp knife. With a slotted spatula, carefully transfer asparagus to a plate lined with paper towels.

Bring shallot mixture to simmer in a saucepan. Reduce heat to low and add one piece of butter, whisking liquid constantly. When butter piece is nearly blended into liquid, add another piece, still whisking. Continue adding butter pieces one or two at a time, whisking constantly. The sauce should be pleasantly warm to the touch. If it becomes too hot and drops of melted butter appear, remove pan immediately from heat and whisk well; add next butter pieces off heat, whisking constantly. When temperature of sauce drops again to warm, return to low heat to continue adding remaining butter pieces. Remove from heat as soon as last butter piece is added. Strain sauce if desired. Taste and adjust seasoning.

Serve sauce as soon as possible. (It can be kept warm for about 15 minutes in its saucepan set on a rack above warm water, but it must be whisked frequently to prevent separation. It can also be kept warm in a vacuum flask.)

To serve, divide asparagus among 6 plates. Serve sauce separately.

STEAMED CARROTS WITH PISTACHIO BUTTER
Carottes à la vapeur au beurre de pistaches

Pistachio nuts add a festive touch to carrots in this quick easy dish. Serve it with chicken, rice or couscous.   MAKES 6 SERVINGS

450 g/1 lb baby carrots, scraped
50 g/2 oz shelled roasted green
    pistachio nuts

75 g/3 oz unsalted butter, slightly
    softened
Salt and freshly ground pepper

Bring at least 2·5 cm/1 inch of water to a boil in base of steamer. Place carrots in steamer top in one layer or on a rack or in a metal colander above boiling water. Cover tightly and steam for about 15 minutes, or until just tender.

Grind pistachios to fine powder in food processor. Set aside 2 teaspoons.

Cream butter until soft. Stir in remaining pistachios and salt and pepper to taste. Leave at room temperature.

Transfer carrots to serving dish. Toss with pistachio butter. Sprinkle with reserved ground pistachios.

BEETROOT WITH ORANGE HOLLANDAISE
Betteraves, sauce maltaise

Beetroot becomes very tender and keeps in its good flavour when steamed. Although orange hollandaise is traditionally served with asparagus it is also delicious in this starter.   MAKES 6 SERVINGS

12 baby beetroot

½ medium-size orange

175 g/6 oz unsalted butter

3 egg yolks

2 tablespoons water

Pinch of salt

Pinch of white pepper or cayenne
  pepper

½ teaspoon strained fresh lemon
  juice, or to taste

Rinse beetroot. Bring at least 2·5 cm/1 inch of water to a boil in base of steamer. Place beetroot in steamer or on a rack or in a metal colander above boiling water. Cover tightly and steam for 50 to 60 minutes, or until tender, adding boiling water occasionally if water evaporates.

Meanwhile, use a vegetable peeler to pare orange peel without including bitter white pith underneath. Cut peel in very thin strips. Squeeze juice of half orange, strain and set aside. Put orange strips in a small saucepan, cover generously with water, and bring to a boil. Cook for 2 minutes and drain thoroughly.

In a small heavy saucepan, melt butter over low heat. Skim white foam from surface and pour remaining clear butter into a bowl, leaving white sediment behind in saucepan. Let cool to lukewarm.

When beetroot is tender, let cool slightly. Run briefly under water and slip off skins. Cut in half, cover, and keep warm while preparing sauce.

In a small heavy-bottomed non-aluminium saucepan, combine egg yolks, water, salt, and pepper, and whisk briefly. Set pan over low heat and cook, whisking vigorously and constantly, until mixture is creamy and thick enough so whisk leaves a trail on base of pan. Remove pan occasionally from heat; it should not become so hot that you can't touch the sides with your hands. Be careful not to let mixture become too hot or egg yolks will curdle. When yolk mixture becomes thick enough, remove it immediately from heat. Continue to whisk for about 30 seconds.

Gradually whisk in clarified butter, drop by drop. After sauce has absorbed about 2 or 3 tablespoons of butter, add the rest in a very thin stream, whisking vigorously and constantly. Gradually whisk in lemon juice and orange juice. Stir in orange peel strips. Taste and adjust seasoning.

Serve sauce as soon as possible. (It can be kept warm for about 15 minutes in its saucepan set on a rack above warm water, but it must be stirred frequently. It can also be kept warm in a vacuum flask.)

Spoon a little orange sauce on each of 6 small plates and top with beetroot. Serve any remaining sauce separately.

Poached and Boiled Vegetables

The most popular method for cooking green vegetables in France is to plunge them into a large saucepan of boiling salted water and cook them uncovered. A generous amount of water enables them to cook very quickly so that they keep their colour and flavour. The vegetable must have plenty of room to cook evenly rather than being crowded.

Root vegetables and dried beans, on the other hand, are started from cold water so that any undesirable strong flavours they contain can gradually escape into the water as it heats. After they are brought to a boil, they are poached or simmered until tender.

After cooking by either method, the vegetables are well drained in a colander, seasoned with salt and pepper, and finished with butter or a flavourful oil; or, for a more festive dish, they are accompanied by a sauce, as in French Beans with Pesto Sauce or Artichokes with Tomato Béarnaise.

If the cooking liquid of the vegetable tastes good, as in the case of carrots, courgettes, mushrooms or asparagus, it can be used for soups or sauces.

If a green vegetable is being cooked for serving later (by being reheated in butter, for example) or for turning into a salad or a more elaborate dish, immediately after cooking it is rinsed in a colander with cold running water until completely cold. This rinsing, sometimes called 'refreshing', preserves the vegetable's colour and prevents it from overcooking and becoming mushy from its own heat.

PROVENÇAL VEGETABLE AND GARLIC FEAST
Le grand aïoli

Aïoli, a versatile garlic sauce, has been important to the cuisine of southern France for hundreds of years. Recently it has gained favour in other countries as well. Not only does it suit our growing fondness for strong, assertive flavours; it also has the advantage of being quick to prepare and requiring no cooking. It makes a wonderful dipping sauce for vegetables, whether they are cooked or raw, hot or cold.

A traditional Provençal serving custom that is perfect for modern entertaining is called *Le grand aïoli*. An assortment of vegetables in season, and sometimes eggs and seafood, are presented on separate plates and are accompanied by a bowl of aïoli. Diners help themselves to the ingredients they like and to a spoonful of the sauce. Because each spoonful packs quite a punch, a little goes a long way.

The spinach and red pepper variations of aïoli are new vegetable interpretations of the famous sauce. I have also flavoured aïoli with chopped fresh basil or coriander and even with chilli peppers and found these versions delicious as well.   MAKES 6 SERVINGS

3 medium-size or 6 small
   artichokes, trimmed
6 small carrots, peeled and left
   whole or cut in half crosswise
6 medium-size potatoes, peeled
   and cut into quarters

450 g/1 lb green beans, ends
   removed
1 cauliflower, divided into
   medium-size florets

AÏOLI

6 medium-size garlic cloves, peeled
2 egg yolks, at room temperature
About 2 tablespoons strained fresh
   lemon juice

350 ml/12 fl oz extra virgin olive
   oil, at room temperature
Salt and freshly ground pepper
1 tablespoon lukewarm water

3 hard-boiled eggs, cut into halves
   or quarters

French bread, as an
   accompaniment

To trim artichokes, cut off top 2·5 cm/1 inch of large artichokes or 1 cm/½ inch of small ones. Trim spikes from tips of leaves. Put artichokes in a medium-size saucepan of simmering salted water and cover with a lid of slightly smaller diameter than that of pan to keep them submerged. Cook over medium heat until a leaf can be easily pulled out; large artichokes will need about 45 to 50 minutes, and small ones about 15 to 20 minutes. Using tongs, remove artichokes from water and turn them upside down to drain thoroughly.

Cook each of the remaining vegetables separately. Start carrots and potatoes in pans of cold salted water and bring to a boil. Cover and simmer potatoes for about 20 minutes and carrots for about 25 minutes, or until tender. Start green beans and cauliflower in pans of boiling salted water. Cook green beans for about 8 minutes and cauliflower for about 7 minutes. Drain all vegetables thoroughly.

AÏOLI

Cut off brown end and any brown spots from garlic. Halve lengthwise and remove any green sprouts from centre.

To make aïoli in food processor, drop garlic cloves through feed tube of food processor fitted with metal blade, with motor running, and process until finely chopped. Add egg yolks, 1 tablespoon lemon juice, 1 tablespoon oil, and a pinch of salt and pepper, and process until thoroughly blended, scraping bottom and sides of processor container several times. With motor running, gradually pour in 3 tablespoons oil in a thin trickle. After this the remaining oil can be poured in a little faster, in a thin stream. With motor still running, gradually pour in remaining tablespoon lemon juice, 1 teaspoon at a time. Add lukewarm water, 1 teaspoon at a time, to make sauce slightly thinner. Taste and adjust seasoning.

To prepare aïoli using mixer or whisk, chop garlic as finely as possible so that it becomes almost a purée. Combine garlic, egg yolks, 1 tablespoon lemon juice, and a pinch of salt and pepper in mixer bowl or a medium-size heavy bowl set on a towel. Beat at high speed or whisk until thoroughly blended. Begin beating in oil, drop by drop. When 2 or 3 tablespoons oil have been added, continue beating in oil in very thin stream until 225 ml/8 fl oz has been incorporated. Beat in 1 teaspoon of remaining lemon juice to thin sauce and make beating easier. Gradually beat in remaining oil in fine stream. Gradually beat in remaining lemon juice, 1 teaspoon at a time, then water, 1 teaspoon at a time. Taste and adjust seasoning and transfer to a serving bowl.

Serve vegetables warm or at room temperature, and sauce at room temperature. Arrange vegetables and eggs in separate piles on a platter or on serving plates. Serve aïoli and French bread separately.

SPINACH AÏOLI

Bring aïoli to room temperature. Remove stems from 350 g/12 oz fresh spinach. Rinse leaves thoroughly and put in a large saucepan containing enough boiling salted water to cover them generously. Return to boil and cook, uncovered, for 1 minute. Drain, rinse with cold running water until cool and drain. Squeeze by handfuls to remove as much water as possible. Purée in a food processor until very finely chopped. Add aïoli and process until smooth. Taste and adjust seasoning.

RED PEPPER AÏOLI

Preheat grill. Grill 3 medium-size red peppers about 5 cm/2 inches from heat, turning them slightly every few minutes, until their skins blister on all sides and turn black; about 15 to 20 minutes. Put peppers in a plastic bag, close bag, and let stand for 10 minutes. Peel, cut in half, and remove cores. Cool completely in colander and pat dry.

Purée peppers in food processor until as fine as possible. Whisk purée into aïoli in three portions. Stir thoroughly to blend. Taste and adjust seasoning. If a smoother sauce is desired, return to food processor and blend until smooth.

BABY VEGETABLES WITH HERB BUTTER SAUCE
Petits légumes au beurre d'herbes

This dish was inspired by a lovely first course I enjoyed at Le Pré Catalan, the beautiful restaurant in the Bois de Boulogne near Paris. The butter sauce was spooned on the plate and the baby vegetables were arranged attractively on top. In this version each type of vegetable is cooked separately so it retains its own flavour and cooks evenly. Other miniature vegetables such as baby sweetcorn or tiny artichokes can also be included.   MAKES 4 APPETIZER SERVINGS

HERB BUTTER SAUCE

2 large shallots, finely chopped
2 tablespoons tarragon vinegar or white wine vinegar
3 tablespoons dry white wine
2 tablespoons double cream
Salt and freshly ground white pepper

225 g/8 oz cold unsalted butter, cut into 16 pieces
1 tablespoon snipped chives
1 tablespoon chopped tarragon
1 tablespoon chopped chervil or parsley

BABY VEGETABLES

8 baby beetroot (about 2·5 cm/ 1 inch or less in diameter)
12 baby carrots with about 1 cm/½ inch green tops

8 baby turnips with green tops
16 baby courgettes
4 cherry tomatoes

HERB BUTTER SAUCE
In a small heavy non-aluminium saucepan, simmer shallots in vinegar and wine over medium heat until liquid is reduced to about 2 tablespoons. Reduce heat, stir in cream, and simmer, whisking occasionally, until mixture is reduced to about 3 tablespoons. Season lightly with salt and white pepper. (The mixture can be kept, covered, for 1 hour at room temperature.) Keep butter and herbs in refrigerator until ready to use.

BABY VEGETABLES
Rinse beetroot. Put 2·5 cm/1 inch of water in a steamer and bring to a boil. Place beetroot in steamer rack or in another rack or metal colander above boiling water. Cover tightly and steam for about 15 to 20 minutes, or until just tender. Let cool slightly and slip off skins. Put in a warm bowl, cover, and keep warm.

Put carrots in a small saucepan and add water to cover and a pinch of salt. Bring to a boil, reduce heat to low, cover, and simmer for about 10 minutes, or until just tender when pierced with a knife. Drain, cover, and keep warm.

Put turnips in small saucepan and add water to cover and a pinch of salt. Bring to a boil, reduce heat to low, cover, and simmer for about 5 minutes, or until just tender when pierced with a knife. Drain thoroughly. Add to carrots and keep warm.

Add courgettes to a medium-size saucepan of boiling salted water and boil for 2 to 5 minutes, or until just tender when pierced with a knife. Drain thoroughly and add to carrots and turnips.

Put cherry tomatoes in a small saucepan of boiling water, return to a boil, and drain, rinse, and peel. Add to pan of carrots, turnips, and courgettes. Cover and keep warm.

To Finish Sauce:
Bring shallot mixture to simmer in its saucepan.

Over low heat, add one piece of butter, stirring liquid constantly with a whisk. When butter piece is nearly blended in, add another piece, still whisking. Continue adding pieces one or two at a time, whisking constantly. The sauce should be pleasantly warm to touch. If it becomes too hot and drops of melted butter appear, immediately remove pan from heat and whisk well; add next butter pieces off heat, whisking constantly. When temperature of sauce drops again to warm, return to low heat to continue adding remaining butter pieces. Remove from heat as soon as last piece is added. Strain sauce into a bowl. Stir in herbs. Taste and adjust seasoning.

Serve sauce as soon as possible. (It can be kept warm for about 15 minutes in its saucepan set on a rack above warm water, but it must be whisked frequently to prevent separation.)

To serve, spoon about 3 tablespoons Herb Butter Sauce on to each of 4 small plates. Arrange vegetables on plates, dividing them evenly and making sure not to add any liquid that may have accumulated as they were waiting to be served. Serve any remaining sauce separately.

CAULIFLOWER IN ROSEMARY-SCENTED TOMATO SAUCE
Chou-fleur en sauce tomate au romarin

A single sprig of rosemary adds a distinctive aroma to this dish. Pair it with roast chicken or meat, or with poached, baked, or hard-boiled eggs.   MAKES 4 TO 6 SERVINGS

1 sprig fresh rosemary	1 large garlic clove, finely chopped
1 sprig fresh thyme, or ¼ teaspoon dried thyme	1·25 kg/2½ lb ripe tomatoes, peeled, seeded, and chopped
1 bay leaf	Salt and freshly ground pepper
2 tablespoons olive or vegetable oil	1 large cauliflower, divided into medium-size florets
½ onion, chopped	

Wrap rosemary, thyme, and bay leaf in a piece of cheesecloth and tie tightly to make a bouquet garni. In a large saucepan, heat oil over low heat, add onion, and cook, stirring occasionally, until soft but not browned. Add garlic, tomatoes, bouquet garni, and salt and pepper to taste. Cook over medium heat, stirring often, for about 20 minutes, or until tomatoes are soft and mixture is thick and smooth. Discard bouquet garni. Taste and adjust seasoning. (The sauce can be prepared 2 days in advance and kept in refrigerator. Reheat before continuing.)

In a large pan of boiling salted water, cook cauliflower florets, uncovered, over high heat for about 3 to 4 minutes, or until nearly tender. Rinse with cold water and drain thoroughly.

Add cauliflower to tomato sauce, cover, and simmer, gently

turning florets over occasionally, for about 2 minutes, or until they are tender. Taste and adjust seasoning. Serve hot or at room temperature.

FRENCH CURRIED CAULIFLOWER
Chou-fleur au curry

Curry is associated with Indian cooking, but French cooks like to use this spice mixture as well, although with a light hand. Fresh coriander is new to French cooking and this is due to the influence of Moroccan food and the many couscous restaurants in France.

MAKES ABOUT 4 SERVINGS

1 medium-size cauliflower, divided
*   into medium-size florets*
15 g/½ oz butter
25 g/1 oz finely chopped onion
1 teaspoon curry powder
3 tablespoons dry white wine

2 tablespoons water
Salt and freshly ground pepper
225 ml/8 fl oz double cream
2 teaspoons chopped coriander or
*   parsley (optional)*

In a large pan of boiling salted water, cook cauliflower, uncovered, over high heat for about 4 or 5 minutes, or until just tender. Drain, rinse with cold water, and drain thoroughly.

In a heavy sauté pan or deep frying pan, heat butter over low heat, add onion, and cook until soft but not browned. Stir in curry powder and cook, stirring, for about 30 seconds. Add wine, water, a pinch of salt and pepper, and simmer over medium heat until liquid is reduced to about 2 tablespoons.

Add cream and bring to a boil. Add cauliflower and simmer, uncovered, over medium heat, stirring and spooning sauce over it, for about 2 minutes, or until tender. Transfer cauliflower to a shallow serving dish, using slotted spoon.

Continue to cook sauce over medium heat, stirring often, for 3 minutes, or until reduced slightly and thick enough to coat a spoon.

Taste and adjust seasoning. Spoon over cauliflower. Sprinkle with coriander or parsley, if desired. Serve hot or at room temperature.

BROCCOLI WITH ROQUEFORT SAUCE
Brocolis au roquefort

Serve this flavourful combination with simply cooked chicken, veal or beef, or with rice or pasta. It makes a great brunch dish when topped with poached eggs.　　　　MAKES ABOUT 4 SERVINGS

15 g/½ oz unsalted butter
2 shallots, finely chopped
6 tablespoons dry white wine
225 ml/8 fl oz double cream
50 g/2 oz crumbled Roquefort
　cheese

Pepper
Pinch of salt (optional)
1 kg/2 lb broccoli, divided into
　fairly large florets with about
　4 cm/1½ inches of stalk

In a heavy medium-size saucepan, melt butter over low heat, add shallots, and cook, stirring, for about 2 minutes, until softened. Add wine and boil, stirring often, until only about 2 tablespoons liquid remain. Stir in cream and cook over medium heat, stirring often, until sauce is thick enough to coat a spoon; about 7 minutes. Reduce heat to low, add Roquefort cheese, and simmer, whisking, just until sauce is smooth. Add pepper to taste; salt may not be needed because Roquefort cheese is salty.

In a large saucepan of boiling salted water, cook broccoli florets, uncovered, for about 7 minutes, or until just tender. Drain thoroughly in colander. Arrange on a platter with florets pointing outward from centre. Reheat sauce if necessary. Spoon a little sauce over broccoli stems. Serve remaining sauce separately.

COURGETTES WITH CAPERS AND HAZELNUT BUTTER
Courgettes au beurre noisette

Hazelnut butter is not made of hazelnuts but rather refers to the aroma of the heated butter, which resembles that of toasted hazelnuts. It goes well with courgettes and is also delicious with cauliflower and broccoli.   MAKES 4 SERVINGS

4 small courgettes (about 450 g/ 1 lb)	*4 teaspoons capers, well drained*
	2 tablespoons chopped fresh parsley
Salt and freshly ground pepper	*75 g/3 oz unsalted butter*

Cut courgettes in 5-cm/2-inch chunks. Cut each chunk in lengthwise slices about 8 mm/⅜ inch thick and each slice in sticks about 8 mm/⅜ inch thick.

Add sticks to a large saucepan containing enough boiling salted water to generously cover. Cook over high heat for about 2 minutes, or until barely tender. Do not overcook or they will be mushy. Drain very thoroughly and transfer to a shallow heatproof serving dish. Sprinkle lightly with salt and pepper, toss gently, and sprinkle with capers and parsley.

In a small heavy saucepan, cook butter over medium heat, shaking pan occasionally, until butter is light brown and has a nutty aroma. Pour evenly over courgettes and serve immediately.

LYONNAISE GREEN BEANS
Haricots verts à la lyonnaise

Like many dishes from Lyon these green beans are flavoured with sautéed onions. Cooked dried white beans can also be seasoned in this way.   MAKES 4 TO 6 SERVINGS

50 g/2 oz butter
1 onion, halved and thinly sliced
700 g/1½ lb young green beans,
   trimmed and broken in half

Salt and freshly ground pepper
2 tablespoons chopped fresh parsley
2 tablespoons white wine vinegar

In a medium-size frying pan or sauté pan, melt butter over low heat, add onion, and cook, stirring, until softened and just beginning to turn golden.

Meanwhile, in a large pan of boiling salted water, cook green beans, uncovered, over high heat for about 8 minutes, or until just tender. Drain thoroughly and add to pan. Over very low heat, toss beans lightly with onions and season to taste with salt and pepper. Transfer to a serving dish and sprinkle with parsley.

Add vinegar to hot pan and bring to a simmer. Immediately pour over beans, toss well, and serve.

GREEN BEANS WITH DELICATE GARLIC BUTTER
Haricots verts au beurre gascon

Serve these beans with poached or grilled fish or with rice. The garlic becomes surprisingly mild after being simmered. The garlic butter is also good with other vegetables, especially grilled mushrooms, courgettes, and poached dried beans.   MAKES 4 SERVINGS

6 large garlic cloves, unpeeled
75 g/3 oz unsalted butter, softened
Salt and freshly ground pepper

700 g/1½ lb young green beans,
   trimmed and broken in half, or
   haricots verts (thin French
   beans), trimmed

Add garlic cloves to a small pan of boiling water and simmer over low heat for about 10 minutes, or until very tender. Peel garlic, put in a bowl, and mash pulp with a fork. The garlic should not be in large pieces but there is no need for it to be completely smooth. Add butter and salt and pepper to taste and mash together until well mixed.

In a large pan of boiling salted water, cook the beans, uncovered, over high heat for about 7 minutes, or until just tender; if using thin French beans, cooking time will be about 4 minutes. Drain thoroughly and return to pan. Add garlic butter and toss lightly over very low heat just until it coats beans but does not melt completely. If beans are very hot, they can be tossed with butter off heat. Taste and adjust seasoning and serve immediately.

FRENCH/YELLOW BEANS WITH PESTO SAUCE
Haricots beurre au pistou

Although French pistou, like Italian pesto, is best known as a zesty flavouring for soup or pasta, it is also wonderful with vegetables. Try it with cauliflower, too.   MAKES 4 TO 6 SERVINGS

3 large garlic cloves
25 g/1 oz fresh basil (about 1 bunch)
50 g/2 oz freshly grated Parmesan cheese
4 tablespoons extra virgin olive oil

700 g/1½ lb yellow or green French beans, trimmed and broken in half
Salt and freshly ground pepper

Chop garlic in a food processor. Discard basil stems. Add basil leaves and cheese and purée until basil is chopped. Gradually add olive oil, with motor running. Scrape down sides and purée again so mixture is well blended. Transfer to a bowl.

In a large pan of boiling salted water, cook beans, uncovered, over high heat for about 8 minutes, or until just tender. Drain thoroughly, reserving 2 tablespoons cooking liquid, and transfer to a serving dish.

Whisk reserved hot cooking liquid into basil sauce and add to beans. Toss until well combined. Add salt and pepper and taste and adjust seasoning. Serve immediately.

BRUSSELS SPROUTS WITH CREAMY
MUSTARD-SAGE SAUCE
Choux de bruxelles, sauce moutarde à la sauge

Brussels sprouts are pretty and delicious when fresh and not over-cooked. To cut down on cooking time and to keep their colour bright green, these Brussels sprouts are cut in half before being boiled. Serve them as a starter or alongside roast chicken or meat.

MAKES 4 SERVINGS

15 g/½ oz butter
½ medium-size onion, finely
    chopped
2 tablespoons white wine vinegar
3 tablespoons water
1 tablespoon chopped fresh sage, or
    1 teaspoon dried sage

Salt and freshly ground pepper
225 ml/8 fl oz double cream
350 g/12 oz small Brussels sprouts
4 teaspoons Dijon mustard

In medium-size heavy saucepan, melt butter over low heat, add onion, and cook, stirring often, for about 5 minutes, or until soft but not brown. Blend in vinegar, water, sage, and small pinch of salt. Increase heat to medium and boil, stirring often, until liquid is reduced to about 2 tablespoons. Stir in cream. Cook, stirring often, until sauce is slightly reduced and thick enough to coat back of spoon; about 7 minutes. (Sauce mixture can be kept, covered, for 2 days in refrigerator.)

Trim Brussels sprouts, removing tough bases and any yellow leaves. Cut sprouts in half lengthwise. In a large pan of boiling salted water, cook sprouts, uncovered, over high heat for about 7 minutes, or until just tender but still bright green. Drain thoroughly.

While sprouts cook, reheat sauce, if necessary, over medium heat, whisking. Reduce heat to low, and whisk in mustard and a pinch of pepper. Taste and adjust seasoning.

To serve, spoon sauce on to plates and set Brussels sprouts on top, alternating some cut side up, some cut side down.

CABBAGE WITH BUTTER AND WINE VINEGAR
La chouée

This bright green, slightly crisp cabbage dish, which originated in the Loire Valley in central France, can be served with almost any poultry, meat, or even seafood.   MAKES 4 SERVINGS

1 small green cabbage (about   *50 g/2 oz butter*
*   700 g/1½ lb)*   *Salt and freshly ground pepper*
4 teaspoons white wine vinegar

Cut cabbage in half, core it, and rinse thoroughly. Cut in thin strips. In a large saucepan of boiling salted water, cook cabbage for 5 minutes, or until just tender. Rinse under cold running water and drain thoroughly. Gently squeeze dry in a colander.

In a large frying pan, heat cabbage with vinegar, half the butter, and salt and pepper to taste over medium heat, stirring, for 3 minutes, or until butter and vinegar are absorbed. Remove from heat. Stir in remaining butter and taste for seasoning.

ARTICHOKES WITH TOMATO BÉARNAISE SAUCE
Artichauts, sauce choron

Artichokes are considered a noble vegetable and are served with hollandaise and other fine sauces. Students in my California cooking classes love this elegant first course, in which the artichokes are accompanied by the zesty, colourful tomato béarnaise.

MAKES 6 SERVINGS

6 medium-size artichokes, or 12
   small artichokes
175 g/6 oz unsalted butter
2 tablespoons white wine vinegar
3 tablespoons dry white wine
½ teaspoon coarsely cracked
   peppercorns
2 shallots, chopped
3 fresh tarragon stems (without
   leaves), chopped

3 egg yolks
Salt
3 tablespoons Fresh Tomato Sauce
   (page 38), or 1 tablespoon
   tomato paste
Pinch of white pepper or cayenne
   pepper
1 tablespoon chopped fresh
   tarragon
1 tablespoon chopped fresh parsley

To trim artichokes, cut off top 2·5 cm/1 inch of large artichokes or 1 cm/½ inch of small ones. Trim spikes from tips of leaves with scissors. Put artichokes in a large saucepan of boiling salted water and cover with a lid of slightly smaller diameter than that of pan to keep them submerged. Cook over medium heat until a leaf can be easily pulled out; large artichokes will require about 45 to 50 minutes and small ones about 15 to 20 minutes. Using tongs, remove artichokes from water, turn them upside down, and drain thoroughly. Cover to keep warm.

To clarify butter, melt in a small heavy saucepan over low heat. Skim white foam from surface. Pour remaining clear butter into a bowl, leaving white sediment behind in saucepan. Let cool to lukewarm.

In a small heavy-bottomed non-aluminium saucepan, combine vinegar, wine, peppercorns, shallots, and tarragon stems. Simmer until only about 2 tablespoons liquid remain. Strain, pressing hard on shallots. Return liquid to saucepan and let cool to room temperature.

With a whisk, stir egg yolks and a pinch of salt into liquid. Set pan over low heat and cook, whisking vigorously and constantly, until mixture is creamy and thick enough so whisk leaves a clear trail on base of pan. Remove pan occasionally from heat; it should not become so hot that you can't touch the sides with your hands. Be careful not to let mixture become too hot or egg yolks will curdle. When yolk mixture becomes thick enough, remove it immediately from heat. Continue to whisk for about 30 seconds.

Gradually whisk in clarified butter, drop by drop. After sauce has absorbed about 2 or 3 tablespoons butter, add remaining butter in a very thin stream, whisking vigorously and constantly. (If sauce separates while you are adding butter, whisk 1 tablespoon of sauce with 1 tablespoon cold water in a bowl. Gradually whisk remaining sauce into mixture. If this doesn't work, start again by whisking 1 egg yolk and 1 tablespoon water in a small heavy-bottomed saucepan over low heat as above; then gradually whisk in separated sauce, in same manner as clarified butter was whisked in.)

If using Fresh Tomato Sauce, purée it in a food processor until it is smooth. Stir tomato sauce or tomato paste into sauce. Add a pinch of pepper and chopped tarragon and parsley. Taste and adjust seasoning. Serve as soon as possible. (Sauce can be kept warm for about 15 minutes in its bowl set on a rack above warm water, but it must be stirred frequently. It can also be kept warm in a vacuum flask.)

If sauce is too thick, stir in 1 to 2 teaspoons water. Serve in sauceboat. Use for dipping artichoke leaves and heart.

MORELS WITH CREAM
Morilles à la crème

One of the best of culinary preparations, morels in cream are served as a festive side dish with chicken or poached eggs, or as a first course inside artichoke hearts, tartlet cases, or puff pastry cases.

MAKES ABOUT 4 SERVINGS

175 to 225 g/6 to 8 oz fresh morels, or 40 g/1½ oz dried morels
1 tablespoon butter
2 medium shallots, finely chopped
6 tablespoons dry white wine

6 tablespoons Chicken Stock (page 333) or Vegetable Stock (page 332)
Salt and freshly ground pepper
350 ml/12 fl oz double cream
1 tablespoon chopped parsley (optional)

If using fresh morels, rinse thoroughly in several changes of water and brush to remove all the dirt that may be in the crevices.

Soak dried morels in hot water to cover for about 30 minutes or until soft. Rinse and drain well. Cut in half or slice any large morels.

In a medium-size saucepan, melt butter over low heat, add shallots, and cook for about 2 minutes, or until they soften. Add fresh morels (but not dried ones) and sauté over medium heat for about 5 minutes, or until tender. Pour in wine and bring it to a boil, stirring. Add stock, dried morels, and salt and pepper; bring to a boil. Reduce heat to medium and simmer until liquid is reduced to about 200 ml/7 fl oz. Stir in cream and bring mixture to a boil. Reduce heat to medium and simmer, stirring occasionally, for 7 minutes, or until cream mixture is thick enough to coat a spoon. Taste and adjust seasoning. (The morels can be kept, covered, for 1 day in refrigerator.)

Serve hot. Sprinkle with chopped parsley, if desired.

WHITE BEANS WITH TOMATOES AND ONIONS
Haricots à la bretonne

This dish from Brittany is a favourite with grilled and roast meats and with eggs. It is sometimes flavoured with diced bacon and can also be prepared with flageolets (light green French dried beans) instead of white beans.   MAKES 6 SERVINGS

450 g/1 lb dried white (haricot) beans
1 celery stick
1 medium-size carrot, peeled
1 medium-size onion, peeled
2 whole cloves
4 sprigs fresh thyme, or 1½ teaspoons dried thyme

2 bay leaves
5 parsley stalks
40 g/1½ oz butter
1 large onion, thinly sliced
2 teaspoons finely chopped shallots
3 large garlic cloves, finely chopped
1 kg/2 lb ripe tomatoes, peeled, seeded, and chopped

Salt and freshly ground pepper   *1 tablespoon tomato paste*
                                                   (optional)
                                                1 tablespoon chopped fresh parsley

Soak beans for 8 hours or overnight in cold water to generously cover; drain thoroughly.

Put beans, celery, carrot, and whole onion in a large pot. Wrap cloves, 2 sprigs fresh thyme or ¾ teaspoon dried thyme, 1 bay leaf, and parsley stalks in a piece of cheesecloth and tie tightly to make a bouquet garni; add to pot. Add enough water to cover ingredients generously. Bring to a boil over medium heat and simmer, uncovered, adding hot water occasionally so beans remain covered, for about 45 minutes. Add pinch of salt and pepper and simmer for another 45 minutes, or until tender. Towards end of cooking time bean mixture should be moist but not soupy. Season to taste with salt and pepper. Reserve beans in their liquid. Discard bouquet garni.

Wrap remaining thyme and bay leaf in a piece of cheesecloth and tie tightly to make a bouquet garni. In a large saucepan, melt butter over low heat, add sliced onion, and cook, stirring occasionally, until soft but not browned. Stir in shallots and garlic. Add tomatoes, bouquet garni, and salt and pepper to taste, and bring to a boil. Add 6 tablespoons liquid from beans and return to a boil. Cook over medium heat, stirring often, for about 25 minutes, or until tomatoes are soft and mixture is thick and smooth. Stir in tomato paste, if desired, for brighter colour. Discard bouquet garni.

Drain beans and add to tomatoes. Bring to a simmer and cook, uncovered, for 2 to 3 minutes. Taste and adjust seasoning. (The beans can be prepared 2 days in advance and kept, covered, in refrigerator.) Sprinkle with parsley and serve hot.

BROAD BEANS IN GARLIC CREAM
Fèves à la crème d'ail

Green beans are also good with this sauce, which has a delicate taste of garlic. Savory is a traditional flavouring for broad beans and in France often grows wild alongside them in the fields.

MAKES 4 SERVINGS

1·5 kg/3½ lb fresh broad beans
  (weight with pods)
1 sprig fresh savory, or pinch of
  dried savory (optional)
5 garlic cloves, chopped
1 bay leaf
5 parsley stalks
4 tablespoons dry white wine

1 tablespoon white wine vinegar
300 ml/½ pint double cream
Salt and freshly ground pepper
1 teaspoon chopped fresh savory,
  or ¼ teaspoon dried savory
  (optional)
Pinch of cayenne pepper
1 tablespoon chopped fresh parsley
  (optional)

Pod the beans. Put beans in a large saucepan of boiling salted water, add sprig of savory, and cook, uncovered, over high heat for about 15 to 20 minutes, or until tender; taste a bean to check. Drain thoroughly, reserving 2 tablespoons of cooking liquid and discarding fresh savory. If the beans are old and large, peel off thick skins.

Combine garlic, bay leaf, parsley stalks, wine, vinegar, and 2 tablespoons reserved cooking liquid in a large saucepan. Bring to a boil and simmer, uncovered, until reduced to about 3 tablespoons.

Add cream and a small pinch of salt and pepper. Bring to a simmer and cook over medium heat, stirring often, until sauce is thick enough to coat a spoon; about 9 minutes.

Strain sauce, add chopped savory and a pinch of cayenne pepper. Taste and adjust seasoning.

To reheat, bring sauce nearly to a boil, add beans, and simmer for 1 or 2 minutes.

Taste and adjust seasoning, sprinkle with parsley, and serve.

NOTE: Two 275-g/10-oz packets of frozen broad beans can be substituted for the fresh beans. Cook according to the packet directions, adding the sprig of savory to the water.

NOTE: This is a product of frozen brand, which can be obtained for the first liquid. Cook according to the packet instructions, adding the required water to the water.

BAKED, GRILLED, SAUTÉED, AND FRIED VEGETABLES

Vegetables often associated with Mediterranean cooking, such as courgettes, aubergines, peppers and tomatoes, are most often cooked by baking, grilling, sautéing or frying. These techniques are also ideal for cooking mushrooms, both cultivated and wild, and potatoes (which are discussed in the chapter Potatoes, Rice, and Pasta).

The cooking methods in this chapter are considered 'dry-heat techniques' and are very popular for several reasons: they are quick and easy and, more important, the vegetable keeps in all its flavour rather than losing some to a liquid.

Baked and Grilled Vegetables

In addition to some of the Mediterranean vegetables, root vegetables also benefit from baking, as in Baked Beetroot with Lemon Cream. Some vegetables are precooked in water and then baked, as in Artichokes and Baby Onions Antiboise.

For grilling vegetables any grilling equipment can be used: an outdoor grill or barbecue, a stove-top grill or an oven grill. The most tender vegetables, such as mushrooms, peppers, courgettes, and small aubergines, are best for grilling.

COURGETTE, AUBERGINE, AND TOMATO SLICES BAKED WITH HERBS
Courgettes, aubergines, et tomates aux herbes

This colourful dish is inspired by a creation of Master Chef Fernand Chambrette. He alternated these vegetables with sautéed monkfish slices for a recipe that appeared in *La Cuisine du Poisson*, the fish cookbook we co-authored in France. MAKES 4 SERVINGS

2 medium-size courgettes (about 350 g/12 oz)
2 slender aubergines (about 350 g/12 oz), unpeeled

225 g/8 oz large ripe plum tomatoes or small ripe ordinary tomatoes
About 25 g/1 oz plain flour

6 tablespoons vegetable oil

Salt and freshly ground pepper

65 g/2½ oz butter

1 large garlic clove, finely chopped

2 teaspoons fresh thyme, or ¾ teaspoon dried thyme

1 tablespoon chopped fresh basil

1 tablespoon chopped fresh parsley

Cut courgettes in rounds about 8 mm/⅜ inch thick and aubergines in slices about 6 mm/¼ inch thick. Core tomatoes and cut in rounds about 6 mm/¼ inch thick; discard ends of tomatoes. Poke out seeds and put slices on plate in one layer.

Lightly flour aubergine slices and put in one layer on plate. In a large heavy frying pan, heat 2 tablespoons oil over medium-high heat. Add half the slices and sauté for about 1½ minutes per side, or until lightly browned. Remove with fish slice to a paper towel-lined tray. Add 2 tablespoons oil to pan, heat and sauté remaining slices. Transfer to tray.

Add another tablespoon of oil to pan and heat. Lightly flour courgette pieces, add half of them to pan, and sauté for about 2 minutes per side. Add another tablespoon of oil and sauté second batch.

Preheat oven to 200°C/400°F/gas 6. Sprinkle aubergine, courgette, and tomato slices evenly with salt and pepper on both sides.

Butter a large oval gratin dish or other large shallow baking dish. Alternate aubergine, courgette, and tomato slices in one layer in pan, overlapping slightly. If any slices remain, arrange them in an individual gratin dish. If desired, all vegetables can be arranged in individual gratin dishes.

In a small frying pan, melt butter over low heat, add garlic, and cook for 10 seconds. Remove from heat and stir in thyme, basil, and parsley. Pour butter evenly over vegetables in gratin dish. Bake for about 15 minutes, or until vegetables are tender. Serve hot or warm, from baking dish.

BAKED MUSHROOMS WITH
ESCARGOT BUTTER AND WALNUTS
Champignons au beurre d'escargots aux noix

Escargot butter is the irresistible garlic and parsley butter that is by far the most popular accompaniment for *escargots*, or snails. Actually, many people admit that this butter is the main reason they like snails. Whether or not you like snails, you will find that this flavoured butter is wonderful with mushrooms.   MAKES 6 SERVINGS

18 medium-size mushrooms   1 small shallot, finely chopped
   (about 350 g/12 oz)   2 medium-size garlic cloves, finely
2 tablespoons walnut pieces   chopped
3 tablespoons small parsley sprigs   75 g/3 oz butter, softened
   (without large stems)   Salt and freshly ground pepper

Preheat oven to 220°C/425°F/gas 7. Remove mushroom stems and discard.

Grind walnuts in a food processor until fine and remove. Add parsley sprigs and chop finely. Combine walnuts, parsley, shallot, garlic, and butter in processor and process until well blended. (To prepare by hand: Chop walnuts and parsley as fine as possible. Combine with shallot, garlic, and butter and beat with wooden spoon until well blended.) Season to taste with salt and pepper.

Arrange mushrooms in a lightly buttered shallow baking dish. Sprinkle them with salt. Spoon 1 to 1½ teaspoons flavoured butter into each one – enough to fill it to top. Spread filling smooth. (If there is extra flavoured butter, freeze it and serve it on other cooked vegetables, rice, or pasta.)

Bake for about 12 minutes, or until mushrooms are just tender when pierced with a small knife and butter begins to bubble. Serve immediately.

ARTICHOKES AND BABY ONIONS ANTIBOISE
Fonds d'artichauts à l'antiboise

In this dish, named for the French Riviera town of Antibes, artichoke hearts and small onions are baked briefly in fresh tomato sauce.   MAKES 4 SERVINGS

1 lemon	Salt and freshly ground pepper
4 artichokes	2 medium-size garlic cloves, finely
2 tablespoons olive oil	chopped
1 kg/2 lb ripe tomatoes, peeled,	100 g/4 oz button onions
seeded, and finely chopped	1 tablespoon unseasoned bread
1 teaspoon chopped fresh thyme or	crumbs
oregano, or ¼ teaspoon dried	
thyme or oregano	

Prepare artichoke hearts according to directions on page 159.

Squeeze any juice remaining in lemon into medium-size saucepan of boiling salted water, add artichoke hearts, cover, and simmer over low heat for about 15 minutes, or until tender when pierced with a knife. Cool to lukewarm in liquid. Using a teaspoon, scoop out choke from centre of each artichoke heart. Return artichokes to liquid until ready to use. Cut each artichoke into 4 pieces.

Preheat oven to 200°C/400°F/gas 6. In a frying pan, heat 1 tablespoon olive oil over medium-high heat, add tomatoes, thyme or oregano, and salt and pepper to taste. Cook, stirring often, for about 15 minutes, or until tomatoes are tender and liquid that comes out of them has evaporated. Stir in garlic and simmer for 30 seconds. Taste and adjust seasoning.

Put onions in a medium-size saucepan, cover with water, and bring to a boil. Cook for 1 minute. Rinse under cold water and drain well. Peel, return to saucepan, and add water to cover and a pinch of salt. Bring to a boil and simmer over medium heat for about 10 to 15 minutes, or until tender when pierced with a knife. Drain thoroughly.

Transfer artichokes and onions to a baking dish. Spoon tomato mixture over them. (Vegetables can be kept, covered, for up to 1 day in refrigerator.)

Sprinkle top with bread crumbs, then with remaining tablespoon olive oil. Bake for about 10 minutes, or until bubbling. Brown under grill about 1 minute.

BAKED ONIONS WITH DILL BUTTER
Oignons au four, beurre d'aneth

Onions should be baked until they are meltingly tender inside. Baked onions are also good simply served with butter, salt and pepper.   MAKES 4 SERVINGS

4 medium-size onions, with skins
intact (about 1 kg/2 lb)
About 225 ml/8 fl oz water
75 g/3 oz unsalted butter, at room
temperature, cut in pieces

3 tablespoons snipped fresh dill
Salt and freshly ground pepper

Preheat oven to 200°C/400°F/gas 6. Cut off root end of onions so they will stand up. Prick skins a few times with a fork. Oil a gratin dish or other heavy baking dish just large enough to hold onions. Add 4 tablespoons water to dish. Put onions in dish and bake, adding more water, about 4 tablespoons at a time, when dish gets dry; about 1¾ hours, or until tender when squeezed and knife can pierce them easily.

Meanwhile, in small bowl cream butter with a wooden spoon until softened. Stir in dill and add salt and pepper to taste.

To serve, peel onions and cut in half. Spoon some dill butter over each one. Serve remaining dill butter separately.

PROVENÇAL BAKED TOMATOES
Tomates à la provençale

This well-known dish is prepared by a combination of sautéing and baking and, for best flavour, should be made when tomatoes are at the height of their season. It is wonderful with grilled fish or meat and with eggs. The garlic flavour is quite strong; if you would like a more delicate taste, use only two cloves.   MAKES 4 SERVINGS

4 medium-size tomatoes, ripe but
    not too soft (about 700 g/
    1½ lb)
3 medium-size garlic cloves, very
    finely chopped
3 tablespoons chopped fresh parsley
2 tablespoons unseasoned bread
    crumbs
Salt and freshly ground pepper
4 tablespoons olive oil

Preheat oven to 220°C/425°F/gas 7. Make a shallow cut to remove green top of core of tomatoes, then cut in half horizontally. Squeeze each half gently to remove seeds and pat dry. Lightly oil a gratin dish or other baking dish in which tomato halves can fit in single layer. In a small bowl, mix garlic, parsley, bread crumbs, and a pinch of salt and pepper.

Heat 2 tablespoons olive oil in a medium-size heavy frying pan over medium-high heat. Sprinkle 4 tomato halves lightly with salt and pepper. Put them, cut side down, in hot oil. Be very careful because oil splatters. Cook for 3 minutes. Turn over and cook for 1 minute. Transfer carefully with fish slice to prepared baking dish and place them cut side up. Repeat with remaining tomato halves.

Spoon garlic mixture over tomatoes and into their cavities. Sprinkle with remaining 2 tablespoons oil. Bake for about 15 minutes, or until tender. Serve hot, warm, or at room temperature.

BAKED BEETROOT WITH LEMON CREAM
Betteraves au four à la crème de citron

Baking beetroot is one of the best ways to keep in the flavour. In France beetroot are usually purchased at the market already baked. Vendors pick them up with a fork and wrap them carefully to avoid stains. In Britain they are often sold ready-boiled, but you may find them over-done. MAKES 4 SERVINGS

8 baby beetroot, about 4 cm/1½
    inches in diameter

LEMON CREAM

15 g/½ oz butter
1 shallot, finely chopped
3 tablespoons dry white wine
225 ml/8 fl oz double cream
4 teaspoons grated or finely
    chopped lemon peel

2½ teaspoons strained fresh lemon
    juice
Salt and freshly ground white
    pepper

A few thin strips lemon peel,
    removed with lemon zester, for
    garnish

Preheat oven to 170°C/325°F/gas 3. Rinse beetroot and trim roots and tops, leaving beetroot whole and skin intact. Put in a gratin dish or other heavy shallow baking dish, cover tightly with foil, and bake for 1½ hours, or until they are tender when pierced with a knife.

LEMON CREAM
In a small saucepan, melt butter over low heat, add shallot, and cook for about 2 minutes. Stir in wine and cook until liquid is reduced to about 2 tablespoons. Stir in cream, bring to a boil, and cook, stirring, over medium heat until sauce is thick enough to coat a spoon. Just before serving, add lemon peel and juice and salt and pepper to taste.

To serve, peel beetroot, spoon Lemon Cream over each, and sprinkle with a little shredded lemon peel.

This dish is also delicious cold. If the chilled sauce is too thick, stir in a few teaspoons cream.

GRILLED PEPPERS WITH GARLIC AND OLIVE OIL
Poivrons grillés à l'ail et à l'huile d'olive

These Provençal peppers are wonderful as a first course with French or Italian bread or as a side dish with grilled chicken.

MAKES 4 SERVINGS

2 medium-size red peppers
2 medium-size green peppers
6 tablespoons extra virgin olive oil
1 to 2 teaspoons strained fresh
* lemon juice*

Salt and freshly ground pepper
4 large garlic cloves, cut into
* quarters.*

Preheat grill. Grill peppers about 5 cm/2 inches from heat source until blistered and charred, turning often, for a total of about 15 to 20 minutes. Transfer to plastic bag and close bag. Let stand for 10 minutes. Peel, cut into quarters, and remove cores. Drain well in colander and pat dry.

Put peppers in shallow serving dish. Whisk olive oil with lemon juice and salt and pepper to taste. Sprinkle peppers with olive oil mixture and garlic. Let stand at room temperature, turning occasionally, for at least 2 hours; or refrigerate overnight. Remove garlic and serve at room temperature.

GRILLED AUBERGINE WITH FRESH HERBS
Aubergines grillées aux herbes

Aubergine is sometimes salted to remove any bitter juices. But if it is fresh the salting process can be omitted; just season lightly with salt before grilling. This dish is best at room temperature. If desired, garnish it with strips of grilled red or green pepper.

MAKES 4 SERVINGS

1 medium-size aubergine (about 600 g/1¼ lb), unpeeled
1½ teaspoons salt
About 3 tablespoons olive oil, for brushing
2 medium-size garlic cloves, finely chopped

2 tablespoons chopped parsley
2 tablespoons coarsely chopped basil
5 tablespoons olive oil, for sprinkling
Freshly ground pepper
Fresh basil leaves, for garnish (optional)

Cut aubergine in 8-mm/⅜-inch slices crosswise, discarding ends. Arrange slices in one layer on a rack set over a tray. Sprinkle them evenly with about ¾ teaspoon salt, turn them over, and sprinkle second side evenly with remaining salt. Let slices drain for 1 hour, turning them over after 30 minutes. Pat them dry very thoroughly with several changes of paper towels.

Preheat grill with rack about 5 cm/2 inches from heat source. Brush oil on both sides of 6 aubergine slices or enough to make one layer in grill pan. Grill for 3 minutes on each side, lightly oiling top after turning, or until aubergine is tender when pierced with a fork.

Combine garlic, parsley, and basil in a small bowl or cup. Transfer aubergine slices to a shallow dish, such as a round gratin dish, so that it makes three layers. Sprinkle each layer evenly with about one-third of herb mixture and oil, and with freshly ground pepper to taste. Cover slices and refrigerate for at least 4 hours or overnight, turning them over once. (The slices can be kept for up to 2 days in refrigerator.)

Serve aubergine at room temperature, garnished with basil leaves, and accompanied with fresh bread.

GRILLED MUSHROOMS WITH GARLIC PURÉE
Champignons grillés à la purée d'ail

Mushrooms serve as cups for the flavourful garlic purée, a must for garlic lovers. They are perfect with grilled lamb chops, but are also superb with beef steaks and even grilled fish. For a vegetable feast they can be served with an assortment of stuffed vegetables.

MAKES 4 SERVINGS

2 medium-size whole garlic bulbs	*8 to 12 large mushroom caps*
15 g/½ oz butter	*2 teaspoons vegetable oil*
Salt and freshly ground pepper	*2 teaspoons chopped parsley*
4 tablespoons double cream	

Separate garlic bulbs into cloves and peel them. Put them in a small heavy saucepan of cold water, bring to a boil, and cook for 5 minutes. Drain thoroughly.

In a medium-size heavy saucepan, heat butter over very low heat, add garlic and salt and pepper to taste, and cook, stirring often, for about 20 minutes, or until nearly all moisture evaporates. Be careful not to let garlic burn.

Purée garlic in a food processor or blender, adding a little cream if necessary; or mash it with a fork. Return it to saucepan. (Garlic purée can be kept, covered, for 1 day in refrigerator.)

Preheat grill. Brush mushroom caps with oil and grill, turning often, for about 7 minutes, or until just tender. Sprinkle lightly with salt and pepper.

Just before serving, reheat garlic purée over low heat, stirring.

Gradually stir in 3 or 4 tablespoons cream to taste, and heat just until hot. Season to taste with salt and pepper. Spoon a little purée into each mushroom. Sprinkle each with a small pinch of parsley and serve hot. Serve any remaining garlic purée separately.

Sautéed and Fried Vegetables

Both sautéing and frying are excellent ways of cooking vegetables because the hot oil or butter gives them a delicious rich taste that cannot be achieved by any other method.

Sautéing is one of the simplest cooking techniques and enables the cook to have many vegetables ready in a few minutes. Only a small amount of fat is required, especially if a good-quality heavy pan is used.

Almost any vegetable can be sautéed. Those that are naturally tender, such as peppers, celery, mushrooms and courgettes, can simply be cut in small pieces and sautéed. Others, such as green beans and carrots, are usually precooked in water so that they soften first. Colourful combinations of vegetables can also be sautéed, as in Medley of Vegetables with Fresh Thyme. Sautéing is an ideal method for heating leftover cooked vegetables and rice, because they heat quickly and do not dry out.

French cooks generally sauté vegetables in butter, oil, or a mixture of both. Olive oil is used to give them a Mediterranean flavour.

For sautéing or frying the vegetables should be dry to prevent steam from forming when they are added to the oil. This is first and foremost a matter of safety for the cook, to prevent the hot fat from splattering in contact with moisture. But in addition steam created by this moisture would prevent the food from being sealed by the hot oil and so diminish its flavour. To help ensure a dry surface on the vegetables cooks often dip them in flour or in a coating, as in Batter-Fried Vegetables with Rémoulade Sauce.

Deep-fried vegetables can be light and not greasy if a few simple rules are followed. Pure, clean oil is crucial for crisp, good-tasting fried foods. Plain vegetable oil of a neutral flavour, such as corn, peanut, or soybean oil, can be used, as can solidified vegetable oil. The fat can be saved and used again once or twice, but it should be carefully strained after use and kept in a cool place. If it smokes during cooking, however, it should not be reused.

A deep-fat fryer or a deep heavy saucepan is needed for deep-frying. The pan should be large enough to hold an adequate amount of oil to cover the food generously but at the same time should not be more than half full of oil. It should be very stable so that there is no danger of it tipping over. A slotted spoon or wire skimmer is best for removing the food from the pan. To maintain the fat at the correct temperature a frying thermometer is most efficient. If the fat is too hot, the food may burn before it is cooked inside. On the other hand, if it is not hot enough, the food will absorb too much oil.

Hints

· When sautéing several batches of food, add more oil or butter to the pan between batches, if necessary, so the pan remains coated. Heat the oil before continuing. Sautéed vegetables can be reheated, although they will be less crisp.

· Give your full attention to deep-frying; do not leave in the middle to do something else.

· Do not fill the pan more than half full of oil or fat.

· If vegetables are to be coated before deep-frying they must be completely covered with the coating material so that no moist surfaces are exposed to the hot fat.

· Be extremely careful not to let any water or vegetable juice get into the oil because it will splatter violently.

· Hold the vegetables near the surface of the oil and slide them in gently. Do not drop them in because they will splash hot oil.

· Do not crowd the pan with food because the oil can bubble up to the top and even overflow. Besides, too much food lowers the temperature of the oil.

· Regulate the heat to keep the oil at the required temperature.

· Do not move the deep-fat fryer when the fat in it is hot.

· To remove excess fat drain fried foods on paper towels before serving and pat their top surfaces with paper towels.

MEDLEY OF VEGETABLES WITH FRESH THYME
Meli-melo de légumes au thym frais

Serve this colourful dish of sautéed vegetables alone as a side dish or on a bed of rice as a main dish. The vegetables are finished with a *persillade*, a mixture of sautéed garlic and parsley, which is a favourite French seasoning.   MAKES 4 SERVINGS

2 medium-size leeks (about 450 g/1 lb)
1 medium-size red pepper
2 medium-size celery sticks
2 small courgettes (about 225 g/ 8 oz)
1 medium-size aubergine (about 450 g/1 lb)

7 tablespoons olive oil
Salt and freshly ground pepper
2 tablespoons chopped fresh thyme, or 2 teaspoons dried thyme
5 medium-size garlic cloves, finely chopped
2 tablespoons chopped parsley

Use white and light green parts of leeks only. Cut leeks in half lengthwise and soak in cold water for 15 minutes. Check between layers to be sure no dirt remains and rinse thoroughly. Cut in 5-cm/2-inch pieces, press with hand to flatten, and cut in 6-mm/ ¼-inch lengthwise slices; separate slices into strips if they remain joined at root end.

Cut pepper in half lengthwise, core, and remove ribs. Cut again crosswise and then cut each quarter into strips 6 mm/¼ inch wide. Peel celery to remove strings. Cut into 50 × 6 × 6-mm/2 × ¼ × ¼-inch strips. Cut each courgette in 3 pieces crosswise, then in lengthwise strips about 6 mm/¼ inch wide and thick. Cut peel from aubergine and discard ends. Cut flesh in strips the same size as celery.

In large frying pan, heat 2 tablespoons olive oil over medium heat, add aubergine, and sprinkle with salt. Sauté, tossing constantly; about 7 minutes, or until just tender. Transfer to bowl.

Heat 3 tablespoons olive oil in large frying pan over medium-low heat. Add leeks and cook, stirring often, for 5 minutes. Add red pepper, celery, salt and pepper, and thyme, and cook, tossing often, for about 5 minutes, or until all vegetables are nearly tender. Add courgette and aubergine and cook, tossing often, for about 3 minutes, or until courgette is crisp-tender. Remove vegetables to serving dish and keep warm.

Wipe pan clean. Add remaining 2 tablespoons olive oil and heat over low heat. Add garlic and cook for about 30 seconds, or until barely tender but not brown. Add parsley and heat for 2 or 3 seconds. Pour mixture over vegetables, toss thoroughly, taste and adjust seasoning. Serve immediately.

GREEN BEANS WITH SAUTÉED WALNUTS
Haricots verts aux noix

Sautéed nuts are a quick, easy and wonderful way to add zip to vegetables. In this dish almonds can be substituted for the walnuts.

MAKES 4 TO 6 SERVINGS

700 g/1½ lb young green beans,
   ends removed, broken in half
25 g/1 oz butter

25 g/1 oz walnut pieces
Salt and freshly ground pepper

In a large saucepan of boiling salted water, cook beans, uncovered, over high heat for about 5 minutes or until just tender but still crisp. Drain and rinse under cold water until cool and drain well.

In a large frying pan, melt half the butter over medium-low heat, add nuts, and a pinch of salt, and sauté for about 2 or 3 minutes, or until lightly browned. Remove with slotted spoon.

Raise heat to medium-high and add remaining butter to pan and melt. Add beans, and salt and pepper, and sauté until tender and hot; do not let them brown. Transfer to a serving dish and sprinkle with walnuts.

CARROTS WITH RASPBERRY VINEGAR
Carottes au vinaigre de framboises

Carrots are precooked before being sautéed so they will be uniformly tender. Serve these fruit-scented carrots with poultry or lamb. Raspberry vinegar also makes a tasty vinaigrette for carrot salad.

MAKES 2 SERVINGS

*225 g/8 oz long, slender carrots,
   peeled or scraped
25 g/1 oz unsalted butter
Salt and freshly ground pepper*

*2 tablespoons raspberry vinegar
1 tablespoon chopped parsley
   (optional)*

Cut carrots in eighths lengthwise, then in 8-cm/3-inch pieces. In a medium saucepan of boiling salted water, cook carrots for 4 minutes. Drain thoroughly.

In a large frying pan, melt butter over medium-low heat, add carrots and salt and pepper to taste, and sauté, stirring often; about 4 minutes, or until tender.

In a very small saucepan, heat vinegar to a simmer. Pour over carrots in pan. Boil, tossing, until carrots are coated with vinegar. Taste and adjust seasoning. Transfer to a serving dish, sprinkle with parsley, if desired, and serve.

SAUTÉED JERUSALEM ARTICHOKES
Topinambours sautés

Sautéing is an excellent technique for cooking Jerusalem artichokes because it preserves their crispness. These Jerusalem artichokes make a pleasant accompaniment for roast chicken or grilled meat. For uniform cooking choose Jerusalem artichokes which are of even size and as smooth as possible. MAKES 3 TO 4 SERVINGS

1 tablespoon fresh lemon juice or   40 g/1½ oz unsalted butter
    white wine vinegar   Salt and freshly ground pepper
450 g/1 lb Jerusalem artichokes

Add lemon juice or vinegar to a bowl containing 1 litre/1¾ pints water. Peel Jerusalem artichokes and put each into the bowl of acidulated water. Cut large ones into about 2·5-cm/1-inch chunks, leaving whole those that are 2·5 cm/1 inch in diameter or smaller. Return them to acidulated water until ready to cook. Rinse, drain in a colander, and pat dry with paper towels.

In a medium-size heavy sauté pan, melt butter over medium heat. Add Jerusalem artichokes and a pinch of salt and pepper. Sauté for about 3 minutes, tossing them with a fish slice. Reduce heat to low, cover, and cook, shaking pan often and turning them over occasionally, for about 15 minutes, or until largest pieces are just tender when pierced with a thin-bladed knife. Serve immediately.

RED AND GREEN CABBAGE SAUTÉ
WITH GOAT CHEESE
Sauté de chou rouge et vert au fromage de chèvre

Greek feta cheese or Roquefort can be used instead of the goat cheese in this colourful dish. MAKES 4 SERVINGS

350 g/12 oz green cabbage (½ small head), cored
450 g/1 lb red cabbage (½ medium-size head), cored
5 tablespoons vegetable oil

Salt and freshly ground pepper
2 tablespoons capers, drained well
3 tablespoons white wine vinegar
75 g/3 oz coarsely crumbled goat cheese

Shred each type of cabbage separately; a food processor fitted with a shredding disc makes this easy.

Heat 2 tablespoons oil in a large heavy frying pan over medium heat. Add green cabbage and salt and pepper, and sauté, tossing often, for about 5 minutes, or until barely tender. Remove from heat. Add capers, taste and adjust seasoning. Cover and keep warm.

Meanwhile, heat 3 tablespoons oil in second large heavy frying pan over medium heat. Add red cabbage and sauté, tossing often, for about 5 minutes, or until barely tender. Remove from heat. Bring vinegar to boil in very small saucepan and pour it over sautéed red cabbage; colour will change dramatically. Toss well. Add half the cheese, pepper, and toss again. Taste and adjust seasoning.

Arrange green cabbage in a ring along outer edge of platter. Spoon red cabbage mixture into centre. Make hollow in centre of red cabbage and spoon in remaining cheese. Serve hot or warm. When serving, spoon some of each mixture separately on to plates.

SAUTÉED CUCUMBERS WITH DILL
Concombres sautés à l'aneth

Cucumbers are used in France not only for salads but also as a lightly cooked hot vegetable. These are perfect with grilled or fried fish.

MAKES 4 SERVINGS

1 large cucumber
25 g/1 oz butter

2 tablespoons chopped fresh dill
Salt and freshly ground pepper

Cut cucumber in half lengthwise and remove seeds. Cut in thin slices.

In a large frying pan, melt butter over medium heat, add cucumber slices and sauté, stirring often, for about 2 minutes, or until just tender. Do not overcook or they will be mushy. Remove from heat and stir in dill. Season to taste with salt and pepper. Serve immediately.

GARLIC-SCENTED COURGETTES WITH CELERY
Courgettes et celeris à l'ail

Courgettes and celery cook very quickly and are ideal for sautéing. Serve this dish with dishes such as sautéed seafood, roast chicken or grilled meat. For a vegetable dish with a more exotic character substitute fresh coriander for the parsley.   MAKES 4 SERVINGS

4 small courgettes (about 450 g/ 1 lb)
3 celery sticks, peeled
1 tablespoon vegetable oil
2 tablespoons olive oil
Salt and freshly ground pepper
1 large garlic clove, very finely chopped
2 tablespoons chopped parsley

Cut courgettes in 4-cm/1½-inch chunks. Cut each chunk in lengthwise slices about 6 mm/¼ inch thick and each slice in sticks about the same width. Cut peeled celery in very thin strips, about the same length but a bit thinner than the courgette sticks.

In a large frying pan, heat both types of oil over medium-high heat, add celery, and sauté for about 2 minutes. Add courgette sticks and pinch of salt and pepper and sauté, tossing often, for about 2 minutes, or until nearly tender.

Reduce heat to medium, add garlic and parsley, and sauté for 1 minute. Taste and adjust seasoning. Serve immediately.

SAUTÉED SALSIFY WITH FRESH HERBS
Salsifis sautés aux fines herbes

Salsify, or oyster plant, is popular in France because of its delicate flavour, which slightly resembles that of asparagus. This long root vegetable is not easy to find in Britain but it is worth tasting if you happen to see it. Sautéing with herbs is a favourite way of preparing salsify in France, but it is also made into gratins and beignets.

MAKES 4 SERVINGS

600 g/1¼ lb salsify
3 tablespoons white vinegar
50 g/2 oz butter
Salt and freshly ground pepper

1 tablespoon chopped parsley
2 teaspoons chopped tarragon
1 teaspoon snipped chives

Rinse salsify. Prepare a bowl of cold water and add 2 tablespoons white vinegar. Put a salsify on a cutting board. Holding one end, peel it thoroughly and immediately put it in the bowl of acidulated water to prevent it from discolouring. Continue with remaining salsify.

Bring a large saucepan of water to a boil, add salt and 1 tablespoon vinegar. Cut salsify in 8-cm/3-inch pieces and add to water. Cook over high heat for about 10 minutes, or until tender when pierced with a knife. Drain thoroughly.

In a large frying pan, melt butter over medium heat, add salsify, and sauté, tossing or turning often, until very lightly browned. Sprinkle it with salt and pepper and add parsley, tarragon, and chives. Toss for a few seconds and remove from heat. Taste and adjust seasoning and serve hot.

SPINACH, LEEK, AND PUMPKIN PANCAKES
Petites crêpes de légumes

The three vegetables combine to become colourful pancakes which make a delicious main course for lunch or brunch or a side dish to accompany roast chicken, veal or lamb.

MAKES 4 TO 6 SERVINGS, 22 TO 24 SMALL PANCAKES

225- to 275-g/8- to 10-oz piece of pumpkin
350 g/12 oz fresh spinach (leaves with stems)
2 large leeks (about 450 g/1 lb)

5 tablespoons vegetable oil
Salt and freshly ground pepper
70 g/2½ oz plain flour
2 eggs
¼ teaspoon salt
Freshly grated nutmeg

Cut pumpkin in 2 or 3 pieces. Put in a medium saucepan with enough salted water to cover. Bring to a boil, cover, reduce heat to low, and simmer for about 15 minutes, or until tender. Drain thoroughly and cut off peel. Cut in pieces and mash with a fork. Press gently in a strainer to remove excess liquid. Transfer to a bowl.

Remove spinach stems and wash leaves thoroughly. In a large pan of boiling salted water, cook spinach, uncovered, over high heat for about 3 minutes, or until tender. Rinse under cold water. Squeeze spinach to remove excess liquid. Chop finely and transfer to bowl of pumpkin.

Discard dark green leaves and roots of leeks. Split twice lengthwise and dip several times in cold water until no dirt remains between layers. Cut in thin slices crosswise. In a large heavy saucepan, heat 1 tablespoon oil over low heat, add leeks, and sprinkle with salt and pepper. Cover and cook, stirring occasionally, for 5 minutes, or until tender. Transfer to bowl of vegetables.

In a medium-size bowl, mix flour, eggs, ¼ teaspoon salt, and pepper and nutmeg to taste to make a very thick batter. Add batter to bowl of vegetables and mix very well. Taste and adjust seasoning.

Preheat oven to lowest setting. In a large heavy frying pan, heat remaining 4 tablespoons oil over medium heat until hot. Fry vegetable mixture by tablespoonfuls, flattening each after adding it, for about 2 minutes, or until golden brown on each side. Turn very carefully using two fish slices. Transfer to paper towels on an ovenproof tray. Keep warm in oven while frying rest of pancakes.

The pancakes are best if served immediately, but they can be kept warm for about 30 minutes. (They can be kept for 1 day in refrigerator; reheat in 1 layer on paper towels on a baking sheet in a 130°C/250°F/gas ½ oven.)

BATTER-FRIED VEGETABLES WITH RÉMOULADE SAUCE
Fritots de légumes, sauce rémoulade

A variety of vegetables can be dipped in this white wine batter and fried. The cauliflower and Jerusalem artichokes are partially pre-cooked so they will not need much time in the hot oil.

MAKES 4 TO 6 SERVINGS

RÉMOULADE SAUCE

225 ml/8 fl oz Mayonnaise (page 379)

1 tablespoon Dijon mustard or herb mustard

2 tablespoons chopped fresh parsley

2 teaspoons chopped fresh tarragon

1 hard-boiled egg, chopped

1 tablespoon capers, drained, rinsed, and chopped

1 tablespoon chopped pickle

1 teaspoon strained fresh lemon juice (optional)

½ teaspoon anchovy paste (optional)

Salt and freshly ground pepper

125 g/4½ oz plain flour

2 large egg yolks

½ teaspoon salt

Pinch of cayenne pepper

1 tablespoon olive oil

200 ml/7 fl oz dry white wine

225 g/8 oz Jerusalem artichokes,
   scrubbed but not peeled
1 small cauliflower, divided into
   medium-size florets
2 large egg whites, at
   room temperature

Pinch cream of tartar
2 medium-size courgettes, cut in
   6-mm/¼-inch slices

Vegetable oil for deep-frying
   (about 1·25 litres/2¼ pints)

Fresh parsley sprigs, for garnish

RÉMOULADE SAUCE

Mix mayonnaise and mustard in a bowl until thoroughly blended. Stir in parsley, tarragon, egg, capers, and pickle. Taste, and add lemon juice, anchovy paste, and salt and pepper, if needed. (Sauce can be kept, covered, for up to 2 days in refrigerator.)

Review the hints on deep-frying on page 231.

Sift flour into a medium-size bowl and make a well in centre. Into well put egg yolks, salt, cayenne pepper, olive oil, and wine. Using a whisk, stir ingredients together in well and gradually stir in flour until mixture is smooth; do not beat it. Cover and chill for 1 hour.

In a medium-size saucepan, boil 1 litre/1¾ pints water and add salt. Add whole Jerusalem artichokes, cover, and cook for about 10 minutes, or until they are barely tender. Drain them in a colander and pat them dry. Using a sharp knife, scrape off peel. (To save time, they may be left unpeeled.) Using a thin-bladed knife, carefully cut them in 6-mm/¼-inch-wide slices. Use only unbroken slices.

In a large saucepan of boiling salted water to generously cover, cook cauliflower, uncovered, over high heat for about 5 minutes, or until barely tender. Rinse and drain thoroughly.

Bring Rémoulade Sauce to room temperature.

Just before frying, beat egg whites with cream of tartar until they hold fairly stiff peaks. Fold them into batter.

In a deep-fat fryer or a medium-size, deep heavy saucepan, heat oil to 190°C/375°F. Do not fill pan more than half full of fat. Heat oven to lowest setting.

Dip pieces of vegetable in batter, a few at a time, coating them completely and shaking them gently so excess drips off. Carefully lower each coated slice into pan, using your fingertips, tongs, or a fork, being careful not to splash hot fat and not to get your fingers too close to it. Handle coated food as little as possible. Fry pieces in batches, without crowding, for 2 minutes, or until golden on all sides, turning them over with a slotted skimmer. As they are done, transfer to paper towels to drain, keeping them in a single layer. Keep them warm in oven while frying remaining pieces.

Sprinkle fried vegetables with salt. Transfer to a heated platter lined with a napkin, garnish with parsley sprigs, and serve immediately. Serve sauce separately.

POTATOES, RICE, AND PASTA

Because of their neutral flavour potatoes, rice, and pasta are perfect accompaniments for most foods and are so versatile they can be seasoned with almost anything. Although it is difficult to imagine French menus without them, all were once imports to France, potatoes originally coming from the Americas, rice from the Orient, and pasta from Italy.

A French chef, planning a menu around shellfish in a savoury sauce, will frequently choose plainly cooked potatoes, rice pilaf, or pasta as a side dish to go with his creation, so their delicate flavour will harmonize with that of the sauce.

This does not mean that potatoes, rice, and pasta are good only with sauced food. They go well with grilled or roast chicken or meat and fried, sautéed or grilled fish.

The French match a very wide range of ingredients with potatoes, rice, and pasta, including fresh herbs; some spices, especially nutmeg, saffron, and curry; and a great variety of cheeses and nuts.

Cooked vegetables such as peas, diced carrots, courgette strips, diced artichoke hearts, broccoli florets, peeled red and green peppers and sautéed sliced or quartered mushrooms enhance rice and pasta dishes by adding freshness and colour.

Potatoes

Although potatoes are central to French cooking, up until two hundred years ago they were hardly used at all. French food writers are often baffled by the fact that their countrymen refused to eat potatoes when they first appeared in France in the sixteenth century. Parmentier, the scientist credited with popularizing the potato late in the eighteenth century, had to resort to a trick: he positioned guards around his field of potatoes, so that people realized that he had something worth protecting. Gradually potatoes began to appear on French menus. As if to make up for lost time the French developed hundreds of recipes for the vegetable and named many of them for Parmentier to show their gratitude.

Potatoes can be prepared by almost every vegetable cooking technique and can be made into creamy gratins, crisp sautés and even elegant soufflés. Their natural properties make it possible for them to hold together in dishes such as Baked Potato Cakes.

One of the most popular basic ways of preparing potatoes is as purée. Although the procedure is simple, the cooking and seasoning should be done carefully. The owner of the famous La Tour d'Argent restaurant in Paris tested prospective chefs by asking them to prepare potato purée, and some French gastronomes say you can judge the quality of a restaurant by tasting its potato purée.

Potato purée is a versatile basic recipe that can be turned into many more elaborate dishes. Adding choux pastry and frying yields Potatoes Dauphine, those puffy delicate fritters with a light crisp coating. Sprinkling potato purée with grated cheese and browning it in the oven produces a crusty gratin. Enriching potato purée with egg yolks and folding in egg whites gives an elegant soufflé. A delicious purée can also be made from baked potatoes and is used as a base for several dishes, such as Potato and Leek Pancakes.

POTATOES WITH VEGETABLE JULIENNE SAUCE
Pommes de terre à la julienne de légumes

The colourful sauce of carrots, leeks and mushrooms turns simple boiled potatoes into a festive dish.   MAKES 4 TO 6 SERVINGS

1 small or ½ large leek	Salt and freshly ground white
1 carrot, peeled	pepper
½ small celery stick	225 ml/8 fl oz double cream
6 very white large mushroom caps	1 kg/2 lb red-skinned potatoes of
3 tablespoons dry white wine	uniform size
1 tablespoon white wine vinegar	2 teaspoons chopped parsley
1 tablespoon finely chopped	(optional)
shallots	

Trim and discard root and top of leek, leaving white part and about 5 cm/2 inches of deep green. Using sharp knife, slit leek lengthwise, starting from centre and cutting towards green end (leave small section in centre uncut to keep leek in one piece). Rinse leek in cold water, separating pieces to remove all dirt.

Cut leek, carrot, and celery into thin julienne about 4 cm/1½ inches long. Slice mushroom caps crosswise into rounds. Cut rounds into thin strips.

Combine wine, vinegar, and shallots in a medium-size heavy saucepan and bring to a simmer over medium heat. Simmer until reduced to about 2 tablespoons, stirring occasionally to prevent burning. Add mushroom julienne and pinch of salt and pepper, and bring to a boil. Stir in cream, reduce heat to medium, and simmer, stirring occasionally, for about 6 minutes, or until mushrooms are tender and sauce is thick enough to coat back of a spoon lightly. Remove sauce from heat and set aside.

Fill large saucepan with water and bring to boil. Add carrot, leek, and celery and boil for 3 minutes. Drain well. (Sauce and vegetable julienne can be prepared several hours ahead and kept in separate containers in refrigerator.)

Scrub and peel potatoes. Cut in halves or quarters. Put potatoes in large saucepan, cover with water by about 1 cm/½ inch, and add some salt. Bring to boil, cover, reduce heat to low, and simmer for about 18 minutes, or until knife pierces centre of largest potato easily and potato falls from knife when lifted. Do not overcook or potatoes will fall apart. Drain thoroughly.

Just before serving, reheat sauce, stir in vegetable julienne, and bring to simmer. Remove from heat. Taste and adjust seasoning.

Pour sauce over potatoes, sprinkle with parsley, and serve.

NOTE: Potatoes can be peeled a few hours ahead and kept in a bowl of cold water to prevent discoloration.

POTATO AND CHEESE GÂTEAU
Pommes de terre voisin

Parmesan cheese adds a lively flavour to this classic variation of potatoes Anna. Instead of being prepared the traditional way in a frying pan and turned out, this version is baked in a springform pan and browned under the grill and thus is easier to make. The starchiness of the potatoes holds them together in an attractive cake.

MAKES 4 SERVINGS

100 g/4 oz unsalted butter
1 kg/2 lb baking potatoes
Salt and freshly ground pepper

175 g/6 oz Parmesan cheese,
    freshly grated

Line base and sides of a 20-cm/8-inch springform pan with 2 layers of foil, each time using a single piece. Set on baking sheet. Spread one-quarter of butter on base and sides of lined pan. Cut remaining butter in about 15 slices and cut each piece in half.

Position rack in lower third of oven and preheat to 200°C/400°F/gas 6. Peel potatoes and cut crosswise in 3-mm/⅛-inch-thick round slices in food processor, with mandoline, or with sharp knife.

Beginning at the centre of bottom of pan, arrange 1 layer of potato slices so they overlap and form a spiral. (The pattern will show on finished dish.) Sprinkle with salt and pepper. Arrange a second layer of potatoes without forming a pattern. Sprinkle with cheese and a little pepper. Scatter 6 butter pieces on top. Continue making layers of potatoes, cheese, and butter in same manner as the second layer, reserving 1 tablespoon of cheese.

Set springform on baking sheet and bake in lower third of oven for 30 minutes, pressing twice on cake with fish slice to make it compact. Cover with foil and continue baking for another 40 minutes, or until potatoes are very tender when pierced with a pointed knife or skewer. (Potato cake can be baked several hours ahead and kept at cool room temperature.) Before serving, reheat in low oven, if necessary.

Cool for 10 minutes. Turn over on to a platter. Release spring and remove pan. Remove first layer of foil. To remove inner layer, peel off top and very carefully peel off sides, using paring knife to free any potatoes that are stuck.

Sprinkle reserved cheese on top and grill until lightly brown. Serve immediately.

STEAMED NEW POTATOES WITH TARRAGON BUTTER
Pommes de terre nouvelles, beurre d'estragon

Steamed potatoes or *pommes vapeur* have long been a favourite in France, especially as a partner for fish.   MAKES 4 SERVINGS

65 g/2½ oz butter, softened | Salt and freshly ground pepper
4 teaspoons chopped fresh tarragon | 700 g/1½ lb new potatoes
leaves

Beat butter in medium-size bowl until very smooth. Stir in tarragon. Season to taste with salt and pepper. Let butter stand at room temperature.

Remove any eyes from potatoes and scrub well or scrape.

Bring at least 2·5 cm/1 inch of water to a boil in base of steamer. (Boiling water should not reach holes in top part of steamer.)

Set potatoes in steamer and sprinkle with salt. Cover tightly and steam over high heat for about 20 minutes, or until very tender when pierced with a sharp knife but not falling apart. Remove potatoes, drain briefly on paper towels, and transfer to a serving bowl.

Add tarragon butter in spoonfuls and toss lightly with potatoes. Serve immediately.

LIGHT POTATO FRITTERS WITH PINE NUTS
Pommes dauphine aux pignons

Various versions of these fritters are served at elegant meals, especially as an accompaniment for roasted or braised meat or poultry. They are made of potato purée and choux pastry and puff slightly when deep-fried because of the eggs in the pastry. Their delicately crisp crust and creamy interior make them one of France's best-loved potato dishes.   MAKES 6 TO 8 SERVINGS

POTATO PURÉE

700 g/1½ lb boiling potatoes | Salt and white pepper
4 tablespoons milk | Freshly grated nutmeg
25 g/1 oz butter

15 g/½ oz butter | 50 g/2 oz pine nuts

CHOUX PASTRY

70 g/2½ oz plus 1 tablespoon plain flour	¼ teaspoon salt
	50 g/2 oz unsalted butter
6 tablespoons water	2 eggs

Vegetable oil for deep-frying (at least 1·25 litres/2¼ pints)

Read the hints on deep-frying (page 231) before beginning.

POTATO PURÉE

Peel potatoes and cut each in 2 or 3 pieces. Put in a non-aluminium saucepan and add enough water to just cover and a pinch of salt. Cover, bring to a boil, and simmer over medium heat for 20 to 25 minutes, or until potatoes are very tender. Drain thoroughly. Purée potatoes in a food mill and return to saucepan. Add milk and butter and season with salt, white pepper, and nutmeg to taste. Over low heat, stir vigorously with a wooden spoon until milk and butter are absorbed. Remove from heat, and let cool.

In a small frying pan, melt 15 g/½ oz butter over low heat, add pine nuts and a pinch of salt, and sauté for about 2 minutes, or until lightly toasted. Set aside.

CHOUX PASTRY

Sift flour on to a piece of greaseproof paper. Heat water, salt, and butter in a medium-size saucepan until butter melts. Raise heat to medium-high and bring to a boil. Remove from heat, add flour immediately, and stir quickly with a wooden spoon until mixture is smooth. Set pan over low heat and beat mixture for about 30 seconds. Remove and let cool for a few minutes. Add 1 egg and beat it thoroughly into mixture. Beat in second egg.

Add potato purée to choux pastry, stir in pine nuts, and taste for seasoning.

Preheat oven to 150°C/300°F/gas 2. Heat oil in a deep-fat fryer or deep heavy saucepan to about 190°C/375°F on a frying thermometer. Do not fill pan more than halfway with oil. If a thermometer is not available, test by putting a drop of potato mixture into oil; when oil is hot enough, it should bubble energetically.

Take a rounded teaspoonful of batter and use a second teaspoon to slide it gently into oil, forming a rounded fritter. Do not crowd pan because fritters need room to puff. While frying, turn them over occasionally, until they are golden brown on all sides. Remove to ovenproof trays lined with paper towels. Keep in oven with door slightly open while frying remaining fritters. Serve as soon as possible.

POTATO GRATIN WITH CREAM
Gratin dauphinois

In France people say that the potato was created in order to be made into this dish. Numerous French restaurants feature it as a side dish and many chefs count this as their favourite potato speciality. In addition to its wonderful taste *gratin dauphinois* has the advantage of being one of the few potato dishes that is good made in advance and reheated. As in the variation the potatoes can also be baked with wild mushrooms.   MAKES 4 SERVINGS

700 g/1½ lb baking potatoes
Salt and white pepper
Freshly grated nutmeg
600 ml/1 pint milk
1 garlic clove, halved

350 ml/12 fl oz double cream or
Crème Fraîche (page 381)
4 to 6 tablespoons grated Gruyère
or Emmental cheese

Peel potatoes and cut them in slices about 3 mm/⅛ inch thick, using a food processor, mandoline cutter, or sharp knife. Season with salt, white pepper, and nutmeg, and toss to distribute seasonings.

Bring milk to a boil in a medium-size heavy saucepan, stirring occasionally. Add potatoes, reduce heat to medium, and simmer, uncovered, for 10 minutes, stirring occasionally. Drain potatoes; milk can be reserved for soup.

Rub a medium-size gratin dish or other shallow baking dish with garlic; then butter dish. Preheat oven to 220°C/425°F/gas 7.

Return potatoes to saucepan and add cream. Bring to a simmer over medium-high heat. Reduce heat to medium and simmer, stirring occasionally, for about 15 minutes, or until potatoes are tender but not falling apart. Taste and add more salt, white pepper, and nutmeg if needed. Spoon potatoes and cream into baking dish. Sprinkle with cheese. (The gratin can be prepared 4 days in advance up to this point, covered, and refrigerated.)

Bake for 15 to 20 minutes, or until hot and golden brown. If top is not brown enough, grill briefly. Serve hot, from dish.

POTATO GRATIN WITH CÈPES

Soak 25 g/1 oz dried cèpes or *porcini* mushrooms in hot water to cover for about 20 minutes, or until tender. Lift into strainer, rinse, and drain well. Cut cèpes into 6-mm/¼-inch pieces. Add to potatoes in saucepan after they have cooked for 10 minutes in cream.

POTATO SOUFFLÉ IN POTATO SKINS
Pommes de terre en robe de chambre soufflées

In this easy-to-make soufflé, an elegant version of stuffed baked potatoes, the potato pulp is made into a soufflé and baked right in the skins. Freshly grated nutmeg is the favourite spice for creamy potato dishes like this and should be used liberally.   MAKES 4 SERVINGS

4 225 to 275 g/8 to 10 oz baking potatoes	4 eggs, separated, at room temperature
25 g/1 oz unsalted butter	Salt and freshly ground pepper
2 tablespoons cream cheese	Freshly grated nutmeg
2 tablespoons double cream	100 g/4 oz Gruyère cheese, grated

Preheat oven to 220°C/425°F/gas 7. Scrub potatoes but do not peel. Bake them for about 50–60 minutes, or until tender. Leave oven on.

Cut a thin slice from top of each potato. Using a teaspoon, carefully remove most of pulp, leaving only a small amount attached to potato skin so it won't fall apart.

Purée potato pulp in a food mill or mash with a potato masher and put it in a small saucepan. Gradually add butter, stirring vigorously with a wooden spoon, and remove from heat. Stir in cream cheese and cream. Then stir in egg yolks, one at a time. Add salt, pepper, and nutmeg to taste. Butter a shallow baking dish and set potato skins in it. Butter two small ramekins generously.

Beat egg whites until stiff but not dry. Fold about one-quarter of whites into potato mixture. Return this mixture to remaining whites, add about 75 g/3 oz of grated Gruyère cheese, and fold all together as lightly but as quickly as possible.

Fill potato skins with soufflé mixture. Spoon any remaining mixture into buttered ramekins. Sprinkle remaining grated cheese on top of soufflé mixture. Bake for about 15 minutes, or until puffed. Serve immediately.

BAKED POTATO CAKES
Pommes Byron

For best flavour and texture these delicate cakes are made from baked potatoes. The potato cakes are sautéed lightly then baked with a luscious topping of cream and Gruyère cheese.

MAKES 10 CAKES; ABOUT 5 SERVINGS

1 kg/2 lb baking potatoes (about 3 large potatoes), scrubbed but not peeled

6 tablespoons double cream or Crème Fraîche (page 381)

Salt and freshly ground white pepper

Freshly grated nutmeg

About 25 g/1 oz plain flour

2 tablespoons vegetable oil

25 g/1 oz butter

65 g/2½ oz Gruyère cheese, grated

Preheat oven to 220°C/425°F/gas 7. Pierce potatoes with a fork. Bake on rack in preheated oven for about 1 hour or until tender.

Cut hot potatoes in half, scoop out pulp, and transfer it to a bowl. Mash it with a fork. Stir in 2 tablespoons cream. Mix well with fork and season to taste with salt, pepper, and nutmeg.

Shape mixture into cakes, making them about 2 cm/¾ inch thick and 5 cm/2 inches across. Put on a tray or plate in one layer.

Roll each potato cake in flour and pat so all sides are lightly coated.

In a medium-size heavy frying pan, melt oil and butter over medium heat. Add half of potato cakes and cook lightly on both sides, turning very carefully with two spatulas.

Using spatula, transfer to gratin dish or shallow baking dish large enough to hold all potato cakes in one layer. Cook remaining potato cakes. (Potato cakes can be prepared about 4 hours in advance and kept at room temperature.)

Preheat oven to 230°C/450°F/gas 8. Pour remaining 4 tablespoons cream over cakes and sprinkle with grated cheese.

Bake for about 8 minutes or until bubbling. If necessary, put under grill to brown lightly. Serve immediately.

SAUTÉED POTATOES WITH PEPPERS AND THYME
Pommes sautées aux poivrons et au thym

Although potatoes can be sautéed raw they are much easier to handle when partially cooked first as in this recipe. These potatoes are a perfect accompaniment for fish, eggs, or meat and can be varied in many ways. Yellow peppers can be substituted for the red or green, or they can be omitted and only the onions added. Oregano or marjoram can replace the thyme.   MAKES 6 SERVINGS

1 kg/2 lb boiling potatoes, scrubbed but not peeled
4 tablespoons olive or vegetable oil
25 g/1 oz butter
3 medium-size onions, halved and thinly sliced
1 red pepper, cored, seeded, and cut in thin strips
1 green pepper, cored, seeded, and cut in thin strips

Salt and freshly ground pepper
2 teaspoons chopped fresh thyme, or ¾ teaspoon dried thyme
2 tablespoons chopped parsley (optional)

Put potatoes in a large saucepan, cover with water, and add salt. Cover, bring to a boil, and cook over medium heat for 15 to 20 minutes, or until softened but not completely cooked. Drain thoroughly. Peel potatoes and cut in thick slices.

In a large heavy frying pan, heat 2 tablespoons oil and the butter over low heat, add onions, and cook for 3 minutes. Add peppers, salt, pepper, and thyme, and cook, stirring, until vegetables are tender. Raise heat to medium and continue cooking until onions brown very slightly. Remove from pan.

Add another tablespoon oil to pan and heat over medium-high heat. Add about half the potatoes and sauté, carefully turning them over occasionally, until browned and tender. Remove from pan. Add remaining oil and sauté remaining potatoes in same way.

Return all of potatoes and pepper mixture to pan. Sauté together over medium heat for about 2 minutes, tossing carefully. Taste and adjust seasoning, transfer to a serving dish, sprinkle with parsley, and serve.

CREAMY POTATO PURÉE
Pommes purée

When the French speak of purée without specifying the vegetable, it is understood that they mean potato. Prepared the French way, potato purée is light, smooth, fluffy, and rich. It is soft, because cooks like to beat in plenty of milk or cream. This exquisite purée is sometimes called potatoes *mousseline*, a reference to its creaminess and richness.

Because the starch of mature potatoes is needed to make a good purée, any type of potato can be used except new ones.

Old-fashioned methods are best when it comes to puréeing the potatoes. The texture can become unpleasantly elastic if they are puréed in a blender or food processor. French chefs prefer to push them through a large drum sieve called a *tamis*. Home cooks often use a hand-operated food mill instead; a potato masher also works well. If none of these is available, the potatoes can be drained very well and crushed with a wooden spoon against the sides of the saucepan in which they were cooked.

The neutral taste of potato purée makes it a good partner for most foods, whether delicate or strong-flavoured. It is a favourite French accompaniment to all meats, chicken and sausages.

MAKES 6 SERVINGS

1 kg/2 lb boiling potatoes	*50 g/2 oz butter*
Salt and white pepper	*Freshly grated nutmeg*
200 ml/7 fl oz double cream or	*A few tablespoons milk (optional)*
milk, or a mixture of both	

Peel potatoes and cut each in 2 or 3 pieces. Put in a non-aluminium saucepan and add enough water to just cover and a pinch of salt. Cover, bring to a boil, and simmer over medium heat for 20 to 25 minutes, or until potatoes are very tender. Drain thoroughly. Purée potatoes and return to saucepan.

In a small saucepan, bring cream, milk, or mixture of cream and milk to a simmer. Add butter and a little hot cream or milk to potatoes and season with salt, pepper, and nutmeg. Over low heat, stir vigorously with a wooden spoon until purée is light and smooth.

Add remaining cream gradually, still stirring vigorously. The purée should be soft but not soupy; if it is too stiff, beat in a few tablespoons milk. Add more salt, pepper, and nutmeg, if desired. (The purée can be prepared 30 minutes in advance. To keep it hot,

pour a few tablespoons cold milk over purée without stirring it in
to prevent a skin from forming on surface; set saucepan of purée
in a pan of hot water over low heat. Before serving, stir in milk.)
Serve hot.

POTATO AND LEEK PANCAKES
Crêpes aux pommes de terre et aux poireaux

Potatoes and leeks are a favourite French pair, not only for soup, but
also for these rich pancakes. Originally developed to use up extra
baked potatoes, these have gained prestige and are often served in
restaurants as a savoury side dish with many main courses.

MAKES 4 TO 5 SERVINGS; ABOUT 16 SMALL PANCAKES

*600 g/1¼ lb baking potatoes (2
large potatoes), scrubbed but
not peeled
450 g/1 lb large leeks
25 g/1 oz unsalted butter
7 tablespoons milk*

*1½ teaspoons salt
Freshly ground pepper
Freshly grated nutmeg
3 eggs
2 tablespoons plain flour
4 tablespoons vegetable oil*

Preheat oven to 220°C/425°F/gas 7. Pierce potatoes with a fork.
Bake for about 1 hour, or until tender.

Use only white and light green parts of leeks. Cut leeks in half
lengthwise, rinse well, and cut in 6-mm/¼-inch slices. Soak sliced
leeks in cold water to cover for 5 minutes to remove any dirt. Lift into
colander or large strainer, rinse, and drain well.

In medium-size heavy frying pan, melt butter over medium heat,
add leeks, and cook, stirring very often, for about 10 minutes, or
until leeks are very soft but not brown. If any liquid remains in pan,
cook leeks over medium-high heat, stirring, until it evaporates.
Transfer leeks to bowl and cool.

Remove pulp of hot potatoes and purée in a food mill or push
through a sieve into a bowl. Stir in milk, salt, pepper, and nutmeg.

Let cool. Stir in leeks. Add eggs, one by one, stirring well after each addition, then flour. Taste and adjust seasoning if necessary.

Preheat oven to lowest setting. In a large heavy frying pan, heat 3 tablespoons oil over medium heat. Using a large tablespoon, add a spoonful of batter to oil and flatten slightly to make a small pancake of 5 cm/2 inches in diameter. Mixture should spread but pancake does not need to be very thin. If mixture is too thick to spread at all, add a little milk to batter. (The amount of milk to add varies according to the absorbing power of the potatoes.) If pancakes do not hold together, add 1 tablespoon more flour to batter.

Make more pancakes of same size and fry until golden brown on both sides (about 5 minutes), turning carefully with two spatulas. Transfer to paper towels on an ovenproof tray. Keep warm in oven while frying rest of pancakes.

The pancakes are best if served immediately, but they can be kept warm for about 30 minutes. (They can be kept for 1 day in refrigerator; reheat in one layer on paper towels on a baking sheet in cool oven.)

FRENCH FRIED SWEET POTATOES
Patates douces frites

Sweet potatoes can be treated like ordinary potatoes to produce special sweet french fries. MAKES 4 SERVINGS

1 kg/2 lb sweet potatoes, peeled   Salt
About 2 litres/3½ pints vegetable
 oil, for deep-frying

Read the hints on deep-frying (page 231) before beginning.

If potatoes are over 10 cm/4 inches long, cut them in half crosswise, then cut in lengthwise slices about 1 cm/½ inch wide. Cut each slice in strips about 6 mm/¼ inch wide. Trim irregular edges.

With paper towels, thoroughly pat potatoes dry in small batches.

This step is very important because if they are even slightly wet, fat will bubble up violently.

Line trays with two layers of paper towels. Heat oil in a deep-fat fryer or deep, heavy saucepan to about 180°C/350°F on a frying thermometer. If no thermometer is available, test oil with a piece of potato; oil should foam up around it.

Dip a frying basket into hot oil to prevent potatoes from sticking. Put about one-third to one-half of potatoes in basket and carefully lower into hot oil. Do not overfill because fat bubbles up vigorously when potatoes are added and can be dangerous. Leave basket in oil during frying.

Fry potatoes for about 4 to 5 minutes, or until tender and light brown. Check by pressing one; it should crush easily. Use slotted spoon to remove potatoes to towel-lined trays. Reheat oil before adding next batch.

Sprinkle potatoes with salt and toss gently. Serve immediately.

Rice

In France there are two basic methods for preparing rice. In the first, rice is cooked like pasta, in a large pan of boiling salted water, then drained well. This method is often used for salads and stuffings. The second technique for cooking rice is pilaf.

Rice pilaf is among the best-travelled recipes. It originated in Persia and spread to the Middle East and the Mediterranean area. In France many classic recipes are called *à la turque* when they are accompanied by pilaf, because Europe probably learned about rice pilaf from the Turks during the Crusades. Pilaf is a favourite formula for preparing rice in France and appears in the finest as well as the simplest restaurants.

Most people think they are familiar with rice pilaf because the name frequently appears on restaurant menus. Unfortunately the rice that passes for pilaf is often a far cry from the buttery, delicate grain dish it should be. There is no excuse for this because rice pilaf is extremely simple to make.

Pilaf has more flavour than boiled or steamed rice due to the preliminary sautéing of the rice with an onion in oil or butter. This sautéing is a key step in preparing pilaf, because the oil or butter coats the grains and helps keep them from sticking. Next the rice is simmered in stock or water over low heat or in the oven. The rice is fluffy and each grain is distinct. It is easy to prepare, reheats well, and can be kept warm, which makes it convenient for both professional and home menu planning.

Vegetables are generally cooked separately and mixed with the cooked rice. This permits each ingredient to cook evenly. Stocks give the richest-tasting rice pilaf, while water yields the whitest rice with the most delicate flavour.

Whether they boil rice or cook it as pilaf, French cooks like to enrich it with a little butter as a final touch. When moistened with vinaigrette instead and accented by the addition of a few fresh vegetables, rice can become a refreshing luncheon salad.

Pilaf is perfect for pairing with grilled foods, roasts and quick sautés and is the classic partner for brochettes of lamb, beef or seafood, which are often set on a bed of the rice. It also makes a savoury stuffing for poultry and vegetables.

An elegant presentation for rice prepared by either method is moulded rice. It can be presented as a ring, with sauced or sautéed food in the centre, as in Rice Ring with Curried Aubergines, or as individual cakes formed by unmoulding the rice from ramekins.

Hints

· A sauté pan or other good-sized heavy pan with a lid is best for preparing pilaf because the wide surface area makes sautéing easier and encourages even cooking. Packaged rice is clean and there is no need to rinse it. Rinsing would interfere with the sautéing.

· Use a fork for stirring butter or any other ingredients, such as vegetables, meats, or seafood, into cooked rice. Be sure any additions to the pilaf are in small pieces, and always stir by tossing the rice as lightly as possible to avoid crushing the grains.

RICE WITH PEAS AND BASIL
Riz aux petits pois au basilic

Rice is often cooked like pasta – in a very large pan of boiling salted water, a method that keeps the grains separate and is known in France as Creole rice. At least four times as much water as rice should be used. It is a favourite technique for preparing rice to use in both hot dishes and salads.   MAKES 4 SERVINGS

225 g/8 oz long-grain white rice
450 g/1 lb fresh peas or 225 g/8 oz
    frozen peas
50 g/2 oz butter
2 medium-size garlic cloves, finely
    chopped

Salt and freshly ground pepper
2 tablespoons chopped fresh basil
Fresh basil leaves, for garnish
    (optional)

In a large saucepan, bring about 1·4 litres/2½ pints water to a boil and add a pinch of salt. Add rice, stir once, and cook, uncovered, for about 12 to 14 minutes, or until tender; check by tasting. Drain in strainer, rinse with cold water until cool, and leave for 5 minutes.

In a medium-size saucepan, bring enough water to generously cover peas to a boil and add a pinch of salt. Add peas and cook, uncovered, until just tender; about 7 minutes for fresh peas and 3 minutes for frozen. Drain thoroughly.

Melt half the butter in a large shallow pan over low heat. Stir in garlic and cook for about 30 seconds. Add peas, rice, and salt and pepper to taste. Heat mixture over low heat, tossing lightly with a fork, until hot.

Add remaining butter. Cover pan and let rice stand for about 2 minutes, or until butter melts. Add chopped basil; toss again lightly. Taste and adjust seasoning. Garnish, if desired, with fresh basil leaves.

RICE WITH SAUTÉED VEGETABLES AND WALNUT OIL
Riz aux légumes sautés à l'huile de noix

Serve this colourful dish for a light main course or as an accompaniment to fish or chicken.   MAKES 4 SERVINGS

225 g/8 oz long-grain white rice
175 to 225 g/6 to 8 oz Swiss
    chard, rinsed thoroughly

2 medium-size carrots, trimmed,
    peeled, and cut in matchsticks

2 medium-size spring onions,
  trimmed
25 g/1 oz butter
2 medium-size shallots, finely
  chopped
Salt and freshly ground pepper

3 tablespoons walnut oil
2 medium-size celery sticks,
  trimmed, peeled, and cut in
  matchsticks
2 tablespoons coarsely chopped
  parsley

In a large saucepan, bring about 1·4 litres/2½ pints water to a boil
and add a pinch of salt. Add rice, stir once, and cook, uncovered, for
about 12 to 14 minutes, or until tender; check by tasting. Drain in
strainer, rinse with cold water until cool, and leave for 5 minutes.

Cut chard leaves from ribs. Peel stringy side of ribs and cut
crosswise into 6-mm/¼-inch slices. Pile chard leaves, cut them in
half lengthwise and cut crosswise in strips 1 cm/½ inch wide. In
medium-size saucepan of boiling salted water, cook chard ribs,
uncovered, for about 5 minutes, or until just tender. Drain
thoroughly.

Put carrots in medium-size saucepan and add enough water to
cover and a pinch of salt. Bring to boil, reduce heat to low, cover,
and simmer for about 4 minutes, or until tender. Drain thoroughly.

Keep white and light green parts of onions separate from dark
parts. Cut each in thin slices.

In saucepan used to cook rice, melt butter over low heat, add
shallots, and cook for 1 minute. Add rice and salt and pepper to
taste. Heat mixture, tossing lightly with a fork, cover partially, and
keep warm.

In large shallow pan, heat 2 tablespoons walnut oil over medium
heat, stir in celery and white and light parts of onions, then chard
leaves, and sauté for 3 minutes. Add chard ribs, carrots, dark parts of
onions, and salt and pepper. Sauté mixture, tossing lightly, for about
1½ minutes, or until hot.

With a fork, gently stir vegetable mixture into rice; add remaining
walnut oil and parsley. Taste and adjust seasoning. Transfer to
serving dish and serve immediately.

SAVOURY RICE PILAF WITH
AUBERGINES
Pilaf aux aubergines

Sautéed mushrooms or cubes of courgette are other good additions to
this pilaf.   MAKES 6 TO 8 SERVINGS

5 parsley stalks (*without leaves*)
2 fresh thyme sprigs, or ½
   teaspoon dried thyme
1 bay leaf
65 g/2½ oz unsalted butter
2 medium-size onions, chopped
1 large garlic clove, crushed
450 g/1 lb long-grain white rice
900 ml/1½ pints hot Vegetable
   Stock (*page 332*) or water

Salt and freshly ground pepper
4 or 5 small aubergines, or 2
   medium-size
3 tablespoons olive or vegetable oil
3 tablespoons chopped parsley

Position rack in lower third of oven and preheat to 180°C/350°F/gas
4. Wrap parsley stems, thyme, and bay leaf in a piece of cheesecloth
and tie tightly to make a bouquet garni. Cut a piece of greaseproof
paper to fit pan to be used for cooking rice (about 23 cm/9 inches)
and butter it.

In a large ovenproof sauté pan, heat 40 g/1½ oz butter over low
heat, add onions, and cook, stirring, for about 10 minutes, or until
soft but not brown. Add garlic and sauté for 30 seconds. Raise heat to
medium, add rice, and sauté, stirring, for about 4 minutes, or until
grains begin to turn opaque.

Bring stock or water to boil over high heat. Pour hot stock or water
over rice and stir once. Add bouquet garni and submerge it in liquid.
Add pinch of salt and pepper. Raise heat to high and bring mixture
to boil. Set buttered paper, buttered side down, on rice, and cover
with tight lid. Bake, without stirring, for 18 minutes.

Meanwhile, rinse and wipe aubergines. Do not peel unless their
skins are tough. Cut aubergines in small dice. In a large frying pan,

heat 1½ tablespoons oil over medium heat, add half of aubergine cubes and pinch of salt and pepper, and sauté for about 7 minutes, or until tender. Remove to a bowl. Repeat with remaining oil and remaining aubergine.

Taste rice; if it is too chewy or if liquid is not absorbed, bake for 2 more minutes. Discard bouquet garni.

(Rice can be kept up to 2 days in refrigerator and reheated in a little melted butter or heated oil in a large frying pan; aubergine can be prepared 4 hours in advance and kept at room temperature.)

When rice is cooked, cut remaining butter in small pieces and scatter them on top. Cover and let stand for 4 minutes for slightly chewy rice, or up to 10 minutes if more tender rice is preferred.

Meanwhile, reheat aubergine cubes in pan. Taste and adjust seasoning.

Use fork to fluff rice and gently stir in minced parsley and aubergine. Taste and adjust seasoning.

MEDITERRANEAN SAFFRON RICE PILAF WITH VEGETABLES
Pilaf safrané aux légumes

Among the spices that go well with pilaf, saffron is the most honoured by tradition and has long been a favourite in France and in other Mediterranean countries. This pilaf can be a main course for a light meal. If you like, instead of sprinkling the rice with almonds, serve a bowl of grated Gruyère or Parmesan cheese on the side.

MAKES 4 TO 6 SERVINGS

1 lemon
4 medium-size artichokes
1 tablespoon strained fresh lemon juice
450 ml/¾ pint boiling water
¼ teaspoon crushed saffron strands

5 parsley stalks (without leaves)
1 fresh thyme sprig, or ¼ teaspoon dried thyme
1 bay leaf
4 tablespoons olive oil
50 g/2 oz onion, finely chopped
225 g/8 oz long-grain white rice

Salt and freshly ground pepper   *1 medium-size courgette (about*
2 medium-size ripe tomatoes,   *100 g/4 oz)*
   peeled, seeded, and cut in about   *1½ teaspoons chopped parsley*
   8-mm/³⁄₈-inch dice
40 g/1½ oz slivered almonds

Prepare artichoke hearts according to directions on page 159.

Add 1 tablespoon lemon juice to medium-size saucepan of boiling salted water. Add artichoke hearts, cover, and cook over low heat for about 15 minutes, or until they are just tender when pierced with knife. Cool to lukewarm in liquid. Using teaspoon, scoop out choke from centre of each artichoke. Cut each in 1-cm/½-inch dice and drain on paper towels.

Combine boiling water and saffron in small saucepan. Cover and keep warm over low heat.

Position rack in lower third of oven and preheat to 180°C/350°F/gas 4. Wrap parsley stems, thyme, and bay leaf in a piece of cheesecloth and tie tightly to make a bouquet garni. Cut a piece of greaseproof paper to fit pan to be used for cooking rice and butter it.

In 23-cm/9-inch-diameter ovenproof sauté pan or deep frying pan with lid, heat 2 tablespoons oil over low heat, add onion, and cook, stirring, for about 7 minutes, or until soft but not brown. Raise heat to medium, add rice, and sauté, stirring, for about 4 minutes, or until grains begin to turn opaque.

While rice is sautéing, bring saffron water to boil over high heat. Pour over rice and stir once. Add bouquet garni and submerge it in liquid. Add ¼ teaspoon salt and pinch of pepper. Raise heat to high and bring mixture to boil. Set buttered paper, buttered side down, on rice, and cover with tight lid. Bake, without stirring, for 18 minutes. Taste rice; if it is too chewy or if liquid is not absorbed, bake for 2 more minutes. Discard bouquet garni. (Rice can be prepared 2 days in advance and refrigerated. Reheat in shallow pan with 1 tablespoon oil, stirring gently with fork, until just warm.)

While rice cooks, put tomatoes in strainer and leave to drain. Toast almonds in small baking dish in oven alongside pilaf for about 4 minutes, or until they are light brown. Transfer almonds to a plate and reserve at room temperature.

Cut courgette into 3 pieces. Cut each piece in lengthwise slices about 6 mm/¼ inch thick, and each slice in lengthwise strips about 6 mm/¼ inch thick. In a medium-size frying pan, warm 2 tablespoons olive oil over medium heat, add courgette and salt and pepper to taste, and sauté for about 1½ minutes, or until barely tender. Transfer courgette pieces with their oil to a plate.

When rice is cooked, scatter tomatoes and artichokes on top. Cover and let stand for 4 minutes for slightly chewy rice, or up to 10 minutes if more tender rice is preferred. Use fork to fluff rice and gently stir in tomatoes and artichokes. Add parsley and courgette and its oil, stir in gently, taste and adjust seasoning.

Transfer rice gently to a serving dish. Sprinkle with half of almonds. Serve remaining almonds in a small dish.

CREAMY RICE PILAF WITH ASPARAGUS
Riz pilaf à la crème et aux asperges

Cream can be used to enrich rice pilaf as in this elegant dish. Serve it on its own or with lobster, prawns or chicken.

MAKES 4 TO 6 SERVINGS

275 to 375 g/10 to 12 oz thin
  asparagus
5 parsley stalks (without leaves)
1 fresh thyme sprig, or ¼ teaspoon
  dried thyme
1 bay leaf
50 g/2 oz butter
50 g/2 oz onion, finely chopped
225 g/8 oz long-grain white rice
450 ml/¾ pint hot Chicken Stock
  (page 333), Vegetable Stock
  (page 332), or water

¼ teaspoon salt
Freshly ground pepper
2 tablespoons double cream, at
  room temperature
2 tablespoons chopped fresh
  tarragon or parsley

Peel asparagus and cut 6-cm/2½-inch-long asparagus tips from stems. Cut stems in pieces about 4 cm/1½ inches long, discarding tough ends.

Position rack in lower third of oven and preheat to 180°C/350°F/gas 4. Wrap parsley stems, thyme, and bay leaf in a piece of cheesecloth and tie tightly to make a bouquet garni. Cut a piece of greaseproof paper to fit pan to be used for cooking rice and butter it.

In an ovenproof sauté pan about 23 cm/9 inches in diameter, melt 40 g/1½ oz butter over low heat, add onion, and cook, stirring, for about 7 minutes, or until soft but not brown. Raise heat to medium, add rice, and sauté, stirring, for about 4 minutes, or until grains begin to turn opaque.

While rice is sautéing, bring stock or water to boil over high heat, pour over rice, and stir once. Add bouquet garni and submerge it in liquid. Add salt and pepper to taste, raise heat to high, and bring mixture to boil. Set buttered paper, buttered side down, on rice, and cover with tight lid. Bake, without stirring, for 18 minutes. Taste rice; if it is too chewy or if liquid is not absorbed, bake for 2 more minutes. Discard bouquet garni. (Rice can be prepared 2 days in advance and refrigerated. Reheat with 1 additional knob of butter, stirring gently with fork, until just warm.)

Meanwhile, put asparagus pieces into large saucepan containing enough boiling salted water to cover them generously. Return to boil. Cook, uncovered, for about 1 minute, or until asparagus is just tender when pierced with a small sharp knife. Drain, rinse with cold running water until cool, and drain thoroughly.

When rice is cooked, pour cream quickly and evenly over it; do not stir. Cover rice with its buttered paper and lid and for slightly chewy rice, let stand for 4 minutes, or just until cream is absorbed; for more tender rice, let stand for up to 10 minutes.

In large pan, melt remaining butter over medium heat, add asparagus, and sauté for about 1 minute, or just until hot. Reserve 8 to 12 asparagus tips for garnish.

Use fork to fluff rice and gently stir in tarragon and remaining asparagus. Taste and adjust seasoning. Transfer pilaf gently to serving dish, garnish with reserved asparagus tips, and serve.

MULTICOLOURED PILAF WITH SWEET RED PEPPERS AND WALNUTS
Pilaf multicolore aux poivrons rouges et aux noix

Nuts and pilaf make a wonderful pair; the crunchiness of sautéed nuts provides a perfect complement to the tender rice.   MAKES 4 SERVINGS

50 g/2 oz butter
75 g/3 oz walnut halves
About ½ teaspoon salt
2 tablespoons vegetable oil
1 medium-size onion, finely
    chopped
1 red pepper, cored and cut in
    small dice

2 celery sticks, peeled and cut in
    thin slices
350 g/12 oz long-grain rice
750 ml/1¼ pints boiling water
Pinch of black pepper

In a small heavy pan, melt one-quarter of butter over medium-low heat, add walnut halves and a pinch of salt, and sauté for about 2 minutes, or until lightly browned. Set aside and reserve at room temperature.

In a large heavy sauté pan, heat oil and one-third of remaining butter over low heat, add onion, red pepper, and celery, and cook, stirring, for about 10 minutes, or until soft but not brown. Add rice and sauté, stirring, for about 4 minutes.

Add boiling water, ½ teaspoon salt, and a pinch of black pepper. Stir once, cover, and cook over low heat, without stirring, for 18 minutes. Taste rice; if not yet tender, simmer for 2 more minutes. (Rice can be prepared 2 days in advance and refrigerated. Reheat with 1 additional knob of butter, stirring gently with fork, until just warm.) Remove from heat and dot with remaining butter. Cover and let stand for 10 minutes. Gently stir with a fork to distribute butter. Taste and adjust seasoning.

Transfer rice to a serving dish and sprinkle with sautéed walnuts.

RICE PILAF WITH ARTICHOKE HEARTS, CARROTS, AND TOASTED ALMONDS

Pilaf aux coeurs d'artichauts, aux carottes, et aux amandes grillées

Although rice pilaf frequently accompanies meat or fish in sauces – whether creamy or spicy – it is rich enough to be paired with plainer dishes as well, such as grilled foods, roasts, and quick sautés.

MAKES 4 SERVINGS

1 lemon (for fresh artichokes)
2 fresh artichokes, or 8 frozen
    artichoke heart pieces, cooked
75 g/3 oz slivered almonds
2 tablespoons vegetable oil
40 g/1½ oz unsalted butter
1 medium-size onion, finely
    chopped

2 medium-size carrots, cut in small
    dice
350 g/12 oz long-grain white rice
750 ml/1¼ pints boiling water
About ½ teaspoon salt
Pinch of pepper

If using fresh artichokes, prepare and cook hearts according to instructions on page 159.

Preheat oven to 200°C/400°F/gas 6. In a shallow baking dish, toast almonds in oven for about 5 minutes, or until lightly browned. Transfer to a plate and leave at room temperature.

In a large heavy sauté pan, warm oil and one-third of butter over low heat, add onion and carrots, and cook, stirring, for about 10 minutes, or until onion is soft but not brown. Add rice and sauté, stirring, for about 2 minutes.

Add boiling water, ½ teaspoon salt, and a pinch of pepper. Stir once, cover and cook over low heat, without stirring, for 18 minutes. Taste rice; if not yet tender, simmer for 2 more minutes. Remove from heat and dot with remaining butter. Cover and let stand for 10 minutes. (Rice can be prepared 2 days in advance and refrigerated.

Reheat with 1 additional knob of butter, stirring gently with fork, until just warm.)

Cut artichoke hearts into quarters if using fresh. With a fork, gently stir into rice. Taste and adjust seasoning. Transfer rice to a serving dish and sprinkle with toasted almonds.

BROWN RICE PILAF WITH TARRAGON
Pilaf de riz complet à l'estragon

Brown rice is rarely used in France, and so I was amazed to find it on the menu at Paul Bocuse's world-famous restaurant. The brown rice was from the Camargue, the area in southern France where rice is cultivated, and was served with casserole-roasted guinea hen, tarragon cream sauce, and an assortment of vegetables. Brown rice is very good when cooked as pilaf and can be substituted for white rice in the other pilafs in this chapter.   MAKES 4 TO 6 SERVINGS

5 parsley stalks (without leaves)
5 tarragon stalks (without leaves)
1 fresh thyme sprig, or ¼ teaspoon dried thyme
1 bay leaf
25 g/1 oz butter, for enrichment (optional)
450 ml/¾ pint hot Chicken Stock (page 333), Vegetable Stock (page 332), or water

3 tablespoons vegetable oil or olive oil
50 g/2 oz onion, finely chopped
225 g/8 oz long-grain brown rice
¼ teaspoon salt
Freshly ground pepper
2 tablespoons chopped fresh tarragon

Position rack in lower third of oven and preheat to 180°C/350°F/gas 4. Wrap parsley, tarragon, thyme, and bay leaf in a piece of cheesecloth and tie tightly to make a bouquet garni. Cut a piece of greaseproof paper to fit pan to be used for cooking rice, and butter it.

Cut optional butter into small pieces and let stand at room temperature while preparing pilaf.

If using stock, keep it hot in small saucepan over low heat, covered; if using water, keep it hot in kettle.

In deep ovenproof sauté pan about 23 cm/9 inches in diameter, warm 3 tablespoons oil over low heat, add onion, and cook, stirring, until soft but not brown; about 7 minutes. Raise heat to medium, add rice, and sauté, stirring, until grains begin to turn opaque; about 4 minutes.

Bring stock or water to boil over high heat, pour over rice, and stir once. Add bouquet garni and submerge it in liquid. Add salt and pepper to taste. Raise heat to high and bring mixture to boil. Press buttered paper, buttered side down, on to rice, and cover with tight lid. Bake, without stirring, for 35 minutes. Taste rice; if it is too chewy or if liquid is not absorbed, bake for 5 more minutes and check again. Discard bouquet garni. (Rice can be prepared 2 days in advance and refrigerated. Reheat with 1 additional tablespoon of oil, stirring gently with fork, until just warm.)

When rice is cooked, scatter reserved butter pieces over it, if using. For slightly chewy rice, fluff by tossing with fork; if more tender rice is preferred, cover rice with its buttered paper and lid, let stand up to 10 minutes, and then fluff with fork. Continue tossing until butter is evenly blended into rice. Add fresh tarragon. Taste and adjust seasoning.

RICE RING WITH CURRIED
AUBERGINES
Couronne de riz aux aubergines, sauce curry

Since rice can be easily moulded into an attractive ring this is a popular presentation of pilaf in France because a rich mixture can be spooned into the centre. If desired add other vegetables such as courgettes, cauliflower, mushrooms, or peas to the sauce.

MAKES 4 SERVINGS

RICE PILAF WITH PEPPERS

50 g/2 oz butter
1 large onion, finely chopped
1 large red pepper, cored, ribs
   removed, finely diced

225 g/8 oz long-grain white rice
450 ml/¾ pint hot water
¼ teaspoon salt
Freshly ground pepper

CURRIED AUBERGINES

25 g/1 oz butter
2 tablespoons finely chopped
   shallots
1 tablespoon finely chopped fresh
   ginger root
2 teaspoons finely chopped garlic
2 teaspoons curry powder
225 ml/8 fl oz Chicken Stock
   (page 333) or Vegetable Stock
   (page 332)

1 bay leaf
Salt and freshly ground pepper
350 ml/12 fl oz double cream
450 g/1 lb small aubergines,
   unpeeled
1 tablespoon vegetable oil

RICE PILAF WITH PEPPERS

In large heavy sauté pan, melt half the butter over low heat, add onion, and cook for 3 minutes. Add red pepper and cook, stirring occasionally, for about 5 minutes, or until softened. Add rice and cook, stirring, for about 4 minutes, or until evenly coated. Add water, salt and pepper to taste, stir once, and bring to boil. Cover and cook over low heat, without stirring, for about 18 minutes, or until liquid is absorbed. Let stand, covered, for 5 minutes.

Cut remaining butter in cubes. Fluff rice with fork. Using fork, gently stir in butter cubes. Taste and adjust seasoning. (Rice can be prepared 2 days in advance and refrigerated.)

CURRIED AUBERGINES

In medium-size heavy saucepan, melt half the butter over low heat, add shallots, and cook, stirring, for about 2 minutes, or until soft but not browned. Add ginger and garlic and cook for 1 minute. Add curry powder and cook, stirring, for 30 seconds. Add stock, bay leaf, and a little salt and pepper. Stir well and bring to boil. Simmer, uncovered, over medium-high heat, stirring occasionally, until mixture is reduced to about 4 tablespoons. Discard bay leaf. Add cream and bring to boil, stirring. Reduce heat to medium and simmer until sauce is thick enough to coat a spoon. (Sauce can be prepared 4 hours in advance and refrigerated.)

Cut aubergines in 2-cm/¾-inch dice and season lightly with salt. In large frying pan, heat oil and remaining butter over medium heat, add aubergine, and sauté, tossing often, for about 5 minutes, or until lightly browned. Reduce heat to low, cover, and cook, stirring occasionally, for about 5 minutes, or until tender. Transfer to bowl and keep warm. (Aubergines can be prepared 2 hours in advance and kept at room temperature. Reheat in covered pan.)

Preheat oven to 150°C/300°F/gas 2. If rice was prepared ahead, reheat it with 1 additional knob of butter, stirring gently with fork, until just warm. Butter medium ring mould. Spoon rice into mould and press it in gently so there are no holes; do not crush grains. Cover with foil and warm in oven for 10 minutes.

Reheat curry sauce to simmer in medium-size heavy saucepan, stirring. Taste and adjust seasoning. Sauce should be quite sharply flavoured. Cover and keep warm.

Unmould pilaf ring on to round platter, put a layer of aubergine in centre, and spoon enough sauce over it to coat it. Top with a layer of aubergine. Repeat layering, arranging aubergine pieces decoratively on top. Filling should be mounded above level of rice ring. With slotted spoon, transfer any remaining aubergine pieces to sauce, mix gently, and spoon into separate dish. Serve immediately.

NOTE: To make individual portions of moulded rice, spoon cooked pilaf into 4 to 6 buttered 8-cm/3-inch ramekins. Press with a spoon so the rice is lightly packed, but do not crush grains. Put moulds in a roasting pan and add enough simmering water to come halfway up. Cover with buttered greaseproof paper. Bake in a pre-heated 180°C/350°F/gas 4 oven for 10 minutes. Unmould the ramekins on to plates. Serve with any sauced mixture. To serve with aubergine dish above, mix aubergine cubes with curry sauce and spoon them around rice moulds.

Pasta

During the five years we lived in Paris, my husband and I enjoyed taking trips throughout France and Italy and sampling a variety of pasta dishes. We discovered to our surprise that the pasta dishes in the best French restaurants were on the whole even better than those on the other side of the border. It was difficult to find pasta dishes in Italy that could match such French creations as ragoût of fresh pasta with black truffles, sole fillets with white wine butter sauce on a bed of pasta, or the unparalleled noodle gratin with foie gras that we savoured at L'Auberge de l'Ill, the world-famous restaurant in Alsace.

When we considered it further we realized that actually this is not a new phenomenon. The French have adopted and refined Italian dishes for centuries. Important ingredients such as spinach and fresh peas and basic preparations such as *genoise* all came to France from Italy and were then used by the French in their own way. Following the same tradition French cooks have recently created marvellous dishes with their neighbour's pasta by adding their special touches – delicious sauces, inspired combinations and unique presentation.

Until modern times pasta lovers who wanted to enjoy their favourite food in France had to travel to Provence and Alsace but now chefs all over France are giving pasta a place of honour on their menus. They have realized that the incomparable *crème fraîche* and the delicate French sauces – exquisite butter sauces, cream-based sauces and traditional velouté sauces prepared from concentrated seafood and chicken stocks – are perfect with pasta. Like the Italians the French also enjoy pasta with tomato sauce made from ripe tomatoes and cooked briefly to preserve their fresh flavour. The smoothness and richness of the sauces are balanced in France by such zesty flavourings as Dijon mustard, fresh tarragon, sorrel, shallots, morels, smoked salmon, and Roquefort, Gruyère and goat cheeses.

Rather than confining pasta to first courses the French prefer to broaden its role and serve it as part of the main course or as a side dish, because it is a wonderful complement to seafood, poultry, and meats. A favourite French presentation is topping a bed of pasta with a portion of seafood or meat.

The French are careful to cook their pasta only until it is *al dente*, or slightly firm to the bite, and they too use this Italian term to refer to properly cooked pasta. To check whether the pasta is done a strand is removed from the pot and tasted; tongs are a convenient tool for doing this.

Hints

· Whether buying fresh or dried pasta, be sure it is thin.
· A wooden pasta fork or other large fork is best for mixing the pasta gently but efficiently with the sauce and the other ingredients.
· Always season sauces well before adding them to pasta so that they provide a flavourful contrast to its subtle taste.

TOMATO PASTA WITH GOAT CHEESE
AND GARLIC
Pâtes rouges au fromage de chèvre et à l'ail

In this very quick, easy and flavourful pasta dish the garlic provides just the right complement for the goat cheese. The sauce is also delicious with spinach noodles.

MAKES 4 SERVINGS AS A SIDE DISH OR FIRST COURSE OR

2 SERVINGS AS A MAIN COURSE

300 ml/½ pint double cream
8 medium-size garlic cloves, lightly
  crushed and peeled
50 g/2 oz creamy French goat
  cheese

225 g/8 oz fresh tomato pasta, or
  175 g/6 oz dried
2 tablespoons chopped parsley
Freshly ground pepper
Salt (optional)

In a small saucepan, bring 225 ml/8 fl oz cream to a boil, add garlic, reduce heat to low, and simmer for about 8 minutes, or until garlic is just tender.

If using a goat cheese with a dark rind, remove rind. Cut cheese in a few pieces. Transfer garlic with a slotted spoon to a food processor or blender, add goat cheese and ½ the hot cream, and purée mixture. Gradually add remaining cream and process until smooth.

Return sauce to pan and heat it gently. If sauce is thin, simmer until thick enough to coat a spoon; if it is too thick, stir in enough of remaining cream to obtain desired consistency. (The sauce can be kept, covered, for 4 hours in refrigerator; thin it out with 1 to 2 tablespoons more cream when reheating.)

In a large pan of boiling salted water, cook pasta over high heat, stirring occasionally, for about 3 minutes for fresh pasta or 7 minutes for dried, or until it is *al dente*, and drain it well. While pasta is cooking, reheat sauce over moderate heat, stirring.

Transfer pasta to a heated serving dish and toss it with sauce. Add parsley and pepper to taste. Add salt if desired; it may not be needed because of cheese. Serve immediately.

PASTA WITH FRESH PEAS AND
SAFFRON BUTTER SAUCE
Pâtes aux petits pois, beurre au safran

Unlike the Italians the French often serve pasta as a side dish. This pasta dish is wonderful with scallops, prawns, lobster, or other seafood.   MAKES 6 SERVINGS AS A SIDE DISH

SAFFRON BUTTER SAUCE

¼ teaspoon crumbled saffron
  strands

2 tablespoons finely chopped
  shallots

2 tablespoons white wine vinegar

3 tablespoons dry white wine

1 kg/2 lb fresh peas, shelled or
  450 g/1 lb frozen peas

450 g/1 lb fresh fettucine, or
  350 g/12 oz dried

25 g/1 oz butter, cut into pieces

3 tablespoons double cream

Salt and freshly ground pepper

225 g/8 oz cold unsalted butter,
  cut into 16 pieces.

2 large ripe tomatoes, peeled,
  seeded, well-drained, and diced

Salt and freshly ground pepper

SAFFRON BUTTER SAUCE

In a small heavy non-aluminium saucepan, simmer saffron and shallots in vinegar and wine over medium heat until liquid is reduced to about 2 tablespoons. Reduce heat to low, stir in cream, and simmer, whisking occasionally, until mixture is reduced to about 2 tablespoons. Season lightly with salt and pepper. Cover and reserve. (The mixture can be kept, covered, for 1 hour at room temperature.) Keep butter in refrigerator until ready to use.

In a saucepan of boiling salted water, cook peas for 7 minutes if fresh, or 3 minutes if frozen, or until they are just tender. Drain well.

In a large pan of boiling salted water, cook pasta over high heat, stirring occasionally, for about 3 minutes for fresh pasta or 7 minutes for dried, or until it is al dente, and drain it well. Transfer it to a large pan. Add 25 g/1 oz butter, peas, tomatoes, and pinch of salt and pepper, and toss mixture over low heat just until it is hot.

To finish sauce, bring saffron mixture to a simmer in its saucepan. Reduce heat to low. Add one piece of butter, whisking liquid constantly. When butter piece is nearly blended into liquid, add another piece, still whisking. Continue adding butter pieces one or two at a time, whisking constantly. The sauce should be pleasantly warm to touch. If it becomes too hot and drops of melted butter appear, remove pan immediately from heat and whisk well; add next butter pieces off heat, whisking constantly. When temperature of sauce drops again to warm, return to low heat to continue adding remaining butter pieces. Remove from heat as soon as last butter piece is added. Taste and adjust seasoning and serve sauce as soon as possible. (Sauce can be kept warm for about 15 minutes in its saucepan set on a rack above warm water, but it must be whisked frequently to prevent separation.)

Transfer pasta mixture to a platter and toss with sauce. Taste and adjust seasoning. Serve immediately.

PASTA WITH CREAMY BROCCOLI PURÉE
Pâtes à la crème de brocolis

By adding cream to vegetable purées it is easy to prepare delicious sauces for pasta, as in this colourful dish.　　　MAKES 4 SERVINGS

1 kg/2 lb broccoli, divided into
　medium-size florets
350 ml/12 fl oz cream
40 g/1½ oz butter, at room
　temperature
2 medium-size shallots, finely
　chopped

Salt and freshly ground pepper
Freshly grated nutmeg
225 g/8 oz fresh fettucine or
　medium-width egg noodles, or
　175 g/6 oz dried

Reserve 16 relatively small florets for garnish. Peel large stalk of each head of broccoli. Cut peeled stalk in slices 2 cm/¾ inch thick. In a large saucepan of boiling salted water, cook broccoli slices for 2 minutes. Add florets (except those reserved for garnish) and cook, uncovered, over high heat for about 5 minutes, or until stems of florets are tender when pierced with a sharp knife. Drain, rinse under cold running water, and drain thoroughly.

Purée cooked broccoli in a food processor, or in batches in a blender, adding a total of 4 tablespoons cream, a little at a time. Purée until very smooth.

In a medium-size saucepan, melt 15 g/½ oz butter over low heat, add shallots, and cook for about 7 minutes, stirring often, until soft but not browned. Add broccoli purée and gradually stir in remaining cream. Bring to simmer. Season to taste with salt, pepper, and nutmeg. Keep warm over low heat. (Sauce can be kept, covered, for up to 2 days in refrigerator.)

In a large pan of boiling salted water, cook pasta over high heat, stirring occasionally, for about 3 minutes for fresh pasta or 7 minutes for dried, or until it is *al dente*, and drain it well. Put in a serving dish.

Meanwhile, in a separate saucepan of boiling salted water, cook reserved broccoli florets over high heat for about 2 minutes, or until flower ends are just tender. Drain thoroughly.

Stir remaining butter into broccoli sauce and toss pasta with two-thirds of sauce. Garnish with florets. Serve remaining sauce separately.

FETTUCINE WITH MORELS AND ASPARAGUS
Fettucine aux morilles et aux asperges

Morels are one of the most flavourful of mushrooms; a small amount of morels can add a wonderfully rich taste to a sauce. This creamy pasta dish is great on its own and makes a delectable accompaniment for veal or chicken.   MAKES 2 TO 3 SERVINGS AS A MAIN COURSE, OR
4 TO 6 SERVINGS AS A FIRST COURSE OR SIDE DISH

20 g/¾ oz dried morels
225 g/8 oz thin asparagus
50 g/2 oz unsalted butter
4 teaspoons finely chopped shallots
6 tablespoons dry white wine

6 tablespoons Chicken Stock
    (page 333) or Vegetable Stock
    (page 332)
Salt and freshly ground pepper
225 ml/8 fl oz cream
225 g/8 oz fresh fettucine, or
    175 g/6 oz dried

Soak morels in hot water to cover for about 30 minutes, or until soft. Rinse and drain well. Cut any large morels in half. Remove asparagus tips and cut stalks in 2·5-cm/1-inch pieces, discarding any thick, white bases. Refrigerate half the butter.

In a medium-size saucepan, melt half the remaining butter over low heat, add shallots, and cook for about 2 minutes, or until softened. Pour in wine and bring to a boil, stirring. Add stock, morels, and salt and pepper to taste. Bring to a boil, reduce heat to medium, and simmer until liquid is reduced to about 200 ml/7 fl oz. Stir in cream and bring mixture to a boil. Simmer, stirring occasionally, over medium heat for 7 minutes, or until mixture is thick enough to coat a spoon. (The sauce can be kept, covered, for 1 day in refrigerator.)

In a saucepan of boiling salted water, cook asparagus for 2 minutes. Drain, rinse under cold water, and drain thoroughly. In a small pan over medium-low heat, melt remaining butter, add asparagus and salt and pepper to taste, and sauté for 2 minutes, or until tender. Reserve some tips for garnish.

In a large pan of boiling salted water, cook pasta over high heat, stirring occasionally, for about 3 minutes for fresh pasta or 7 minutes for dried, or until it is *al dente*, and drain it well. Transfer to a bowl. While pasta is cooking, reheat sauce over medium heat, stirring. Add refrigerated butter to sauce and stir over low heat just until blended. Taste and adjust seasoning.

To serve, toss pasta with sauce and asparagus and transfer to a heated platter. Garnish edge of platter with reserved asparagus tips.

SPAGHETTI WITH AUTUMN VEGETABLES AND TOMATO-TARRAGON SAUCE
Spaghetti aux légumes d'automne, sauce tomate à l'estragon

Any vegetable in season can be used in this dish. Tarragon adds a pleasant accent to both the sauce and the vegetables.

MAKES 3 TO 4 SERVINGS

TOMATO-TARRAGON SAUCE

5 tarragon stalks (optional)	Pinch of thyme
1 bay leaf	Salt and freshly ground pepper
1 tablespoon olive oil	2 tablespoons chopped fresh
15 g/½ oz butter	tarragon, or 2 teaspoons dried
1·5 kg/3½ lb ripe tomatoes,	tarragon
peeled, seeded, and chopped	

1 celery stick	Salt and freshly ground pepper
1 small aubergine (about 75 g/	1 small or ½ large cauliflower
3 oz), unpeeled	(about 450 g/1 lb), divided into
1 medium-size carrot, peeled	small florets
1 tablespoon olive oil	225 g/8 oz spaghetti
50 g/2 oz butter	
1 tablespoon chopped fresh	
tarragon, or 1 teaspoon dried	
tarragon	

TOMATO-TARRAGON SAUCE

Tie tarragon stalks and bay leaf in a piece of cheesecloth to make a bouquet garni. (If using dried tarragon, cheesecloth is not needed.) In a large frying pan, heat oil and butter over medium heat, add tomatoes, thyme, bouquet garni or bay leaf, and salt and pepper. Cook, stirring often, for about 25 minutes, or until tomatoes are soft and mixture is thick and smooth. Discard bouquet garni or bay leaf. (Sauce can be kept, covered, for 3 days in refrigerator.)

Add chopped tarragon leaves, taste and adjust seasoning.

Peel celery stick to remove strings. Cut celery, aubergine, and carrot into thin strips about 4 cm/1½ inches long. Put vegetable strips in a large pan of boiling salted water and cook, uncovered, for about 3 minutes. Drain, rinse under cold running water and drain thoroughly. Return to pan and add olive oil, 15 g/½ oz butter, and tarragon. Heat, stirring gently, for about 2 minutes, or until just tender. Season to taste with salt and pepper.

In a large pan of boiling salted water, cook cauliflower florets, uncovered, for about 5 minutes, or until just tender. Drain thoroughly.

In a large pan of boiling salted water, cook spaghetti, uncovered, over high heat for about 7 minutes, or until just tender but still *al dente*, or slightly firm to bite; check by tasting. Drain thoroughly and add to pan of vegetable strips. Add remaining butter and half the cauliflower and toss gently over low heat, using pasta spoons or two forks, just until hot. Taste and adjust seasoning.

Reheat tomato sauce if necessary. Transfer spaghetti mixture to a platter or to plates and spoon tomato sauce over centre. Set remaining cauliflower pieces on tomato sauce and serve.

PASTA WITH VEGETABLE 'NOODLES'
Pâtes aux 'nouilles' de légumes

French cooks like to cut colourful vegetables, such as the carrots and courgette here, in strips and toss them with white noodles, giving the illusion of mixing different coloured noodles. For a delicious main course serve these surrounded by sautéed prawns.

MAKES 2 TO 3 SERVINGS

About 225 g/8 oz carrots,
  preferably large, peeled
1 medium-size courgette (about
  150 g/5 oz)
2 tablespoons finely chopped
  shallots

6 tablespoons dry white wine
225 ml/8 fl oz double cream
Salt and freshly ground pepper
225 g/8 oz fresh medium-width
  noodles, or 175 g/6 oz dried
2 tablespoons snipped fresh dill

Cut carrots in thin strips about 5 cm/2 inches long and of same width as noodles. Cut courgette in strips of same size as carrot strips.

In a saucepan, combine shallots and wine and bring to a boil. Cook over low heat for about 5 minutes, or until liquid is reduced to about 2 tablespoons. Stir in cream, add a pinch of salt and pepper, and bring sauce to a boil. Cook it over medium heat for 6 minutes, or until it is thick enough to coat a spoon.

In a large pan of boiling salted water, cook pasta over high heat, stirring occasionally, for about 3 minutes for fresh pasta or 7 minutes for dried, or until it is *al dente*, and drain it well. Transfer it to a heated platter.

In another saucepan of boiling salted water, cook carrots for about 3 minutes, or until just tender. Add courgette and cook for 1 minute. Rinse and drain thoroughly.

Bring sauce to a boil, remove it from heat, and stir in dill, courgette, and carrots. Pour mixture over noodles and toss gently, using a large fork or tongs. Taste and adjust seasoning.

CREAMY PASTA GRATIN WITH CHEESE
Gratin de pâtes à la crème et au fromage

This dish is inspired by potato gratin dauphinois. French chefs also make pasta gratins with black truffles and even with foie gras.

MAKES 6 SERVINGS AS SIDE DISH

225 g/8 oz dried fettucine
450 ml/¾ pint Crème Fraîche
(page 381)
¼ teaspoon freshly grated nutmeg
Salt and freshly ground white pepper

100 g/4 oz Gruyère cheese, grated
1 cut garlic clove (optional)

Preheat oven to 200°C/400°F/gas 6. In a large pan of boiling salted water, cook fettucine over high heat, stirring occasionally, for about 7 minutes, or until it is *al dente*, and drain it well.

In a large bowl, mix crème fraîche with nutmeg and salt and white pepper to taste. Add pasta and half grated cheese and toss. Taste and adjust seasoning, if necessary, so mixture is well-flavoured.

Rub a shallow 20-cm/8-inch round gratin dish or other baking dish with cut garlic clove. Butter dish, transfer pasta mixture to it, and sprinkle with remaining Gruyère. Bake for about 10 minutes, or until pasta absorbs cream. If necessary, put under a hot grill to brown lightly.

BAKED PASTA WITH AUBERGINES
Macaronis aux aubergines au four

This vegetable and pasta dish is hearty enough to be served as a main course. A fresh tomato sauce like the one served with Aubergine Savarin (see page 38) is a good complement and provides both colour and flavour. Or serve with Provençal Baked Tomatoes (see page 224).   MAKES 4 TO 6 SERVINGS

450 g/1 lb aubergines
6 tablespoons vegetable oil
Salt
25 g/1 oz butter
1 small onion, finely chopped
2½ tablespoons plain flour
350 ml/12 fl oz milk

Freshly ground white pepper
Freshly grated nutmeg
175 g/6 oz elbow macaroni
2 eggs, beaten
100 g/4 oz Gruyère or Emmental
cheese, grated
Fresh Tomato Sauce (page 38)

Peel aubergines and cut in 1-cm/½-inch cubes. Preheat oven to 190°C/375°F/gas 5. Generously butter a large soufflé dish or deep baking dish.

In a medium-size frying pan, heat 3 tablespoons oil over medium heat, add half of aubergine cubes, sprinkle them with salt, and sauté for about 7 minutes, or until tender; since oil is absorbed quickly, reduce heat and stir constantly so aubergine doesn't burn. Remove cubes and repeat with remaining oil and aubergine cubes.

In a medium-size heavy saucepan, melt butter over low heat, add onion, and cook for about 5 minutes, or until soft but not brown. Sprinkle with flour and cook, stirring, about 2 minutes. Remove from heat. Gradually whisk in milk. Bring to a boil over medium-high heat, stirring constantly with a whisk, add a small pinch of salt, white pepper, and nutmeg, and reduce heat to low. Cook, whisking often, for 5 minutes. Transfer to a bowl.

In a large pan of boiling salted water, cook macaroni over high heat, stirring occasionally, for about 9 minutes, or until it is *al dente*. Rinse with cold water and drain well.

Add macaroni and aubergine to sauce and mix gently. Gently stir in eggs and cheese. Add more salt, pepper, and nutmeg, if needed. (Mixture can be prepared 1 day in advance; in this case dab surface with a small piece of butter to prevent a skin from forming. Cover and keep in refrigerator.) Transfer to buttered dish. Set in a shallow pan and put in oven. Add enough very hot water to pan to come halfway up sides of dish. Bake for about 40 minutes, or until mixture sets.

Remove from pan of water. Serve hot with Fresh Tomato Sauce.

PASTA WITH BROCCOLI, CAULIFLOWER, AND ROQUEFORT SAUCE
Pâtes aux brocolis et chou-fleur, sauce roquefort

Serve this pasta dish on its own or to accompany chicken or veal.

MAKES 4 TO 6 SERVINGS

25 g/1 oz unsalted butter
2 medium-size shallots, finely chopped
6 tablespoons dry white wine
350 ml/12 fl oz double cream
50 g/2 oz Roquefort cheese, crumbled
Freshly ground pepper
½ medium-size head cauliflower, divided into medium-size florets

350 g/12 oz broccoli, divided into medium-size florets
450 g/1 lb fresh good-quality fettucine, or 350 g/12 oz dried
Salt (if needed)

In a large heavy saucepan, melt half the butter over low heat, add shallots, and cook, stirring, for 2 minutes. Add wine and simmer, stirring often, until liquid is reduced to about 2 tablespoons. Stir in cream and cook over medium-high heat, stirring often, for about 7 minutes, or until sauce is thick enough to coat a spoon. Reduce heat to low, whisk in Roquefort cheese, and cook sauce, stirring, just until smooth. Add pepper to taste.

In a large pan of boiling salted water, cook cauliflower florets, uncovered, for about 7 minutes, or until just tender. Drain thoroughly. In a pan of boiling salted water, cook broccoli florets for about 5 minutes, or until just tender. Drain thoroughly.

In a large pan of boiling salted water, cook pasta over high heat, stirring occasionally, for about 3 minutes for fresh pasta or 7 minutes for dried, or until it is *al dente*, and drain it well. Transfer to bowl, add remaining butter and about 6 tablespoons sauce, toss, and season to taste with pepper; salt may not be needed.

Transfer pasta to a heated platter and set broccoli and cauliflower florets on top. Coat them partially with sauce. Serve any remaining sauce separately.

COUSCOUS PILAF WITH CARROTS, PEAS, AND SAUTÉED MUSHROOMS
Pilaf de couscous aux carottes, aux petits pois et aux champignons sautés

Although a Tunisian woman in Israel taught me to prepare couscous the traditional way, my first taste of couscous pilaf was in Paris, where it was cooked by a French chef. He quickly poured hot stock over the couscous and enriched it with butter. The couscous was ready in 5 minutes and was delicious.　　MAKES 5 TO 6 SERVINGS

75 g/3 oz blanched almonds
2 medium-size carrots
225 ml/8 fl oz Chicken Stock
　(page 333), Vegetable Stock
　(page 332), or water
Salt and freshly ground pepper
600 g/1 1/4 lb fresh peas, shelled, or
　225 g/8 oz frozen peas

75 g/3 oz unsalted butter, at room
　temperature
100 g/4 oz mushrooms, halved and
　thinly sliced
1 large onion, finely chopped
200 g/7 oz couscous

Preheat oven to 200°C/400°F/gas 6. Toast almonds in small baking pan or baking dish in oven, stirring occasionally, for 8 minutes, or until they are golden brown. Transfer to plate and reserve at room temperature.

Cut carrots in half lengthwise and then into slices 3 mm/1/8 inch thick. In a medium-size saucepan, combine carrots with stock or water and bring to a boil. Add salt to taste and cook over medium heat for about 7 minutes, or until they are just tender. Drain, reserving cooking liquid. Measure liquid from carrots, add enough hot water to make 225 ml/8 fl oz, and pour it into a small saucepan.

In a second saucepan of boiling salted water, cook fresh peas for 7 minutes, or frozen peas for 3 minutes, or until they are just tender. Drain well.

In a medium-size frying pan, melt 25 g/1 oz butter over medium heat, add mushrooms and salt and pepper, and sauté, stirring, for 3 minutes, or until lightly browned. Add carrots and peas and cook over low heat, stirring, for 1 minute. Cover and keep warm.

In a large shallow pan, melt 25 g/1 oz butter over low heat, add onion, and cook, stirring, for 10 minutes, or until it is soft but not brown. Add 15 g/½ oz butter and heat until butter melts. Add couscous and stir with a fork until blended. Remove pan from heat and shake to spread couscous in an even layer. Bring measured carrot cooking liquid to a boil, pour it evenly over couscous, immediately cover pan tightly, and let mixture stand for 5 minutes. Cut remaining butter into 4 pieces. Scatter butter pieces over couscous and let it stand, covered, for 1 minute. Fluff with a fork to break up any lumps in couscous, tossing until butter is blended in. Add vegetables, toss, and taste it for seasoning.

Transfer couscous to a serving dish or mound it on a platter and garnish it with almonds.

VEGETABLE SOUPS

Vegetable soup is one of the most appealing first courses, whether it is warm and comforting on a cold day or cool and refreshing on a hot day.

French cooks prepare soups from nearly every vegetable. These soups can contain chunks of vegetables or can be smooth purées. Generally the smooth type is made of a single vegetable but sometimes several vegetables are combined harmoniously. I particularly remember a lovely cream of asparagus and broccoli soup at Alain Chapel restaurant near Lyon.

Although vegetables do not need to be as crisp for soups as for salads the flavour of the soup will be best if all ingredients are fresh. This does not mean that leftovers have no place in soups. Yesterday's cooked cauliflower, spinach, peas, or carrots, for example, can certainly be added to today's vegetable soup. To save time frozen vegetables can also be simmered in soups. But in this case it is important that some of the ingredients be fresh to give the soup zest.

Soups can play different roles in a meal. A chunky soup, such as Southwestern Vegetable Soup with Vegetable Croutons, makes a lovely light lunch and is best served in larger bowls. Cream soups, however, are so rich they should be presented in small, dainty bowls. Many soups, such as Country Spinach Soup, are equally good hot or cold.

Some of the following soups are thickened. Only a small quantity of potato, rice, or flour is required in soups to help produce a smooth, creamy consistency. The right amount of properly cooked flour does not make soups pasty. Without one of these thickeners, large quantities of cream are often needed to achieve the same degree of smoothness. When these soups are brought to the right consistency with stock or milk, so that they barely coat a spoon, they are never heavy.

Soups that are served cold require more seasoning than those served hot and should be tasted again before they are served. They should not be enriched with butter because it would congeal when chilled and mar their consistency.

Whether a soup is brought to the table in an elegant tureen or ladled into bowls in the kitchen, it is a good idea to warm or chill the tureen or bowls first, depending of course on the type of soup and the weather.

Hearty Vegetable Soups

Hearty soups are the symbol of simple, wholesome country cooking. They can contain a variety of vegetables, as well as rice and pasta, and are served as a satisfying first course or main dish.

These soups can be varied infinitely, gaining liveliness from almost any herb, from many spices, and from seasonal vegetables. Sauces such as aïoli, rouille, and pistou, the French version of pesto, can enrich a vegetable soup.

VEGETABLE BOUILLABAISSE
Bouillabaisse de légumes

Provençal cooks make vegetable bouillabaisse seasoned like its cousin, fish bouillabaisse. This sumptuous vegetable soup is flavoured with saffron, garlic and thyme and is served with rouille sauce. Other vegetables such as green beans can be added instead of or in addition to the peas.   MAKES 4 TO 6 SERVINGS

ROUILLE SAUCE

½ fresh chilli pepper
3 medium-size garlic cloves, peeled
1 egg yolk, at room temperature
Salt
2 to 3 teaspoons strained fresh
   lemon juice

200 ml/7 fl oz extra virgin olive oil,
   at room temperature
1 to 2 tablespoons tomato paste
Freshly ground pepper
Pinch of cayenne pepper (optional)

SAFFRON-VEGETABLE SOUP

225 g/8 oz boiling potatoes, peeled
3 tablespoons extra virgin olive oil
1 large onion, halved and thinly
  sliced
6 large garlic cloves, chopped
1 litre/1¾ pints water
Salt and freshly ground pepper
¾ teaspoon chopped fresh thyme,
  or ¼ teaspoon dried thyme

1 bay leaf
½ teaspoon fennel seed
Scant ½ teaspoon saffron strands
700 g/1½ lb fresh peas, shelled
  and rinsed
2 small courgettes (about 100 g/
  4 oz), diced

Slices of French baguette, left
  whole, or 8 slices of Italian
  bread, about 6 mm/¼ inch
  thick, cut in half

ROUILLE SAUCE

Wear rubber gloves if you are sensitive to hot peppers. Discard seeds
and ribs from chilli pepper. Handle it carefully and be sure to wash
your hands, the knife, and the board immediately afterwards. Chop
garlic and chilli as finely as possible so that they become almost a
purée.

In a medium-size heavy bowl set on a towel, whisk egg yolk with
garlic, chilli, a pinch of salt, and 2 teaspoons lemon juice. Using a
whisk or hand mixer, begin stirring or beating in the oil, drop by
drop. When 2 or 3 tablespoons oil have been incorporated, whisk in
remaining oil in a very thin stream. After adding 6 tablespoons,
whisk in ½ teaspoon lemon juice to thin sauce and make stirring
easier. When all of oil is added, gradually stir in tomato paste. Add
salt, pepper, cayenne pepper, and more lemon juice, if desired. (The
sauce can be made 2 days in advance and kept, covered, in
refrigerator.) Serve it at room temperature.

SAFFRON-VEGETABLE SOUP

Cut potatoes lengthwise into quarters if they are round. If using long,
oval potatoes, cut them lengthwise in half. Cut potato quarters or
halves in 6-mm/¼-inch slices.

In a medium-size saucepan, warm oil over low heat, add onion, and cook, stirring often, about 15 minutes, or until soft but not brown. Add garlic and cook, stirring, 30 seconds.

Add potatoes and stir. Add water and salt and pepper to taste. Wrap thyme, bay leaf, and fennel seed in a piece of cheesecloth and tie tightly to make a bouquet garni; add to soup. Bring to a simmer, crumble in saffron, and stir. Bring to a boil, reduce heat to low, cover, and cook for 10 minutes. Stir in peas and courgette, cover, and cook for about 25 to 30 minutes or until vegetables are tender. Discard bouquet garni. Taste soup and adjust seasoning. (Soup can be kept, covered, 1 day in refrigerator. Reheat over low heat.)

Toast bread and spread a little rouille sauce on 4 to 6 slices. Serve separately. Pass remaining toast and sauce separately. Toast spread with rouille can be floated in soup or eaten separately.

RICH ONION SOUP WITH PORT
Soupe à l'oignon au porto

Although onion soup is a restoring midnight snack to enjoy at cafés or small restaurants in Paris, it is also a favourite for lunch or supper and makes a wonderful light meal at home. The secrets of delicious onion soup are cooking the onions slowly in butter and using a good homemade stock and a good cheese; French or Swiss Gruyère yield the best results.   MAKES 6 SERVINGS

50 g/2 oz unsalted butter
700 g/1½ lb onions, thinly sliced
Salt and freshly ground pepper
1·15 litres/2 pints Chicken Stock
    (page 333), Vegetable Stock
    (page 332), or a mixture of
    stocks
1 bay leaf

3 sprigs fresh thyme
6 thick slices French or Italian
    bread (about 2 cm/¾ inch thick
    and 8 cm/3 inches in diameter)
2 egg yolks, at room temperature
4 tablespoons port
175 g/6 oz Gruyère cheese, grated

Prepare 6 ovenproof soup bowls or large ramekins.

In a large heavy saucepan melt butter over low heat, add onions and pinch of salt and pepper. Cover with buttered foil and with a lid and cook, stirring occasionally, for about 20 minutes, or until onions are tender. Uncover and continue cooking over medium heat until onions are golden brown. Add stock. Wrap bay leaf and thyme in a piece of cheesecloth and tie tightly to make a bouquet garni; add to soup. Bring to a boil, cover, reduce heat to low, and simmer for at least 30 minutes, or up to 1 hour, until well flavoured. Discard bouquet garni and taste and adjust seasoning. (Soup can be kept, covered, for up to 2 days in refrigerator. Reheat, covered, over medium heat.)

Meanwhile, preheat oven to 170°C/325°F/gas 3. Put sliced bread on a baking sheet and bake for about 5 minutes on each side, or until dry. Beat egg yolks with port and put in a sauceboat.

To serve, put 1 slice bread in each ovenproof soup bowl. Ladle soup over bread. Sprinkle with cheese. Grill until cheese is lightly browned. Serve immediately. (If you do not have ovenproof soup bowls, you can sprinkle the cheese on the bread slices, set them on a baking sheet, brown them under the grill, and pass them separately.) Serve port mixture separately so that those who wish can stir it into their soup under the topping.

CREAMY ONION SOUP WITH PASTA
Potage thourins Roumanille

This easy-to-prepare soup requires no stock. Simmering the onions in milk and adding thin pasta to cook directly in the mixture give it a creamy texture and a delicious flavour.   MAKES 6 SERVINGS

50 g/2 oz butter	1 bay leaf
5 medium-size onions, halved and cut in very thin slices	5 parsley stalks
2 sprigs fresh thyme	1 large garlic clove, finely chopped
	1 tablespoon plain flour

450 ml/¾ pint water
About 750 ml/1¼ pints milk
Salt and white pepper

50 g/2 oz very thin short noodles
Freshly grated Parmesan cheese, as
an accompaniment

In a medium-size heavy saucepan, melt butter over low heat, add onions, and cook, stirring often, for about 30 minutes, without letting onions brown. If onions seem to be beginning to brown, cover pan after 10 minutes of cooking so that steam will help prevent browning, but continue stirring often. Wrap thyme, bay leaf, and parsley stalks in a piece of cheesecloth and tie tightly to make a bouquet garni.

Add garlic to onions and cook for 1 minute. Sprinkle flour over mixture and cook over low heat, stirring, for 2 minutes.

Gradually add water to mixture, stirring. Pour in milk, stirring. Add bouquet garni and a little salt and white pepper. Bring to a boil, reduce heat to low, and cook, stirring often, for 10 minutes.

Add noodles and continue cooking for 5 minutes, or until they are just tender. Add more pepper, taste, and adjust seasoning. Discard bouquet garni. If soup is too thick, stir in a little more milk.

When serving, pass grated cheese for sprinkling on soup.

COUNTRY SPINACH SOUP
Potage campagnard aux épinards

For this rustic soup the ingredients are not puréed and thus retain their texture. The soup can be served hot or cold. For a vegetable feast, follow it with Spaghetti with Autumn Vegetables and Tomato-Tarragon Sauce (page 282) and a fresh green salad.

MAKES 4 SERVINGS

450 g/1 lb fresh spinach (leaves
  with stems)
50 g/2 oz butter
½ onion, finely chopped
350 ml/12 fl oz water
2 tablespoons uncooked long-grain
  white rice

Salt and freshly ground pepper
225 ml/8 fl oz milk
Freshly grated nutmeg
2 egg yolks, at room temperature
4 tablespoons double cream

Discard spinach stems and rinse leaves thoroughly. Hold a handful of
leaves on cutting board and cut them crosswise in thin strips.
Continue with remaining leaves.

In a medium-size saucepan, heat 40 g/1½ oz butter over low heat,
add onion, and cook, stirring, for about 5 minutes, until softened but
not browned. Add spinach and stir until coated with butter. Add
water, rice, and salt and pepper, and bring to a boil over high heat.
Reduce heat to low, cover, and simmer for about 15 minutes, or until
rice is tender. Stir in milk, add nutmeg, and simmer, uncovered, for
5 minutes. Remove from heat.

Whisk egg yolks and cream in a bowl until blended. Gradually
pour about 6 tablespoons soup into egg yolk mixture. Stir this
mixture into soup remaining in saucepan. Warm over low heat,
stirring, for about 2 minutes, or until slightly thickened; do not boil.
Remove from heat, stir in remaining butter, and add more salt,
pepper, and nutmeg, if needed. Serve immediately.

PROVENÇAL VEGETABLE SOUP WITH
PASTA AND PISTOU
Soupe au pistou

Pistou, the French version of the Italian pesto, gives zest to this
popular Provençal soup. Basil is the essential ingredient in pistou
and thus makes this soup primarily a summer treat. But the soup is so
well loved in Provence that pistou is often made in large quantities,
covered with olive oil, and kept for use in a winter version of the soup

as well. Traditionally a mortar and pestle were used to blend the ingredients for the sauce. Today pistou is prepared in seconds with the aid of a food processor.

In addition to or instead of some of the vegetables below, the soup can include spinach, Swiss chard, potatoes, pumpkin, or a small amount of turnip. Although traditional recipes call for cooking all the vegetables together, modern cooks prefer to add the most tender ones last so that they retain their character. MAKES 8 SERVINGS

100 g/4 oz dried haricot beans
3 litres/5 pints water
3 tablespoons olive oil
2 garlic cloves, chopped
2 large leeks (white and green
   parts), cleaned and chopped
350 g/12 oz ripe tomatoes, peeled,
   seeded, and chopped
1 medium-size carrot, peeled and
   diced

50 g/2 oz green beans, ends
   removed, cut in 3 pieces
Salt and freshly ground pepper
4 small courgettes (about 450 g/
   1 lb), cut in cubes
175 g/6 oz fresh peas, shelled
100 g/4 oz medium-width noodles
Freshly grated Parmesan cheese, as
   an accompaniment

PISTOU

6 large garlic cloves
About 50 g/2 oz basil, leaves only
75 g/3 oz freshly grated Parmesan
   cheese

150 ml/¼ pint extra virgin olive oil

Soak dried beans overnight in cold water to generously cover; drain thoroughly. Put beans in a large saucepan with 1·25 litres/2¼ pints water. Bring to a boil over medium heat. Simmer, uncovered, for 1 hour, adding hot water occasionally so beans remain covered. Reserve beans in 200 ml/7 fl oz of their liquid.

In a saucepan, warm 2 tablespoons olive oil over medium heat, add garlic and leeks, and stir briefly. Add tomatoes and cook, stirring, for about 5 minutes. Add carrot, green beans, white beans in their reserved liquid, remaining 1·25 litres/2¼ pints water, remaining tablespoon olive oil, and a pinch of salt and pepper and bring to a boil. Cover and simmer for 20 minutes. Add courgettes and simmer for about 20 minutes longer, or until vegetables are very tender.

PISTOU
Chop garlic in a food processor. Add basil and cheese and purée with garlic until basil is chopped. Gradually add olive oil, with motor running. Scrape down sides and purée again so mixture is well blended.

Add peas and noodles to soup and simmer for about 10 minutes or until just tender. Remove from heat, stir in pistou, taste and adjust seasoning; serve immediately. Serve grated Parmesan cheese separately. (It is best not to reheat this soup because pistou loses its fresh flavour, but any leftovers are very good cold.)

NOTE: Frozen peas (about 50 g/2 oz) can be substituted for fresh; add them 5 minutes after adding noodles.

MUSHROOM CREAM SOUP WITH
FRESH HERBS
Crème de champignons aux fines herbes

Like a velouté soup, this soup is made with a light velouté sauce but is chunky with slices of mushrooms rather than being puréed. Cultivation of white mushrooms, which are known as *champignons de Paris* in French, began in France about two hundred years ago, and with it came the development of numerous recipes. What a contribution they have made to Western menus!   MAKES 4 SERVINGS

2 medium sprigs fresh thyme, or ½   2 medium-size shallots, finely
   teaspoon dried thyme   chopped
3 tarragon stalks (optional)   350 g/12 oz small button
1 bay leaf   mushrooms, halved and thinly
40 g/1½ oz butter   sliced

Salt and freshly ground pepper
2 tablespoons plain flour
225 ml/8 fl oz Chicken Stock
   (page 333), Vegetable Stock
   (page 332), or water
450 ml/¾ pint milk

200 ml/7 fl oz double cream
1 tablespoon chopped fresh
   tarragon (optional)
1 tablespoon chopped fresh parsley
Freshly grated nutmeg

Wrap thyme sprigs, tarragon stalks, and bay leaf in a piece of cheesecloth and tie tightly to make a bouquet garni.

In large heavy saucepan, melt butter over medium heat, stir in shallots, and cook for 1 minute. Stir in mushrooms and add salt and pepper to taste. Cover and cook, shaking pan occasionally, for about 5 minutes, or until tender. Uncover and cook over medium heat, stirring, until liquid rendered by mushrooms evaporates.

Reduce heat to low, stir in flour, and cook, stirring constantly, for about 3 minutes, or until mixture is well blended and bubbly.

Remove from heat and gradually pour stock and milk into mushroom mixture, stirring and scraping bottom of saucepan thoroughly. Add bouquet garni and bring to a boil over medium-high heat, stirring constantly. Stir in cream and bring to a simmer, stirring. Reduce heat to low and simmer, uncovered, stirring often, until thickened to taste; about 10 minutes. Discard bouquet garni. (Soup can be kept, covered, for up to 2 days in refrigerator. Reheat, uncovered, over low heat.)

Stir in half the tarragon and parsley, and nutmeg to taste. Add salt and pepper, if needed. Serve hot, sprinkled with remaining tarragon and parsley.

VEGETABLE BOURRIDE WITH AÏOLI
Bourride de légumes

Traditionally bourride is prepared with fish, but it is also superb when made with vegetables. It has a zesty flavour and a creamy consistency because of the addition of aïoli, or garlic sauce, at the end. Broccoli

or cauliflower florets can be added instead of or in addition to the
other vegetables.   MAKES 5 TO 6 SERVINGS

AÏOLI

4 large garlic cloves, chopped	6 tablespoons extra virgin olive oil
4 egg yolks	Salt and freshly ground pepper
1 teaspoon strained fresh lemon juice	

100 g/4 oz small courgettes	50 g/2 oz chopped onion
225 g/8 oz carrots	1 garlic clove, finely chopped
225 g/8 oz leeks, light green and white parts only	1 litre/1¾ pints Vegetable Stock (page 332), Chicken Stock (page 333), or unsalted vegetable stock powder mixed with water
2 celery sticks, peeled	
2-inch sprig fresh rosemary	
2 sprigs fresh thyme	Salt and freshly ground pepper
1 tablespoon olive oil	

AÏOLI

Drop garlic cloves through feed tube of a food processor fitted with
metal blade, with motor running, and process until finely chopped.
Add egg yolks, lemon juice, 1 tablespoon oil and a little salt and
pepper and process until very thoroughly blended, scraping bottom
and sides of container several times. With motor running, gradually
pour in oil in a thin trickle. After adding 4 tablespoons, remaining
oil can be poured in a little faster, in a fine stream.

Cut courgettes into pieces 4 cm/1½ inches long, then into
6-mm/¼-inch lengthwise slices. Cut each slice lengthwise into
sticks 6 mm/¼ inch wide. Cut carrots, leeks, and celery in pieces of
same size as courgettes. Wrap rosemary and thyme in a piece of
cheesecloth and tie tightly to make a bouquet garni.

In a medium-size heavy saucepan, heat oil over low heat, add
onion, and cook, stirring often, for about 5 minutes, or until soft but
not brown. Add garlic and cook for 30 seconds, stirring.

Add stock, bouquet garni, and salt and pepper to taste. Stir and bring to a boil. Add carrots, reduce heat to low, and simmer, uncovered, for 5 minutes. Add celery and leeks, cover, and return to a simmer. Cook over low heat for 15 minutes, or until carrots are just tender. Add courgette and cook for 8 minutes, or until just tender.

Remove soup from heat. Discard bouquet garni. Using slotted spoon, transfer vegetables to medium-size bowl, letting as much soup as possible drain back into pan. Holding solids back with large slotted spoon, drain any liquid from bottom of bowl back into pan.

Spoon aïoli into a medium-size heavy bowl and gradually whisk in about 450 ml/¾ pint of soup. With saucepan of soup off heat, gradually whisk mixture into remaining soup. Return soup to low heat and warm, whisking constantly, for 4 or 5 minutes; be careful not to let it come near a boil.

Remove from heat and gently add vegetable mixture with a slotted spoon, leaving behind any liquid in bowl. Taste and adjust seasoning. Serve hot. (Leftover bourride can be reheated in a double boiler, very carefully and with constant stirring, until just warm; or it can be served at room temperature but not cold.)

SOUTHWESTERN VEGETABLE SOUP WITH VEGETABLE CROUTONS
Potage garbure

This soup originated in the Pyrenees area of southwest France and is made from a variety of vegetables. Fresh peas, courgettes, green beans, or other vegetables in season can be added. The soup is sometimes flavoured with goose fat and meat and used to be made thick enough so a spoon could stand up in it, but today many prefer this lighter version. Vegetable croutons, made of vegetable purée spread on bread, sprinkled with grated Gruyère, and browned in the oven, are the special accompaniment. They involve very little extra work because their topping is made from vegetables that cook in the soup.   MAKES 6 SERVINGS

50 g/2 oz dried haricot beans
1 whole onion
2 cloves
2 sprigs fresh thyme, or ½
    teaspoon dried thyme
1 bay leaf
40 g/1½ oz butter
2 leeks, white part only, cleaned
    and cut in thin slices
3 medium-size celery sticks, peeled
    and cut in thin slices; or 1 small
    celeriac, peeled and cut in small
    dice
350 g/12 oz carrots, peeled and cut
    in thin slices

1 medium-size turnip, peeled and
    cut in thin slices
¼ small cabbage, cut in thin slices
    (optional)
2 medium-size potatoes, peeled,
    halved and cut in thin slices
2 garlic cloves, chopped
About 1·25 litres/2¼ pints
    Vegetable Stock (page 332) or
    water
Salt and freshly ground pepper
1 thin French bread (baguette), or
    4 long French rolls, cut in thin
    slices
50 g/2 oz grated Gruyère cheese
Pinch of cayenne pepper
2 tablespoons chopped fresh parsley

Soak beans about 8 hours or overnight in cold water to generously cover; drain thoroughly. Put beans and onion in a large saucepan and add enough water to cover by about 2·5 cm/1 inch. Wrap cloves, thyme, and bay leaf in a piece of cheesecloth and tie tightly to make a bouquet garni, and add to pan. Bring to a boil over medium heat and simmer, uncovered, for 1½ hours, adding hot water occasionally so beans remain covered. Discard bouquet garni. Reserve beans in 200 ml/7 fl oz of their liquid.

In a large saucepan, melt 25 g/1 oz butter over low heat. Add leeks, celery, carrots, turnip, and cabbage. Cook, stirring often, for 15 minutes.

Add potatoes, garlic, stock, beans in their liquid, and pinch of salt and pepper. Bring to a boil, reduce heat to low, cover, and cook for about 30 minutes, or until all vegetables are very tender.

Meanwhile, preheat oven to 190°C/375°F/gas 5. Put sliced bread on a lightly buttered baking sheet and bake for about 3 minutes on each side or until lightly toasted.

Remove about one-quarter of vegetables from saucepan with a slotted spoon. Purée them in a blender or food processor until very smooth. Transfer to a small saucepan and cook over low heat, stirring, until mixture is very thick. Taste and adjust seasoning. Spread mixture generously on bread slices and sprinkle with grated cheese. Bake for about 10 minutes or until cheese melts and browns lightly; if necessary, grill briefly to brown. (Soup and topping for croutons can be prepared 2 days in advance and kept, covered, in refrigerator; but croutons should be baked a short time before serving.)

Reheat soup before serving. If soup is too thick, stir in a little more stock. Stir in remaining butter, if desired, add a pinch of cayenne pepper, taste and adjust seasoning. Sprinkle with chopped parsley and serve. Serve croutons separately.

NOTE: After croutons are made, remaining vegetables can also be puréed until smooth and served as a purée soup.

Vegetable Purée Soups

Puréed vegetables are what give these quick easy soups their characteristic flavour and thickness. The vegetables are cooked in stock or water before being puréed with their cooking liquid. Some French cooks prefer to use water rather than stock to emphasize the natural flavour of the vegetables.

Most vegetables require the addition of a small amount of rice or potatoes to give the soup enough body. For vegetables that contain a relatively high proportion of starch, such as green peas, chestnuts, or dried beans, the thickener can be omitted. A light version of purée soups can be made from non-starchy vegetables by simply increasing the amount of vegetable purée, as in Light Cauliflower Soup. Whichever technique is chosen, a little cream or fresh butter provide the ideal final enrichment.

Hints

· A food processor, blender, or food mill with a fine disc can be used to purée vegetables for soups. When using a food processor it is best to add the vegetables and a few tablespoons of the liquid. In a blender, the soup can be puréed most efficiently if all the liquid is added along with the cooked vegetables. A food mill is useful for puréeing fibrous vegetables such as watercress, so that the strings do not go through into the soup. Another way to eliminate the fibres is to purée the soup in a blender or food processor and then strain it.

· If substituting stock-cube stock for homemade stock in soups, use volume of recommended-strength stock equal to amount of stock called for in the recipe. Do not add salt – cubes are often salty.

· Fresh herbs, especially tarragon, dill, basil, parsley, chives and chervil, can be added to purée, cream and velouté soups for extra flavour and colour. Stir 2 to 3 tablespoons into the soup just before serving; or after ladling the soup into a tureen or into bowls, sprinkle with about 1 tablespoon for garnish.

· Purée, cream and velouté soups thicken on standing. After reheating them or when serving them cold, gradually add 1 or 2 tablespoons cream, milk, stock, or water to the soup to bring it back to the desired consistency.

FRESH PEA SOUP WITH MINT CREAM
Purée de petits pois à la crème de menthe

Serve this rich bright-green soup in small portions, either hot or cold.

MAKES 4 SERVINGS

6 tablespoons Crème Fraîche
  (page 381) or bought crème
  fraîche or sour cream
1 tablespoon chopped fresh mint
1·75 kg/4 lb fresh or 600 g/1¼ lb
  frozen peas
450 ml/¾ pint Vegetable Stock
  (page 332) or water

Salt and freshly ground pepper
225 ml/8 fl oz milk
225 ml/8 fl oz double cream
Small sprigs of mint, for garnish
  (optional)

To make mint cream, mix crème fraîche or sour cream with chopped mint. Let stand for 30 minutes at room temperature if serving soup hot, or in refrigerator if serving it cold.

In a medium-size saucepan, combine peas with stock or water and salt and pepper to taste. Bring to a boil, reduce heat to medium-low, cover, and simmer for about 5 minutes, or until barely tender. Remove 2 tablespoons peas with a slotted spoon and reserve for garnish. Continue cooking remaining peas for about 3 minutes, or until very tender.

Transfer peas and their cooking liquid to a blender or food processor. Purée peas until very fine. With machine running, gradually pour in milk. Continue to purée until very smooth. Return to saucepan and simmer over low heat for 2 minutes, stirring often.

Stir in cream. Bring to a boil, stirring, and simmer soup to desired consistency; about 5 minutes. Taste and adjust seasoning. (The soup may be kept, covered, for up to 1 day in refrigerator.)

Just before serving, reheat soup over medium-low heat, stirring. To reheat reserved peas, put them in a pan of boiling water for 30 seconds; drain well. Ladle soup into shallow bowls. Spoon mint cream into centre of each bowl. Garnish with reserved peas and sprigs of mint.

TOURAINE CHESTNUT SOUP
Potage aux marrons à la tourangelle

This soup from the Loire Valley south of Paris makes a rich elegant first course. Fresh herbs are added to the finished soup to balance the delicate naturally sweet taste of the chestnuts.

MAKES 4 SMALL SERVINGS

450 g/1 lb fresh chestnuts
15 g/½ oz butter
1 medium-size leek, white part only, chopped
350 ml/12 fl oz Chicken Stock (page 333), Vegetable Stock (page 332), or water
1 small celery stick, broken in two pieces
1 bay leaf

Salt and freshly ground pepper
750 ml/1¼ pints milk, plus a little more if needed
4 tablespoons double cream or Crème Fraîche (page 381)
2 teaspoons snipped chives
2 teaspoons chopped tarragon
1 tablespoon plus 2 teaspoons chopped parsley

In a medium-size saucepan, combine half the chestnuts with enough water to cover them by about 2·5 cm/1 inch. Bring to full boil and cook for 1 minute. Remove one with slotted spoon and peel: first cut base and pull off outer skin, and then pull and scrape off inner skin. Continue with remaining chestnuts, removing from water one by one.

In a medium-size saucepan, melt butter over low heat, add leek, and cook, stirring, for about 5 minutes, or until soft but not brown. Add chestnuts, stock or water, celery, bay leaf, and salt and pepper to taste. Bring to a boil, reduce heat to low, cover, and simmer until chestnuts are just tender when pierced with point of knife; about 15 minutes.

Bring milk to a boil in a separate saucepan. Stir 450 ml/¾ pint hot milk into soup. (Cover remaining milk and reserve.) Simmer soup, uncovered, over medium heat, for about 20 minutes, or until chestnuts are very tender. Discard celery pieces and bay leaf. Purée soup in blender or purée chestnuts in a food processor and add rest of soup liquid to food processor with motor running. Return puréed soup to clean saucepan.

Bring soup to a boil, stirring, add remaining milk, and return to a boil. Add cream and return to a boil. Remove from heat. If preparing soup in advance, stir as it cools. (Soup can be kept, covered, for up to 2 days in refrigerator.)

Soup thickens on standing. If soup was cold, reheat it, whisking. If soup is too thick after reheating, stir in 1 or 2 tablespoons milk to bring it to desired consistency.

Stir in chives, tarragon, and 1 tablespoon parsley. Taste and adjust seasoning; be generous with the seasoning so soup will not be bland. Serve hot. Sprinkle remaining parsley on each serving.

ASPARAGUS SOUP WITH OLIVE OIL
Soupe d'asperges à la languedocienne

Asparagus is delicious both in a cream soup in the style of northern France (as in the variation) and in this southern version, from Languedoc.   MAKES 3 TO 4 SERVINGS

2 egg yolks, at room temperature	1 kg/2 lb medium-size asparagus
1 teaspoon strained fresh lemon	spears
juice	900 ml/2½ pints water
Salt	White pepper
6 tablespoons extra virgin olive oil	

CROUTONS (OPTIONAL)

4 thick slices white bread, crusts
  removed
4 to 6 tablespoons vegetable oil

In a medium-size heavy bowl set on a towel, whisk egg yolks with lemon juice and a pinch of salt. Begin whisking or beating in oil, drop by drop. When 2 or 3 tablespoons have been added, whisk in remaining oil in a very thin stream. Transfer to a large bowl.

Peel asparagus spears and cut in 5-cm/2-inch pieces, discarding tough ends. Reserve 16 to 20 tips for garnish.

In medium-size saucepan, bring the water to boil and add salt. Add asparagus pieces (except tips reserved for garnish) and return to a boil. Simmer, uncovered, over medium heat for about 15 minutes, or until stalks are very tender when pierced with a small sharp knife. Drain, reserving 450 ml/¾ pint cooking liquid.

Purée asparagus in food processor until very smooth. Gradually add reserved cooking liquid, with machine running. (If using blender, combine asparagus with reserved liquid and purée.) Strain into a medium-size heavy saucepan, pushing and stirring hard and repeatedly and using rubber spatula to scrape mixture from underside of strainer.

In a medium-size saucepan of boiling salted water, cook asparagus tips, uncovered, over high heat for about 2 minutes, or until barely tender. Rinse and drain well.

CROUTONS

Cut bread in 1-cm/½-inch squares.

In a large heavy pan, heat 4 tablespoons oil. Test oil by adding a bread square; if oil is hot enough, it should bubble vigorously around bread. Remove bread piece with fish slice.

Add enough of remaining bread squares to hot oil to make one layer. Toss or turn them frequently so they will brown evenly. Fry them until they are golden brown.

Transfer to paper towels to drain. If pan is dry, add another 2 tablespoons oil and heat thoroughly. Repeat frying remaining bread squares. (The croutons can be made 2 hours in advance and kept at room temperature.)

Bring soup to a boil and remove from heat. Gradually whisk soup into egg yolk mixture. Return to saucepan and cook over low heat, stirring, for about 2 minutes, or until slightly thickened; do not let soup come near boil or it will curdle. Add white pepper and taste and adjust seasoning. Stir in asparagus tips. Serve immediately in shallow bowls; pass croutons separately.

CREAMY ASPARAGUS SOUP

Beat the 2 egg yolks with 6 tablespoons double cream. Omit oil, lemon juice, and croutons. Finish soup as above, thickening it with the cream mixture.

LIGHT CAULIFLOWER SOUP
Potage léger au chou-fleur

This soup is light in texture because no thickening ingredients are added. It is good hot or cold. If you like, serve it with Cheese Puffs (see page 327).   MAKES 4 TO 6 SERVINGS

1 small cauliflower (about 600 g/
    1¼ lb)
25 g/1 oz butter
1 onion, thinly sliced
¼ teaspoon fresh thyme, or pinch
    of dried thyme
1 bay leaf

Salt and freshly ground pepper
350 ml/12 fl oz water
225 ml/8 fl oz milk
Freshly grated nutmeg
6 tablespoons double cream
1½ to 2 tablespoons snipped chives

Divide cauliflower into medium-size florets. Reserve a few small florets for garnish. Peel and slice cauliflower stalk. In a medium-size saucepan, melt butter over low heat, add onion, and cook, stirring occasionally, for about 10 minutes, or until tender. Add cauliflower (except florets reserved for garnish), thyme, bay leaf, and salt and pepper to taste. Stir briefly over low heat, cover, and cook for 2 to 3 minutes. Add water, cover, bring to a boil, reduce heat to low, and simmer, stirring often so all cauliflower pieces come in contact with water; about 20 minutes, or until cauliflower is very tender.

Discard bay leaf. Transfer cauliflower and onion pieces to a food processor; reserve cooking liquid. Purée cauliflower and onion until smooth and return purée to saucepan of cooking liquid. (If using a blender, purée cauliflower and onion with cooking liquid and return to pan.) Bring to a boil, stirring, add milk and nutmeg to taste, and bring to a boil. Stir in cream and bring again to a boil. Simmer, stirring, for about 3 minutes, or until soup thickens to desired consistency. Add half the chives and more salt, pepper, and nutmeg, if needed. (The soup can be kept, covered, for up to 1 day in refrigerator.)

A short time before serving, cook reserved florets in a pan of boiling salted water for about 4 minutes, or until just tender. Reheat soup if necessary. To serve, set 1 or 2 florets in centre of each soup bowl. Sprinkle remaining chives around florets.

PUMPKIN AND PASTA SOUP
Purée de potiron à la bourgeoise

While American cooks have been stimulated by the sweet flavour and smooth texture of pumpkin to make pie fillings, the French find those same characteristics perfect for making savoury dishes, including a soup with the poetic name of *crème d'or* or 'golden cream'.

MAKES 4 SERVINGS

1·25 kg/2½ lb fresh pumpkin
350 ml/12 fl oz water
4 teaspoons sugar
Salt and freshly ground pepper

350 ml/12 fl oz milk
50 g/2 oz thin noodles or
   vermicelli, broken in
   5-cm/2-inch lengths
50 g/2 oz butter, cut into 4 pieces

Cut pumpkin in pieces and cut off peel. Remove any seeds or stringy flesh. Cut flesh in about 4-cm/1½-inch cubes and rinse them. In a saucepan, combine pumpkin with water, sugar, and salt and pepper. Cover and bring to a boil, reduce heat to medium-low, and simmer, turning pieces over often, for about 20 minutes, or until tender.

With a slotted spoon, transfer pumpkin pieces to a food processor or blender and purée until smooth. Return purée to pan of cooking liquid and bring to a boil. Cook, uncovered, over low heat for 5 minutes, stirring often. Add milk and bring to a simmer. Cook over low heat, stirring often, for 5 more minutes. (The soup can be prepared 1 day in advance up to this point and kept, covered, in refrigerator.)

Reheat soup if necessary. Add noodles, stir gently, and cook over low heat for about 7 minutes, or until they are just tender; do not overcook or they will lose their texture. Taste and adjust seasoning.

Remove from heat and add butter, a small piece at a time. Stir and serve immediately.

PUMPKIN, POTATO, AND LEEK SOUP
Potage de potiron aux poireaux et aux pommes de terre

This light, delicate soup is more colourful than its famous cousin, potato and leek soup. The green part of the leek should not be used because it gives the soup an odd colour.   MAKES 4 SERVINGS

450 g/1 lb fresh pumpkin	*Salt*
2 leeks, white part only, rinsed thoroughly	*225 ml/8 fl oz milk*
2 medium-size potatoes	*6 tablespoons double cream*
350 ml/12 fl oz water	*White pepper*
	Freshly grated nutmeg
	1 tablespoon chopped parsley

Cut pumpkin in pieces and cut off peel. Remove any seeds or stringy flesh. Cut pumpkin in cubes. Thoroughly rinse and slice leeks. Peel potatoes and cut them in pieces.

In a saucepan, combine pumpkin, leeks, potatoes, water, and a pinch of salt. Cover and bring to a boil, reduce heat to low, and simmer for about 30 minutes, or until vegetables are very tender.

With a slotted spoon, transfer vegetables to a food processor and add a few tablespoons of their cooking liquid; purée until smooth and return to saucepan containing remaining cooking liquid. If using a blender, purée vegetables together with their liquid.

Bring soup to a boil and simmer for 5 minutes. Stir in milk, reduce heat to low, and simmer for 2 minutes. Stir in cream and bring to a simmer. Add white pepper and nutmeg to taste. Add more salt, pepper, and nutmeg, if needed. (Soup can be kept, covered, for 1 day in refrigerator.)

Reheat soup over low heat if necessary. Sprinkle each serving with chopped parsley.

PROVENÇAL TOMATO SOUP
Soupe de tomates à la provençale

This soup is made with the favourite ingredients of Provence: tomatoes, garlic, basil and olive oil. It is important to use very ripe tomatoes at the peak of their season. The pesto-like herb oil added just before the soup is served gives it extra zest. MAKES 4 SERVINGS

2 tablespoons extra virgin olive oil
1 large onion, thinly sliced
3 small garlic cloves, finely
   chopped
1·75 kg/4 lb very ripe soft tomatoes,
   cored and cut in eighths
Salt
½ to ¾ teaspoon sugar

2 tablespoons coarsely chopped
   fresh basil
¾ teaspoon chopped fresh thyme,
   or ¼ teaspoon dried thyme
Freshly ground pepper
1 clove
1 bay leaf

HERB OIL

1 large garlic clove
4 tablespoons fresh parsley

4 tablespoons fresh basil
3 tablespoons extra virgin olive oil

1 tablespoon thin strips of fresh
   basil, or a few small whole basil
   leaves, for garnish (optional)

In a large heavy saucepan, heat oil over low heat, add onion, and cook, stirring often, for about 20 minutes, or until soft and just beginning to brown. Add garlic and cook, stirring, for 1 minute.

Add tomatoes, sprinkle them with salt, and stir. Add ½ teaspoon sugar, basil, thyme, and a pinch of pepper. Tie clove and bay leaf in cheesecloth, add to saucepan, and push into tomatoes. Bring to a boil, cover, and simmer over medium heat, stirring often, for 20 minutes, or until very soft. Discard cheesecloth bag.

Purée tomato mixture in a food mill, using fine disc. Push through as much as possible until pulp remaining in food mill is dry. Scrape off any mixture remaining on underside of disc. Rinse saucepan. Return purée to pan and bring to a boil, reduce heat to low, and simmer, uncovered, stirring often, for about 15 minutes, or until soup is of desired thickness. (Soup can be kept, covered, for 1 day in refrigerator.)

HERB OIL

In a food processor, chop garlic clove, add basil and parsley, and process until finely chopped. Add oil and purée until blended. The mixture will not be smooth and emulsified. Transfer to a bowl and stir briefly to blend in oil.

Just before serving, reheat soup if necessary. Remove from heat and stir in herb oil. Taste and adjust seasoning, adding remaining sugar if desired. Serve garnished with basil.

LIGHT COURGETTE SOUP WITH CURRY PUFFS
Purée de courgettes aux gnocchis

This light soup is thickened by a generous amount of courgette purée. The curry puffs are made of a mixture similar to a rich *pâte à choux* and can be flavoured with paprika or herbs (added to finished dough) instead of curry powder. These types of puffs can be used to garnish other vegetable purée soups, especially cauliflower, broccoli and spinach soups.   MAKES 4 TO 6 SERVINGS

CURRY PUFFS

75 g/3 oz plain flour	40 g/1½ oz unsalted butter, cut in
6 tablespoons milk	cubes
¼ teaspoon salt	1 egg
½ teaspoon curry powder	1 egg yolk

LIGHT COURGETTE SOUP

700 g/1½ lb small courgettes	Salt and freshly ground pepper
25 g/1 oz butter	350 ml/12 fl oz water
1 onion, thinly sliced	6 tablespoons milk
1 sprig fresh thyme, or ¼ teaspoon dried thyme	4–6 tablespoons double cream
	Pinch of cayenne pepper
1 bay leaf	

CURRY PUFFS

Sift flour on to a piece of greaseproof paper.

Combine milk, salt, curry powder, and butter in a small heavy saucepan. Cook over low heat, stirring constantly, until butter melts. Raise heat to medium-high and bring to a boil. Remove from heat, immediately add flour all at once, and stir quickly with a wooden spoon until mixture is smooth. Set pan over low heat and beat mixture for about 30 seconds.

Remove from heat and cool for about 3 minutes. Beat egg and yolk in a small bowl. Gradually beat egg mixture into dough. Beat with a wooden spoon until mixture is very smooth. (The mixture can be kept, covered, for up to 4 hours in refrigerator.)

LIGHT COURGETTE SOUP

Cut courgettes into medium-size slices. In a medium-size saucepan, melt butter over low heat, add onion, and cook, stirring occasionally, for about 10 minutes, or until soft. Add courgette, thyme, bay leaf, and salt and pepper to taste. Stir briefly over low heat so courgette absorbs flavour from butter, add water, and bring to a boil. Reduce heat to low, cover, and simmer for 7 to 10 minutes, or until courgette is tender.

Discard bay leaf and thyme sprig, if using fresh. Transfer courgette and onion pieces to blender or food processor, reserving cooking liquid. Purée until smooth. Return purée to saucepan of cooking liquid; bring to boil, stirring. Stir in milk and bring to boil. Stir in 4–6 tablespoons cream and bring again to boil. Add cayenne pepper, taste and adjust seasoning. (Soup can be kept, covered, for 1 day in refrigerator.)

A short time before serving, boil a generous amount of salted water in a large wide saucepan. Reduce heat to medium so water simmers. Take a half teaspoonful of curry dough on a teaspoon; dip a second teaspoon in simmering water and use it to push mixture from first spoon into water. Continue making puffs in this way; try to give them a fairly even oval shape. Do not crowd; they need room to puff.

Reduce heat to low and cook puffs, uncovered, for about 10 to 15 minutes. To check whether they are done, remove one and cut it; if dough sticks to knife, it is not cooked enough.

Remove with a slotted spoon and drain on paper towels.

To serve, bring soup to a boil, stirring. Ladle it into bowls and put two or three puffs in each.

NORMAN POTATO-SHALLOT SOUP
Potage de pommes de terre aux échalotes à la normande

This simple country potato soup is accented by a delicate shallot flavour and enriched with cream.   MAKES 3 TO 4 SERVINGS

2 thyme sprigs, or ½ teaspoon
    dried thyme
1 bay leaf
25 g/1 oz butter
10 medium-size shallots, chopped
    (about 225 g/8 oz)
2 medium-size potatoes, peeled
    and diced (about 350 g/12 oz)

750 ml/1¼ pints water
Salt and white pepper
6 tablespoons Crème Fraîche
    (page 381) or bought crème
    fraîche or double cream
1 or 2 tablespoons milk or cream
    (optional)

Wrap thyme sprigs and bay leaf in a piece of cheesecloth and tie tightly to make a bouquet garni.

In a large saucepan, melt butter over low heat, add shallots, and cook, stirring often, for about 3 minutes, or until they soften. Add potatoes, water, bouquet garni, and salt and white pepper to taste, and bring to a boil. Reduce heat to low, cover, and cook for about 25 minutes, or until potatoes are tender.

Discard bouquet garni. Stir cream into soup and bring to a simmer. With a slotted spoon, transfer vegetables to a food processor and add a few tablespoons of their cooking liquid; purée them until smooth and gradually add remaining cooking liquid. If using a blender, purée vegetables together with all their cooking liquid.

Return soup to saucepan and bring to a boil, add more pepper, taste and adjust seasoning. (Soup can be kept, covered, for 1 day in refrigerator.)

Reheat soup over medium heat, stirring often. If soup is too thick, stir in a few tablespoons milk or cream.

CARROT SOUP WITH CHIVES
Purée de carottes à la ciboulette

This sensational soup has a great flavour and superb colour. A small amount of cooked rice puréed with the carrots imparts a velvety texture to the soup.   MAKES 4 SERVINGS

25 g/1 oz butter
450 g/1 lb carrots, finely diced
450 ml/³⁄₄ pint water or Vegetable
    Stock (page 332)
2 tablespoons uncooked rice
Salt and freshly ground pepper
Pinch of sugar

¹⁄₄ teaspoon dried thyme
1 bay leaf
About 225 ml/8 fl oz milk
4 tablespoons double cream
4 teaspoons snipped chives

In a medium-size heavy saucepan, melt butter over low heat, add carrots, and cook, stirring often, for about 3 minutes.

Add water or stock, rice, salt, pepper, sugar, thyme, and bay leaf to saucepan and bring to a boil. Reduce heat to low, cover, and cook for about 30 minutes, or until carrots and rice are very tender. Discard bay leaf.

Using a slotted spoon, transfer carrots and rice to a blender or food processor, reserving their cooking liquid. Purée carrots until fine. With machine running, gradually pour in carrot cooking liquid. Purée until very smooth. Return to saucepan and simmer over low heat for 5 minutes, stirring often.

Add enough of milk to bring soup to desired consistency. Bring to a boil, stirring. Add cream and bring again to a boil, stirring. Taste and adjust seasoning. (Soup can be kept, covered, for 2 days in refrigerator.)

Just before serving, reheat soup over medium-low heat, stirring. Ladle soup into bowls and garnish with chives.

Vegetable Cream and Velouté Soups

Velouté in French means velvety and is the perfect description of the texture of cream and velouté soups. They acquire a smooth, silky texture from a roux made of butter and flour cooked together, which also thickens them. These delicious festive soups are a French culinary treasure.

The traditional technique for preparing cream soups calls for a thin béchamel sauce, made from milk and a roux, combined with a puréed vegetable, as in Swiss Chard Soup with Toasted Hazelnuts. This method can be used to create a cream soup from almost any vegetable, but the favourites are asparagus, broccoli, cauliflower, carrots, leeks, lettuce, mushrooms, spinach, tomatoes, turnips, watercress and courgettes.

Velouté soups are based on a light version of velouté sauce, which is composed of stock thickened with a small amount of roux. For vegetable veloutés either chicken stock or vegetable stock can be used. Like cream soups veloutés can be prepared from a purée of nearly any vegetable. In classic cuisine velouté soups are enriched with a mixture of cream and egg yolks, which gives them a wonderful flavour and a beautiful light yellow colour. Many contemporary cooks omit the egg yolks because of their tendency to curdle during reheating.

Delicacy of taste is characteristic of these soups and extra flavourings are usually avoided so the flavour of the major ingredient will remain pure.

The favourite decoration for cream and velouté soups is a small quantity of the main element, which is left in pieces instead of being puréed or strained. In Red Pepper Velouté Soup, for example, a little diced red pepper is added at the last moment. To highlight the garnish and prevent it from sinking, shallow bowls are preferred for serving this kind of soup.

'Soup is to a dinner what the entrance portico is to a building,' wrote Grimod de la Reynière, a noted French gastronomic writer. Because cream and velouté soups are rich, they should be served in rather small portions. They are not meant to play the role of a main course, but rather of an elegant beginning that should stimulate the appetite for the rest of a fine meal.

Hints

· Soups that contain flour should be cooked in a heavy saucepan to prevent sticking. A whisk is most practical for stirring soups that do not contain any chunks; otherwise use a wooden spoon. These soups should be stirred often while they simmer, by moving the whisk or spoon over the entire surface of the saucepan and around the edges, to prevent the flour from causing lumps.

· To ensure complete smoothness cream and velouté soups can be strained.

· Cream and velouté soups should be delicately flavoured but not bland. Season them well.

· Reheat soups gently over low heat, whisking or stirring. If a soup containing egg yolks must be reheated, set it over low heat in a double boiler or a pan above hot, not boiling, water and heat it carefully, stirring constantly. Remove the soup from the heat as soon as it is warm. It should not boil.

SWISS CHARD SOUP WITH TOASTED HAZELNUTS
Crème de blettes aux noisettes

A sprinkling of toasted hazelnuts on each serving contributes elegance, flavour, and a crunchy contrast to this smooth and creamy pale green soup.   MAKES 4 SERVINGS

600 g/1¼ lb Swiss chard
750 ml/1¼ pints water
50 g/2 oz butter
30 g/1¼ oz plain flour
450 ml/¾ pint milk, plus a few
*   tablespoons more if needed*

Salt and freshly ground pepper
Freshly grated nutmeg
40 g/1½ oz hazelnuts
4 tablespoons double cream

Discard chard stems and rinse leaves thoroughly. In a medium-size saucepan, bring 750 ml/1¼ pints water to a boil and add chard. Boil for 3 minutes or until just tender. Drain, reserving liquid. Rinse chard under cold water and drain thoroughly. Squeeze out excess liquid. Measure 450 ml/¾ pint chard cooking liquid.

In medium-size saucepan, melt 15 g/½ oz butter over low heat, add chard, and cook, stirring, for about 2 minutes to dry.

In a medium-size heavy saucepan, melt remaining butter over low heat, add flour, and cook, whisking constantly, for 2 minutes. Remove from heat, gradually whisk in milk and reserved chard cooking liquid, and cook over medium-high heat, whisking constantly, until mixture comes to boil. Add chard and season with salt, pepper, and nutmeg to taste. Reduce heat to low and cook, stirring often, for about 10 minutes.

Preheat oven to 180°C/350°F/gas 4. In a shallow baking pan, toast hazelnuts in oven for about 8 minutes, or until skins begin to split. Transfer to a large strainer. Rub hot nuts against strainer with clean tea towel to remove most of skins. Cool nuts completely. Chop coarsely with a knife.

Purée soup in a blender, food processor, or food mill with a fine disc. Return soup to saucepan. Bring to a boil, stirring. Add cream and return to boil. Simmer, stirring often, for about 6 minutes, or until thickened slightly; it should be slightly thick so the hazelnuts will not sink. (Soup can be kept, covered, for 2 days in refrigerator; keep toasted hazelnuts separately in covered container at room temperature.)

Reheat soup if serving hot. Stir in a few tablespoons milk if soup is too thick. Taste and add more salt, pepper and nutmeg if needed. Serve hot or cold. Spoon into bowls and sprinkle hazelnuts over each serving.

LEEK CREAM SOUP WITH DICED TOMATOES
Crème de poireaux aux dés de tomates

Ripe tomatoes add bright flecks of red to this delicate rich soup.

MAKES 4 SERVINGS

2 medium sprigs fresh thyme, or ½
 teaspoon dried thyme
1 bay leaf
40 g/1½ oz butter
8 medium or 4 large leeks, white
 and light green parts only, split
 and cleaned
Salt and freshly ground pepper
2 tablespoons plain flour

225 ml/8 fl oz Chicken Stock
 (page 333), Vegetable Stock
 (page 332), or water
600 ml/1 pint milk
6 tablespoons double cream
1 large ripe tomato, peeled, seeded,
 drained well, and diced
Freshly grated nutmeg
1 tablespoon chopped parsley

Wrap thyme sprigs or dried thyme and bay leaf in a piece of cheesecloth and tie tightly to make a bouquet garni.

In a large heavy saucepan, melt butter over medium heat, stir in leeks, and add salt and pepper. Reduce heat to low and cook, stirring often, for about 10 minutes, or until leeks are softened but not brown.

Stir in flour and cook, stirring constantly, for about 2 minutes, or until mixture is well blended and bubbly.

Remove from heat; gradually pour stock and milk into leek mixture, stirring and scraping bottom of saucepan thoroughly. Add bouquet garni and bring to a boil over medium-high heat, stirring constantly. Reduce heat to low and simmer, uncovered, stirring often, for about 15 minutes, or until leeks are tender.

Discard bouquet garni. Purée soup in a blender or food processor until smooth. If soup is too thick, stir in a little extra milk to thin it so it lightly coats a spoon. Stir in cream and bring to a boil. Simmer, if necessary, to desired consistency. (Soup can be kept, covered, for 2 days in refrigerator.)

Reheat soup, if necessary, over medium heat, reduce heat to low, add tomato, and simmer for 1 minute.

Stir in nutmeg to taste and half the parsley. Add more salt, pepper, and nutmeg if needed. Serve hot; sprinkle each serving with a little of remaining parsley.

SORREL VELOUTÉ SOUP
Velouté d'oseille

Creamy, tangy, refreshing sorrel soup is a favourite throughout northern France, from Brittany to Alsace and south to the Loire Valley. Sorrel is not often seen in British greengrocers', but is easily grown from seed. It also grows wild throughout Britain, especially on acid soils.   MAKES 4 SERVINGS

100 g/4 oz fresh sorrel (leaves with stems)
40 g/1½ oz unsalted butter
2 tablespoons plain flour
450 ml/¾ pint Vegetable Stock (page 332), Chicken Stock (page 333), or water
Salt and freshly ground pepper

350 ml/12 fl oz milk, plus a few tablespoons more if needed
4 tablespoons double cream or Crème Fraîche (page 381) or bought crème fraîche
1 egg yolk
Croutons, sautéed in oil, if desired (see page 310)

Remove sorrel stems and wash leaves thoroughly. Chop leaves coarsely.

In a medium-size saucepan, melt butter over low heat, add sorrel, and cook, stirring often, for about 10 minutes, or until sorrel is wilted and most of liquid has evaporated. Sprinkle with flour and cook, stirring, until flour is absorbed. Remove from heat.

Gradually stir in stock or water with a whisk. Add a little salt and pepper to taste. Return to medium-high heat and bring to a boil, whisking constantly. Reduce heat to low and simmer, uncovered, whisking often, for 20 minutes, or until well flavoured. Add milk and bring to a boil, whisking. Remove from heat. (Soup can be kept, covered, for 1 day in refrigerator.)

Reheat soup if necessary; if it has become too thick, stir in a few tablespoons milk.

In a medium-size bowl, beat cream with egg yolk. Gradually add about 150 ml/¼ pint of soup. Pour this mixture in a thin stream into remaining soup. Return to low heat and cook, stirring, for about 2 minutes, or until hot; do not boil or yolks will curdle. Add more pepper and taste and adjust seasoning.

Ladle into bowls and serve hot. Pass croutons separately.

WATERCRESS VELOUTÉ SOUP WITH CHEESE PUFFS
Velouté de cresson, petits choux au fromage

Watercress becomes delicate when made into a creamy soup in this way, and cheese puffs provide a perfect flavour complement. The watercress purée is strained to remove the stems and stringy parts. Be sure to use very fresh watercress. MAKES 3 TO 4 SERVINGS

CHEESE PUFFS

40 g/1½ oz Gruyère cheese	50 g/2 oz unsalted butter, cut in
50 g/2 oz plus 1 tablespoon plain	pieces
flour	3 eggs
6 tablespoons water	1 egg, beaten with a pinch of salt,
¼ teaspoon salt	for glaze

WATERCRESS SOUP

About 350 g/12 oz watercress	Salt and white pepper
50 g/2 oz butter	2 tablespoons plain flour
1 large onion, thinly sliced	350 to 400 ml/12 to 14 fl oz milk
400 ml/14 fl oz Chicken Stock	Freshly grated nutmeg
(page 333), Vegetable Stock	3 to 6 tablespoons double cream
(page 332), or water	

CHEESE PUFFS

Preheat oven to 200°C/400°F/gas 6. Lightly butter two baking sheets. Use food processor fitted with shredding disc to shred cheese, or grate it by hand. Sift flour on to a piece of greaseproof paper.

In a small heavy saucepan, heat water, salt, and butter until butter melts. Raise heat to medium-high and bring to a boil. Remove from heat, add flour immediately and stir quickly with a wooden spoon until mixture is smooth. Set pan over low heat and beat mixture for about 30 seconds. Remove from heat and let cool for a few minutes.

Add 1 egg and beat it thoroughly into mixture. Add second egg and beat mixture until it is smooth. Reserve 2 tablespoons of shredded cheese for sprinkling on top. Add remaining cheese to dough and beat until blended.

In a small bowl beat third egg with a fork. Gradually beat enough of this egg into dough until dough becomes very shiny and is soft enough so it just falls from spoon.

Using a piping bag and small plain tip, or two teaspoons, shape small mounds of dough, spacing them about 4 cm/1½ inches apart on baking sheets. Brush them with egg glaze and sprinkle with remaining cheese. Bake in preheated oven for about 15 minutes, or until dough is puffed and browned.

Transfer puffs to a rack to cool. (They can be baked 1 day in advance and kept in an airtight container, but taste best on day they are baked.)

WATERCRESS SOUP

Thoroughly rinse watercress, discard large stems and reserve only upper, leafy third of each bunch. Reserve a few attractive leaves for garnish.

Plunge watercress into a large pan of boiling water. Bring back to a boil, drain, and rinse under cold running water. Squeeze dry in handfuls.

In a medium-size heavy saucepan, melt 15 g/½ oz butter over low heat, add onion, and cook, stirring often, until soft but not brown. Add watercress and cook, stirring, for 2 more minutes. Add stock and a pinch of salt and pepper and bring to a boil. Cover, reduce heat to low, and simmer, stirring occasionally, for about 20 minutes, or until onion is very tender.

Purée soup in a food mill. Alternatively, purée it in a blender or food processor, then strain to remove stringy parts of watercress.

In a medium-size heavy saucepan, melt remaining butter over low heat, add flour, and stir it into butter. Cook over low heat, whisking constantly, for 2 minutes. Remove from heat and gradually add watercress mixture, followed by 350 ml/12 fl oz milk. Cook over medium-high heat, whisking constantly, until soup comes to boil. Adjust seasoning and add nutmeg to taste. Reduce heat to low and cook, stirring often, for about 10 minutes.

Stir in 3 tablespoons cream and bring again to a boil. If soup is too thin, simmer until it reaches desired consistency; it should lightly coat a spoon. If soup is too thick, stir in extra cream or milk. Add nutmeg; taste and add more salt, pepper and nutmeg if needed. (The soup can be kept, covered, for 1 day in refrigerator.)

If desired, reheat cheese puffs in a 150°C/300°F/gas 2 oven. Reheat soup over low heat, stirring. Stir in 1 to 2 tablespoons milk if needed.

For garnish, put reserved watercress leaves in a small strainer and dip in a small pan of boiling water for 30 seconds. Rinse and drain.

To serve, ladle soup into bowls and garnish with watercress leaves. Serve cheese puffs, hot or at room temperature, separately.

CAULIFLOWER VELOUTÉ SOUP WITH BROCCOLI
Velouté de chou-fleur aux brocolis

Bright green briefly cooked broccoli florets garnish this rich creamy cauliflower soup. The soup can also be done in reverse: the broccoli can be made into a velouté soup and garnished with cauliflower florets. Each soup can instead be garnished by florets of the same vegetable.   MAKES 4 TO 5 SERVINGS

2 small heads cauliflower (about 1·25 kg/2½ lb total), cut into medium-size florets	*Salt and white pepper*
	Freshly grated nutmeg
25 to 50 g/1 to 2 oz butter	*About 350 ml/12 fl oz milk*
2 tablespoons plain flour	*4 tablespoons double cream*
350 ml/12 fl oz Vegetable Stock (page 332) or Chicken Stock (page 333)	*About 20 small broccoli florets*

Peel cauliflower stalks and slice. Fill large saucepan with water and bring to boil. Add salt, cauliflower florets, and stalks and return to boil. Remove to a colander and rinse under cold water.

In medium-size heavy saucepan, melt 25 g/1 oz butter over low heat, add flour, and combine it with butter. Cook over low heat, whisking constantly, for 2 minutes. Remove from heat and gradually whisk in stock. Cook over medium-high heat, whisking constantly, until mixture thickens and comes to boil. Add a pinch of salt, pepper, and nutmeg to taste.

Add cauliflower florets to stock mixture. Add 225 ml/8 fl oz milk; liquid will not cover cauliflower. Bring to boil, stirring. Reduce heat to low, cover, and simmer, stirring often so that all pieces come in contact with liquid and so flour does not stick to bottom of pan. As cauliflower becomes more tender, crush slightly with spoon while stirring. Simmer for about 25 minutes, or until cauliflower is very tender.

Using a slotted spoon, remove cauliflower and purée it (in batches if necessary) in a blender, food processor, or food mill with a fine disc. If using blender or food processor, gradually add rest of soup to purée, while machine is running. Purée until very smooth. Return soup to saucepan and bring to a boil, stirring.

Add enough of remaining milk to bring soup to desired consistency; it should lightly coat a spoon. Bring to a boil, stirring, add cream, and bring again to a boil, stirring. Simmer for 1 or 2 minutes to thicken slightly. Taste and adjust seasoning; soup should be generously flavoured with salt, pepper, and nutmeg. (Soup can be kept, covered, for 2 days in refrigerator.)

Just before serving, in a medium-size saucepan of boiling salted water, boil broccoli florets, uncovered, over high heat for about 3 minutes, or until just tender. Drain thoroughly.

If soup was made in advance, reheat it over medium-low heat, stirring. Remove soup from heat and stir in remaining butter, if desired. Ladle soup into a tureen or into bowls and garnish with broccoli florets.

COLD CAULIFLOWER VELOUTÉ SOUP WITH BROCCOLI

Omit optional extra butter. If soup is too thick, stir in a few tablespoons cream. Taste for seasoning before serving. Garnish with broccoli as above.

RED PEPPER VELOUTÉ SOUP
Velouté de poivrons rouges

Red peppers are a fashionable ingredient today. Yet their vibrant colour and sweet taste have long been loved in the French kitchen. This classic soup is made of peppers simmered in stock and is garnished with rice.   MAKES 4 SERVINGS

3 medium-size red peppers (about
    600 g/1¼ lb), cut in half,
    cored, and seeded
75 g/3 oz unsalted butter
900 ml/1½ pints Chicken Stock
    (page 333) or Vegetable Stock
    (page 332)

2 tablespoons uncooked long-grain
    rice
Salt and freshly ground pepper
2 tablespoons plain flour
2 tablespoons double cream
Pinch of cayenne pepper

Cut peppers in thin strips, about 1 cm/⅜ inch wide. In a large pan, melt half the butter over low heat and stir in pepper strips. Cover and cook, stirring occasionally, for about 7 minutes, or until softened. Remove 8 pepper strips with slotted spoon and reserve for garnish. Add 200 ml/7 fl oz stock to pan, cover, and bring to simmer. Reduce heat to low and cook until peppers are very tender; about 15 minutes.

Put 350 ml/12 fl oz boiling salted water in a small saucepan, add rice, and cook, uncovered, over medium-high heat for about 12 minutes, or until just tender; taste to check. Drain thoroughly, rinse, and reserve for garnish.

Transfer peppers and their cooking liquid to a blender or food processor. Purée for 2 minutes, or until very smooth.

In a medium-size heavy saucepan, melt remaining butter over low heat, add flour, and cook, whisking constantly, until mixture turns a light beige colour; 2 to 3 minutes. Remove from heat.

Gradually ladle remaining stock into flour mixture, whisking. Bring to a boil, whisking constantly, over medium-high heat. Add a pinch of salt and pepper. Reduce heat to medium-low and simmer, uncovered, whisking often, for 5 minutes. Add puréed peppers and simmer, stirring often, for 5 minutes.

Stir in cream and bring to a boil, add cayenne pepper, and simmer, stirring, about 1 minute, or until soup thickens slightly. Taste and adjust seasoning.

Gently peel skin off pepper strips reserved for garnish. Dice peppers. (Soup can be prepared in advance up to this point and kept, covered, for up to 1 day in refrigerator; refrigerate pepper strips and rice in separate containers.)

Bring pepper dice to room temperature and reheat soup, if

necessary, over medium-low heat, stirring. Stir rice into hot soup and heat briefly. Ladle soup into bowls and garnish with pepper dice.

VEGETABLE STOCK
Fond de légumes

Vegetable stock is made of aromatic vegetables and mild herbs. Because it is a base for a great number of dishes and should not clash with the taste of other ingredients, it should have a relatively neutral taste. Salt is not added, because often stock is used in a dish that already contains salty ingredients. Rather, the dishes using the stock are seasoned to taste.

The purpose of stock is to provide depth of flavour to dishes; vegetables with an assertive flavour, such as cauliflower, cabbage, and turnips, should not be used.

Small pieces of onion, carrot, leeks, mushrooms, and celery can be frozen in bags or containers and saved for stock.

The cook who is in a great hurry can substitute stock cubes, diluted with water according to the directions, but these are usually quite salty.   MAKES ABOUT 1 LITRE/1¾ PINTS

25 g/1 oz unsalted butter
3 medium-size onions, coarsely
  chopped
1 medium-size carrot, scraped and
  diced
2 celery sticks, chopped
Dark green part of 1 leek, rinsed
  thoroughly and sliced (optional)
1·4 litres/2½ pints water

1 bay leaf
2 sprigs fresh thyme, or ½
  teaspoon dried thyme
3 medium-size garlic cloves, peeled
  and crushed
5 parsley stalks (optional)
½ teaspoon black peppercorns
175 g/6 oz sliced mushrooms or
  mushroom stalks (optional)

In a large saucepan, melt butter over low heat, add onions, carrot, celery, and leek, and cook, stirring, for about 10 minutes. Add water, bay leaf, thyme, garlic, parsley stems, peppercorns, and mushrooms and mix well. Bring to a boil.

Reduce heat to low and simmer, uncovered, for 1 hour. Strain, pressing on ingredients in strainer; discard these ingredients. (Stock can be kept for up to 3 days in refrigerator, or it can be frozen.)

CHICKEN STOCK
Fond de volaille

Chicken stock is a useful, all-purpose light stock that adds a good flavour to a great variety of French soups and sauces. With just a little salt, pepper, chopped fresh herbs, and perhaps a few cooked vegetables added, homemade chicken stock is a very good soup on its own. It is convenient to prepare a large quantity of chicken stock and keep it in the freezer in small or medium-size containers.

MAKES ABOUT 2·5 LITRES/4½ PINTS

1·5 kg/3 lb chicken wings and necks, or a mixture of wings, backs, necks, and giblets (except livers)
2 medium-size onions, cut into quarters
Green part of 1 leek, cleaned (optional)
2 medium-size carrots, cut into quarters
2 bay leaves
10 parsley stalks
About 4 litres/7 pints water
2 sprigs fresh thyme, or ½ teaspoon dried thyme
½ teaspoon black peppercorns

Combine chicken, onions, leek, carrots, bay leaves, and parsley stalks in a stockpot or other large pan. Add enough water to cover ingredients. Bring to a boil, skimming foam that collects on top. Add thyme and peppercorns.

Reduce heat to very low so that stock bubbles very gently. Partially cover and cook, skimming foam and fat occasionally, for at least 2 or up to 3 hours.

Strain stock into large bowl; discard ingredients in strainer. If not using immediately, cool to lukewarm. Refrigerate until cold and skim fat off top. (Stock can be kept, covered, for 3 days in refrigerator, or it can be frozen.)

VEGETABLE SALADS

In France in the past decade the role of salads has become much more central. With the growing interest in light foods and the beginning of nouvelle cuisine salads became very popular when they gained an important place on the menus of the finest restaurants. While the starred restaurants compete with each other to invent new and original salads, including warm salads that feature meat or seafood, the small bistros and cafés still serve simple salads such as *crudités*. A wide variety of freshly prepared salads can be found at the *charcuteries* as well. These are mainly traditional salads that have long been favourites, such as French potato salad, sweetcorn and pepper salad and macédoine, a salad of diced cooked vegetables with mayonnaise. Often a few exotic newcomers are included as well, such as the Lebanese *tabbouleh*.

There are two basic types of salads: simple salads consisting of one major ingredient, and composed salads made up of two or more main components. Generally a composed salad is more substantial than a simple one.

Serving Salads

Salads are not served very cold in France, but rather at cool room temperature, because cold vegetables have less flavour.

Fresh French bread, especially the long, thin baguette, is an important accompaniment for salads and is nearly always on the table. At cafés in France a colourful salad served with fresh bread is a popular light lunch.

Traditionally in France the time to serve a green salad is after the main course in order to refresh the palate before the cheese course or dessert. But today menus are more flexible. Green salads often accompany the main course, especially one of grilled meat or fish. Other salads, depending on their size, can be a first course or even a main course.

Salad Dressings

The favourite salad dressing in France is the simplest, a vinaigrette made of only four ingredients: oil, vinegar, salt and pepper. Vinaigrette is always the choice when a light dressing is desired, and it shows off the colourful ingredients.

The oil and vinegar can be varied to your taste. The traditional dressing in France is a neutral-flavoured vegetable oil and a wine vinegar, but often olive oil is used and sometimes the more exotic walnut or hazelnut oils. Herb or garlic vinegars or sometimes fruit vinegars can also add zip to salads. Many variations on the basic vinaigrette are given in the following chapter.

Homemade mayonnaise is the second most important salad dressing, for richer more substantial salads. Crème fraîche is another popular salad enhancer. Both recipes are given in this chapter for your reference.

Dijon mustard is a good addition to both mayonnaise and vinaigrette, for its flavour and because it helps thicken them. Fresh herbs are also popular additions. But always remember that the purpose of the dressing is to enhance the flavours of the salad ingredients, not to overpower them. The French almost never add sugar to salad dressings and are horrified when they hear of such an idea.

Hints

· When preparing cooked vegetables for salad, cook them until they are tender but still retain a touch of crunchiness. Rinse green vegetables with cold water immediately after cooking until they are cold; if allowed to stand in hot water they will continue to cook.

· After cooking vegetables or rinsing raw salad ingredients be sure to drain and dry them very thoroughly. If any water remains, it dilutes the dressing, makes it run off the vegetables, and results in a watery, flavourless salad.

· Add enough dressing to coat the salad ingredients; do not drench them. Do not dress green salads until ready to serve or they will go limp.

· Always taste a salad after tossing with the dressing to be sure it is well seasoned. Even if the dressing itself is seasoned, after the addition of a generous amount of vegetables the salad might be bland.

· For elegant meals toss the salad in a mixing bowl and then transfer it to a serving bowl so that the edges of the bowl remain clean.

Simple Vegetable Salads

These salads can be made of raw or cooked vegetables. A favourite way of presenting raw vegetables for a first course is as a plate of crudités, a colourful combination of several vegetables. Which vegetables to include depends on the season and on personal taste. Vegetables served raw *must* be absolutely fresh; some say that a favourite way for restaurant reviewers to judge small restaurants is by the freshness of their crudités platter.

For salads of cooked vegetables, the vegetables are generally steamed or cooked in water, then drained and mixed with the dressing.

WATERCRESS SALAD WITH GOAT CHEESE AND WALNUTS
Salade de cresson au fromage de chèvre et aux noix

Creamy goat cheese is a popular addition to green salads. Often the cheese is warmed in the oven or sautéed, but it is also very good at room temperature. Do not buy watercress more than one day in advance; it quickly turns yellow.　　　MAKES 4 SERVINGS

WALNUT OIL VINAIGRETTE

2 tablespoons white wine vinegar
Salt and freshly ground pepper

6 tablespoons walnut oil

175 g/6 oz very fresh watercress
1 small butterhead lettuce
225 g/8 oz creamy French goat
　　cheese

50 g/2 oz walnut pieces, coarsely
　　chopped

WALNUT OIL VINAIGRETTE

Put vinegar with salt and pepper in a small bowl; stir in walnut oil with a whisk. Taste and adjust seasoning and set aside.

Use upper part of watercress – tiny sprigs and leaves only – and discard large stems. Thoroughly rinse and dry watercress and lettuce. Put both in a bowl.

If goat cheese has a dark rind, cut it off, then crumble cheese.

Stir vinaigrette again and add enough to salad to moisten it and then toss. Taste and adjust seasoning.

When serving salad, sprinkle each serving with goat cheese and walnuts.

GREEN SALAD WITH PINE NUTS AND SHERRY VINAIGRETTE
Salade verte aux pignons

The traditional green salad served in France after the main course is now often embellished with nuts and with vinaigrettes made of exotic vinegars and oils. This salad can also be served as an accompaniment for roast chicken or grilled steak.　　　　　MAKES 6 SERVINGS

SHERRY VINAIGRETTE

2 tablespoons sherry vinegar or white wine vinegar	1 teaspoon Dijon-style mustard (optional)
Salt and freshly ground pepper	6 tablespoons vegetable oil
2 butterhead lettuces, or 1 cos lettuce	25 g/1 oz pine nuts
½ head radicchio (optional)	Salt
2 teaspoons vegetable oil	1 tablespoon chopped parsley (optional)

SHERRY VINAIGRETTE

Stir vinegar, salt, pepper, and mustard in a small bowl until blended. Gradually add oil, stirring with a whisk. Taste and adjust seasoning; vinaigrette should be highly seasoned to flavour lettuce. (Vinaigrette can be kept for 2 weeks in covered jar in refrigerator.)

Discard any yellow lettuce leaves and tough bases. Rinse lettuce leaves and radicchio well in a sinkful of water. Remove leaves from water so that any dirt sinks to bottom. Dry well in a salad spinner or in a towel. The leaves can be kept in a towel for 1 to 2 hours in refrigerator.

In a small shallow pan, heat 2 teaspoons oil over low heat, add pine nuts and a pinch of salt, and sauté for about 2 minutes, or until lightly toasted. Transfer to a bowl and cool.

Leave small lettuce leaves whole; tear large leaves in a few pieces. Put in a bowl.

Stir vinaigrette with a whisk. Add parsley, if desired. Add enough vinaigrette to lettuce leaves, tossing them, to coat. Taste and adjust seasoning. Do not add so much vinaigrette that a pool of it remains at bottom of bowl. When serving, sprinkle pine nuts over each serving.

NOTE: Other lettuces in season can be added. *Mâche* (also called lamb's lettuce) will add a festive note and wonderfully delicate flavour to green salad, but remember to rinse it very thoroughly.

CELERIAC SALAD WITH MUSTARD DRESSING
Celeri-rave rémoulade

Celeriac salad is often served as part of crudités, a selection of colourful salads. When garnished with walnuts and eggs, as in this version, it can make a first course on its own. For further colour surround it with a ring of cherry tomato halves.

MAKES 4 TO 6 SERVINGS

225 ml/8 fl oz Mayonnaise (page 379)
2 to 3 teaspoons Dijon mustard
About 450 g/1 lb celeriac
½ lemon
Salt and freshly ground pepper

3 tablespoons chopped parsley
2 hard-boiled eggs, quartered (optional)
50 g/2 oz walnut halves (optional)

To make dressing, mix mayonnaise with 2 teaspoons mustard. Taste and adjust seasoning and add another teaspoon mustard if desired.

Use a sharp knife to peel celeriac, removing all brown parts. Rub peeled celeriac with cut side of lemon half to prevent it from discolouring. Cut peeled celeriac in thin strips, using a sharp knife or julienne blade of a food processor.

Put celeriac in a pan of water and bring to a boil. Cook, uncovered, for 1 to 2 minutes, or until slightly softened so celeriac is crisp but not unpleasantly hard. Drain thoroughly and dry on paper towels. Put in a bowl.

Add enough dressing to moisten celeriac and 2 tablespoons parsley. Taste and adjust seasoning. Serve at room temperature or cold. (Salad can be kept for up to 2 days in refrigerator.) Garnish with quartered hard-boiled eggs, remaining parsley, and walnut halves, if desired.

FENNEL SALAD WITH HERBED CRÈME FRAÎCHE
Fenouil à la crème

Salting fennel slightly softens it so that it is good in salad. Cream is a good match for fennel's distinctive flavour, but fennel salad can also be seasoned with vinaigrette or mayonnaise. This salad is white and is best served with a selection of other colourful salads.

MAKES 4 TO 6 SERVINGS

2 medium-size fennel bulbs
Salt
225 ml/8 fl oz Crème Fraîche
   (page 381) or purchased crème
   fraîche, or 150 ml/¼ pint sour
   cream mixed with 4 tablespoons
   double cream

Freshly ground pepper
3 to 4 teaspoons strained fresh
   lemon juice
1 tablespoon chopped parsley
1 tablespoon snipped chives

Remove stalks and tough outer layers of fennel bulbs. Slice lengthwise, then cut in sticks about 6 mm/¼ inch thick and place in a colander or on a rack. Sprinkle with salt on both sides and let stand for 30 minutes. Rinse well and pat dry with paper towels.

To make dressing, mix cream with salt, pepper, lemon juice to taste, parsley, and 2 teaspoons chives in a medium-size bowl.

Put fennel in a bowl and add enough dressing to moisten it. Fold until blended. Taste and adjust seasoning. Refrigerate for at least 30 minutes or as long as overnight. Sprinkle with remaining chives and serve.

CUCUMBER SALAD WITH YOGURT HERB DRESSING
Salade de concombres au yaourt

This refreshing salad is a summer favourite. The long European cucumbers are best because they have few or no seeds.

MAKES 6 SERVINGS

1 small garlic clove, crushed and finely chopped
1 teaspoon salt
6 tablespoons plain yogurt
6 tablespoons sour cream
3 tablespoons double cream

2 tablespoons chopped parsley, chives, or dill
1 large seedless cucumber (about 450 g/1 lb)
Small sprigs of parsley or dill, for garnish (optional)

In a bowl, mash garlic with salt, using back of a spoon. Add yogurt, sour cream, and double cream and blend well. Stir in parsley, chives, or dill.

Peel cucumber and cut it in half lengthwise. Cut it in thin slices and add to yogurt mixture. Fold in gently. Taste and adjust seasoning. Refrigerate for at least 15 minutes or up to 4 hours before serving.

To serve, garnish with small sprigs of parsley or dill.

ESCAROLE SALAD WITH ROQUEFORT CHEESE
Salade de scarole au roquefort

Unlike other green salads, this one is made ahead so that the escarole leaves become tenderized by the dressing. If desired, Bleu d'Auvergne or other French blue cheese can be used instead of Roquefort.

MAKES 4 TO 6 SERVINGS

1 head escarole (frilly lettuce)
Walnut Oil Vinaigrette (page
   340), using 3 tablespoons white
   wine vinegar to 9 tablespoons
   walnut oil

50 g/2 oz Roquefort cheese,
   crumbled
50 g/2 oz walnut pieces (optional)

Rinse and dry escarole leaves thoroughly. Tear large leaves in half but leave small ones whole.

Prepare Walnut Oil Vinaigrette according to the instructions in recipe for Watercress Salad with Goat Cheese and Walnuts.

Mix escarole leaves with vinaigrette, add most of cheese and walnuts, leaving a little of each for garnish, and toss. Taste and adjust seasoning. Cover and refrigerate for 30 minutes to wilt slightly.

Just before serving, garnish with remaining Roquefort cheese and walnuts.

SUMMER TOMATO SALAD WITH
FRESH HERBS
Salade de tomates aux herbes

When tomatoes are at the peak of their season, this salad is made at many homes and small restaurants in France. If desired, the vinaigrette can be made with less vinegar or lemon juice than usual because the tomatoes have their own natural acidity.

MAKES 6 TO 8 SERVINGS

6 medium-size ripe tomatoes

2 spring onions

FRESH HERB VINAIGRETTE

2 tablespoons strained fresh lemon
   juice or white wine vinegar
Salt and freshly ground pepper
6 tablespoons extra virgin olive oil

1 garlic clove, crushed
1 tablespoon chopped parsley
1 tablespoon chopped basil or
   oregano (optional)

Slice tomatoes and arrange overlapping in a shallow dish.

Slice white part of onions and sprinkle over tomatoes. Chop green part of onions.

FRESH HERB VINAIGRETTE

In a small bowl, stir lemon juice with salt and pepper and add oil, using a whisk. Add green part of onions, garlic, parsley, and basil; taste and adjust seasoning.

Pour enough vinaigrette over tomatoes to moisten them.

This salad can be kept, covered, for 4 hours in refrigerator but is best served immediately and at cool room temperature. Serve any remaining vinaigrette separately.

TOMATO AND EGG SALAD

Arrange tomato slices alternating with slices of hard-boiled egg.

LEEKS MIMOSA WITH HAZELNUTS
Poireaux mimosa aux noisettes

This dish is a new, nut-flavoured version of the classic leeks mimosa, in which 'mimosa' refers to the yellow and white decoration of chopped eggs. In France leeks are sometimes called 'asparagus of the poor' because they are delicious but inexpensive and, indeed, this salad is also made with asparagus, as in the variation.

MAKES 4 SERVINGS

25 g/1 oz hazelnuts   *Salt*
1 kg/2 lb small leeks   *2 hard-boiled eggs*

PARSLEY VINAIGRETTE

2 tablespoons white wine vinegar   *2 tablespoons chopped parsley*
Salt and freshly ground pepper
3 tablespoons hazelnut oil and 3
  tablespoons vegetable oil, or 6
  tablespoons vegetable oil

Preheat oven to 180°C/350°F/gas 4. In a shallow baking pan, toast hazelnuts in oven for about 8 minutes, or until skins begin to split. Transfer to a large strainer. Rub hot nuts against strainer with tea towel to remove most of skins. Cool nuts completely. Chop coarsely with a knife.

Remove dark green ends of leeks and discard. Slit each leek lengthwise twice, beginning halfway through centre of white part and slitting upward in direction of green tops. Dip repeatedly in a sinkful of cold water to remove any dirt. Cut off roots.

In a large saucepan of boiling salted water, cook leeks, uncovered, over medium heat for about 10 minutes, or until tender. Drain thoroughly. Cut in 2 or 3 pieces crosswise. Arrange on a platter, reconstructing each leek and arranging so all point in same direction.

Cut hard-boiled eggs in half and remove yolks. Chop egg whites separately from yolks.

PARSLEY VINAIGRETTE
In a small bowl, stir vinegar with salt and pepper, and whisk in oil. Add parsley, taste and adjust seasoning.

To serve, spoon enough dressing over leeks to moisten them. Sprinkle egg whites in a row across their bases, then a row of hazelnuts next to whites, then a row of chopped yolks. Leave top ends of leeks showing. Serve at room temperature. Serve remaining dressing separately.

ASPARAGUS MIMOSA WITH HAZELNUTS

Substitute asparagus for leeks. Peel asparagus stems and cut off bases. Rinse well. Put asparagus in a deep pan with enough boiling salted water to cover. Cook, uncovered, over high heat for about 5 minutes, or until just tender when pierced with a sharp knife. With a slotted spoon transfer asparagus carefully to a plate lined with paper towels and let cool to room temperature.

To serve, arrange asparagus on a platter, with tips all pointing in same direction. Dress as above. When sprinkling nuts and eggs, leave asparagus tips showing.

MARINATED GREEN BEAN SALAD
WITH SPRING ONIONS
*Salade de haricots verts marinés aux oignons
nouveaux*

For a colourful assortment, serve this salad together with Grilled Peppers with Garlic and Olive Oil (page 226) and with a rice, pasta, or potato salad.   MAKES 4 SERVINGS

600 g/1¼ pounds green beans or
   mixed green beans and yellow
   beans, ends discarded
1 small garlic clove, crushed
Salt and freshly ground pepper
2 tablespoons strained fresh lemon
   juice

3 tablespoons extra virgin olive oil
1 to 2 tablespoons chopped parsley
2 spring onions, white part and a
   little of green, chopped

Break beans in roughly 5-cm/2-inch pieces. In a medium-size saucepan of boiling salted water, cook, uncovered, over high heat for about 5 minutes, or until just tender but still slightly crisp. Drain and rinse under cold water until cool.

In a small bowl, mash garlic with salt until very fine, stir in lemon juice, olive oil, parsley, and chopped onions. Toss with green beans. Taste and adjust seasoning. Let stand for about 30 minutes to marinate. Serve at room temperature.

WARM DANDELION SALAD WITH MUSHROOMS AND POACHED EGGS
Salade de pissenlits aux champignons et à l'oeuf poché

Dandelions are an acquired taste, but those who like them find their characteristic bitterness refreshing. Warm dandelion salads are generally topped with sautéed bacon; in this recipe mushrooms are used instead, but diced sautéed bacon can be added as well. Poached eggs are a favourite finishing touch among some French cooks and turn the salad into a richer dish. MAKES 3 TO 4 SERVINGS

225 g/8 oz dandelions
6 tablespoons vegetable oil
2 tablespoons very finely chopped
 onion

225 g/8 oz small mushrooms, cut
 into quarters
Salt and freshly ground pepper
3 tablespoons white wine vinegar

POACHED EGGS
1·4 litres/2½ pints water
3 tablespoons vinegar

3 or 4 very fresh eggs

French bread, for accompaniment

Remove stalks of dandelion from bases and discard bases. Thoroughly rinse and drain dandelion leaves. Break each stalk in 5-cm/2-inch pieces. Put them in a large heatproof bowl.

Heat 3 tablespoons vegetable oil in a heavy medium-size shallow pan, over medium heat. Add onion and sauté over low heat until soft but not browned. Add mushrooms and salt and pepper to taste and sauté until tender and light brown. Transfer mushrooms and their oil to bowl with dandelion. With pan off heat, pour in vinegar, then bring to a boil, stirring. Pour over dandelion, add remaining oil, and mix thoroughly. Return to pan and toss over medium heat for 1 minute, or until just wilted. Return to bowl and taste and adjust seasoning. Keep warm while poaching eggs.

POACHED EGGS
Prepare a bowl of cold water for cooling poached eggs.

Combine water and vinegar in a large non-aluminium sauté pan or deep frying pan and bring to a boil. Reduce heat to medium-low so that water just simmers. Break an egg into a small cup or ramekin and slide egg into water where it is bubbling. With a spoon, bring white over yolk. Repeat with another egg. Reduce heat to low and poach eggs, uncovered, for 2½ minutes. Lift each egg carefully with fish slice and touch it; white should be firm and yolk still soft. Transfer egg to bowl of cold water. Continue poaching remaining eggs.

Transfer eggs to paper towels and trim off uneven parts.

To serve, quickly divide dandelion salad among 3 or 4 small plates. Carefully set one egg in centre of each salad. Serve immediately, with French bread.

BABY ARTICHOKES WITH HAZELNUT OIL VINAIGRETTE
Petits artichauts, vinaigrette à l'huile de noisettes

Large artichokes, broccoli and tender lettuce are also good with the nut-flavoured dressing. It contains less vinegar than usual so that it will best complement the delicate baby artichokes.

MAKES 4 SERVINGS

8 to 12 baby artichokes (about 4
    cm/1½ inches in diameter at
    their widest part)

HAZELNUT OIL VINAIGRETTE
2 tablespoons white wine vinegar   6 tablespoons hazelnut oil
Salt and freshly ground pepper

There is no need to trim baby artichokes. Rinse them and put them in a medium-size saucepan of boiling salted water. Cover and cook over medium heat for about 18 minutes, or until a leaf can be pulled out easily. Remove them and drain them thoroughly, upside down.

HAZELNUT OIL VINAIGRETTE

In a small bowl, stir vinegar with salt and pepper and whisk in oil. Taste and adjust seasoning.

Serve artichokes warm or at room temperature, accompanied by the vinaigrette.

Composed Vegetable Salads

There are no fixed rules for creating these salads. The flavours and textures can be either complementary or contrasting. Often a great combination will be discovered by chance, by mixing ingredients that happen to be at hand. Salads of ingredients of similar shape and different colour, such as cauliflower with broccoli, are attractive, and so are green and yellow beans; red, yellow, and green peppers; and even chick-peas and white beans.

Fine-quality cheese such as Roquefort, goat cheese, and Gruyère add richness and flavour to contemporary French salads, while peppers, cucumbers, celery, walnuts, and almonds add crispness. When lettuce is part of a composed salad, or arranged as a bed for the other ingredients, it is combined with the rest of the salad at the last minute to avoid wilting.

Many French salads have a regional theme, mixing the typical ingredients of a certain French province. Provençal potato salad, for example, includes peppers and olives. A bean salad from Brittany in northwestern France combines cold-weather vegetables – cooked white beans, cubes of beets, mixed greens, and parsley vinaigrette.

BRETON VEGETABLE SALAD WITH CHIVE MAYONNAISE
Salade bretonne de légumes, mayonnaise à la ciboulette

Artichokes, cauliflower, and peas flourish in the western French province of Brittany and are used to make this salad. To turn this into a main course salad, hard-boiled eggs, prawns or lobster can be added to the platter. MAKES 4 SERVINGS

1 large lemon (if using fresh artichokes)
2 large artichokes, or 8 pieces frozen artichoke hearts
Salt and freshly ground pepper
225 g/8 oz green beans, ends removed, broken in half
1 medium-size cauliflower (about 700 g/1½ lb), divided into medium-size florets

12 baby carrots, scraped
200 g/7 oz cooked peas (fresh or frozen)
4 tablespoons Mayonnaise (page 379)
1 tablespoon snipped chives

VINAIGRETTE
1 tablespoon white wine vinegar
Salt and freshly ground pepper

3 tablespoons vegetable oil

1 head cos lettuce, leaves rinsed and dried thoroughly

If using fresh artichokes, prepare hearts according to directions on page 159.

Squeeze any juice remaining in lemon into medium-size saucepan of boiling salted water, add artichoke hearts, cover, and simmer over low heat until tender when pierced with a knife; about 15 minutes for fresh ones, 7 minutes for frozen ones. Cool to lukewarm in liquid. Using a teaspoon, scoop out choke from centre of each fresh artichoke heart. Cut each fresh artichoke into 8 pieces and each piece of frozen artichoke heart into 2 pieces. Return artichokes to liquid until ready to use.

In a medium-size saucepan of boiling salted water, cook green beans, uncovered, over high heat for about 5 minutes, or until just tender but still slightly crisp. Drain, rinse under cold water until cool, and drain thoroughly.

In a large saucepan of boiling salted water, cook cauliflower, uncovered, over high heat for about 5 minutes, or until just tender but still slightly crisp. Drain, rinse under cold water until cool, and drain thoroughly. Divide half the cauliflower florets into smaller florets.

Put baby carrots in a saucepan, cover with water, and add salt. Bring to a boil, cover, and simmer over medium heat for about 5 minutes, or until just tender when pierced with a knife; size of baby carrots varies greatly and this affects cooking time. Drain thoroughly.

Combine cooked artichokes, peas, and small cauliflower florets in a bowl. Mix mayonnaise with 1 teaspoon chives. Add enough mayonnaise to vegetables to moisten them. Mix gently, taste and adjust seasoning. (Salad can be kept, covered, for 1 day in refrigerator.)

VINAIGRETTE
In a small bowl, whisk vinegar with salt and pepper; whisk in oil. Taste and adjust seasoning.

Make a bed of lettuce on a large platter. Spoon artichoke and pea mixture into centre. Arrange green beans, baby carrots, and remaining cauliflower florets in piles around mixture and sprinkle them with vinaigrette. Sprinkle remaining chives over artichoke and pea mixture and over separate cauliflower florets.

SWEETCORN SALAD WITH PEPPERS
Salade de maïs aux poivrons

This quick, colourful salad can be found displayed in the windows of many *charcuteries* throughout Paris under the name *salade mexicaine* or *salade américaine*, a tribute to the origin of its major ingredients. Sometimes black olives or tuna in olive oil is added.

MAKES 6 SERVINGS

About 450 g/1 lb sweetcorn
   kernels, either cut from fresh
   cobs or frozen

VINAIGRETTE

3 tablespoons white wine vinegar
   or fresh strained lemon juice
Salt and freshly ground pepper

9 tablespoons vegetable oil or olive
   oil

1 medium-size or large red pepper,
   cored, seeded, and finely diced
1 medium-size or large green
   pepper, cored, seeded, and
   finely diced
2 celery sticks, peeled and finely
   diced (optional)

100 g/4 oz Gruyère cheese, finely
   diced
12 lettuce leaves, rinsed, dried
   well, and cut in thin strips
   (optional)

Add sweetcorn to a large saucepan of boiling water and simmer, uncovered, for about 5 minutes, or until just tender. Drain thoroughly.

VINAIGRETTE
In a small bowl, whisk vinegar with salt and pepper; whisk in oil. Taste and adjust seasoning.

A short time before serving, combine sweetcorn, peppers, celery, and cheese in a bowl and add enough vinaigrette to moisten. Toss well and taste and adjust seasoning. (Salad can be kept, covered, for up to 1 day in refrigerator.) Just before serving, add lettuce and toss salad again.

TOMATOES STUFFED WITH MUSHROOM SALAD
Tomates farcies salade de champignons

The contrast of colours between the red tomatoes and the white mushroom salad makes this an attractive first course. It is essential to use very white fresh button mushrooms.   MAKES 6 SERVINGS

MUSHROOM SALAD

1½ tablespoons white wine vinegar or strained fresh lemon juice

1 garlic clove, very finely chopped

Salt and freshly ground white pepper

3 large ripe tomatoes

6 tablespoons sour cream or Crème Fraîche (page 381)

150 g/5 oz button mushrooms, wiped

1 tablespoon chopped parsley

MUSHROOM SALAD

In a medium-size bowl, whisk vinegar with garlic and salt and pepper to taste. Add sour cream. Cut mushrooms in very thin slices. Add to dressing immediately and mix well. Taste and adjust seasoning; add a few drops more vinegar or lemon juice if needed. Cover and refrigerate for at least 2 hours so mushrooms absorb flavour from dressing. (Salad can be kept, covered, for 8 hours in refrigerator.)

If necessary, cut a thin slice from each end of each tomato so it can stand up without rolling. Cut each tomato in half horizontally. Using a small spoon, carefully remove pulp from tomatoes. Sprinkle tomatoes with salt and pepper. Turn them upside down on a plate and let stand for 30 minutes so the excess juices can drain off.

Spoon mushroom salad into tomatoes to fill them generously. Just before serving, sprinkle with parsley.

CHICORY AND BEETROOT SALAD
Salade d'endives aux betteraves

The sweetness of the beetroot is a perfect complement for the slight bitterness of the chicory in this salad. If desired, other salad vegetables, such as pieces of cos lettuce, can be added as well. Because beetroot has a tendency to colour everything near it purple, it is added to the salad at the last minute so that the other ingredients keep their colour.   MAKES 6 SERVINGS

5 baby beetroot (about 4 cm/1½   *2 celery sticks, peeled and cut in*
* inches in diameter)*   *thin slices*
350 g/12 oz chicory

CHAMPAGNE VINAIGRETTE
2 tablespoons champagne vinegar   *2 teaspoons champagne mustard or*
* or white wine vinegar*   *Dijon mustard*
Salt and freshly ground pepper   *6 tablespoons vegetable oil*

50 g/2 oz walnut pieces

Rinse beetroot, put 2·5 cm/1 inch of water in a steamer, and bring to a boil. Place beetroot on steamer rack or on another rack or in a colander above boiling water. Cover tightly and steam for 50 to 60 minutes, or until tender, adding boiling water occasionally if water evaporates. Let cool. Run under cold water and slip off skins.

Wipe chicory and trim the bases. Cut leaves in fairly thin slices crosswise. Combine with celery in a bowl.

CHAMPAGNE VINAIGRETTE
In a small bowl, whisk vinegar with salt, pepper, and mustard until blended. Stir in oil, taste, and adjust seasoning.

Toss chicory and celery with vinaigrette. Leave to marinate for 5 to 10 minutes. Just before serving, dice beetroot, add to salad, and toss gently. Adjust seasoning, sprinkle with walnuts, and serve.

CHICK-PEA AND BEAN SALAD WITH TOMATOES AND BASIL
Salade de pois chiches et haricots aux tomates et au basilic

This colourful salad, dressed with sautéed onions and an olive oil and lemon dressing, is best served warm.   MAKES 4 SERVINGS

225 g/8 oz haricot beans
225 g/8 oz chick-peas (also called garbanzo beans), rinsed
1 litre/1¾ pints water
Salt and freshly ground pepper
2 bay leaves
225 g/8 oz green beans, ends removed, broken in half
6 tablespoons extra virgin olive oil

1 large onion, halved and cut in thin slices
225 g/8 oz ripe tomatoes, diced
75 g/3 oz Niçoise olives or other oil-cured black olives, halved and stoned
3 tablespoons coarsely chopped fresh basil
1 tablespoon plus 1 teaspoon strained fresh lemon juice

Put haricot beans and chick-peas in separate bowls, cover with cold water and leave in a cool place for 8 hours, or overnight.

Drain and rinse beans and chick-peas. Put them in separate medium-size saucepans with 450 ml/¾ pint water and bay leaf. Bring to boil, reduce heat to low, cover, and simmer for 45 minutes. Add pinch of salt and simmer for 30–45 minutes more, or until tender. (Both types beans can be kept in their cooking liquid for 1 day in refrigerator.)

Reheat both types beans together to simmer before serving. Drain beans, discarding bay leaves. Cover and keep warm.

Meanwhile, in medium-size saucepan of boiling salted water, cook green beans, uncovered, over high heat for about 7 minutes, or until just tender. Drain thoroughly.

In medium-size frying pan, heat 2 tablespoons olive oil over low heat, add onion, and cook, stirring often, for about 12 minutes, or until soft but not brown.

Combine chick-peas, beans, green beans, cooked onion with its oil, tomatoes, olives, and basil in a glass bowl and toss lightly. Whisk lemon juice with 4 tablespoons olive oil and salt and pepper to taste; use salt lightly because olives are salty. Add to bowl and toss until ingredients are coated. Taste and adjust seasoning. Serve warm or at room temperature. (Leftover salad can be kept, covered, for 1 day in refrigerator; serve at room temperature.)

NOTE: Substitute 400 g/14 oz can chick-peas for dried, if desired. Drain them well, add them to cooked haricot beans, and heat gently.

AVOCADO AND MUSHROOM SALAD
WITH SWISS CHARD
Salade d'avocats et de champignons aux blettes

This beautiful salad makes a wonderful main course for a warm day. It consists of a bed of lettuce topped with sautéed mushrooms and Swiss chard, slices of avocado and egg and halved cherry tomatoes, all moistened with a creamy chive dressing. MAKES 4 SERVINGS

8 to 10 leaves salad bowl lettuce	Salt and freshly ground pepper
About 275 g/10 oz Swiss chard	100 g/4 oz small mushrooms, cut
3 tablespoons vegetable oil	in quarters

CREAMY CHIVE VINAIGRETTE

½ teaspoon Dijon mustard	3 tablespoons vegetable oil
1 tablespoon white wine vinegar	3 tablespoons double cream
Salt and freshly ground pepper	2 tablespoons thinly sliced chives

1 *medium-size avocado*   4 to 8 *cherry tomatoes, cut in half,*
3 *hard-boiled eggs, sliced*   *for garnish*

Wash lettuce and dry thoroughly. Tear each leaf in 3 or 4 pieces.
Chill until ready to use.

Remove chard stalks from leaves and discard. Rinse leaves
thoroughly. Pile chard leaves, cut them in half lengthwise and then
crosswise into 1-cm/½-inch-wide strips.

In a large frying pan, heat 2 tablespoons oil over low heat, add
about half the chard and a pinch of salt and pepper, and cook,
stirring often, for about 6 minutes, or until tender. Remove with
tongs, add remaining chard and a little salt and pepper, and cook it
also until tender. Return all of chard to pan and heat, stirring, for 1
minute. Transfer to a plate and cool to room temperature.

In a large frying pan, heat 1 tablespoon oil over medium-high
heat, add mushrooms, salt, and pepper, and sauté, tossing often, for
about 3 minutes, or until tender and light brown. Remove with a
slotted spoon and reserve at room temperature. (Chard and mushrooms can be kept for about 4 hours at room temperature.)

CREAMY CHIVE VINAIGRETTE
In a small bowl, whisk together mustard, vinegar, and salt and
pepper to taste. Gradually stir in oil; dressing will thicken slightly.
Using a fork, mix 2 tablespoons of dressing into chard. Taste and
adjust seasoning.

Gradually whisk cream into remaining dressing, stir in chives;
taste and adjust seasoning.

Cut avocado in half and remove stone by hitting it with heel of a
heavy knife. Peel avocado and slice it crosswise.

Arrange lettuce leaves on a platter. Set chard in centre. Arrange
avocado and egg slices in a ring around chard. Arrange mushrooms
around them, discarding any liquid. Whisk dressing and spoon it
over avocado and egg. Garnish with cherry tomato halves. Serve
immediately.

CAULIFLOWER AND TOMATO SALAD WITH GARLIC AND WALNUT DRESSING
Salade de chou-fleur et tomates, sauce aillade

The garlic and walnut dressing, or sauce aillade, is adapted from a cookbook that is very special to me – *French Regional Cooking* by Anne Willan and La Varenne. The dressing always reminds me of a garlic fair my husband and I visited near Toulouse, where the sauce originated. The wreaths of purple, pink, and white garlic were huge, beautiful and impressive. Many people were buying them as their garlic supply for the next few months. MAKES 6 TO 8 SERVINGS

GARLIC AND WALNUT DRESSING

2 large garlic cloves, peeled and cut
   in half
2 tablespoons parsley sprigs
75 g/3 oz walnut halves
Salt and freshly ground pepper

2 tablespoons cold water
200 ml/7 fl oz walnut oil
1 to 2 teaspoons strained fresh
   lemon juice, or to taste
   (optional)

1 medium-size cauliflower, divided
   into medium-size florets
1 red pepper
1 green pepper

1 butterhead lettuce
4 medium-size ripe tomatoes, cut
   in wedges

GARLIC AND WALNUT DRESSING

Drop garlic cloves into food processor one at a time, with blades turning, and process until finely chopped. Add parsley sprigs and continue to process until fine. Add walnuts, salt, and pepper, and process until walnuts are finely ground. Add water and process to a smooth paste.

With blades turning, add walnut oil in a very thin stream. Stop occasionally to scrape down sides and bottom of work bowl. Transfer to a bowl, whisk in lemon juice, if desired, taste and adjust seasoning. Transfer to a jar and keep in refrigerator. (Sauce can be kept for up to 2 weeks.) Bring to room temperature before using.

In a large saucepan of boiling salted water, cook cauliflower, uncovered, over high heat for about 5 minutes, or until just tender. Drain, rinse, and drain thoroughly.

Preheat grill. Grill peppers about 5 cm/2 inches from heat source, turning often, for about 20 minutes, or until blistered and charred. Transfer to plastic bag and close bag. Let stand for 10 minutes. Peel, cut in half, and remove cores. Drain well in colander, pat dry, and cut them in about 2-cm/¾-inch strips.

Arrange a bed of lettuce leaves on one large or two medium-size platters. Stir dressing. Pour about 4 tablespoons dressing over lettuce. Arrange cauliflower, tomato wedges, and peppers decoratively on top; cauliflower in centre, tomato wedges around it, and pepper strips around them, radiating outwards. Pour a ring of dressing around outer edge of ring of tomatoes and serve. Serve remaining dressing separately.

ARTICHOKE, ASPARAGUS, GREEN BEAN, AND FRESH PEA SALAD WITH TARRAGON MAYONNAISE
Salade Saint-Jean

For this springtime salad use freshly cooked vegetables and home-made mayonnaise to obtain the best results.   MAKES 4 TO 6 SERVINGS

FRESH TARRAGON MAYONNAISE

1 egg yolk, at room temperature
Salt and white pepper
½ teaspoon Dijon mustard
1 tablespoon strained fresh lemon juice or tarragon vinegar

6 tablespoons vegetable oil
1 tablespoon warm water (optional)
1 tablespoon chopped fresh tarragon

1 lemon (if using fresh artichokes)
4 small fresh artichokes or 12
    pieces frozen artichoke hearts
8 medium-size asparagus spears,
    peeled and cut in 5-cm/2-inch
    pieces

225 g/8 oz green beans, cut in
    thirds
150 g/5 oz green peas
2 hard-boiled eggs, sliced
1 or 2 cornichons (tiny French
    pickles) or small gherkins, sliced
A few tarragon leaves, for garnish

FRESH TARRAGON MAYONNAISE

Stir egg yolk in a medium-size heavy bowl with a pinch of salt, white pepper, mustard, and 1 teaspoon lemon juice. With a whisk, begin beating in oil, drop by drop. When 2 or 3 tablespoons oil have been added, beat in remaining oil in a very thin stream. Whisk in remaining lemon juice. If mayonnaise is very thick, whisk in about 1 tablespoon warm water. Stir in chopped tarragon and taste and adjust seasoning. Let stand for 1 hour at room temperature, or refrigerate up to overnight to blend flavours.

If using fresh artichokes, prepare hearts according to the directions on page 159.

Squeeze any juice remaining in lemon into medium-size saucepan of boiling salted water, add artichoke hearts, cover, and simmer over low heat until tender when pierced with a knife; about 15 minutes for fresh ones, 7 minutes for frozen ones. Cool to lukewarm in liquid. Using a teaspoon, scoop out choke from centre of each fresh artichoke heart. Cut each fresh artichoke heart into 4 pieces. Return artichokes to liquid until ready to use.

In a medium-size saucepan of boiling salted water, cook each of the remaining vegetables separately, uncovered, until just tender; asparagus will need about 3 minutes, green beans about 7 minutes, fresh peas about 7 minutes, and frozen peas about 3 minutes. Rinse and drain thoroughly. Cool completely.

Combine vegetables in a bowl and toss with mayonnaise. Spoon into a serving dish. Garnish with egg slices alternating with slices of cornichon. Put tarragon leaves on egg slices for garnish. Serve at room temperature.

NOTE: If you have homemade mayonnaise already prepared, flavour 6 tablespoons mayonnaise with the tarragon. Whisk in a little water to thin it out if necessary.

PROVENÇAL MARINATED VEGETABLES
Légumes marinés à la provençale

Delicately sweet and sour, this colourful dish is made of vegetables that cook directly in their dressing of tomatoes, olive oil, white wine, and lemon juice, along with a few raisins. If you prefer, the raisins can be omitted.   MAKES 4 SERVINGS

100 g/4 oz button onions
100 g/4 oz small cauliflower florets
50 g/2 oz yellow or French beans, ends removed, broken in 2 or 3 pieces
200 ml/7 fl oz olive oil
1 medium-size onion, finely chopped
3 large ripe tomatoes, peeled, seeded, and chopped (about 700 g/1½ lb)
50 g/2 oz raisins (optional)
Salt and freshly ground pepper

100 g/4 oz small mushrooms, cut into quarters
1 celery stick, peeled and thinly sliced
50 g/2 oz diced fennel (optional)
2 teaspoons fresh thyme leaves, or ½ teaspoon dried thyme
200 ml/7 fl oz dry white wine
3 tablespoons strained fresh lemon juice

Put button onions in a medium-size saucepan, cover with water, and bring to a boil. Cook 1 minute, rinse under cold water, drain well, and peel.

In a medium-size saucepan of boiling salted water, cook cauliflower and beans, uncovered, over high heat for 2 minutes. Rinse with cold water and drain thoroughly.

In a medium-size sauté pan, warm 1 tablespoon olive oil over low heat, add chopped onion, and cook for about 7 minutes, or until soft but not brown. Add tomatoes, raisins, and salt and pepper to taste, and cook over medium heat, stirring often, for about 12 minutes, or until tomatoes are soft and most of their liquid has evaporated.

Add 7 tablespoons oil to tomato mixture and bring to a boil, stirring. Stir in mushrooms, button onions, celery, fennel, and thyme, and cook over high heat for 2 minutes. Stir in wine and bring to a boil. Add cauliflower, beans, and 2 tablespoons lemon juice.

Reduce heat to low, cover, and cook for about 25 minutes, or until vegetables are very tender; check by piercing button onion with knife.

Add remaining 4 tablespoons oil and 1 tablespoon lemon juice and bring to a boil. Remove from heat. Taste and adjust seasoning. Let cool completely. (Vegetables can be kept, covered, for up to 3 days in refrigerator.) Serve cold or at room temperature.

Potato, Rice, and Pasta Salads

In France potato and rice salads are a standard item at *charcuteries*, but pasta salads are gaining favour among home cooks. Both home cooks and professional chefs vary the salads to suit their own taste and produce a great array with many different flavours.

The simplest form of potato, rice or pasta salad is composed of the main ingredient, dressing, and often chopped onions or shallots. An infinite number of combinations can be created from this basic formula because the neutral taste of potatoes, rice, and pasta enables them to harmonize with nearly all foods, whether of mild or strong flavour. Colourful cooked vegetables such as beetroot, carrots, and peas are a welcome addition. Zesty condiments such as pickled cucumbers, capers, black olives, or chopped anchovies add zip to all types of salads.

Whether the salad is plain or elaborate, it is the dressing that determines its character. For potato salad the French prefer vinaigrette, although mayonnaise is sometimes used to make a creamy salad similar to American-style potato salad. Potato salad is often served cold but is best at room temperature.

Besides occupying the centre of a salad buffet table or accompanying cold meats or hot sausages a potato, rice or pasta salad can play the role of a light main course if it contains meat, fish, cheese, or eggs.

Rice is so associated with the cuisines of the East that some people might find it surprising that Escoffier, author of the 'bible' of French cuisine, devotes a major section of his chapter on first courses to rice salads. He even wrote a whole book of recipes for cooking rice. His salads often combine just a few ingredients to make a lovely balance. For example Salade Andalouse combines rice flavoured with vinaigrette, garlic, onion, and parsley with a julienne of sweet red peppers and small tomato wedges; Salade des Moines is rice, asparagus tips, strips of chicken and mustard vinaigrette sprinkled with black truffles.

Hints

· For potato salads be sure the potatoes are cooked just right. Undercooked potatoes do not taste good; if potatoes are overcooked, they fall apart when cut and tossed with the dressing. If the potatoes are not all of one size, check each with a knife to see if it is tender and remove the smaller ones first.

· Potatoes, rice and pasta should be freshly cooked for salad but other vegetables can be cooked one day in advance.

POTATO AND BEETROOT SALAD
Salade de pommes de terre aux betteraves

The most suitable potatoes for salad are relatively small, preferably new, boiling potatoes. These have firm, waxy flesh, unlike mealy old potatoes, and therefore do not fall apart in the water during cooking and do not crumble when cut. The potatoes are cooked whole in their skins to keep in their taste. This potato and beetroot salad is colourful, light, and perfect for any season.   MAKES 4 SERVINGS

4 beetroot, about 4 cm/1½ inches in diameter
2 tablespoons dry white wine
1 tablespoon white wine vinegar
1 tablespoon vegetable oil

Salt and freshly ground pepper
1 kg/2 lb red-skinned potatoes of uniform size, scrubbed but not peeled
2 tablespoons finely chopped spring onion or chives

VINAIGRETTE

3 tablespoons white wine vinegar   9 tablespoons vegetable oil
Salt and freshly ground pepper

Put beetroot in medium-size saucepan, cover with water, and bring to boil. Cover, reduce heat to low, and cook for about 35 minutes, or until just tender when pierced with knife. Drain and slip off skins.

Combine wine, vinegar, oil, and salt and pepper to taste in small bowl and whisk until blended.

Put potatoes in large saucepan, cover with water by about 1 cm/½ inch, and add salt. Bring to boil, cover, reduce heat to low, and simmer for about 25 minutes, or until knife pierces centre of largest potato easily and potato falls from knife when lifted; to be sure potato is cooked enough: check by cutting largest potato in half at widest point, cut a slice from centre of potato and taste. Do not overcook, or potatoes will fall apart when cut.

Drain potatoes in colander and peel while hot. Hold them with a kitchen fork, to avoid burnt fingers, and peel with a small sharp knife. Cut potatoes into medium dice.

Put potatoes in large bowl. Stir wine mixture until blended and pour it over potatoes. Toss or fold gently to mix, separating any potato pieces that are stuck together. Fold in onion. Cool to room temperature.

VINAIGRETTE

In a small bowl, whisk vinegar with salt and pepper; whisk in oil. Taste and adjust seasoning.

Add 6 tablespoons vinaigrette to potato mixture and fold it in gently, using a rubber spatula. Add more vinaigrette if needed. (Salad tastes best on day it is made but it can be prepared 1 day in advance, covered, and refrigerated.) If salad was prepared in advance and has absorbed all the dressing, add about 2 tablespoons more vinaigrette, or enough to moisten.

Just before serving, dice beetroot and fold into salad. Taste and adjust seasoning. Transfer salad to serving dish and serve at room temperature.

SUMMER POTATO AND GREEN BEAN SALAD
Salade de pommes de terre aux haricots verts

In French potato salads the potatoes are sliced and tossed with a simple white wine marinade immediately after cooking, because they absorb seasonings best when they are still warm.

MAKES 4 SERVINGS

2 tablespoons dry white wine
1 tablespoon vegetable oil
Salt and freshly ground pepper
1 kg/2 lb red-skinned or other
  boiling potatoes of uniform size,
  scrubbed but not peeled

2 tablespoons finely chopped spring
  onion

VINAIGRETTE
3 tablespoons tarragon vinegar or
  white wine vinegar

Salt and freshly ground pepper
9 tablespoons vegetable oil

225 g/8 oz green beans, ends
  trimmed, broken in thirds
2 tablespoons chopped fresh
  tarragon (optional)

1 tablespoon capers, rinsed and
  drained
2 small ripe tomatoes, cut into
  quarters

Combine wine, oil, and salt and pepper in small bowl and whisk until blended.

Put potatoes in large saucepan, cover with water by about 1 cm/½ inch, and add salt. Bring to boil, cover, reduce heat to low, and simmer for about 25 minutes, or until knife pierces centre of largest potato easily and potato falls from knife when lifted.

Drain potatoes in colander and peel while hot. Cut off any dark parts of potato. Cut potatoes into medium dice.

Put potatoes in large bowl. Stir wine mixture until blended and pour it over potatoes. Toss or fold gently to mix, separating any potato pieces that are stuck together. Fold in onion. Cool to room temperature.

VINAIGRETTE
In a small bowl, whisk vinegar with salt and pepper; whisk in oil.
Taste and adjust seasoning.

Add 6 tablespoons vinaigrette to potato mixture and fold it in
gently, using a rubber spatula. Taste and adjust seasoning.

In a medium-size saucepan of boiling salted water, cook green
beans, uncovered, over high heat for about 5 minutes, or until just
tender. Rinse with cold water and drain thoroughly.

Fold beans, tarragon, and capers into salad. If salad was prepared
ahead and absorbed all the dressing, add about 2 tablespoons more
vinaigrette, or enough to moisten. Taste and adjust seasoning and
transfer salad to serving dish. Garnish with tomato quarters and
sprinkle them with a little vinaigrette. Serve salad at room temperature. (Salad tastes best on day it is made but it can be prepared 1 day
in advance, covered, and refrigerated.)

CLASSIC SALADE NIÇOISE
Omit tarragon and garnish salad with black olives and anchovy
fillets.

POTATO-PEPPER SALAD À LA
PROVENÇALE
Salade de pommes de terre et poivrons à la provençale

Peppers of three hues make this one of the most colourful of potato
salads. It is flavoured with three favourites of southern France – olive
oil, black olives, and anchovies.   MAKES 4 SERVINGS

2 tablespoons dry white wine	2 tablespoons finely chopped spring
1 tablespoon extra virgin olive oil	onion
Salt and freshly ground pepper	1 medium-size red pepper
1 kg/2 lb red-skinned potatoes of	1 medium-size green pepper
uniform size, scrubbed but not	1 medium-size yellow pepper
peeled	

VINAIGRETTE

3 tablespoons white wine vinegar
9 tablespoons extra virgin olive oil

4 anchovy fillets in olive oil
  (optional)

100 g/4 oz black olives, preferably
  Niçoise olives, halved and
  stoned

Combine wine, olive oil, and salt and pepper to taste in small bowl and whisk until blended.

Put potatoes in large saucepan, cover with water by about 1 cm/½ inch, and add salt. Bring to boil, cover, reduce heat to low, and simmer about 25 minutes, or until knife pierces centre of largest potato easily and potato falls from knife when lifted.

Drain potatoes in colander and peel while hot. Cut off any dark parts of potato. Cut potatoes into medium.dice.

Put potatoes in large bowl. Stir wine mixture until blended and pour it over potatoes. Toss or fold gently to mix, separating any potato pieces that are stuck together. Fold in onion. Cool to room temperature.

Preheat grill. Grill peppers about 5 cm/2 inches from heat source, turning often with tongs, for about 15 to 20 minutes, or until they are blistered and charred. Transfer to plastic bag and close bag. Let stand for 10 minutes. Peel, cut in half, remove cores, and pat dry. Cut pepper halves crosswise in half. Cut each half lengthwise into strips about 1 cm/½ inch wide.

Make vinaigrette according to the instructions given in previous recipe. Put anchovy fillets in small bowl, cover with warm water, and soak for 5 minutes. Drain, pat them dry, and chop very finely. Add to 6 tablespoons vinaigrette and taste and adjust seasoning.

Fold the anchovy-flavoured vinaigrette into potato mixture. Reserve 6 olive halves for garnish. Fold peppers and remaining olives gently into salad and adjust seasoning. (Salad can be kept, covered, for 1 day in refrigerator.)

If salad was prepared in advance and has absorbed all the dressing, add about 2 tablespoons more vinaigrette, or enough to moisten salad. Taste and adjust seasoning and transfer salad to serving dish. Garnish with reserved olives. Serve salad at room temperature.

AUVERGNE POTATO SALAD WITH CANTAL CHEESE
Salade auvergnate

This is a favourite lunchtime salad in French cafés. Walnuts are often used in salads in the region of Auvergne in central France, but other nuts are fine. Cantal is one of France's oldest cheeses, produced only in the Auvergne. If Cantal cheese is not available, it can be replaced by fine quality Gruyère or Cheddar.   MAKES 4 TO 6 SERVINGS

1 kg/2 lb red-skinned potatoes	Salt

VINAIGRETTE

3 tablespoons white wine vinegar	9 tablespoons olive oil, walnut oil,
Salt and freshly ground pepper	or vegetable oil
225 g/8 oz Cantal or good-quality Gruyère or Cheddar cheese, cut in thin strips	1 head lettuce 100 g/4 oz walnut pieces

Scrub potatoes but do not peel them. Put them in a saucepan, cover them generously with water, and add a pinch of salt. Cover, bring to a boil, and simmer for 25 minutes, or until tender when pierced with a sharp knife.

VINAIGRETTE
In a medium bowl, whisk vinegar with salt and pepper; whisk in oil. Taste and adjust seasoning.

When potatoes are tender, drain them and leave until cool enough to handle. Peel potatoes, cut them in half lengthwise, and slice. Put them in a large bowl. Whisk dressing briskly, spoon 4 tablespoons dressing over potatoes, and mix gently. Let cool to room temperature. Add cheese. (Salad tastes best on day it is made but it can be prepared 1 day in advance, covered, and refrigerated.)

Rinse and dry lettuce leaves thoroughly. Tear large leaves in half but leave small ones whole.

A short time before serving, toss lettuce leaves with 3 tablespoons vinaigrette and taste and adjust seasoning. Arrange on a platter.

Add enough of remaining dressing to potato mixture to lightly coat ingredients. Add all but 2 tablespoons of walnuts. Mix gently, taste and adjust seasoning.

To serve, spoon potato salad on to bed of lettuce. Garnish with remaining walnuts.

POTATO SALAD WITH WATERCRESS
Salade de pommes de terre au cresson

A generous amount of fresh watercress accents this potato salad with a bright green colour and a lively flavour.   MAKES 4 SERVINGS

2 tablespoons dry white wine	1 kg/2 lb red-skinned potatoes of
1 tablespoon vegetable oil	uniform size, scrubbed but not
Salt and freshly ground pepper	peeled
	2 tablespoons finely chopped spring onion

VINAIGRETTE

3 tablespoons white wine vinegar	9 tablespoons vegetable oil
Salt and freshly ground pepper	

1 bunch watercress, washed,
   trimmed and chopped

Combine wine, oil, salt, and pepper in small bowl and whisk until blended.

Put potatoes in large saucepan, cover with water by about 1 cm/½ inch, and add salt. Bring to boil, cover, reduce heat to low, and simmer for about 25 minutes, or until knife pierces centre of largest potato easily and potato falls from knife when lifted.

Drain potatoes in colander and peel while hot. Cut potatoes into medium dice.

Put potatoes in large bowl. Stir wine mixture until blended and pour it over potatoes. Toss or fold gently to mix, separating any potato pieces that are stuck together. Fold in onion. Cool to room temperature.

VINAIGRETTE
In a small bowl, whisk vinegar with salt and pepper; whisk in oil. Taste and adjust seasoning.

Add 6 tablespoons vinaigrette to potato mixture and fold it in gently, using a rubber spatula. Taste and adjust seasoning. (Salad tastes best on day it is made but it can be prepared 1 day in advance, covered, and refrigerated.) If salad was prepared in advance and has absorbed all the dressing, add about 2 tablespoons more vinaigrette, or enough to moisten salad.

Just before serving, fold in watercress, taste and adjust seasoning. Transfer salad to serving dish and serve at room temperature.

POTATO, ASPARAGUS, AND ARTICHOKE SALAD
Salade Rachel

Classic versions of this salad also add as many truffles as potatoes, but here they are obviously optional.   MAKES 4 SERVINGS

2 tablespoons dry white wine
1 tablespoon white wine vinegar
1 tablespoon vegetable oil
Salt and freshly ground pepper

1 kg/2 lb red-skinned or other
boiling potatoes of uniform size,
scrubbed but not peeled
1 lemon (if using fresh artichokes)

4 fresh artichokes, or 16 frozen
   artichoke heart pieces
275 g/10 oz cooked fresh or frozen
   asparagus tips
2 celery sticks, peeled and very
   thinly sliced

300 ml/½ pint Mayonnaise (page
   379)
2 tablespoons chopped tarragon,
   chives, or parsley

Combine wine, vinegar, oil, and salt and pepper in small bowl and whisk until blended.

Put potatoes in a large saucepan, cover with water by about 1 cm/½ inch, and add salt. Bring to a boil, cover, reduce heat to low, and simmer for about 25 minutes, or until knife pierces centre of largest potato easily.

Drain potatoes in colander and peel while hot. Cut potatoes into medium dice.

Put potatoes in large bowl. Whisk wine mixture until blended and pour it over potatoes. Toss or fold gently to mix, separating any potato pieces that are stuck together. Cool to room temperature.

If using fresh artichokes, prepare hearts according to the directions on page 159.

Squeeze any juice remaining in lemon into medium-size saucepan of boiling salted water, add artichoke hearts, cover, and simmer over low heat until tender when pierced with a knife; about 15 minutes for fresh ones, 7 minutes for frozen ones. Cool to lukewarm in liquid. Using a teaspoon, scoop out choke from centre of each fresh artichoke heart. Cut each fresh artichoke into 4 pieces. Return artichokes to liquid until ready to use.

Reserve 8 asparagus tips for garnish. Add artichokes, celery, and remaining asparagus tips to potato salad. Add mayonnaise and tarragon and fold them in gently, using a rubber spatula. Taste and adjust seasoning. (Salad tastes best on day it is made but it can be prepared 1 day in advance, covered, and refrigerated.) Transfer salad to serving dish, garnish with reserved asparagus tips, and serve at room temperature.

RICE SALAD WITH PEAS AND PEPPERS
Salade de riz aux petits pois et aux poivrons

This is one of the prettiest of salads – the snowy white rice is dotted with green peas, diced grilled red peppers, and pieces of black olives.

MAKES 6 TO 8 SERVINGS

2 red peppers (about 350 g/12 oz)
Salt
350 g/12 oz long-grain white rice
50 g/2 oz thinly sliced spring
   onion, green and white parts
225 g/8 oz cooked peas

100 g/4 oz stoned black olives, cut
   lengthwise in 4 pieces
1 tablespoon chopped parsley
2 teaspoons drained capers

VINAIGRETTE

3 tablespoons white wine vinegar
Salt and freshly ground pepper

9 tablespoons olive oil

Preheat grill. Grill peppers about 5 cm/2 inches from heat source, turning often, for about 15 to 20 minutes, or until blistered and charred. Transfer to plastic bag and close. Let stand for 10 minutes. Peel, cut peppers in half, and remove cores. Drain well in colander, pat dry, and dice.

In a large saucepan, boil about 2 litres/3½ pints water and add a pinch of salt. Add rice, stir once, and cook, uncovered, for about 12 to 14 minutes, or until tender; check by tasting. Drain, rinse with cold water, and leave in strainer for about 15 minutes.

Combine rice, onion, peas, peppers, olives, parsley, and capers in a large bowl; mix well.

Make vinaigrette according to the instructions in recipe for Breton Vegetable Salad with Chive Mayonnaise, page 353.

Add vinaigrette to rice mixture, stir gently, taste and adjust seasoning. Cover and refrigerate for at least 1 hour. (Salad can be kept, covered, for 2 days in refrigerator.) Serve at room temperature.

RICE SALAD WITH PYRÉNÉES CHEESE, MUSHROOMS, AND TOMATOES
Salade de riz au fromage des Pyrénées, aux champignons, et aux tomates

Use a fine-quality cheese, very fresh mushrooms, and ripe tomatoes for best results.   MAKES 6 TO 8 SERVINGS

Salt   2 celery sticks
350 g/12 oz long-grain white rice

VINAIGRETTE

3 tablespoons white wine vinegar   9 tablespoons vegetable oil
Salt and freshly ground pepper
1 teaspoon Dijon mustard
  (optional)

75 g/3 oz small white mushrooms   2 large ripe tomatoes, diced
2 hard-boiled eggs, chopped   2 tablespoons chopped fresh parsley
  (optional)
75–100 g/3 to 4 oz Pyrénées,
  Cantal, or Gruyère cheese, cut
  in thin strips

In a large saucepan, boil about 2 litres/3½ pints water and add a pinch of salt. Add rice, stir once, and cook, uncovered, for about 12 to 14 minutes, or until tender; check by tasting. Drain, rinse with cold water, and leave in strainer for about 15 minutes.

Peel strings from celery and cut in 6-mm/¼-inch dice.

VINAIGRETTE
Whisk vinegar with mustard, salt and pepper in a bowl. Gradually whisk in oil. Taste and adjust seasoning.

Cut mushrooms in half and thinly slice, transfer to a small bowl, and sprinkle immediately with about 1 tablespoon vinaigrette to prevent them from discolouring. Toss gently.

Combine rice, celery, eggs, cheese, and mushrooms in a large bowl and mix well.

Whisk vinaigrette, add to rice mixture, and fold in gently. Fold in tomatoes and parsley and mix. Taste and adjust seasoning, cover, and refrigerate for at least 1 hour. (Salad can be kept, covered, for 1 day in refrigerator.) Serve at room temperature.

PASTA SALAD WITH RED PEPPERS, BROCCOLI, AND GARLIC DRESSING
Salade de pâtes aux poivrons rouges et aux brocolis, sauce à l'ail

Pasta salads are not all that popular in France but can be found occasionally in Alsace and Provence, the areas known for their pasta dishes. The dressing in this salad resembles a light mayonnaise flavoured with garlic, and is also good with cooked vegetables.

GARLIC DRESSING

2 large garlic cloves	3 tablespoons vegetable oil
1 egg, at room temperature	1 ½ tablespoons white wine vinegar
Salt and freshly ground pepper	
3 tablespoons olive oil	

700 g/1 ½ lb broccoli	225 g/8 oz wide egg noodles
1 red pepper	100 g/4 oz black olives

GARLIC DRESSING

In a food processor, chop garlic until very fine. Add egg, salt and pepper to taste, then 1 tablespoon olive oil and process until blended. With blades of processor turning, pour in remaining olive oil and vegetable oil in a very thin stream. Pour in vinegar gradually. Taste and adjust seasoning. (To prepare dressing using a blender, first chop garlic with a knife, then combine with egg, salt, pepper, and 1 tablespoon oil and proceed as above.)

Divide broccoli into small florets. Peel large stem, removing all woody parts and leaving only tender core. Slice peeled stem, put in a pan of boiling salted water, and cook for 1 minute. Add broccoli florets and boil for about 4 minutes, or until just tender. Drain, rinse under cold running water, and drain thoroughly.

Cut pepper in half lengthwise, remove core and thick ribs, and cut again crosswise. Cut pepper in short strips. Put pepper strips in a medium-size saucepan of boiling salted water and cook for 1 minute. Drain, rinse, and drain thoroughly.

Add noodles to a large pan of boiling salted water and cook, uncovered, over high heat for 6 to 7 minutes, or until just tender but still *al dente*, or slightly firm to bite; check by tasting. Rinse under cold running water and drain thoroughly.

Reserve about 3 tablespoons red pepper strips for garnish. In a large bowl, toss noodles with broccoli and remaining pepper strips. Add dressing, taste and adjust seasoning. Transfer to a serving bowl and garnish centre with reserved pepper strips and edges with olives. Serve at room temperature or cool, but not chilled.

MAYONNAISE
Mayonnaise

Homemade mayonnaise is delicious with a great variety of cooked and raw vegetables and is the base of many dressings and cold sauces.

MAKES ABOUT 300 ml/½ PINT

2 egg yolks, at room temperature
Salt and white pepper
1 teaspoon Dijon mustard, or more
   to taste (optional)
2 tablespoons white wine vinegar
   or strained fresh lemon juice, or
   more to taste

300 ml/½ pint vegetable oil, or 6
   tablespoons vegetable oil mixed
   with 9 tablespoons olive oil, at
   room temperature
1 tablespoon plus 1 teaspoon
   lukewarm water

To prepare mayonnaise in a blender or food processor, combine egg yolks, pinch of salt, white pepper, mustard, 1 tablespoon vinegar and 1 tablespoon oil in blender or food processor fitted with metal blade. Process mixture until well blended. With motor running, pour in about 3 tablespoons oil in thin trickle. After this has been added, remaining oil can be poured in a little faster, in thin stream. With motor still running, gradually add remaining vinegar. Taste and adjust seasoning; gradually add a little more vinegar if desired. Gradually add enough water to thin mayonnaise so that it holds soft, not stiff, peaks.

To prepare mayonnaise in a bowl with a whisk or a mixer, beat egg yolks with a pinch of salt, white pepper, mustard, and 1 tablespoon vinegar. Begin beating in oil, drop by drop. When 2 or 3 tablespoons oil have been added, beat in remaining oil in a very thin stream. Stir in remaining vinegar and taste and adjust seasoning. Gradually, add enough water to thin mayonnaise so that it holds soft, not stiff, peaks.

(Mayonnaise can be kept, covered, for about 4 days in refrigerator.) Bring to room temperature before using. If mayonnaise thickened on standing, gradually add a few drops more water.

NOTES

· If mayonnaise separates during preparation, whisk the separated mixture very gradually into 1 teaspoon Dijon mustard or 1 egg yolk; then continue adding any remaining oil according to the recipe.

· If preparing mayonnaise in a large food processor, do not try to make half a recipe.

· If preparing mayonnaise in a blender or food processor, egg yolks can be replaced by 1 whole large egg. This mayonnaise will be slightly less rich and a bit thinner than that made with egg yolks.

CRÈME FRAÎCHE
Crème fraîche

Thick, slightly tangy crème fraîche is a wonderful French ingredient. Fortunately it is becoming more easily available. But it is quite simple and much cheaper to make your own.

MAKES ABOUT 450 ml/¾ PINT

450 ml/¾ pint double cream   *3–4 tablespoons whole-milk yogurt*

Stir cream and yogurt together in a medium-size saucepan. Heat over very low heat, stirring constantly, for 1 minute. Pour into a jar, partially cover, and leave overnight, or for at least 8 hours, at room temperature until thickened. Stir gently, cover, and refrigerate. (Crème fraîche keeps for about 2 weeks in refrigerator.)

A Note About The Author

Faye Levy, an internationally published cookery book author and certified cookery teacher, has been described by the food editor of *Gourmet* magazine as 'one of the finest cooks in the country'.

Born and brought up in Washington, D.C., Faye has the distinction of being the first American ever to have been commissioned to write a cookery book by Flammarion, the most prestigious cookery book publisher in France, the original publisher of Escoffier, Bocuse, and Lenotre. *La Cuisine du Poisson*, the seafood cookery book Faye co-authored with Fernand Chambrette, was published in 1984.

Faye holds the 'Grand Diplome' of the first graduating class of the famous Parisian cookery school La Varenne, where she spent five years. She is the author of the school's first cookery book, *The La Varenne Tour Book*. As La Varenne's editor, Faye planned the school's curriculum and developed and drafted the recipes for the award-winning cookery books, *French Regional Cooking*, *The Observer French Cookery School*, and *Basic French Cookery*.

Faye has been writing 'The Basics' column for *Bon Appétit* magazine since 1982. Her creative dishes have been featured on the covers of *Bon Appétit* and *Gourmet*, America's top cookery magazines. Faye is the only person to have contributed to the finest collections of both magazines; her recipes appear in *The Best of Gourmet* and *The Best of Bon Appétit* series. Articles by Faye have also been published in other national magazines, as well as in *The Washington Post*, the *Chicago Tribune*, the *Boston Globe*, the *New York Post*, the *Los Angeles Herald Examiner* and in numerous other major newspapers.

Faye now lives in Santa Monica, California, with her husband/associate Yakir Levy.

Index

Aïoli. *See* Sauces

Almonds, Toasted, Artichoke Hearts, Carrots, and, Rice Pilaf with, 270–1

Alsatian Onion and Cream Cheese Tart, 98–9

Appetizers
  Baked Broccoli Gnocchi with Parmesan Cheese Sauce, 82–4
  Brie Beignets, 81–2
  Cèpe Turnovers, 109–11
  Country Leek Tart, 94–6
  Spring Onion and Parmesan Croissants, 100–2
  Mushroom and Olive Pastry Rolls, 102–4
  See also Canapés

Apples and Cider, Cabbage with, 181–2

Artichoke(s)
  Asparagus, Green Bean, and Fresh Pea Salad with Tarragon Mayonnaise, 362–4
  Baby, with Hazelnut Oil Vinaigrette, 350–1
  and Baby Onions Antiboise, 222–3
  in Breton Vegetable Salad with Chive Mayonnaise, 353–4
  in Colourful Vegetable Blanquette, 186–8
  Filled with Peas, 160–1
  hearts
    Carrots and, Toasted Almonds, Rice Pilaf with, 270–1
    to cook, 2
    to shape, 2
  Jerusalem. *See* Jerusalem artichokes
  in Mediterranean Saffron Rice Pilaf with Vegetables, 265–7
  with Onion Compote, 159–60
  Potato, Asparagus, and, Salad, 374–5
  in Provençal Vegetable and Garlic Feast, 198–200

and Rice Salad, Tomatoes Filled with, 167–8
  with Tomato Béarnaise Sauce, 210–12

Asparagus
  Artichoke, Green Bean, and Fresh Pea Salad with Tarragon Mayonnaise, 362–4
  with Beurre Blanc, 192–3
  and Carrots with Madeira, 184
  Cheese Puff Crown with, 76–8
  Creamy Rice Pilaf with, 267–8
  -filled Pastry Cases with Watercress Sauce, 104–6
  Mimosa with Hazelnuts, 347
  Morels and, Fettucine with, 280–1
  to peel, 3
  Potato, and Artichoke Salad, 374–5
  and Roquefort Canapés, 126–7
  Soup(s)
    Creamy, 311
    with Olive Oil, 310–11
  Timbales with Hollandaise Sauce, 13–16
  in Vegetable Terrine with Mushroom Mousse and Fresh Tomato Vinaigrette, 33–5

Aubergine(s)
  Baked Pasta with, 285–6
  Courgettes, and Tomato Slices Baked with Herbs, 219–20
  Curried, Rice Ring with, 272–4
  with Fresh Herbs, Grilled, 227–8
  in Medley of Vegetables with Fresh Thyme, 232–3
  Savarin with Fresh Tomato Sauce, 37–9
  Savoury Rice Pilaf with, 264–5
  Soufflé-filled Crêpes with Red Pepper Sauce, 122–4
  Stuffed
    with Duxelles, 165–6

Aubergine(s)
Stuffed – *cont.*
with Pine Nut Pilaf and Tomato Curry Sauce, 161–3
with Tomatoes, Saffron and Garlic, 163–5
Auvergne Potato Salad with Cantal Cheese, 372–3
Avocado
Mousse, 45–6
and Mushroom Salad with Swiss Chard, 359–60

Baby Vegetables
with Herb Butter Sauce, 201–3
See also Names of vegetables
Baked Beets with Lemon Cream, 225–6
Baked Broccoli Gnocchi with Parmesan Cheese Sauce, 82–4
Baked Mushrooms with Escargot Butter and Walnuts, 221
Baked Onions with Dill Butter, 223
Baked Pasta with Aubergines, 285–6
Baked Potato Cakes, 253–4
Baking vegetables, notes on, 219
Basil
Courgette Purée with, 150
-Garlic Sauce, Creamy, Tricoloured Vegetable Terrine with, 29–33
Peas and, Rice with, 261–2
Tomatoes and, Chick-pea and Bean Salad with, 358–9
Batter-fried Vegetables with Rémoulade Sauce, 240–2
Bavarian, Broccoli, 46–8
Bean(s)
Broad, in Garlic Cream, 215–16
Chick-pea and, with Tomatoes and Basil, 358–9
Flageolets with Green and Yellow Beans and Green Onion Butter, 185–6
green. *See* Green beans
white
in Southwestern Vegetable Soup with Vegetable Croutons, 303–5
with Tomatoes and Onions, 213–14
yellow. *See* Yellow beans
Beet(s)
baby, *in* Baby Vegetables with Herb Butter Sauce, 201–3
Baked, with Lemon Cream, 225–6
Endive and, Salad, 357–8
with Orange Hollandaise, 194–6
Potato and, Salad, 367–8
Timbales, 11–13
Beignets, Brie, 81–2

Belgian endives. *See* Endives
Beurre Blanc, Asparagus with, 192–3
Blanquette, Vegetable, Colourful, 186–8
Boiling vegetables, notes on, 197
Bouillabaisse, Vegetable, 293–5
Bourride, Vegetable, with Aïoli, 301–3
Braised Chestnuts, 179–80
Braised Fennel with Peppers and Olives, 183
Braising vegetables, notes on, 179
Breton Vegetable Salad with Chive Mayonnaise, 353–4
Brie Beignets, 81–2
Bright Green Spinach Tart, 63–6
Broad Beans in Garlic Cream, 215–16
Broccoli
Bavarian, 46–8
in Buckwheat Crêpes with Creamy Vegetables, 114–15
Cauliflower
and Roquefort Sauce, Pasta with, 287–8
Velouté Soup with, 329–30
Velouté Soup with, Cold, 330
Gnocchi, Baked, with Parmesan Cheese Sauce, 82–4
Gratin
with Light Cheese Sauce, 140–1
Quick, with Celery and Nuts, 142–3
and Mushroom Soufflé with Chives, 57–8
Purée, Creamy, Pasta with, 279–80
Red Peppers, and Garlic Dressing, Pasta Salad with, 378–9
with Roquefort Sauce, 205
Timbales with Garlic Butter Sauce, 17–19
Brown Rice Pilaf with Tarragon, 271–2
Brussels sprouts
Baked in Mornay Sauce, 143–4
with Creamy Mustard-Sage Sauce, 209
Buckwheat Crêpes with Creamy Vegetables, 114–15
Butter(s)
-braised endives, 182–3
Dill, Baked Onions with, 223
Escargot, and Walnuts, Baked Mushrooms with, 221
Garlic
Delicate, Green Beans with, 207–8
-glazed Carrots, 175–6
Sauce, Broccoli Timbales with, 17–19
Green Onion, Green and Yellow Beans and, Flageolets with, 185–6
Hazelnut, Capers and, Courgettes with, 206
Mint
Courgettes with, 191–2
Green Pea Purée with, 155–6
Pistachio, Steamed Carrots with, 194

salted vs. unsalted, 6
Tarragon, Steamed New Potatoes with, 248–9
Tomato, Sauce, Cauliflower Timbales with, 24–6
and Wine Vinegar, Cabbage with, 210

Cabbage
with Apples and Cider, 181–2
with Butter and Wine Vinegar, 210
Cream-braised, with Leeks, 180–1
Gratin with Light Cheese Sauce, 140–1
and Mushroom Gratin, Layered, 141–2
Red and Green, Sauté with Goat Cheese, 235–6
in Southwestern Vegetable Soup with Croutons, 303–5
Tart with Caraway Seeds, 68–9
Cakes, Baked Potato, 253–4
Canapés
Asparagus and Roquefort, 126–7
Cucumber and Herbed Goat Cheese, 127–8
Radish Flower, 128
Roasted Pepper, 129–30
Cantal Cheese, Auvergne Potato Salad with, 372–3
Capers and Hazelnut Butter, Courgettes with, 206
Caraway Seeds, Cabbage Tart with, 68–9
Carrot(s)
Artichoke Hearts, and Toasted Almonds, Rice Pilaf with, 270–1
Asparagus and, with Madeira, 184
baby
in Baby Vegetables with Herb Butter Sauce, 201–3
in Colourful Vegetable Blanquette, 186–8
in Breton Vegetable Salad with Chive Mayonnaise, 353–4
Butter-glazed, 176–7
in Festive Vegetable Tart, 96–8
in Pasta with Carrot 'Noodles', 283–4
Peas, and Sautéed Mushrooms, Couscous Pilaf with, 288–9
in Provençal Vegetable and Garlic Feast, 198–200
Purée(s)
Cream Puffs with, 79–80
Creamy, 154–5
with Raspberry Vinegar, 234
in Rice with Sautéed Vegetables and Walnut Oil, 262–3
Soufflé, Cold, with Peas, 48–50

Soup with Chives, 319–20
in Southwestern Vegetable Soup with Vegetable Croutons, 303–5
Steamed, with Pistachio Butter, 194
Timbales, 16–17
in Tricoloured Vegetable Terrine with Creamy Basil Garlic Sauce, 29–33
and Turnips, Ginger-glazed, 175–6
in Vegetable Bourride with Aïoli, 301–3
in Vegetable Terrine with Mushroom Mousse and Fresh Tomato Vinaigrette, 33–6
Cauliflower
in Batter-fried Vegetables with Rémoulade Sauce, 240–2
in Breton Vegetable Salad with Chive Mayonnaise, 353–4
Broccoli, and Roquefort Sauce, Pasta with, 287–8
in Buckwheat Crêpes with Creamy Vegetables, 114–15
Curried, French, 204–5
Gratin with Light Cheese Sauce, 139–41
and Potato Purée, 150–1
in Provençal Marinated Vegetables, 364–5
in Provençal Vegetable and Garlic Feast, 198–200
Quiche with Onion and Gruyère Cheese, 72–3
in Rosemary-scented Tomato Sauce, 203–4
Soufflé Pudding with Gruyère Cheese, 58–60
Soup, Light, 312–13
Timbales with Tomato Butter Sauce, 24–6
and Tomato Salad with Garlic and Walnut Dressing, 361–2
Velouté Soup with Broccoli, 329–30
Cold, 330
Celeriac
Purée, 153–4
Salad with Mustard Dressing, 342
in Southwestern Vegetable Soup with Vegetable Croutons, 303–5
Celery
Garlic-scented Courgettes with, 237
Gratin with Tomato Sauce, 139
in Medley of Vegetables with Fresh Thyme, 232–3
in Provençal Marinated Vegetables, 364–5
in Rice with Sautéed Vegetables and Walnut Oil, 262–3
root. See Celeriac
in Southwestern Vegetable Soup with Vegetable Croutons, 303–5
in Vegetable Bourride with Aïoli, 301–3

Cèpe(s)
in Mixed Mushroom Ragoût, 188–9
Potato Gratin with, 252
Tartlets, 68
Turnovers, 109–11
Champagne Vinaigrette, 357
Chard. *See* Swiss chard
Cheese
Creamy Pasta Gratin with, 284–5
Potato and, Gâteau, 247–8
Puff(s)
Crown with Asparagus, 76–8
Watercress Velouté Soup with, 326–8
sauces. *See* Sauces
See also Names of cheese
Cherry tomatoes, in Baby Vegetables with Herb Butter Sauce, 201–3
Chestnut(s)
Braised, 179–80
Soup, Touraine, 308–9
Chick-pea
and Bean Salad with Tomatoes and Basil, 358–9
Pancake, Baked, Niçoise, 124–5
Chicken Stock, 333–4
Chicory
and Beet Salad, 357–8
Butter-braised, 182–3
Gratin with Cream Sauce and Walnuts, 136–7
Chive(s)
Broccoli and Mushroom Soufflé with, 57–8
Carrot Soup with, 319–20
Creamy Mushroom Tart with, 70–1
Mayonnaise, Breton Vegetable Salad with, 353–4
to snip, 4
Vinaigrette, Creamy, 359–60
Cider, Apples and, Cabbage with, 181–2
Classic Salade Niçoise, 370
Cold Carrot Soufflé with Peas, 48–50
Cold Cauliflower Velouté Soup with Broccoli, 330
Colourful Vegetable Blanquette, 186–8
Compote, Onion, Artichokes with, 159–60
Corn oil, to use, 6
Country Leek Tart, 94–6
Country Spinach Soup, 297–8
Courgettes
baby, in Baby Vegetables with Herb Butter Sauce, 201–3
Baby Onions and, Glazed, 177–8
Baked in Mornay Sauce, 144
in Batter-fried Vegetables with Rémoulade Sauce, 240–2

with Capers and Hazelnut Butter, 206
in Colourful Vegetable Blanquette, 186–8
Aubergine, and Tomato Slices Baked with Herbs, 219–20
in Festive Vegetable Tart, 96–8
Garlic-scented, with Celery, 237
in Green Vegetable Quenelles with Mushroom Cream, 84–7
in Mediterranean Saffron Rice Pilaf with Vegetables, 265–7
in Medley of Vegetables with Fresh Thyme, 232–3
with Mint Butter, 191–2
in Pasta with Vegetable 'Noodles', 283–4
Purée with Basil, 150
Soup, Light, with Curry Puffs, 316–18
Stuffed with Red Pepper Purée, 166–7
in Vegetable Bouillabaisse, 293–5
in Vegetable Bourride with Aïoli, 301–3
Couscous
Pilaf with Carrots, Peas, and Sautéed Mushrooms, 288–9
Cream(s)
-braised Cabbage with Leeks, 180–1
Morels with, 212–13
Potato Gratin with, 251–2
Sauce
Spinach Gratin with, 137
and Walnuts, Chicory Gratin with, 136–7
soups. *See* Soups
Garlic, Broad Beans in, 215–16
Lemon, Baked Beets with, 225–6
Mint, Fresh Pea Soup with, 307–8
Mushroom, Green Vegetable Quenelles with, 84–7
Cream Cheese, Onion and, Tart, Alsatian, 98–9
Cream Puffs with Carrot Purée, 79–80
Creamy Asparagus Soup, 311
Creamy Basil-Garlic Sauce, Tricoloured Vegetable Terrine with, 29–33
Creamy Carrot Purée, 154–5
Creamy Chive Vinaigrette, 360
Creamy Mushroom Sauce, Spinach-Cauliflower Gâteau with, 40–2
Creamy Mushroom Tart with Chives, 70–1
Creamy Mustard-Sage Sauce, Brussels Sprouts with, 209
Creamy Onion Soup with Pasta, 296–7
Creamy Pasta Gratin with Cheese, 284–5
Creamy Potato Purée, 255–7
Creamy Rice Pilaf with Asparagus, 267–8
Crème Fraîche, 381

Herbed, Fennel Salad with, 343
Spinach-filled Crêpes with, 115–18
Crêpe(s)
Aubergine Soufflé-filled, with Red Pepper
Sauce, 122–4
Buckwheat, with Creamy Vegetables,
114–15
Leek and Mushrooms, 118–19
notes on, 112–13
pan(s)
to clean, 113
to season, 113
types of, 113
with Peppers, Onions, and Peas in Curry
Sauce, 120–22
Spinach-filled, with Crème Fraîche,
115–18
Croissants, Spring Onion and Parmesan,
100–2
Croûtes, Spinach Purée on, 152
Croutons, Vegetable, Southwestern
Vegetable Soup with, 303–5
Cucumber(s)
and Herbed Goat Cheese Canapés,
127–8
Salad with Yogurt Herb Dressing, 344
Sautéed, with Dill, 236–7
Cumin, Hollandaise Sauce, Quick, Spinach
Timbales with, 22–4
Curry
Puffs, Light Courgette Soup with, 316–18
Sauce, Crêpes with Peppers, Onions, and
Peas in, 120–2
Tomato, Sauce, Pine Nut Pilaf and, Stuffed
Aubergine with, 161–3

Dandelion Salad, Warm, with Mushrooms
and Poached Eggs, 349–50
Deep-frying vegetables, notes on, 230–2
Delicate Garlic Butter, Green Beans with,
207–8
Dill
Butter, Baked Onions with, 223
Sautéed Cucumbers with, 236–7
to snip, 4
Dressing(s)
Garlic
Red Peppers, Broccoli, Pasta Salad with,
378–9
and Walnut, Cauliflower and Tomato Salad
with, 361–2
Mustard, Celeriac Salad with, 342
notes on, 337–8
Yogurt Herb, Cucumber Salad with, 344
See also Mayonnaise; Vinaigrettes

Duxelles
Aubergines Stuffed with, 165–6
Leek and, Gratin, 134–6

Egg(s)
large, to use, 6
Poached, Mushrooms and, Warm
Dandelion Salad with, 349–50
Tomato
and, Canapés, 129
Salad, 346
Escargot Butter and Walnuts, Baked
Mushrooms with, 221
Escarole Salad with Roquefort Dressing,
344–5

Fat for deep frying, notes on, 230–2
Fennel
Braised, with Peppers and Olives, 183
in Provençal Marinated Vegetables, 364–5
Salad with Herbed Crème Fraîche, 343
Festive Vegetable Tart, 96–8
Fettucine with Morels and Asparagus, 280–1
Flageolets with Green and Yellow Beans and
Spring Onion Butter, 185–6
Flour, as soup thickener, 291, 321
French Curried Cauliflower, 204–5
French-fried Sweet Potatoes, 258–9
Fresh Pea Soup with Mint Cream, 307–8
Fritters, Potato, Light, with Pine Nuts,
249–51

Garlic
Basil-, Sauce, Creamy, Tricoloured
Vegetable Terrine, 29–33
Butter
Delicate, Green Beans with, 207–8
Sauce, Broccoli Timbales with, 17–19
to chop or mince, 3
Cream, Broad Beans in, 215–16
Dressing, Red Peppers, Broccoli, and, Pasta
Salad with, 378–9
Goat Cheese and, Tomato Pasta with,
276–7
and Olive Oil, Grilled Peppers with, 226
to peel, 3
Purée, Grilled Mushrooms with, 228–9
-scented Courgettes with Celery, 237
Tomatoes, Saffron, and, Aubergine with,
163–5
Vegetable and, Feast, Provençal, 198–200
and Walnut Dressing, Cauliflower and
Tomato Salad with, 361–2
Gâteau
Cheese and Potato, 247–8

Gâteau – *cont.*
  Spinach-Cauliflower, with Creamy
    Mushroom Sauce, 40–2
Ginger-glazed Carrots and Turnips, 175–6
Glazed Baby Onions and Courgettes, 177–8
Glazing vegetables, notes on, 158–9
Gnocchi, Broccoli, Baked, with Parmesan
    Cheese Sauce, 82–4
Goat cheese
  and Garlic, Tomato Pasta with, 276–7
  Herbed, Cucumber and, Canapés, 127–8
  Red and Green Cabbage Sauté with, 235–6
  Spinach and, Soufflé, 52–3
  Tomato and, Tartlets, with Fresh Thyme,
    66–8
  and Walnuts, Watercress Salad with,
    339–40
Gratin(s)
  Broccoli, with Light Cheese Sauce, 140
  Brussels Sprouts Baked in Mornay Sauce,
    143–4
  Cabbage
    with Light Cheese Sauce, 140–1
    and Mushroom, Layered, 141–2
  Cauliflower, with Light Cheese Sauce,
    139–41
  Celery, with Tomato Sauce, 139
  Chicory, with Cream Sauce and Walnuts,
    136–7
  Courgettes Baked in Mornay Sauce, 144
  dishes, notes on, 134
  Leek and Duxelles, 134–6
  notes on, 133–4
  Pasta, Creamy, with Cheese, 284–5
  Potato
    with Cèpes, 252
    with Cream, 251–2
  Pumpkin, with Fresh Tomato Sauce, 137–9
  Spinach, with Cream Sauce, 137
  Swiss Chard and Pepper, with Tomatoes,
    144–6
  Turnip and Onion, with Parmesan, 146–7
Green bean(s)
  Artichoke, Asparagus, and Fresh Pea Salad
    with Tarragon Mayonnaise, 262–4
  in Breton Vegetable Salad with Olive
    Mayonnaise, 353–4
  with Delicate Garlic Butter, 207–8
  Lyonnaise, 206–7
  Potato and, Salad, Summer, 369–70
  in Provençal Vegetable and Garlic Feast,
    198–200
  Salad, Marinated, with Spring Onions, 348
  with Sautéed Walnuts, 233–4
  in Vegetable Terrine with Mushroom

  Mousse and Fresh Tomato Vinaigrette,
    33–6
  and Yellow Beans and Spring Onion Butter,
    Flageolets with, 185–6
Green pepper(s)
  in Grilled Peppers with Garlic and Olive
    Oil, 226
  in Peppers Stuffed with Rice, Mushrooms,
    and Olives, 170–1
  in Potato-Pepper Salad à la Provençale,
    370–2
  in Sautéed Potatoes with Peppers and
    Thyme, 254–5
  in Sweetcorn Salad with Peppers, 355–6
  in Swiss Chard and Pepper Gratin with
    Tomatoes, 144–6
Green Pea Purée with Mint Butter, 155–6
Green Salad with Pine Nuts and Sherry
    Vinaigrette, 340–1
Green vegetables. *See* Vegetables
Grilled Aubergine with Fresh Herbs, 227–8
Grilled Mushrooms with Garlic Purée, 228–9
Grilled Peppers with Garlic and Olive Oil,
    226
Grilling vegetables, notes on, 219
Gruyère (cheese)
  Cauliflower Soufflé Pudding with, 58–60
  in Creamy Pasta Gratin with Cheese, 284–5
  and Nuts, Quick Broccoli Gratin with,
    142–3
  Onion and, Cauliflower Quiche with, 72–3

Hazelnut(s)
  Asparagus Mimosa with, 347
  Butter, Capers and, Courgettes with, 206
  Leeks Mimosa with, 346–7
  Oil, Vinaigrette, Baby Artichokes with,
    350–1
  Toasted, Swiss Chard Soup with, 323–4
Herb(s)
  Butter Sauce, Baby Vegetables with, 201–3
  fresh
    to chop or mince, 3–4
    Grilled Aubergines with, 227–8
    Mushroom Cream Soup with, 300–1
    Sautéed Salsify with, 238
    as seasoning for soups, 307
    Summer Tomato Salad with, 345–6
    Vinaigrette, 345–6
  Oil, 316
  Yoghurt, Dressing, Cucumber Salad with,
    344
  Courgette, Aubergines, and Tomato Slices
    Baked with, 219–20
  See also Names of herbs

Hollandaise sauce. *See* Sauces

Individual Onion Soufflés, 55–6

Jerusalem artichoke(s)
 in Batter-fried Vegetables with Rémoulade
   Sauce, 240–2
 Sautéed, 235

Layered Cabbage and Mushroom Gratin,
  141–2
Layered Vegetable Tourte, 106–9
Leek(s)
 Cabbage with, Cream-braised, 180–1
 to clean, 4
 Cream Soup with Diced Tomatoes, 324–5
 and Duxelles Gratin, 134–6
 in Festive Vegetable Tart, 96–8
 in Medley of Vegetables with Fresh Thyme,
   232–3
 Mimosa with Hazelnuts, 346–7
 and Mushroom Crêpes, 118–19
 Potato and, Pancakes, 257–8
 Pumpkin, Potato, and, Soup, 314–15
 in Southwestern Vegetable Soup with
   Vegetable Croutons, 303–5
 Spinach, and Pumpkin Pancakes, 239–40
 Tart, Country, 94–6
 in Vegetable Bourride with Aïoli, 301–3
Lemon Cream, Baked Beets with, 225–6
Light Cauliflower Soup, 312–13
Light Potato Fritters with Pine Nuts, 249–51
Light Courgette Soup with Curry Puffs,
  316–18
Lyonnaise Green Beans, 206–7

Madeira, Asparagus and Carrots with, 184
Marinated Green Bean Salad with Spring
  Onions, 348
Mayonnaise, 379–80
 Chive, Breton Vegetable Salad with,
   353–4
 separated, to correct, 380
 Tarragon, Artichoke, Asparagus, Green
   Bean, and Fresh Pea Salad with,
   262–4
 See also Dressings
Mediterranean Saffron Rice Pilaf with
  Vegetables, 265–7
Medley of Vegetables with Fresh Thyme,
  232–3
Milk, whole, to use, 6
Mint
 Butter
   Green Pea Purée with, 155–6
   Courgettes with, 191–2

Cream, Fresh Pea Soup with, 307–8
Mixed Mushroom Ragoût, 188–9
Morels
 and Asparagus, Fettucine with, 280–1
 with Cream, 212–13
Mornay sauce. *See* Sauces
Mousse(s)
 Avocado, 45–6
 Broccoli Bavarian, 46–8
 Mushroom, and Fresh Tomato Vinaigrette,
   Vegetable Terrine with, 33–6
 Tomato, Two-Tone, 43–5
 See also Soufflés
Multicoloured Pilaf with Sweet Red Peppers
  and Walnuts, 269
Mushroom(s)
 to clean, 4
 Avocado and, Salad with Swiss Chard,
   359–60
 Baked, with Escargot Butter and Walnuts,
   221
 Broccoli and, Soufflé with Chives, 57–8
 in Buckwheat Crêpes with Creamy
   Vegetables, 114–15
 Cabbage and, Gratin, Layered, 141–2
 in Colourful Vegetable Blanquette, 186–8
 Cream
   Green Vegetable Quenelles with, 84–7
   Soup with Fresh Herbs, 300–1
 in Festive Vegetable Tart, 96–8
 Grilled, with Garlic Purée, 228–9
 in Layered Vegetable Tourte, 106–9
 Leek and, Crêpes, 118–19
 Morels
   and Asparagus, Fettucine with, 280–1
   with Cream, 212–13
 Mousse and Fresh Tomato Vinaigrette,
   Vegetable Terrine with, 33–6
 and Olive Pastry Rolls, 102–4
 and Poached Eggs, Warm Dandelion Salad
   with, 349–50
 in Provençal Marinated Vegetables, 364–5
 Pyrenees Cheese, and Tomatoes, Rice
   Salad with, 377–8
 Salad, Tomatoes Stuffed with, 356–7
 Sauce, Cream,
   Spinach-Cauliflower Gâteau with, 40–2
 Sautéed, Carrots, Peas, and Couscous Pilaf
   with, 288–9
 to slice, 4
 Stuffed with Fresh Tomato Purée, 158–9
 Tart, Creamy, with Chives, 70–1
 See also Duxelles
Mustard
 Dressing, Celeriac Salad with, 342

Mustard – *cont.*
-Sage Sauce, Creamy, Brussels Sprouts
with, 209
Sauce, 13

Niçoise Baked Chick-pea Pancake, 124–5
'Noodles', Vegetable, Pasta with, 283–4
Norman Potato-Shallot Soup, 318–19
Nuts, Gruyère and, Quick Broccoli Gratin
with, 142–3

Oil(s)
Hazelnut, Vinaigrette, Baby Artichokes
with, 350–1
Herb, 316
Olive
Asparagus Soup with, 310–11
Garlic and, Grilled Peppers with, 226
peanut, to use, 6
safflower, to use, 6
Walnut
Sautéed Vegetables and, Rice with,
262–3
Vinaigrette, 340
Olive(s)
Mushroom and, Pastry Rolls, 102–4
Oil
Asparagus Soup with, 310–11
Garlic and, Grilled Peppers with, 226
Peppers and, Braised Fennel with, 183
Onion(s)
Baby
Artichokes and, Antiboise, 222–3
and Courgettes, Glazed, 177–8
Baked, with Dill Butter, 223
to chop or mince, 4–5
Compote, Artichokes with, 159–60
and Cream Cheese Tart, Alsatian, 98–9
and Gruyère Cheese, Cauliflower Quiche
with, 72–3
pearl, *in* Provençal Marinated Vegetables,
364–5
to peel, 4
Peppers, and Peas, Crêpes with, in Curry
Sauce, 120–2
to slice, 4
Soufflés, Individual, 55–6
Soup
Creamy, with Pasta, 296–7
Rich, with Port, 295–6
Stuffed with Spinach, 171–2
Tomatoes and, White Beans with,
213–14
Turnip and, Gratin with Parmesan, 146–7
Orange Hollandaise, Beetroots with, 194–6

Pancake(s)
Chick-pea, Baked, Niçoise, 124–5
Potato and Leek, 257–8
Spinach, Leek, and Pumpkin, 239–40
Parmesan (cheese)
in Potato and Cheese Gâteau, 247–8
Sauce, Baked Broccoli Gnocchi with,
82–4
Spring Onion and, Croissants, 100–2
Turnip and Onion Gratin with, 146–7
Parsley
Purée, 153
Sauce, Parsnip Timbales with, 20–2
Vinaigrette, 346–7
Parsnip Timbales with Parsley Sauce, 20–2
Pasta
Baked with Aubergine, 285–6
with Broccoli, Cauliflower, and Roquefort
Sauce, 287–8
with Creamy Broccoli Purée, 279–80
Creamy Onion Soup with 296–7
Fettucine with Morels and Asparagus,
280–1
with Fresh Peas and Saffron Butter Sauce,
277–9
Gratin, Creamy, with Cheese, 284–5
notes on, 275–6
and Pistou, Provençal Vegetable Soup
with, 298–300
Pumpkin and, Soup, 313–14
salad(s)
notes on, 366–7
with Red Peppers, Broccoli, and Garlic
Dressing, 378–9
Spaghetti with Autumn Vegetables and
Tomato-Tarragon Sauce, 282–3
Tomato, with Goat Cheese and Garlic,
276–7
with Vegetable 'Noodles', 283–4
Pastry(ies)
Cases, Asparagus-filled, with Watercress
Sauce, 104–6
Cèpe Turnovers, 109–11
Layered Vegetable Tourte, 106–9
for quiches and tarts, notes on, 63
Rolls, Mushroom and Olive, 102–4
Spring Onion and Parmesan Croissants,
100–2
See also Puffs
Pâté(s)
Spinach, Quick, 36–7
See also Terrines
Pea(s)
Artichokes Filled with, 160–1
and Basil, Rice with, 261–2

in Breton Vegetable Salad with Chive
    Mayonnaise, 353–4
Carrots, and Sautéed Mushrooms,
    Couscous Pilaf with, 288–9
Cold Carrot Soufflé with, 48–50
Fresh
    Artichoke, Asparagus, Green Bean, and,
      Salad with Tarragon Mayonnaise,
      362–4
    and Saffron Butter Sauce,
      Pasta with, 277–9
    Soup, with Mint Cream, 307–8
    Green, Purée with Mint Butter, 155–6
Peppers, Onions, and, Crêpes with, in
    Curry Sauce, 120–2
and Peppers, Rice Salad with, 376
in Vegetable Bouillabaisse, 293–5
in Vegetable Terrine with Mushroom
    Mousse and Fresh Tomato Vinaigrette,
    33–6
Peanut oil, to use, 6
Pearl onions, *in* Provençal Marinated
    Vegetables, 364–5
Peppers. *See* Red, green, yellow peppers
Pesto Sauce, French, Yellow Beans with, 208
Pilaf(s)
    Couscous with Carrots, Peas, and Sautéed
      Mushrooms, 288–9
    rice. *See* Rice
Pine nuts
    Light Potato Fritters with, 249–51
    Pilaf and Tomato Curry Sauce, Stuffed
      Aubergines with, 161–3
    and Sherry Vinaigrette, Green Salad with,
      340–1
Pipérade Pizza, 93–4
Pistachio Butter, Steamed Carrots with, 194
Pistou, Pasta and, Provençal Vegetable Soup
    with, 298–300
Pizza(s)
    Pipérade, 93–4
    Provençal, 88–92
    Ratatouille, 90–2
Plum Tomatoes with Shallot Purée, 169–70
Poaching vegetables, notes on, 197
Port, Rich Onion Soup with, 295–6
Potato(es)
    Baked, Cakes, 253–4
    Cauliflower and, Purée, 150–1
    and Cheese Gâteau, 247–8
    Fritters, Light, with Pine Nuts, 249–51
    Gratin
      with Cèpes, 252
      with Cream, 251–2
    and Leek Pancakes, 257–8

New, Steamed, with Tarragon Butter,
    248–9
notes on, 245–6
in Provençal Vegetable and Garlic Feast,
    198–200
Pumpkin, and Leek Soup, 314–15
purée(s)
    Creamy, 255–7
    uses for, 245–6
salads. *See* Salads
for salads, to cook, 366–7
Sautéed, with Peppers and Thyme,
    254–5
-Shallot Soup, Norman, 318–19
Skins, Potato Soufflé in, 252–3
as soup thickener, 291, 306
in Southwestern Vegetable Soup with
    Vegetable Croutons, 303–5
Sweet, French-fried, 258–9
in Vegetable Bouillabaisse, 293–5
with Vegetable Julienne Sauce, 246–7
Provençal Baked Tomatoes, 224
Provençal Marinated Vegetables, 364–5
Provençal Pizza, 88–90
Provençal Tomato Soup, 315–16
Provençal Vegetable and Garlic Feast,
    198–200
Provençal Vegetable Soup with Pasta and
    Pistou, 298–300
Pudding, Soufflé, Cauliflower, with Gruyère
    Cheese, 58–60
Puffs
    Cheese, Watercress Velouté Soup with,
      326–8
    Cream, with Carrot Purée, 79–80
    Curry, Light Courgette Soup with,
      316–18
Pumpkin
    Gratin with Fresh Tomato Sauce, 125–6
    and Pasta Soup, 313–14
    Potato, and Leek Soup, 314–15
    Soufflé, 50–52
    Spinach, Leek, and, Pancakes, 239–40
Purée(s)
    Broccoli, Creamy, Pasta with, 279–80
    Carrot
      Cream Puffs with, 79–80
      Creamy, 154–5
    Cauliflower and Potato, 150–1
    Celeriac, 153–4
    Fresh Tomato, Mushrooms Stuffed with,
      158–9
    Garlic, Grilled Mushrooms with, 228–9
    Green Pea, with Mint Butter, 155–6
    methods for, 148–9

Purée(s) – *cont.*
  notes on, 148–9
  Parsley, 153
  Potato, Creamy, 255–7
    uses for, 245–6
  Red Pepper, Courgettes Stuffed with,
    166–7
  to season, 149
  Shallot, Plum Tomatoes with, 169–70
  soups, notes on, 306–7
  Spinach, on Croûtes, 152
  Courgettes, with Basil, 150
Pyrenees Cheese, Mushrooms, and Tomatoes,
    Rice Salad with, 377–8

Quenelles, Green Vegetable, with Mushroom
    Cream, 84–7
  Cauliflower, with Onion and Gruyère
    Cheese, 72–3
  pastry for, notes on, 63
  See also Tarts
Quick Broccoli Gratin with Gruyère and
    Nuts, 142–3
Quick Hollandaise Sauce, 15–16
Quick Spinach Pâté, 36–7

Radish Flower Canapés, 128
Ragoût, Mixed Mushroom, 188–9
Raspberry Vinegar, Carrots with, 234
Ratatouille Pizza, 90–2
Red and Green Cabbage Sauté with Goat
    Cheese, 235–6
Red pepper(s)
  Aïoli, 200
  in Braised Fennel with Peppers and Olives,
    183
  Broccoli, and Garlic Dressing, Pasta Salad
    with, 378–9
  in Crêpes with Peppers, Onions, and Peas
    in Curry Sauce, 120–2
  in Festive Vegetable Tart, 96–8
  in Grilled Peppers with Garlic and Olive
    Oil, 226
  in Layered Vegetable Tourte, 106–9
  in Medley of Vegetables with Fresh Thyme,
    232–3
  in Peppers Stuffed with Rice, Mushrooms,
    and Olives, 170–1
  in Potato-Pepper Salad à la Provençale,
    370–2
  Purée, Courgettes Stuffed with, 166–7
  in Rice Salad with Peas and Peppers, 376
  in Roasted Pepper Canapés, 129–30
  Sauce, Aubergine Soufflé-filled Crêpes
    with, 122–4

  in Sautéed Potatoes with Peppers and
    Thyme, 254–5
  Sweet and Walnuts, Multicoloured Pilaf
    with, 269
  in Sweetcorn Salad with Peppers, 355–6
  in Swiss Chard and Pepper Gratin with
    Tomatoes, 144–6
  Velouté Soup, 330–2
'Refreshing' vegetables, notes on, 197
Rémoulade Sauce, Batter-fried Vegetables
    with, 240–2
Rice
  Brown, Pilaf, with Tarragon, 271–2
  with Peas and Basil, 261–2
  Pilaf(s)
    with Artichoke Hearts, Carrots, and
      Toasted Almonds, 270–1
    Creamy, with Asparagus, 267–8
    Multicoloured, with Sweet Red Peppers and
      Walnuts, 269
    notes on, 260–1
    Pine Nut, and Tomato Curry Sauce,
      Stuffed Augergine with, 161–3
    Saffron, with Vegetables, Mediterranean,
      265–7
    Savoury, with Aubergine, 264–5
    Ring with Curried Aubergine, 272–4
    salads. *See* Salads
    with Sautéed Vegetables and Walnut Oil,
      262–3
    as soup thickener, 291, 306
Rich Onion Soup with Port, 295–6
Root vegetables, to purée, 149
Roquefort (cheese)
  Asparagus and, Canapés, 126–7
  Escarole Salad with, 344–5
  Sauce
    Broccoli with, 205
    Broccoli, Cauliflower, and, Pasta with,
      287–8
Rosemary-scented Tomato Sauce, Cauliflower
    in, 203–4
Rouille Sauce, 293–4

Safflower oil, to use, 6
Saffron
  Butter Sauce, Fresh Peas and, Pasta with,
    277–9
  Rice Pilaf with Vegetables, Mediterranean,
    265–7
  Tomatoes, and Garlic, Aubergines with,
    163–5
Sage, Mustard-, Sauce, Creamy, Brussels
    Sprouts with, 209

Salad(s)
  Artichoke
    Asparagus, Green Bean, and Fresh Pea
      Salad with Tarragon Mayonnaise,
      362–4
    Baby, with Hazelnut Oil Vinaigrette,
      350–1
    and Rice, Tomatoes Filled with, 167–8
  Asparagus Mimosa with Hazelnuts, 347
  Avocado and Mushroom, with Swiss
    Chard, 359–60
  Cauliflower and Tomato, with Garlic and
    Walnut Dressing, 361–2
  Celeriac, with Mustard Dressing, 342
  Chick-pea and Bean, with Tomatoes and
    Basil, 358–9
  Classic Salade Niçoise, 370
  Chicory and Beetroot, 357–8
  composed, notes on, 337–8, 352
  Cucumber, with Yogurt Herb Dressing, 344
  Dandelion, Warm, with Mushrooms and
    Poached Eggs, 349–50
  dressings
    notes on, 338
    See also Dressings
  Escarole, with Roquefort Cheese, 344–5
  Fennel, with Herbed Crème Fraîche, 343
  Green, with Pine Nuts and Sherry
    Vinaigrette, 340–1
  Green Bean, Marinated with Spring
    Onions, 348
  Leeks Mimosa with Hazelnuts, 346–7
  Mushroom, Tomatoes Stuffed with, 356–7
  notes on, 337–8
  pasta, notes on, 366–7
  Potato
    Asparagus, and Artichoke, 374–5
    Auvergne, with Cantal Cheese, 372–3
    and Beetroot, 367–8
    and Green Bean, Summer, 369–70
    notes on, 366–7
    -Pepper à la Provençale, 370–2
    with Watercress, 373–4
  Rice
    notes on, 366–7
    with Peas and Peppers, 376
    with Pyrénées Cheese, Mushrooms, and
      Tomatoes, 377–8
  to season, 367
  to serve, 338
  simple, notes on, 338, 367
  Sweetcorn, with Peppers, 355–6
  Tomato
    and Egg, 346
    Summer, with Fresh Herbs, 345–6
  Vegetable, Breton, with Chive
    Mayonnaise, 353–4
  Watercress, with Goat Cheese and
    Walnuts, 339–40
Salsify, Sautéed, with Fresh Herbs, 238
Sauce(s)
  Aïoli, 198–200
    Red Pepper, 200
    Spinach, 200
  Basil-Garlic, Creamy, Tricoloured
    Vegetable Terrine with, 29–33
  Beurre Blanc, Asparagus with, 192–3
  Cheese, Light
    Broccoli Gratin with, 140
    Cabbage with, 140
    Cauliflower Gratin with, 139–40
  Cream
    Spinach Gratin with, 137
    and Walnuts, Chicory Gratin, 136–7
    Curry, Crêpes with Peppers, Onions, and
      Peas in, 120–2
  Garlic Butter, Broccoli Timbales with,
    17–19
  Herb Butter, Baby Vegetables with, 201–3
  Hollandaise
    Asparagus Timbales with, 13–16
    Cumin, Quick, Spinach Timbales with,
      22–4
    Orange, Beetroot with, 194–6
    Quick, 15–16
  Mornay
    Brussels Sprouts Baked in, 143–4
    Courgettes Baked in, 144
  Mushrooms, Creamy, Spinach-Cauliflower
    Gâteau with, 40–2
  Mustard, 12–13
    -Sage, Creamy, Brussels Sprouts with,
      209
  Parmesan Cheese, Baked Broccoli
    Gnocchi, 82–4
  Parsley, Parsnip Timbales with, 20–2
  Pesto, French Yellow Beans with, 208
  Remoulade, Batter-fried Vegetables with,
    240–2
  Roquefort
    Broccoli, Cauliflower, and, Pasta with,
      287–8
    Broccoli with, 205
  Rouille, 294
  Saffron Butter, Fresh Peas and, Pasta with,
    277–9
  Tomato
    Béarnaise, Artichokes with, 210–12
    Butter, Cauliflower Timbales with, 24–6
    Celery Gratin with, 139

Sauce(s)
Tomato – *cont.*
Curry, Pine Nut Pilaf, Stuffed Aubergine with, 161–3
Fresh, Aubergine Savarin with, 37–9
Rosemary-scented, Cauliflower in, 203–4
Tarragon, Autumn Vegetables and, Spaghetti with, 282–3
Vegetable Julienne, Potatoes with, 246–7
Watercress, Asparagus-filled Pastry Cases with, 104–6
See also Butters; Dressings
Sauté, Red and Green Cabbage with Goat Cheese, 235–6
Sautéed Cucumbers with Dill, 236–7
Sautéed Jerusalem Artichokes, 235–6
Sautéed Potatoes with Peppers, 254–5
Sautéed Salsify with Fresh Herbs, 238
Sautéing vegetables, notes on, 230–2
Savarin, Aubergine, with Fresh Tomato Sauce, 37–9
Savory Rice Pilaf with Aubergine, 264–5
Shallot(s)
to peel, slice, and chop or mince, 4–5
Potato-, Soup, Norman, 318–19
Purée, Plum Tomatoes with, 169–70
Sherry Vinaigrette, Pine Nuts and, Green Salad with, 340–1
Sorrel Velouté Soup, 325–6
Soufflé(s)
Broccoli and Mushroom, with Chives, 57–8
Aubergine-filled Crêpes with Red Pepper Sauce, 122–4
notes on, 51
Onion, Individual, 55–6
Potato, in Potato Skins, 252–3
Pudding, Cauliflower, with Gruyère Cheese, 58–60
Spinach and Goat Cheese, 52–3
See also Mousses
Soup(s)
Asparagus
Creamy, 311
with Olive Oil, 310–11
Carrot, with Chives, 319–20
Cauliflower, Light, 312–13
Chestnut, Touraine, 308–9
cold, to season, 292
cream
to garnish, 321–2
Leek, with Diced Tomatoes, 324–5
Mushroom, with Fresh Herbs, 300–1
to reheat, 322

to season, 306–7, 322
to thicken, 321
Fresh Pea, with Mint Cream, 307–8
Onion
Creamy, with Pasta, 296–7
Rich, with Port, 295–6
Potato-Shallot, Norman, 318–19
Pumpkin
and Pasta, 313–14
Potato, and Leek Soup, 314–15
purée
notes on, 306–7
to season, 306–7
Spinach, Country, 297–8
Swiss Chard, with Toasted Hazelnuts, 323–4
to thicken, 291, 304–5
Tomato, Provençal, 315–16
Vegetable
Bouillabaisse, 293–5
Bourride with Aïoli, 301–3
Provençal, with Pasta and Pistou, 298–300
Southwestern, with Vegetable Croutons, 303–5
vegetables for, 291–2
Velouté
Cauliflower, with Broccoli, 329–30
Cauliflower, with Broccoli, Cold, 330
to garnish, 321–2
notes on, 321–2
Red Pepper, 330–2
to reheat, 324
to season, 306–7, 322
Sorrel, 325–6
to thicken, 321–2
Watercress, with Cheese Puffs, 326–8
Courgettes, Light with Curry Puffs, 316–18
Southwestern Vegetable Soup with Vegetable Croutons, 303–5
Spaghetti with Autumn Vegetables and Tomato-Tarragon Sauce, 282–3
Spinach
Aïoli, 200
in Buckwheat Crêpes with Creamy Vegetables, 114–15
-Cauliflower Gâteau with Creamy Mushroom Sauce, 40–2
to clean, 5
-filled Crêpes with Crème Fraîche, 115–18
and Goat Cheese Soufflé, 52–3
Gratin with Cream Sauce, 137
in Green Vegetable Quenelles with Mushroom Cream, 84–7
in Layered Vegetable Tourte, 106–9

Leek, and Pumpkin Pancakes, 239–40
  Onions Stuffed with, 171–2
  Purée on Croûtes, 152
  Soup, Country, 297–8
  to substitute frozen for fresh, 5
  Tart, Bright Green, 63–6
  Timbales with Quick Cumin Hollandaise
    Sauce, 22–4
  in Tricoloured Vegetable Terrine with
    Creamy Basil-Garlic Sauce, 29–33
Spring onion(s)
  Butter, Green and Yellow Beans and
    Flageolets with, 185–6
  Marinated Green Bean Salad with, 348
  and Parmesan Croissants, 100–2
  in Rice with Sautéed Vegetables and
    Walnut Oil, 262–3
Steamed Carrots with Pistachio Butter, 194
Steamed New Potatoes with Tarragon Butter,
  248–9
Steaming vegetables, notes on, 173–4, 190–1
Stewing vegetables, notes on, 179
Stock(s)
  Chicken, 333–4
  Vegetable, 332–3
Stuffed Aubergines with Pine Nut Pilaf and
  Tomato Curry Sauce, 161–3
Stuffed vegetables, notes on, 157
Summer Potato and Green Bean Salad,
  369–70
Summer Tomato Salad with Fresh Herbs,
  345–6
Sunflower oil, to use, 6
Sweet Potatoes, French-fried, 258–9
Sweetcorn Salad with Peppers, 355–6
Swiss chard
  Avocado and Mushroom Salad with,
    359–60
  in Buckwheat Crêpes with Creamy
    Vegetables, 114–15
  in Colourful Vegetable Blanquette, 186–8
  and Pepper Gratin with Tomatoes, 144–6
  in Rice with Sautéed Vegetables and
    Walnut Oil, 262–3
  Soup with Toasted Hazelnuts, 323–4
  and Tomato Tart, 73–5

Tarragon
  Brown Rice Pilaf with, 271–2
  Butter, Steamed New Potatoes with, 248–9
  Mayonnaise, Artichoke, Asparagus, Green
    Bean, and Fresh Pea Salad with,
    362–4
  Tomato-, Sauce, Autumn Vegetables and,
    Spaghetti with, 282–3

Tart(s)
  Caraway, Cabbage Tart with, 68–9
  Leek, Country, 94–6
  Mushroom, Creamy, with Chives, 70–1
  pastry for, notes on, 63
  Spinach, Bright Green, 63–6
  Vegetable, Festive, 96–8
  See also Pastries; Pizza; Quiches; Tartlets
Tartlets
  Cèpe, 68
  Tomato and Goat Cheese, with Fresh
    Thyme, 66–8
  See also Tarts
Terrine(s)
  Aubergine Savarin with Fresh Tomato
    Sauce, 37–9
  Spinach-Cauliflower Gâteau with Creamy
    Mushroom Sauce, 40–2
  Vegetable
    with Mushroom Mousse and Fresh
      Tomato Vinaigrette, 33–6
    Tricoloured, with Creamy Basil-Garlic
      Sauce, 29–33
  See also Pâtés
Thyme
  Fresh
    Medley of Vegetables with, 232–3
    Tomato and Goat Cheese Tartlets with,
      66–8
    Peppers and, Sautéed Potatoes with,
      254–5
Timbales
  Asparagus, with Hollandaise Sauce, 13–16
  Beetroot, 11–13
  Broccoli, with Garlic Butter Sauce, 17–19
  Carrot, 16–17
  Cauliflower, with Tomato Butter Sauce,
    24–6
  to check if done, 10–11
  as main course, 9–10
  notes on, 9–11
  Parsnip, with Parsley Sauce, 20–2
  sauces for, 9–10
  Spinach, with Quick Cumin Hollandaise
    Sauce, 22–4
  Turnip, 27–8
  to unmold, 11
  water bath for, 10
Tomato(es)
  Baked, Provençal, 224
  and Basil, Chick-pea and Bean Salad with,
    358–9
  Cauliflower and, Salad with Garlic and
    Walnut Dressing, 361–2
  Chard and, Tart, 73–5

Tomato(es) – *cont.*
  cherry, *in* Baby Vegetables with Herb
      Butter Sauce, 201–3
  Curry Sauce, Pine Nut Pilaf and, Stuffed
      Aubergines with, 161–3
  Diced, Leek Cream Soup with, 324–5
  and Egg
      Canapés, 129
      Salad, 345–6
  Filled with Artichoke and Rice Salad,
      167–8
  Fresh
      Purée, Mushrooms Stuffed with, 158–9
      sauces. *See* Sauces
      Vinaigrette, Mushroom
      Mousse and, Vegetable Terrine with,
          33–6
  and Goat Cheese Tartlets with Fresh
      Thyme, 66–8
  in Mediterranean Saffron Rice Pilaf with
      Vegetables, 265–7
  Mousse, Two-Tone, 43–5
  and Onions, White Beans with, 213–14
  Pasta with Goat Cheese and Garlic, 276–7
  to peel, seed, and chop, 6
  Plum, with Shallot Purée, 169–70
  in Provençal Marinated Vegetables, 364–5
  Pyrenees Cheese, Mushrooms, and, Rice
      Salad with, 377–8
  Saffron, and Garlic, Aubergines with,
      163–5
  salads. *See* Salads
  sauces. *See* Sauces
  Slices, Courgette, Aubergine, and, Baked
      with Herbs, 219–20
  Soup, Provençal, 315–16
  Stuffed with Mushroom Salad, 356–7
  Swiss Chard and Pepper Gratin with,
      144–6
  -Tarragon Sauce, Autumn Vegetables and,
      Spaghetti with, 282–3
Touraine Chestnut Soup, 308–9
Tourte, Vegetable, Layered, 106–9
Tricoloured Vegetable Terrine with Creamy
    Basil-Garlic Sauce, 29–33
Turnip(s)
  baby, *in* Baby Vegetables with Herb Butter
      Sauce, 201–3
  Carrots and, Ginger-glazed, 175–6
  and Onion Gratin with Parmesan, 146–7
  in Southwestern Vegetable Soup with
      Vegetable Croutons, 303–5
  Timbales, 27–8
  in Tricoloured Vegetable Terrine with
      Creamy Basil-Garlic Sauce, 29–33

Turnovers, Cèpe, 109–11
Two-Tone Tomato Mousse, 43–5

Vegetable(s)
  Baby, with Herb Butter Sauce, 201–3
  baked, notes on, 219
  Batter-fried, with Rémoulade Sauce,
      240–2
  Blanquette, Colourful, 186–8
  boiled, notes on, 197
  Bouillabaisse, 293–5
  Bourride with Aïoli, 301–3
  cooked, to season, 173–4
  Creamy, Buckwheat Crêpes with, 114–15
  Croutons, Southwestern Vegetable Soup
      with, 303–5
  deep-fried, notes on, 230–1
  Autumn, and Tomato-Tarragon Sauce,
      Spaghetti with, 282–3
  and Garlic Feast Provençal, 198–200
  glazed, notes on, 175
  green
      to purée, 148–9
      Quenelles with Mushroom Cream, 84–7
  to 'refresh', 197
  grilled, notes on, 219
  Julienne
      Sauce, Potatoes with, 246–7
  Marinated, Provençal, 364–5
  Medley of, with Fresh Thyme, 232–3
  'Noodles', Pasta with, 283–4
  oil, types of, to use, 6
  root, to purée, 149
  Saffron Rice Pilaf with, Mediterranean,
      283–4
  Salad, Breton, with Chive Mayonnaise,
      353–4
  for salads, to cook, 339
  Sautéed
      notes on, 230–2
      and Walnut Oil, Rice with, 262–3
  Soup
      Provençal, with Pasta and Pistou,
          298–300
      Southwestern, with Vegetable Croutons,
          303–5
  for soups, 291–2
      to purée, 306–7
  steamed, notes on, 173–4, 190–1
  Stock, 322–3
  stuffed, notes on, 157
  Tart, Festive, 96–8
  Tourte, Layered, 106–9
  See also Names of vegetables
Velouté soups. *See* Soups

Vinaigrette(s)
Champagne, 357
Chive, Creamy, 360
Fresh Herb, 345–6
Fresh Tomato, Mushroom Mousse and,
Vegetable Terrine with, 33–6
Hazelnut Oil, Baby Artichokes with,
350–1
Parsley, 347
Sherry, Pine Nuts and, Green Salad with,
340–1
Walnut Oil, 340
See also Dressings
Vinegar(s)
Raspberry, Carrots with, 234
Wine, Butter and, Cabbage with, 210

Walnut(s)
Cream Sauce and, Celery Gratin with,
136–7
Escargot Butter and, Baked Mushrooms
with, 221
Garlic and, Dressing, Cauliflower and
Tomato Salad with, 361–2
Goat Cheese and, Watercress Salad with,
339–40
Oil
Sautéed Vegetables and, Rice with,
262–3
Vinaigrette, 340
Sautéed, Green Beans with, 233–4

Sweet Red Peppers and, Multicoloured Pilaf
with, 269
Warm Dandelion Salad with Mushrooms and
Poached Eggs, 349–50
Water bath, for timbales, 10–11
Watercress
in Green Vegetable Quenelles with
Mushroom Cream, 84–7
Potato Salad with, 373–4
Salad with Goat Cheese and Walnuts,
339–40
Sauce, Asparagus-filled Pastry Cases with,
104–6
Velouté Soup with Cheese Puffs, 326–8
White Beans. *See* Beans
Wine
for cooking, 6
Vinegar, Butter and, Cabbage with, 210

Yellow beans
in Flageolets with Green and Yellow Beans
and Spring Onion Butter, 185–6
with Pesto Sauce, 208
in Provençal Marinated Vegetables, 364–5
in Vegetable Terrine with Mushroom
Mousse and Fresh Tomato Vinaigrette,
32–6
Yellow peppers, *in* Potato Pepper Salad à la
Provençale, 370–2
Yogurt Herb Dressing, Cucumber Salad with,
344